DATE DUE

MAR 25			
NOV 18 '84			

GAYLORD   PRINTED IN U.S.A.

THE POLITICAL ECONOMY
OF LATIN AMERICA

THE POLITICAL ECONOMY OF LATIN AMERICA

WENDELL C. GORDON

University of Charleston Library
Charleston, WV 25304

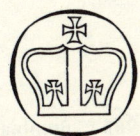

COLUMBIA UNIVERSITY PRESS
NEW YORK AND LONDON

330.98
G659p

Copyright © 1965 Columbia University Press
Columbia Paperback Edition 1966
International Standard Book Number: 0-231-08572-9
Third printing and second Paperback printing 1970
Printed in the United States of America

To CLARENCE AYRES
and E. E. HALE

PREFACE

In this book I am attempting much the same task as was attempted in *The Economy of Latin America* in 1950, general coverage of the economic problems of Latin America. However, the treatment of the material has been rather substantially modified, and it seems desirable to look on the present work as a new book rather than as a revision of the 1950 volume.

Professional economic jargon has been avoided as far as possible in the hope that the book may be of use to the general reader and to the social science student who is interested in Latin American problems but is not an economics specialist. Royalties for this book have been waived so that it can reach the greatest number of students.

The descriptive material of the book is oriented around the argument that substantial institutional change is necessary in Latin America if the development of the region is to be accelerated. But the Latin Americans themselves will have to be the chief architects of these institutional changes. This theoretical framework is chiefly the work of Clarence Ayres and of Thorstein Veblen.

A brief selective bibliography is included as an appendix. And brief, specialized bibliographies appear as footnotes at various places in the text where such an inclusion seems appropriate.

For aid in laboring on the more prosaic and thankless aspects of the task I am indebted to Analeslie Unfried, Margaret Armstrong, Gwyndolen Vail, Betty L. DeWitt, Elizabeth Seufer, and Janet Gordon. Carey Thompson, Gertrude Gordon, and Bonnie Whittier have been most helpful.

WENDELL GORDON

September, 1964
Austin, Texas

CONTENTS

Introduction		1
Part One: Evolution of Economic Systems		
ONE	Evolution of Economic Systems to 1860	5
TWO	Evolution of Economic Systems since 1860	17
Part Two: Market Organization		
THREE	Types of Business Organization	39
FOUR	Market Behavior: Private Practices	55
FIVE	Market Behavior: Government Regulation	66
SIX	Market Behavior: International Raw Commodity Control Schemes	78
SEVEN	Market Behavior: Government Business and Public Utilities	94
Part Three: Welfare		
EIGHT	Labor Movement	109
NINE	Wages and Security	122
TEN	Level of Living, Income, and Production Patterns	133
Part Four: Economic Development		
ELEVEN	Basis for Industrialization: Institutions	155
TWELVE	Basis for Industrialization: Technology and Resources	172
THIRTEEN	Planning	189
FOURTEEN	Capital Formation: Domestic	213
FIFTEEN	Capital Formation: Foreign Resources	231
SIXTEEN	Priorities and Complementarity	250
SEVENTEEN	Priorities: Infrastructure and Social Overhead	265
EIGHTEEN	Industrial Priorities	277

Part Five: Trade and Finance

NINETEEN	International Trade Patterns	295
TWENTY	Trade and Development	307
TWENTY-ONE	Common Markets	325
TWENTY-TWO	The Monetary Standard and the Foreign Exchanges	335
TWENTY-THREE	Banking	344
TWENTY-FOUR	Public Finance	356
TWENTY-FIVE	Cycles, Growth, and the Money Supply	372
	Conclusion	386

Selected Bibliography   389

Index   393

THE POLITICAL ECONOMY
OF LATIN AMERICA

INTRODUCTION

This book is a survey of the political economy of Latin America. This means that economic conditions are described in a theoretical framework which, it is hoped, has valid implications for public policy.

The description of the behavior of business enterprise, of the market, and of business-government relations is Part Two. The description of the economy viewed from the standpoint of the people, their standard of living, and the institutions they have to protect their welfare is Part Three. The elaboration of the theoretical model in which economic development is analyzed, the institutional theory of Ayres and Veblen, is presented at the beginning of Part Four. The latter chapters of Part Four are concerned with a reinterpretation of the Latin American development problem in the light of this theoretical model. Planning, capital formation, foreign investments, and priorities in the development of industries are discussed. Part Five singles out several of the economic problem areas (international trade, money and banking, and public finance). Effort is made to apply the theoretical model to indicate appropriate policies for dealing with both economic development and business cycle problems.

But as a preliminary to the discussion of the current economic problems of Latin America, it has seemed desirable in Part One to attempt an interpretation of the economic history of the region. The interpretation is in terms of the institutional theory which is later developed in Part Four.

Latin America is in ferment at the same time that various age-old institutional arrangements are demonstrating an obdurate survival value. The defensive machinations of those institutions are frustrating constructive change. Why is this possible? In an attempt to throw light on

INTRODUCTION

an answer, Part One is a hurried economic history of Latin America which tries to provide the outlines of a theory of history, or at least of Latin American economic history. In broad outline the theme is that, at least since the Spaniards came, Latin America has been living under a set of alien institutions—institutions whose nature and role have not been understood by the mass of the Latin American population. To large degree the economic lag and the political instability are a result of the manner in which these alien institutions have played out their role.

PART ONE

EVOLUTION OF ECONOMIC SYSTEMS

CHAPTER ONE

EVOLUTION OF ECONOMIC SYSTEMS TO 1860

This chapter and the one following represent an effort to sketch the economic history of Latin America and to interpret that history in the light of the institutional theory. The argument presented involves an approach which has already become the concern of some of the most constructive of the Latin American economists. For example, someone at the Economic Commission for Latin America, perhaps Raúl Prebisch, wrote recently: "What has to be done is to overcome the ideological poverty that prevails in our countries . . . the traditional propensity to introduce from abroad nostrums that are largely alien to the real requirements of Latin America's situation." [1]

Analytical Model

INSTITUTIONAL THEORY. It is risky to attempt to fit the history of a society representing a substantial segment of mankind into a simple model. And yet a certain understanding of that society may be gained by making the effort—even if one is not entirely satisfied with the result in the end. The simplified, theoretical model will almost certainly not succeed in explaining all aspects of a complicated and disparate culture. But if the model is reasonably satisfactory, it should explain a good deal.

In the pages which follow, then, effort will be made to interpret the

---

[1] United Nations, *Towards a Dynamic Development Policy for Latin America* (New York, 1963), p. 14.

economic history of Latin America in terms of institutional theory, a theory in the development of which Clarence Ayres and Thorstein Veblen have played major roles.[2]

The institutional theory may be summarized in the following manner. Economic progress is conditioned by:

(1) The static resistance to change, and especially to the assimilation of new technology, which exists because of the institutional organization of society;

(2) The dynamic forces inherent in the process of accumulation of technical knowledge;

(3) The appropriateness of the available raw material resources to the state of technical knowledge. (The implications of this theoretical model will be discussed at greater length in Chapter Eleven.)

THE VIABILITY OF THE SYSTEM. The institutional theory attempts to explain how social and economic change evolves over time. But at any given stage in historical evolution there is the additional question as to whether the system "works." A society certainly needs to "work," but it also needs to do something more. A society may "work" without doing anything. This is the case with the traditional, primitive societies which have existed in a static institutional form over many generations.

However, a society may also be afflicted with institutional arrangements which are poorly integrated, are not understood by the people, and are in a state of confusion and even chaos. The people living in the system may not understand it. Arrangements are in danger of breaking down. One might say that the system lacks viability or does not work.

It will be argued subsequently that it is generally necessary, in order for a set of institutional arrangements to be viable, that those arrangements be indigenous, that they have evolved from within the society itself. It will also be argued that the institutional pattern needs to be coherent or homogeneous. The various institutions of a society (corporate organization, the banking system, the tax system) need to interrelate in a manner that can be understood by the population living under the system. The meaning of the institutional relations needs to be appreciated by the people.

[2] C. E. Ayres, *Theory of Economic Progress* (Chapel Hill, University of North Carolina Press, 1944); Thorstein Veblen, *The Theory of the Leisure Class* (New York, Modern Library, 1934 [first published in 1899]); Thorstein Veblen, *Theory of Business Enterprise* (New York, Scribner's, 1927 [first published in 1904]).

A society, then, to operate satisfactorily needs both (1) to be dynamic, in the sense of having a flexible institutional order that permits the assimilation of new technology, and (2) to be viable, in the sense that it does not break down in the course of performing its day-to-day chores.

Explanations of the capitalistic economy have been made by men brought up in such an economy. And policy has been formulated in capitalistic economies by men who have had a feeling of participation. However well or badly the developed countries may have served themselves as a result of their use of the philosophy of laissez-faire capitalism, the laissez-faire school of thought provided, during the nineteenth century in England and the United States, some basis upon which individuals could work, act, and justify their actions. The system was developed domestically in those countries and was reasonably comprehensible to the people involved.

In Latin America the situation has been far otherwise for over four hundred years. From about 1500 until 1910, there was no indigenous economic philosophy—however bad—to serve as an understandable explanation of the working of the institutional order under which the people were, perforce, living.

Preconquest

INSTITUTIONS. The advanced Indian empires of pre-Spanish times (the Aztec, Maya, Chibcha, and Inca) were possessed until 1500, each, of an indigenous and reasonably coherent economic system. This system provided a code to live by, which was at least intelligible to the people living under it. The individual knew and understood his position and what he could, or could not, do about it.

On the political side, the system was an absolutism involving regimentation from above. (1) There was a highly developed hierarchical organization in which a predominantly agricultural society was organized under the control of priest and warrior classes. But the hierarchical arrangements seem to have been fairly coherent and understandable so far as the bulk of the population was concerned. (2) On the economic side, it involved a type of communism. In general, in those Indian empires the village land was held in common. It was worked sometimes in common and sometimes in small plots. This was as true in the Inca *ayllu* in Peru as in the Aztec *altepetlalli* or *calpulli* in Mexico.[3] These empires were surprisingly alike in economic organization, despite the distance between them and the dearth of transportation facilities.

There may have been, there probably was, exploitation of the Indian villagers by the priesthood and warrior classes. In Mexico the Aztecs, who seem to have been a minority group of Nahuatl background, had been exploiting assorted other tribes on the central plateau for a century or two before the Spaniards came. Along the west coast of South America, the Incas, also a small tribe, had succeeded, by the time the Spaniards came, in establishing their hegemony over a region extending from Ecuador to central Chile. They, like the Aztecs, had asserted themselves perhaps two or three hundred years before the Spaniards came by conquering an already existing civilization: the Aymará. But, perhaps, the Aztec or Inca exploitation was something which the mass of the Indian population had a chance of understanding. There were customary, long-accepted ways of doing things which Aztec and Inca conquerors did not substantially disturb. And perhaps in such a setting the people could live in reasonable harmony with their environment, whether or not they relished particular tyrants. But, whether or not these pre-Columbian civilizations were arrangements with which the mass of the population could live in sufficient harmony so that there was effective rapport with the institutional environment, there certainly was no longer meaningful harmony between the people and that environment after the Spaniards (and the Portuguese) came.

The institutional arrangements seem to have been indigenous and reasonably workable during the period before 1500. But to say that they thus met some of the conditions necessary for viability is not to claim that they met all the conditions sufficient to ensure a pleasant way of life.

TECHNOLOGY. Before 1500 most of the area that was to become Latin America was inhabited by Indian tribes in the hunting and fishing stage of development. These tribes, in isolated cases, possessed some remarkable bits of technical knowledge. The Jivaro tribe of interior Ecuador,

---

[3] *Ayllu* was the name of the pre-Spanish communal, landholding village in Peru. In Mexico the *altepetlalli* was much the same thing; the *calpulli,* apparently, was the clan or kinship group, of which there might be two or three in a village, which actually administered the land, allotting specific plots to heads of families, and so on.

for example, could shrink heads. But on the whole, the stage of technical advance of these tribes was extremely backward relative to the Europe of 1500.

There was, however, a very considerable degree of technical advance present in the Inca civilization in Peru, the Aztec on the central plateau of Mexico, the Maya in Guatemala and Yucatan, and the Chibcha in Colombia. These were societies based on sedentary agriculture. They did not understand the use of the wheel; but the Aztecs and Mayas had calendars which seem to have represented at least as sophisticated an understanding of astronomy as did the calendar in use at the time in western Europe. Also, the irrigation system in use in southern Peru seems to have been a remarkable engineering performance, one which was allowed to fall into disuse after the coming of the Spaniards. Minerals were worked, but used only for ornamentation.

At all events, the Indian military technology could not match gunpowder, the blunderbuss, and the horse. Technological inferiority, not the legend of the white god returning from the East, cost the Indians of America their independence.

The Colonial Period

TECHNOLOGY. The Spanish and Portuguese conquered the New World because they had a militarily superior technology. They brought gunpowder and firearms. They also brought horses, as well as cattle, swine, sheep, mules, and chickens. They brought citrus fruit, sugar, cotton, and coffee, items which were later to become extremely important in Latin America. They found tobacco and the potato, which later found its way from the highlands of Peru to Ireland. Most important of all, they brought the wheel.

Initially also, the Spaniards introduced the manufacturing of wool, cotton, and leather goods. They introduced ironworking. They established a tile-manufacturing industry at Puebla, Mexico, blanketmaking at Saltillo, lacquer work at Pátzcuaro, and gold and silver filigree work.

But they also brought a set of institutional arrangements that subsequently inhibited the growth of those early industries and even resulted in the effort to eliminate some of them. Technical progress lagged in Latin America for the next four hundred years.

INSTITUTIONS. The Spaniards and Portuguese came, following 1492, and imposed an alien culture on what remained a predominantly Indian population. In contrast, the area that was to become the United States did not have the problem of absorbing an alien culture because most of the population was immigrant. The Anglo-Americans brought with them a culture to which they were reasonably well adjusted. But such was not the case with the Indian-mestizo population of Latin America.

The Spanish and Portuguese brought with them from western Europe the economic system, mercantilism, and the logical method, Scholasticism; and they imposed these systems on a population whose experience provided little basis for assimilating them.[4]

Scholasticism. The deductive method of Scholasticism tended to inhibit scholars from engaging in field research and experimentation. It was thought that fundamental principles were identified by revelation or insight, not by experimentation. In imposing such restraints on the scholars in the newly acquired colonies, Spain went so far as to prohibit anyone in the New World from publishing or selling books written on "matters concerning the Indies."[5] It would not be accurate to allege that restrictions as stringent as these applied consistently to Latin America through the whole colonial period. But such restrictions certainly operated in Latin America as a major restraint on technical progress during the seventeenth and eighteenth centuries, when the development of the scientific method in England was setting the stage for the Industrial Revolution in northern Europe.

Mercantilism. Spain and Portugal, as was also true of the other great mercantilistic empires of those years, desired colonies in order that they

---

[4] *Mercantilism.* A system involving close governmental regulation of production and commerce in an effort to build up national power. It was thought that an export trade balance and an inflow of gold would contribute to this purpose.

Scholasticism. This was the philosophical system of Thomas Aquinas (1225–74?). It has played an important role in the dogma of the Catholic Church. At the heart of the system is the syllogistic logic, a system of reasoning which analyzes problems in the pattern: thesis-antithesis-synthesis or major-premise—minor-premise—conclusion. The conclusion necessarily follows from the premises. An example is: All dogs are black; this thing is a dog; therefore, it is black. In general, the major premises used in scholastic argument were assumed rather than being derived from observation or experimentation. The deductive method involved in the syllogistic logic is in contrast to the inductive method (or scientific approach) of Francis Bacon.

[5] *Recopilación de Leyes de los Reynos de las Indias* (1680), Ley 1, Tit. 24, Lib. 1. The Ley 1 actually read to the effect that the publication had to be cleared with the Real Consejo de Indias.

might obtain the precious metals from them. From the wealth in precious metals, the Crown received typically a fifth and the adventurers kept the rest. Subsistence agriculture was permitted; but beyond mining and agriculture, Spain and Portugal discouraged the economic development of the colonies. It was thought best that they have little industry. They would then be more profitable markets for the products of the mother country.[6]

There were two chief aspects to the mercantilistic system of controls: (1) trade regulation and (2) industrialization policy.

(1) *Trade Regulation.* The broad outlines of the mercantilistic trade policy are well known. Since it was difficult to control innumerable ships sailing to and from innumerable harbors, that difficulty was met by specifying a small number of harbors which must be used and by making the ships sail together in great fleets at rare intervals. The ports of Spain that came to serve the New World trade were Cádiz and Seville. The ports in the New World were Havana, Vera Cruz, Porto Bello, and Cartagena. Large fleets sailed once a year between these ports and Spain. Great fairs were held at the ports in the New World while the fleets were in. There is ample evidence that this system had a throttling influence on trade. How could that help but be true, since goods from Argentina, at least during certain periods, instead of going directly by water from Buenos Aires to Spain, had to go overland to Lima, up the west coast to Panama, and thence by the fleet to Spain? Or, goods from the Philippines, in one galleon a year, came to Acapulco in Mexico, went overland to Vera Cruz, and thence proceeded by the fleet to Spain. Whether or not this system meant any real protection, even from the pirates, is open to question. If captured, the fleet was a major prize.

The English had begun to undermine this tight system of trade control before the end of the colonial period. In 1713, at the close of the War of the Spanish Succession, the English forced upon Spain the *Asiento* agreement. It provided that the English could send one ship a year in the Porto Bello and Vera Cruz trades and also could sell Negro slaves in Spanish America. The one ship came to serve as a smuggling base and was repeatedly reloaded by other English ships. To this practice the

[6] Leopoldo Solís M., "La Influencia del Mercantilismo Español en la Vida Económica de América Latina: Un Intento de Interpretación," *Trimestre Económico,* XXXI (April, 1964), 200–9.

colonists gave tacit consent, for they desired to augment the insufficient quantity of goods provided by the annual fleets, and they desired to sell to other than Spanish merchants if that could be done with greater profit. Despite these minor breaches, however, the system of trade controls was the dominating economic fact of the times. And Spain and Portugal were intent on maintaining that system as best they could.

(2) *Industrialization Policy.* Wherever the interests of local industry or agriculture in the New World crossed the interests of the industry and agriculture of Spain and Portugal, the New World industry was doomed for trouble. In those cases, the home government was not only in a position to enact legislation beneficial to the "peninsular" (Spanish and Portuguese) interests, but consistently did so. In various colonies at various times, there were many examples of such practices. The raising of grapes in the New World might lead to a wine-making industry that would compete with that in Spain; so, the raising of grapes in the New World was prohibited. On another occasion, olive groves were destroyed; the textile and leather industries were burdened with restrictions. In the seventeenth century in Mexico the manufacture of silk was prohibited and mulberry groves were destroyed. A steel industry in Brazil might compete with that in Portugal; so, a new steel industry in Brazil was ordered out of existence by Portugal and smithies were closed at São João de Ipanema. Those efforts reached a peak in a comprehensive attempt to abolish the textile industry in Spanish America in 1800.

The motive for this activity was simple, although not particularly commendable. Spanish and Portuguese producers desired to make as much profit as they could; therefore, they suppressed competition whenever possible. Spanish producers were in a better position for influencing the king of Spain than were the producers in the New World. Consequently, royal decrees tended to favor Spanish and Portuguese producers at the expense of the New World producers.[7]

Spanish Law. Spanish law, heavily influenced by canon law, was transferred virtually intact to become the legal system of Spanish America. The impact was all pervasive. But it should be particularly noted that it influenced the nature of titles to minerals. Minerals in the ground were owned by the state rather than by the surface owner. Private

---

[7] This type of exploitation was not a unique vice of the Iberians. The English applied a similar system in their relations with their colonies—such as the thirteen in North America. To speak even more broadly, nations in general have tended to put such systems into effect when and where they could.

mining companies, then, would have to obtain the concessions permitting them to operate from the governments rather than from the surface owners.

Many laws brought from Spain, such as the price-control laws, were intended by the Crown to protect the Indians and the people generally. Effort was made to regulate wages and conditions of labor in the interest of the Indian. The guild system, a relic of medieval Europe, found a place in some of the craft industries of the New World. Its paternalistic structure was also designed to provide some protection for labor. But generally their ignorance of these institutional arrangements prevented the Indians from taking advantage of them.

Land Tenure and Forced Labor. Individual conquistadores received great tracts of land to exploit much as they chose; and the Crown also gave to them "in trust" the Indians who lived on the land. These were the encomiendas. The royal grant said: "To you are entrusted [*se os encomienda*] the Indians, and they are to be instructed in the precepts of the Holy Catholic faith." A moral responsibility toward the Indians was thus expressed in the grant—however badly the Indians may have been treated in specific cases, especially in the mines where forced labor and virtual slavery prevailed.

About 1720 the encomienda system, as such, was abolished, and land titles assumed more nearly their modern form. Emphasis was on the ownership of the land rather than being centered on the relation with the Indian. The new landholding units came to be called hacienda in Mexico, *estancia* in Argentina, and *fazenda* in Brazil. Leverage over the Indians was maintained by the system of debt peonage.

EVALUATION. Indian discontent with these arrangements during the colonial period led to such incidents as the Tupac Amaru revolt in Peru. But the incomprehensibility of the system is probably an important part of the explanation of the inefficacy of the Indians in either resisting the system or adjusting to it.

The Independence Period (to 1860)

By 1800 Latin America was ripe for revolt; and it was, anyway, the fashion to rebel, following the United States and French revolutions. But what do you do when revolting against something you do not understand? Perhaps you are likely to turn to something else you do not understand but which is ostensibly the opposite of the thing rejected. At any rate, Latin America embraced the political ideals of the French Revolution and the economics of Adam Smith, both something less than indigenous, home-grown-to-the-culture phenomena in Latin America. The free trade idea of Adam Smith was an appealing contrast to the restrictive practices of mercantilism, as was the concept of competitive free private enterprise.

But the group that dominated the Latin American societies after independence had been gained was not the Indian but rather the Creole (the person of pure Spanish blood, born in the New World). The people who understood something of the system against which they were fighting were in a position to supplant it. So, the Creole took power from the *gachupín* (the Spaniard born in Spain). And the Indian remained an outsider in the land of his ancestors.

INSTITUTIONS. *Political Democracy and the Rights of Man.* The leaders of the independence movement, Bolívar and Miranda from Venezuela, Belgrano, Moreno, and San Martín from Argentina, made much of the principle that they were fighting for political democracy and the rights of man against tyranny and kings. But, as it turned out, neither the Indian masses nor their new leaders, the Creoles, had much conception as to what was required to make a political democracy work so as to protect the individual in his "rights." Political chaos and the failure to establish democracy was characteristic of nineteenth-century Latin America.

Land Tenure. Initially in Mexico the independence movement involved a mass Indian revolt in an effort to get the land back. The symbol was the Grito de Dolores of Father Hidalgo in 1810: "My children, this day comes to us a new dispensation. Are you ready to receive it? Will you be free? Will you make the effort to recover from the hated Spaniards the lands stolen from your forefathers three hundred years ago?"[8] But when independence was consummated in the early 1820s, it was the Creoles (and the Church) who had the land.

In the early independence period, the Creoles and the Indians could agree on one thing, opposition to large landholding by the Catholic Church. In fact, between 1750 and 1860 considerable effective action

---

[8] Hubert Howe Bancroft, *History of Mexico* (San Francisco, Bancroft, 1885), IV, 117.

was taken in Latin America against the power position of the Church. Even before independence was obtained, in many parts of Latin America, the Jesuits had been expelled. A dramatic movement against the position of the Church occurred in the 1850s in Mexico. It was called the Reform, and Benito Juárez, a full-blooded Zapotec Indian was the leader. But the result was merely that the Creoles, and the rising mestizo (mixed Spanish and Indian) class, got the land. And the Indians were increasingly dispossessed.

Laissez Faire and Free Trade. It is not difficult to see why there was tremendous pressure in Latin America for a change by 1800. The Creoles had had just enough contact with the English and Dutch to know that better, cheaper, and more abundant merchandise could be obtained from them than from Spain and Portugal. Also, they knew that other countries represented a more profitable market for the products of Latin America than did Spain and Portugal—if only the systems of prohibitions could be broken down.

Adam Smith in England in *The Wealth of Nations* (1776) had, by argument, apparently devastated the mercantilistic position. The new school in economics emphasized the general gain that accrues as a result of greater trade freedom accompanied by geographical specialization. Smith also advocated laissez faire, a concept referring to the independence of private business from governmental regulation and control.

In Latin America some of the most important writers on economics in this period were exponents of the new liberal economics. In Argentina in the 1790s there was Manuel Belgrano, who inveighed against the shackles of mercantilism and espoused a freer type of trade. And Mariano Moreno, in *La Representación de los Hacendados* (1809), argued for opening the port of Buenos Aires to the English because of the general gains that would result from increased imports and exports and also (and this was the bait to gain official approval) because the customs collections would be larger. Viceroy Cisneros did open the port shortly thereafter.

In Brazil several public figures wrote in this vein about 1800. One was José da Silva Lisboa, Visconde de Cayrú. Even before independence was effected, a report on the economic and financial situation of the country, which was made by the Conde da Ponte in 1807, recommended commercial liberty in the style of laissez faire. Indeed, José Bonifacio, the father of the Brazilian independence movement, was himself an adherent of the doctrines of Smith. Similarly in Mexico there was José María Luis Mora (1794–1850); and in Cuba there was Francisco de Arango y Parreño.[9]

TECHNOLOGY. There was little or no scientific progress in Latin America during the nineteenth century. The institutional arrangements did not provide a welcoming environment. And the consequent technological weakness of the society provided much of the explanation of the influence of foreigners and of foreign investments and of the political weakness of the region relative to western Europe.

EVALUATION. To the Indian, the Creoles, following 1810, had little to offer except their own supremacy in the place of the supremacy of the gachupines. But the economic philosophy was still alien and incomprehensible so far as the indigenous population was concerned. And the Creoles had no more interest in instructing the Indians than the gachupines had had before them.

Even if there had not been political chaos in Latin America in the first half of the nineteenth century, it is doubtful that a competitive laissez-faire economic system would have been sufficiently comprehensible to the bulk of the Latin American population to operate as a viable system. At all events, there was during those years in Latin America a noncomprehensible economic system accompanied by considerable political and economic confusion.

[9] Arango y Parreño opposed the mercantilistic controls Spain was exercising in Cuba. But he went one step further and favored the protection of Cuban industry to Cuba's benefit. Such views anticipated what was later to become standard public policy in Latin America.

CHAPTER TWO

EVOLUTION OF ECONOMIC SYSTEMS SINCE 1860

The Late Nineteenth Century

POSITIVISM. By the latter part of the nineteenth century, there were politically effective regimes in several Latin American countries (Mexico, Argentina, and Brazil, at least). And these regimes were attempting to assimilate yet another alien ideology, the Positivism of a Frenchman, Auguste Comte.[1]

Forerunners of the movement were, in Argentina, Juan Bautista Alberdi and Domingo Sarmiento. Later exponents were José Victoriano Lastarria and Valentín Letelier in Chile; José Ingenieros in Argentina; Eugenio María de Hostos y Bonilla in Puerto Rico; and Francisco Bulnes and José Limantour in Mexico. In fact, in Mexico a group of positivists, the Científicos, was responsible for economic planning during the Díaz regime (1876-1911). Brazil, during the middle of the nineteenth century when the Visconde de Mauá was the principal figure, was also under the influence of the positivist viewpoint. A symbol of this influence is the term Ordem e Progresso on the Brazilian flag.

Comte believed that human thinking was evolving into a positive or

---

[1] Works dealing with positivism and with other aspects of the history of economic ideas in Latin America include: W. Rex Crawford, *A Century of Latin American Thought* (Cambridge, Harvard University Press, 1944); *Pensamiento Económico Latinoamericano* (México, Fondo de Cultura Económica, 1945); Jesús Silva Herzog, *El Pensamiento Económico en México* (Mexico, Fondo de Cultura Económica, 1947); and Leopoldo Zea, *El Positivismo en México,* (México, El Colegio de México, 1943).

scientific stage. Positivism involves observation and experience as the basis of the logical process, rather than deductive logic in the manner of Scholasticism. It is, thus, oriented to the scientific method and inductive logic.

The Latin American positivists observed that life was better, in terms of the possession of material goods, in western Europe and the United States than it was in Latin America. They therefore advocated, as good for Latin America, the various things which they believed to be characteristic of the civilizations they admired. Some of the results of this analysis may seem a trifle odd. Bulnes thought he observed that the only truly progressive people ate bread made from wheat. So, he concluded that Mexicans should shift from tortillas to wheat bread.

On a more serious level, it should be mentioned that such observations led them to favor industrialization for Latin America. And, to implement the industrialization, they favored the importation of foreign capital. They had observed, they thought, that capital accumulation was the basis for the strength and prosperity of Western civilization. Therefore, they advocated the encouragement of the migration of capital to Latin America by all possible means. Alberdi said: "The peso is an immigrant that demands concessions and privileges. Grant them, because capital is the left arm of progress." [2]

Alberdi was also a forceful advocate of the desirability of inundating Argentina with a flood of skilled immigrants from Europe: "To govern is to populate." [3] As an aspect of this program, he denounced the native Indian population of Argentina in strong terms as being a useless and barbarous people. The latter attitude toward the native Indian population was, in fact, rather generally characteristic of positivist writers from Argentina to Mexico. A Mexican government publication of the Díaz period called the Indian *un lastre,* a burden on the economy.[4] It was advocated that he should be displaced and his communities destroyed.

IDEALISM. By 1900 there was a strong reaction against Positivism. The reactionary movement has been called idealism. The Uruguayan

---

[2] Juan Bautista Alberdi, *Bases y Puntos de Partida para la Organización de la República Argentina* (Buenos Aires, La Cultura Argentina, 1923), pp. 98–99, 214. First published in 1852.

[3] *Ibid.,* p. 214.

[4] Frank Tannenbaum, *Mexico: The Struggle for Peace and Bread* (New York, Knopf, 1950), p. 139.

Rodó, a major idealist in the years immediately preceding World War I, alleged the Latin American nature to be "Ariel triumphant"; and "Ariel triumphant signifies idealism and order in life, noble inspiration in thought, lack of dogmatism in moral questions, good taste in art, heroism in action, consideration in habits." [5] This appeal to spiritual values and for disregard of material considerations did not contribute greatly to the resolution of Latin American difficulties in the early twentieth century, in spite of Rodó's assertion that

it has been noticed more than once that the great advances of history, the great epochs, the brightest and most fruitful periods in the evolution of humanity, are almost always the result of two distinct but interacting forces which generate, as a result of the concentrated force of their opposition, a living dynamism and stimulation—which disappear, exhausted, when absolute unity exists.[6]

A conflict of opposing ideologies may lead to progress, but the conflict of positivism with idealism did not.

Because they were searching for a mystical ideal, such writers have been prone to criticize capitalistic and United States society on the grounds that they have been based on the pursuit of material gain. The crass, crude, materialistic culture of the United States, where the production of goods by the brute machine was emphasized, represented a culture to be spurned by one searching after the "ideal."

It was natural that this group of writers should attack the manifestations of foreign, capitalistic imperialism which were an important influence in Latin America by the close of the nineteenth century. The strong-arm tactics, sometimes used by foreign capital, provided a basis for such a denunciation; it became popular to denounce Tío Sam and his "big stick."

As a result of such attitudes, the idealist school of philosophy, which had little indeed to contribute toward the genuine improvement of the region, came to occupy an influential position in a Latin America which was, to a large measure, both jealous of and dominated by foreign capital.

It is one of the great tragedies of the Latin American culture that the positivists, the group which to some extent was earnestly trying to

[5] José Enrique Rodó, *Ariel* (Buenos Aires, Ediciones Jackson, 1945), p. 97. The work was originally published in 1900.
[6] *Ariel*, p. 63.

advance the well-being of the region, became associated with foreign imperialism and that idealism unfortunately became the most popular school of philosophy because of a very doubtful contribution in terms of ego gratification.

As of 1910, the Indian and mestizo in Latin America still remained nonunderstanding outsiders in the land of their ancestors. They could scarcely understand what this succession of alien ideologies had meant to them. No doubt, they understood certain things all too well. For example, the loss of the communal land to the landlords was something of which the Indians generally were sullenly resentful. But most of the rest of what was happening to them in the social and economic sphere must have been quite beyond their comprehension.

SYSTEMS OF LAND TENURE. The pittance of agricultural land which is so important as a source of sustenance in Latin America, and from which half of the population derives its livelihood, by 1910 had come to be owned under several different systems of landholding: (1) the *latifundio,* (2) community holding, (3) small individual properties, (4) land colonization projects.

(1) The *latifundio* is the large estate. It is called, in various parts of Latin America: hacienda, estancia, or fazenda. By 1910 it was the predominant type of landholding in Latin America. One estimate had it that in that year 834 *hacendados* owned two thirds of Mexico. And the situation was much the same in Chile, Argentina, and Brazil.

Despite the fact that land was owned in large units, the hacienda system (at least in the region stretching from Mexico to Chile, if not in Argentina and São Paulo) was characterized by subsistence farming in small plots. The hacendado assigned plots of a very few acres to individual peons, who then farmed them with primitive methods, involving frequently only a wooden hoe or a forked stick—and no fertilizer.

The peon was bound to the hacienda by the system of debt peonage which centered on the procedures of the hacienda store, the *tienda de raya.* In pre-1910 Mexico, so long as a peon was in debt to the hacendado, he could not leave the hacienda, and his chance of getting out of debt was almost nonexistent. Peons who attempted to run off to work in the mines were frequently caught and brought back by force, the federal police (*rurales*) being used for this purpose.

(2) By 1910 the community type of landholding, which had dom-

inated Aztec Mexico and Inca Peru, was almost nonexistent. Only in remote mountain regions, where the soil was likely to be rocky and unproductive, did communal landholding villages remain.

(3) Small individual holdings, called *peonías* or *caballerías,* had played a minor role following the Conquest. And, called ranchos in Mexico, or *chacras* in Argentina, they have continued to play a minor role in the Latin American landholding scheme of things. Also, various arrangements involving leaseholds and farming on shares have been used in Latin America, especially in Argentina.

(4) Sporadically, great hopes have been placed in the possibilities offered by colonization projects, either for resettling farmers working plots that are too small or for attracting groups of immigrants. Great areas of unused national domain, *baldíos,* have been the object of such efforts. And projects such as the settlement of Mennonites in Paraguay and of White Russians at Varpa in São Paulo, Brazil, have been implemented on a rather minor scale.

But, in general, as of 1910, the large landholding unit, inefficiently farmed in small plots, was the characteristic agricultural form in Latin America.

Catholic Economic Philosophy

The Catholic Church has been one of the most influential institutions introduced from Europe into Latin America. In view of this influence, it seems worthwhile to catalog some of the Catholic views, especially on economic matters.

Fundamentally, the Catholic Church has approached economic problems from (1) a moral viewpoint. Its economic doctrines have not, therefore, involved economic *laws,* as laissez faire purports to do, nor have they involved an attempt to describe the world as it actually is. Rather, they describe how the world should be.

The Church has believed that (2) private property rights in land should be protected. The possessor of land should not abuse his rights, but he does not lose his property rights merely because he does misuse the property.

It also has believed that (3) there may be inequality in the distribution of income. The individual who receives more than an equal share should give "of" his excess as charity. But the Church does not consider that the individual is obligated to give away all of the excess.

The Catholic Church has believed that in connection with loans of money (4) it is proper to charge a small interest to cover the cost of making the loan available. This now includes loans for both production and consumption. Thus, the taking of interest is not condemned absolutely, as was the case during the Middle Ages.

The Church still subscribes to a concept called (5) the "just" price. During the Middle Ages, the "just" price was a set price in terms of money. To sell an item of goods for anything other than the "just" price was both criminal and immoral. At present, the concept of the "just" price has a slightly different meaning. It is a price set as a result of free bargaining between buyer and seller under conditions guaranteeing that each has equal bargaining power.

In many of the countries of Europe and Latin America, the Catholic Church has sponsored (6) a labor movement. But unions sponsored by the Church do not emphasize the use of strikes, picketing, and assorted kinds of strong-arm pressures. The members are not encouraged to "kick against the pricks." The members attempt, rather, to help themselves by systems of mutual insurance and mutual assistance.

(7) The Church's bitter opposition to Communism has been widely publicized. Not so well known is the position of the Church with respect to capitalism. (8) The Church opposes capitalism on the ground primarily, it would seem, that exploitation is involved in accumulating capital funds and in distributing profits. The capitalists have a bargaining position which is immensely stronger than that of the workers. The Church believes that it is immoral for individuals at key positions in the capitalistic process to make excessive profits as the result of their position. Pope Pius XI said: "It [capitalism] is not by nature vicious, but it violates the proper order of justice to have capital enslave workers or members of the proletariat." [7]

(9) The Church also believes that society should be well ordered. This belief would seem to be tacit, if not explicit, in the position of the Church on many of the world's political and economic problems. The individual should know his "place"; he should be reasonably content therein; and he should refrain from troublemaking. The Catholic intellectual Luigi Sturzo quotes evidence that Pope Pius XI was probably of the opinion that the authoritarian form of government was not only

---

[7] Joaquín Azpiazú, *Moral Profesional Económica* (Buenos Aires, E. Poblet, 1943), p. 72.

best for the Church but best for the state as well.[8] And many Catholic thinkers have thought that nations should be organized into corporations of different industries, with employers organized in one group and employees in another—much after the model of the corporate state that Mussolini actually established in Italy.

In these troubled times, it is difficult to bring about the well-ordered society. The more responsible element in the Church undoubtedly believes that man's good will to man should lead people into such a society, but hardly considers it desirable to use strong-arm methods to bring about that result. Various groups closely connected with the Catholic Church viewpoint, however, are not so scrupulous. The Franco government in Spain, supported by much of the Catholic Church hierarchy in that country, seems to have imposed a "well-ordered society" on the people by force. The *falange* movement in Latin America has attempted, under the sponsorship of Franco, to do the same thing for the various New World countries. The *sinarquismo* movement in Mexico has been an offshoot of this sort of thinking. And the Perón regime in Argentina, at least for a time, seemed to be in this tradition, as did the Vargas government of the late 1930s in Brazil.

Twentieth-century Philosophies

THE MEXICAN REVOLUTION. Since 1910 there have been indications that a great change might be occurring in Latin America. The first major manifestation of this possibility was the Mexican Revolution. It began as a spontaneous, indigenous movement, being directed primarily against the hacendados and the foreign investors. This revolutionary movement, unlike the Marxist and the fascist, has been eclectic. It has drawn its doctrines from many different sources as it has needed them. Much of the strength of the movement would seem to lie in the circumstance that it has been indigenous and eclectic.

Among the eclectic elements in the process are the following:

(1) The idea of the communal landholding village, which came to be called the *ejido,* was derived from the Aztec *altepetlalli* and *calpulli.*

(2) From the Spanish law was drawn the idea that the government is the owner of the minerals in the ground. In Article 27 of the Constitution of 1917, the Mexican government reclaimed the ownership

---

[8] *Nationalism and Internationalism* (New York, Roy, 1946), p. 67.

of such minerals, which had very largely passed to foreign control as a result of special legislation during the Díaz period.

(3) From Marxian Socialism has been drawn the idea of a class struggle and much socialistic jargon.

(4) From progressive education, influenced by John Dewey in the United States, has come much of the inspiration for reform of the Mexican education system.

(5) In the best positivist tradition, the attempt to industrialize has become a major facet of the program.

(6) From the new cosmopolitan profession of economic development planners, Mexico has acquired a respect for such planning.

But more important than any one of these derived doctrines is the fusion of doctrines itself.

In recent decades economic development in Mexico has been among the most rapid in Latin America. This is what the institutional theory would indicate should be the case. The revolution destroyed or undermined the influence of many of the long-established institutions and gave development a chance such as it has not had in various of the countries which have remained dominated by the hacendado class.

LAND REFORM. At this point it may well be desirable to say something more about land reform in general and the Mexican agrarian reform in particular. Land redistribution procedures were formalized in Article 27 of the Constitution of 1917. Provision was made for four processes: (a) the repossession of land "illegally" acquired by the hacendados and its return to the Indian villages from which it had been taken (restitution); (b) the expropriation of land (with the promise of compensation) from the haciendas and the giving of such land to the Indian villages having need of land (dotation); (c) the breaking up of the large estates, as an end desirable in itself (*fraccionamiento*); (d) colonization of people needing land on the public domain. The second of the processes, dotation, became by far the most important. The first process, restitution, was chiefly directed at land taken from the villages during the Díaz period under what came to be called a misinterpretation of the Laws of the Reform of the 1850s. Fraccionamiento and colonization have played lesser roles.[9]

[9] Two very different types of books about Latin American agriculture are:

Land redistribution reached a peak of activity during the Cárdenas presidency between 1934 and 1940.

As an indication of how far this Mexican land reform has gone, it may be said that, at the end of 1962, 46 million hectares (a hectare is about 2.5 acres) had been redistributed.[10] Title to some 23 percent of the area of the country had changed hands. Involved were 1,900,000 *ejidatarios* living in 26,000 ejidos. The average area of crop land per ejidatario had come to be between five and six hectares. This is not a great deal of land from which to obtain subsistence. The millennium has not arrived in Mexico; but the country has been confronting a major problem.

There have been two chief types of ejidos: (a) those in which the land is distributed to the ejidatarios to be worked in small plots and (b) those in which the whole ejido is farmed as a unit. The latter procedure permits division of labor and the opportunity to make greater use of machinery than would otherwise be the case.

The Mexican land redistribution program has undoubtedly done much psychologically for the Indian and the peon. It has provided the basis for increased self-respect and self-reliance. But the plots into which much of the land has been broken are wastefully small.

There is no particular point in arguing whether these plots grow a microscopic amount more or less now than they grew in the time of Díaz. The issue is not the relative productiveness of the hacienda and the ejido. Both the hacienda and the small-plot ejido have been inefficient units. The land itself needs to be farmed as a large unit to take advantage of the possibilities provided by modern farming methods. Perhaps organizational arrangements can be worked out that will permit the farming of most of the ejidos as units of respectable size.

This was what was intended in the collectivization of the Laguna area around Torreón, the *henequén* plantations of Yucatan, and the sugar-growing area around Los Mochis in Sinaloa. The troubles of the ejidos in the Laguna area have been one of the major tragedies of the agrarian reform. The trouble seems, in part, to have been due to drought and

Edmundo Flores, *Tratado de Economía Agrícola* (México, Fondo de Cultura Económica, 1961); Eyler Simpson, *The Ejido, Mexico's Way Out* (Chapel Hill, University of North Carolina Press, 1937).

[10] James V. Cornehls, *Mexico's Rural Road to Progress* (Austin, Texas, University of Texas Ph.D. dissertation, 1964), pp. 17–43.

the drying up of the Nazas River. Also there have been administrative failures, especially in the Ejido Bank in Torreón.[11]

Another unsatisfactory feature of the Mexican arrangements has been the manner in which the legal ties have bound the ejidatario to the individual plot. If he leaves the plot or does not farm it for a time, he loses his stake completely. If he is discouraged by drought and poor crops, he cannot sell his land to obtain a nest egg to maintain his family while he establishes himself in the city. This is important since it is in the natural course of events that a substantial number of rural people should migrate to the industrial centers during the next few years.

Many, if not most, Latin American countries have made gestures in the direction of land reform during the past fifty years. Following many of the innumerable successful revolutions that have occurred in Latin America during this period, the leader has promised land reform. He has frequently gotten a land reform law through the legislature. But after this early flurry of activity, the new leader has been likely to let the program drag, except for confiscation of the estates of the former president and some of his friends.

The Alliance for Progress at its inception in 1961 called for substantial social and economic reform in Latin America—and especially for land reform. And a new law of the same old sort is one of the criteria as to whether there is satisfactory fulfillment of Alliance for Progress goals.

In spite of all the lip service that has been paid to the principle of land reform during recent years, it remains vague as to just what should go into a worthwhile land reform. Breaking up the great estates into ten-acre plots, which are then given to inadequately helped and inadequately financed ex-peons, is hardly the right prescription. If the peon can mortgage the land, he is all too likely to lose it to the holder of the mortgage. If he cannot mortgage the land or sell it, he is then tied to it in a kind of servitude that in some ways is more vicious than the old debt peonage.

The communal farm, without individually assigned plots, but using large-scale farming methods and considerable amounts of equipment,

---

[11] Juan Ballesteros Porta, *Explotación Individual o Colectiva?—El Caso de los Ejidos de Tlahualilo* (México, Centro de Investigaciones Agrarias, Instituto Mexicano de Investigaciones Económicas, 1964).

is a distinct possibility. But much remains to be done in terms of working out the appropriate administrative machinery for such arrangements. The Mexican experience since 1910 offers a good deal of information; but the Mexican collectively farmed ejidos do not yet seem to have found satisfactory solution to the administrative problem. The ejido banks, which have assumed responsibility for much of the administration as well as much of the financing, may represent a tool which can be made to serve this purpose satisfactorily. But apparently their record up to now has left a good deal to be desired. They have been weak especially at the very lowest level in terms of day-to-day technical advice and assistance to the ejidatarios.

Another possibility is to leave the ownership situation much as it is so far as the large estates are concerned, but to enforce the laws (or enact some new ones) requiring effective utilization of the land as an alternative to forfeiture. Then, in addition, the social security laws and the minimum wage laws should be effectively applied to the large estates.

A third possibility is increased emphasis on the medium-sized family farm of 160 to 640 acres. This is the unit with least basis in the Latin American tradition. But it may offer some real possibilities, if adequate credit arrangements could be established both to finance the purchase of the land and to finance the farmer after the land has been purchased.

State-owned and directly managed farms are another possibility. Cuba is experimenting with this sort of thing. It is no doubt possible that a state farm with a dedicated manager could be a fine, productive place to work. But, except in the state farms which are also agricultural experiment stations, the chance that administration will be decently competent and conscientious seems to remain in doubt. This may be the particular setting where government operation would be at its worst, where bureaucracy would really earn its reputation.

It may well be true that in the land reform proposals too much attention has been given to the land ownership question and too little attention to the effort to see to it that the standard of living of people working the land rises. It might be a good idea to let the land titles rest the way they are (except for enforcement of the laws requiring efficient farming of the land as an alternative to losing it). Adequate credit, technical assistance, and the use of improved production methods (fertilizer and equipment) should be encouraged. And the social security and minimum wage laws should be conscientiously applied in agriculture.

SOCIALISM. The Mexican Revolution may or may not be "socialistic" —depending upon one's meaning for the term. But it cannot be identified with Marxian Socialism. Cuba, under Fidel Castro since 1958, is the only Latin American country to identify itself overtly with Marxian Socialism. However, there are active Marxist groups with differing primary loyalties in most of the countries. Some are oriented to the Soviet Union, some to Communist China. Some are oriented to the Second International, some to the Third International (Lenin), some to the Fourth International (Trotsky), and so on.

It is virtually impossible to separate the fact from the fiction and wishful thinking in connection with the Cuba of Fidel Castro. The truth is in neither the detractors nor the eulogizers. They are much too involved emotionally. Nor is significant truth probably to be found in the texts of the laws which have been passed since 1958. Having been in the Havana airport once since 1958 (in the rain in the middle of the night for a couple of hours) is probably not much more of a disqualification for talking about the impact of the reform than is the spending of a few days being shown the farms the government wants one to see or a few days searching up the other kind. I think I shall limit myself to a few impressionistic comments that may be misguided.

The announcement by Castro, during the summer of 1963, that for the next few years his regime was going to emphasize agriculture in general and sugar production in particular (rather than industrialization) may be taken as a significant indication of various things. Of course, pretty crudely, it means that Khrushchev has told Castro that the Soviet Union will not underwrite significant Cuban industrialization. And this has left him in a "sugar or else" position, whether he likes it or not.

Despite considerable talk to the effect that land would be redistributed from the great estates into small holdings, it seems that in fact the expropriated land is being organized for the most part (1) into cooperatives and (2) into state farms (so-called people's farms). Very little land has been distributed to individual small farmers (*colonos*). Thus the administrative organization and the competence of the managers of the cooperatives and state farms acquire overriding importance in influencing the efficacy of the new arrangements. The whole operation seems to be run by a giant state agency called INRA (Instituto Nacional de Reforma Agraria). There have been stories of administrative bungling. And the fact that Castro and other important leaders have denounced the bungling would seem to confirm its existence. In fact, when a shift in emphasis from cooperatives to people's farms occurred in 1962, Castro explained that it was due to the fact that cooperative members had "suddenly turned into semiexploiters of the work of others." [12] Apparently, the chief trouble was that the permanent members of the cooperatives were exploiting the seasonal workers. Castro could feel for the seasonal workers since he has occasionally made a point of going out and being one of them during the harvest. Just what is to keep the bureaucrats managing the people's farms from being semi-exploiters remains to be seen. But one should be slow to conclude that this means that the system is in danger of imminent collapse. The Russians repeatedly since 1918 have practiced this same sort of self-castigation. They have practiced some bloody purges in the process. But, whether one likes it or not, the Russian system has emerged stronger from its periods of trial. Whether Cuba has the stomach to develop in this sort of an evolutionary pattern and whether Castro has the ability and determination to make the process work, only time can tell.

Meantime, there seems to have been a significant decline in sugar production in Cuba, despite major effort to keep production up. But there may have been a significant increase in truck-gardening production which, in terms of effect on level of living, may largely have offset the sugar decline.

It should have been possible for the aerial reconnaissance over Cuba to provide some pretty comprehensive data on growing crops and on acreage harvested. But if the United States government has worthwhile information of this sort, it has not been revealed.

Whether the Cuban people really like the new land-tenure arrangements is in the realm of pure conjecture. And whether they will like them ten years from now (if they still have them ten years from now) is even more conjectural.

THE CORPORATE STATE. National Socialism and Fascism, written with capital letters, have come and gone; but the corporate state, which

[12] New York *Times,* August 26, 1962.

was the basic economic ingredient in those politico-economic systems, remains as an influence in Latin America.

The set of relations among the government, the unions, and the employer organizations that has come to exist in several Latin American countries is suggestive of the corporate state. There is enough lack of uniformity from country to country in these relations so that the analyst might well hesitate to allege a pattern. And yet some very similar characteristics have emerged in Mexico, Brazil, and Argentina in spite of very different historical backgrounds. In Mexico they have evolved out of the leftward-oriented Revolution; in Brazil they have evolved out of the Estado Novo of Vargas; in Argentina, out of Peronism. But behind these recent influences, the corporate state may basically be a natural development in countries with the Spanish and Portuguese legal traditions (derived out of the southern European sort of Code-Napoleon, Roman-law background). But it is certainly not part of the Don Quixote tradition.

First, let us look at the employer association aspect of the picture. Employers are highly organized in Latin America up to and including hemisphere-wide organizations such as the Asociación de Industriales de Latinoamérica, established in 1962. There is a tendency (approaching being a requirement) that employers must join the appropriate trade association. The association is then used as a semiofficial, or even official, instrument through which the government can implement decisions it makes about production practices, pricing policies, labor-management relations. But by the same token, the association then becomes the recognized spokesman for the industry in influencing the government into applying policies desired by the industry. This verges on being formal administrative channels for action, both ways, in many Latin American countries. This may be contrasted with the situation in the United States, where the trade associations function as lobbying organizations and may even be asked for their views by the government. But, except for the brief NRA period (circa 1933), the trade associations have not had a legally established role in relation to the government apparatus.

Just as the relation of the government to the trade association is more formalized in Latin America than it is in the United States, so also is the pattern of arrangements by which labor-management disputes are supposed to be settled more formalized in Latin America. The law is likely to provide in some detail for the negotiating and conciliation procedures through which the parties must proceed, or for the role of government in conciliation and arbitration. There is considerable variation from country to country as to just what these procedures are. But the general proposition is that the procedures are formalized in a three-way employer-union-state relationship in a setting that may be contrasted with the situation in the United States, where free collective bargaining is ostensibly independent of government interference. This formalization of the labor-management bargaining machinery through the government is important enough to be identified as a characteristic of the Latin American politico-economic scene.

One may find signs of the existence of the corporate state in Mexico in the manner in which the dominant political party, Partido de la Revolución Institucional, breaks down into functional groups. To the extent that there is a popular voice in selecting the presidential nominee of the party, for example, that voice is expressed through the participation of these functional groups in the confidential processes through which the nominee is selected. Also in Mexico both the trade associations and the labor unions have a formalized existence in terms of their relationship with the government. With regard to this situation in connection with labor unions, Raymond Vernon has written: ". . . it does not violate reality too much to think of Mexico's labor unions as an arm of government through which it seeks to affect the conduct of the private sector." [13]

In Argentina, under Perón, both the employer associations and the labor unions came under the effective control of the government. And the legal form of much of this control mechanism has remained even though Perón has departed the scene.

In setting up his New State in the late 1930s, Vargas, instead of using a system of controls operating through the already existing employer associations and trade unions, chose to establish a wholly new hierarchy of organization (the formal corporate state after the model of Fascist Italy). The government would presumably direct the operation of the whole economy through this "corporate" structure. Much of this organization was still only on paper when the regime was overthrown in 1945. But, more important to note, is that a good deal of the organization, including aspects reaching down to some of the grass roots of the eco-

[13] Raymond Vernon, *The Dilemma of Mexico's Development* (Cambridge, Harvard University Press, 1963), p. 65.

nomic system, was a functioning organization; and this organization was not abolished with the overthrow of Vargas. It remains as a vehicle through which the government influences the economy and is influenced in its turn by labor and employers.

Fortunately (I trust I can say fortunately), this corporate state structure in Latin America has lacked the paramilitary aspect that it assumed in Fascist Italy and in Nazi Germany. Also, the legislative bodies have not been elected out of the hierarchy of labor-employer organizations. This is an important difference from Fascist Italy or Nazi Germany.

Nevertheless, as a general evaluation of the economic systems in Latin America, I think there is a substantial element of truth in something like the following statement: The Latin American economies are not more socialistic than the United States economy. Nationalized industry characterizes no larger percentage of the economy than is the case in the United States. But the Latin American government plays, or tries to play, a far more all-pervasive role in the regulation of the economy down to very minor details than is the case in the United States. At the same time, the relations among business, labor, and the government tend to have a formalized character. In applying a name to a system of this sort, when one is especially impressed by what it means in terms of all-embracing organization plus paper-work drudgery, this system may be called, as it has been in Brazil, the cartorial (or paper-shuffling) state. But it also has an importance as an institutional form that justifies calling it by a more substantial name. And it has enough of the features of the corporate state so that the possible appropriateness of that name should not be overlooked. It may be worthwhile for some self-styled Latin American leftists to speculate as to whether that is the sort of a regime they are developing, a sort of politico-economic system generally identified with the right. The Don Quixote predilection for anarchy may keep such a system from really strait-jacketing the economy—just as Mussolini in Italy never quite made the corporate state a reality. Nevertheless the corporate state, Latin American style, implemented by people who consider themselves leftists, has some interesting possibilities.

Whether the existence of competition and laissez faire makes a positive contribution to development is a debatable point. Whether the corporate state is a satisfactory economic instrument is not clear. Whether the Latin American economic regimes are tending to become corporate states is not established. Whether economic development planners have a predilection for corporate states is a question that has not generally been put that way in recent years. That corporate states are a device by which businessmen, labor unions, and the government connive against the people as consumers is a real possibility.

I hope I have phrased these comments in such a way as to indicate my own uncertainty as to what is actually going on and as to what will come of it all.

Despite the uncertainties, one needs to be aware of various possibilities. A union between the development planners (frustrated by the politicians), the oligarchy, and the army is one route Latin America may follow. The result might have some of the characteristics of the "rationalization" which was in vogue in the 1930s and made its small contribution to the emergence of fascism. Victor Alba has written that: ". . . the dictatorship of the technocrats or of the impatient soldiers is history's punishment for the failure of the democratic left in Latin America." [14]

The Present Problem

One thing is, I believe, clear. There has not yet come into being a homogeneous social and economic system which Latin Americans in general accept as their own. Rather, there remain these manifestations: a wealthy class still desperately protecting its vested interests, a great amount of general ferment, a commonly held feeling that major changes are imminent, and a quite widespread feeling that such changes are desirable. It is, then, a discontented, troubled land which stretches from Tijuana to Tierra del Fuego.

The sheer economic anarchy, as well as the resultant political unrest, of the last 130 years in Latin America can very largely be blamed on the fact that in that region there has been no economic order with a claim to general support, and, in the absence of such a system, no new theory of economic order has developed.

"In Latin America the propensity to import ideologies is still very strong. . . ." [15]

---

[14] Victor Alba, "Latin America's Future Leaders," in *New Republic*, September 21, 1963, p. 13.
[15] United Nations, *Towards a Dynamic Development Policy for Latin America* (New York, 1963), p. 17.

Appendix: Political Program

Economic development in Latin America is unlikely to be a smashing success without political viability. A stable, accepted, and respected political regime needs to be part of the pattern of indigenously evolving institutions. It may well be that the social and political underpinning of economic development can contribute more to that development than can economic planning per se.

At any rate, the preceding argument may serve as a justification to permit an economist to say something about the political order in Latin America.

Reconsideration of United States attempts to form a solid front of American countries against Communism might be discreet. Perhaps we had better concentrate on removing the conditions that induced the anti-United States and consequent pro-Communist attitudes rather than treating the Communist menace as the primary problem.

We are not going to rally to our side a bloc of effective anti-Communist countries by the strong-arm methods tried in Guatemala in 1954 and in Cuba in 1961. Having the membership of a responsible international organization voluntarily and enthusiastically behind us (or rather in front of us) might well be a *sine qua non* before we embark on another effort to overthrow an installed regime in a Latin American country. Actually the international agency had better be the initiatory and active instrument. Our role might well be to try to mobilize effective opposition to dictatorship, tyranny, and political murder. A major project in our foreign policy could be encouragement of effort to codify rules for identifying a government which should be socially outcast and for dealing with such a government. We had better not assume that Latin America should or will join with us in a great anti-Communist crusade, and is acting improperly if it does not. Latin America is not going to join us in such a crusade. And the society of nations is not going to identify Communism as per se grounds for ostracism. And Latin Americans are going to resent our efforts to get anti-Communist commitments which will not mean much even if obtained.

The advocacy by the Kennedy Administration of revolutionary social and economic reform in Latin America may sound like the appropriate change in policy. But to advocate revolution as policy for Latin America is a little like carrying coals to Newcastle. It would be more relevant to inquire why nothing has come of repeated revolutions in the land that invented revolutions. Revolution is not enough. And the contemporary, official view of the Alliance for Progress that we should endorse revolution in Latin America misses the point. We, in the United States, have always endorsed revolution in Latin America (or condemned it) according to our lights. In any event, Latin American revolutions have always commanded considerable sympathetic support in this country. And Latin American revolutions have accomplished so little!

Perhaps support of revolution is not nearly as important as effective aid in implementing the reforms after the revolution. The United States has been historically remiss in this regard (Guatemala in 1955, Cuba in 1958, and the Dominican Republic in 1962 are examples of this neglect). The proponents of revolutions have some obligation to see the job through.

But to return to the main political-policy argument, the United States can properly oppose dictatorship, it can properly oppose tyranny, it can properly oppose wholesale murder. However, if it is going to make an international policy out of such opposition, it had better be consistent in implementing the policy.

We need to move down the long and difficult path that must be followed in the effort to create an international machinery that can effectively identify and deal with tyranny rather than with Communism. We just have to gamble that Communism will be attended to, automatically or not, on its merits.

Perhaps what the United States should argue for is something like this: No member of the United Nations (or the Organization of American States) will diplomatically recognize any but a democratically elected government in the future. All governments now in being are recognized, unless the United Nations takes positive action to condemn. And perhaps it should condemn a few in this sense, such as the governments of Paraguay and Haiti. But the past is not the major consideration; the major consideration is the establishment of orderly, supranational procedures for passing judgments on new governments. No government established by revolution should be recognized by anybody. This is not necessarily to condemn revolutions. But the pressure should be strong for prompt elections. All economic contact, trade, and the movement of private citizens to and from the nonrecognized governments might well be suspended. Such action, by the Organization of American States or by the United Nations, might be surprisingly effective, especially in relation to new governments.

It is high time that the international community assumed the obligation of guaranteeing to the people of all countries governments of their own choosing. "I am my brother's keeper." ("But I should not impose my judgment as to what is good for my brother unless the world community endorses my biases.") The difficult trail the United States should follow is to try to obtain this power for the United Nations or the Organization of American States, not for itself. Meanwhile, the United States might well scrupulously abstain from unilateral action that seems to presume that the United States has the wit and wisdom to sit in judgment on other countries and then implement its judgment unilaterally.

Once this is done, the position of the United States vis-à-vis the domestic, political, and economic systems in the Latin American countries (and perhaps in all underdeveloped countries) had better be that the nature of such systems is primarily a domestic concern. The Latin American countries (and especially the young idealists in those countries) had better, for their part, think rather more in terms of the building from within of a viable system. Swinging like a pendulum from advocacy of one foreign ideology to advocacy of another has been going on all too long in Latin America. Also, the aid gotten first by begging in one foreign camp and then in another may well not make as much contribution to economic development as a determined, intelligent, domestic effort would make. It is odd that the young idealist in the land of Rodó does not have a more imaginative expression for his anti-yankeeism than a swing to uncritical advocacy of Communism.

PART TWO

MARKET ORGANIZATION

CHAPTER THREE

TYPES OF BUSINESS ORGANIZATION

Setting

It has been estimated that there are about two million business enterprises in Latin America, agriculture excluded.[1] This figure compares with six million for the United States. The labor force in the services, business, and industry, outside of agriculture, is about 25 million in Latin America. In the United States, the figure is well over 60 million. In Latin America over 50 percent of the firms are engaged in trade and commerce, about 20 percent in manufacturing. But this latter 20 percent includes many of the largest enterprises.

In a very basic sense, Latin American governments exercise "control of entry" in connection with the establishment of new firms. Of course, control of entry could be used as an effective tool in economic development planning. But, historically, that has not been the role the Latin American governments have played in exercising this power. Rather, the power to permit or prohibit operation has been the tool the low-level administrative official or policeman has been able to use to obtain bribes from the small merchant or tradesman, or stall holder in the market. The intimate relation between the small merchant and the associated administrative official is one of the most important characterizing institutional features of the Latin American scene. If the businessman is strong enough, he intimidates the official. If he is weak, he is intimidated by the official. But in either case, the formalizing of the relationship results in a fantastic amount of paper work. The paper work ostensibly provides

[1] *Latin American Business Highlights* (Chase Manhattan Bank), Fourth Quarter, 1957, p. 8.

the basis for effective government supervision and regulation of the activities of the businessman. And it thus provides some of the justification for inquiring whether Latin American economies may appropriately be called corporate states. Actually, the results of the paper work are almost entirely bootless. Or they would be bootless except for the fact that the documents are never destroyed. And the preparation and preservation of the paper represents an administrative boondoggle of major proportions.

If this documentation had been accurately prepared, all of this paper would represent a rich source of data for the study of the business history of Latin America. And perhaps the assiduous research worker may be able to glean something from these records. But for the most part, the evidence that all of this paper has to offer is inaccurate and substantially worthless. Such is the cartorial state; and it may reasonably be said that the cartorial (or paper-shuffling) state is itself an institutional barrier to economic development.

Legal Organization of Firms

The possible forms of business organization are somewhat more numerous, and somewhat more precisely differentiated by the basic law, in the various Latin American countries than is the case in the United States.

In the following discussion, most of the specific information given is applicable to Mexico. The Spanish names for the different types of organizations are the Mexican names. But the legal provisions are almost identical in the other countries, and the names are generally similar, although not always identical. For example, the word *compañía* is frequently substituted for *sociedad*. There is even a remarkable similarity in the Portuguese (Brazilian) and French (Haitian) expressions.[2]

SINGLE PROPRIETORSHIP. In Latin America, as in the United States, the single proprietorship, the enterprise that identifies an individual owner with the firm, characterizes agriculture and is also found quite

[2] Two readily available sources of information on business organization in Latin America should be mentioned: Pan American Union, *A Statement of the Laws of Venezuela in Matters Affecting Business* (3d ed., Washington, 1962); United States, Department of Commerce, *Overseas Business Reports, Establishing a Business in Venezuela* (Washington, 1962). There are publications in both of these series for virtually all of the Latin American countries.

TYPES OF BUSINESS ORGANIZATION

commonly in the retail trades, but less commonly in mining and in manufacturing. In general, as a prerequisite for establishing a single proprietorship, the individual must be legally competent to sign contracts. Beyond this there is little restriction.

SOCIEDAD EN NOMBRE COLECTIVO (S. en N.C.). This form of organization is equivalent to the simple partnership in the United States. All of the partners are equally responsible for all of the debts of the partnership to an unlimited extent. Any agreement to limit the liability of one of the partners has validity only among the partners. A third-party creditor may collect from whichever of the partners has money—much as is the case in the United States.

SOCIEDAD EN COMANDITA SIMPLE (S. en C.). This is a partnership with two types of partners. One, called the *comanditado,* is responsible in the same sense as applies to all the partners in the sociedad en nombre colectivo. Only the names of the comanditados may be used in the title of the business. The other partners, called *comanditarios* (silent partners), are liable only for the amount of their contribution to the partnership. Their private fortunes are not touched in case the partnership goes bankrupt.

SOCIEDAD DE RESPONSABILIDAD LIMITADA (S. de R.L.). This type of organization differs markedly from any found in the United States. In Mexico it is composed of not more than twenty-five members. In the event of bankruptcy, the members are liable only for their contribution to the business (or if it is so provided, for double their original contribution) and not for additional sums. The capital contribution of all the members must total at least 5,000 pesos, a rather modest $400 (U.S.). The contributions are evidenced by shares of stock, called *partes sociales,* which are not negotiable in the sense that ordinary corporate stock may be bought and sold on stock exchanges. In general, the vote is allotted among the members in proportion to the amount of stock which they possess.

This type of business does not automatically dissolve with the death of one of the members as is the case with the simple forms of partnership. The share of a deceased member may be passed to an heir without affecting the functioning of the business.

The organizational structure is much like that of the corporation. An advantage of this type of organization by comparison with the corporation is in the lack of formality and publicity attendant upon its formation and operation. Numerically, this seems to be a more popular form of organization than the corporation in Brazil and various other countries, although, if economic importance is measured by value of assets, it is surely less important.

SOCIEDAD ANÓNIMA (S.A.). This type of organization compares with the incorporated business in the United States, except that it is created (acquires legal existence) by contract (among the stockholders) rather than by charter. And yet important prerogatives, such as may be very important in doing business, may be acquired only after registration. The number of members, or stockholders, is unlimited, except for the provision of a minimum (in Mexico this minimum is five). The stockholders, in the event of bankruptcy, are liable only for their original contribution. The original capital contribution must amount to at least some minimum figure: 25,000 pesos, about $2,000 (U.S.) in Mexico. A claim on ownership is represented by a share of stock. Unlike the *sociedad de responsabilidad limitada,* the *sociedad anónima* offers the stock for initial public subscription, and thereafter the shares may be bought and sold without the prior approval of the company. Voting power in the company is proportioned to the amount of stock held.

The controlling unit in the organization is the stockholders' meeting, the *asamblea general de accionistas*. The stockholders, at their meeting, select a board of directors, the *consejo de administración,* to represent their interests in the supervision of corporate policy. The actual officers of the business, the *gerentes,* are hired employees who are directly responsible to the board of directors. Individuals called *comisarios,* selected by the stockholders, have the general function of checking upon the operation of the company in the interests of the stockholders. There are no directly analogous functionaries in the case of the United States corporation, although auditors play a related role.

SOCIEDAD MIXTA. The *sociedad mixta* involves joint government-private ownership. Some of the major industrial developments in Latin America in recent years involve this kind of sponsorship. Examples have included the Mexican steel mill at Monclova and the Argentine steel mill at San Nicolás. Apart from the dual ownership and the important implications such ownership suggests for the decision-making process, the sociedad mixta is, otherwise, merely a special case of the sociedad anónima.

There are several other possible forms of business organization. But those mentioned above are the most important and should serve as an indication of the range of possibility.

Foreign Investor

CHANNELS OF CONTROL. (1) *Personal.* Businesses or the businessmen of one country may control businesses in other countries by various means. The most obvious such process involves the establishment of an individual proprietorship in one country by a citizen of another. In such cases, the general rule is that the foreigners have equal rights with native citizens in engaging in business. But there are exceptions. For example, the rule in Mexico is that a foreigner who wishes to establish an independent business may do so only if his country extends a similar right to Mexicans. Several of the Latin American countries, for example Panama, have general restrictions upon the entry of foreigners into the retail trades. Article 234 of the Panamanian Constitution of 1946 provided that the retail trades may be entered by nationals of those countries which maintain on the Isthmus of Panama enterprises in which Panamanian citizens find facilities for employment. This provision gave United States citizens the right to engage in the retail trades in Panama but prohibited many other foreigners from doing so. Somewhat similarly, the Constitution of Haiti (Article 10) decrees that foreigners may not function as landlords, although they may own their own homes; and Article 19 decrees that "only Haitians by birth may engage in retail trade, direct enterprises of small industry, and carry out any other commercial or professional activities that the law determines." One of the generally prevalent restrictions is against the owning of land by foreigners close to the land frontier or the seacoast, within, say, 50 or 100 kilometers.

Apart from the single proprietorship possibility, the foreigner might, having met the proper legal requirements, utilize any of the legal forms of organization mentioned earlier. In fact, he is most likely to use the sociedad anónima form. If he does so, there are various possibilities as to where he may incorporate.

(2) *Branch Plant.* The branch-plant situation involves incorporation in the home country of the investor and the registration of the activity in the country where the investment is made. The pros and cons of the branch-plant procedure might be catalogued somewhat in this fashion:

(a) Administratively speaking, it may be slightly easier, but not much, to establish a branch plant than a locally incorporated subsidiary. Registration may be quite complicated.

(b) The branch plant is exposed automatically to all of the formal discrimination that a country may practice against foreigners. (In Brazil a branch plant has been the object of an additional 15 percent income tax rate, applicable unless the profits are plowed back in Brazil.) But antiforeign discrimination is frequently not clearly defined in terms of the home base of the corporation. And subsidiaries incorporated in Latin America may fall as much victim to this sort of thing as do branch plants.

(c) So far as United States tax law is concerned, the earnings of the branch plant abroad are consolidated with the earnings of the company in the United States; and the corporate income tax of the United States is assessed against the whole. (Or, as will be mentioned below, the United States tax is the balance after the income tax paid to the host government has been deducted from the ostensible amount of the tax owed to the United States government.) The branch plant is consequently a rather attractive form of organization in the case of the risky venture, especially in mining where heavy initial losses are expected. In such cases it is desirable to be able to deduct those losses from total income before estimating the income base for purpose of the tax owed in the United States. In the case of the less risky venture, a subsidiary incorporated in Latin America would probably be best from the tax point of view. Such a subsidiary pays no United States tax on profits made in Latin America until such time as those profits are actually transferred to the United States.

(d) The branch-plant method gives administrative unity, or the possibility of it, since the control of all operations is in the hands of one board of directors. But the decentralization that goes with the existence of a separate board of directors in Latin America (in the case of the foreign-incorporated subsidiary) may, on the contrary, also be an advantage if it is important to have effective, independent action on the spot. Frequently, hindsight is better than foresight in determining which of these considerations is more important.

(e) A major advantage to the branch-plant procedure is that it is legal under United States antitrust legislation for the home office to dictate the price and production policies of the branch plant. By contrast, if a parent company in the United States tries to dictate the prices and production policies of a subsidiary, it may fall afoul of the United States antitrust law.

(f) Both the branch plant and the subsidiary may take advantage of the depletion allowance provisions of the United States tax laws. So there does not seem to be much difference between them on that score.

(3) (a) *Subsidiary Incorporated in Home Country.* At first glance, this alternative would seem to be the worst of all possible worlds. Why should a United States corporation incorporate a subsidiary in the United States to operate in Latin America? Such a subsidiary would be treated as foreign in the Latin American country and would automatically be subjected to whatever discriminations there might be against foreigners. Also, the subsidiary incorporated in the United States would be subject to the tax disadvantages of the branch in the sense that the whole operation, in both countries, would be subject to the incidence of the United States tax law, whether profits were repatriated to the United States or not.

But a procedure of this type will, if the company is chartered as a Western Hemisphere Trade Corporation, have one major tax advantage, which will be discussed below. And this advantage has generally been considered sufficient to give this organizational form considerable popularity.

(b) *Subsidiary Incorporated in Latin America.* The incorporation of a subsidiary in a Latin American country would seem to be one of the more likely organizational forms. Even though foreign-owned, the corporation would take on some of the coloration of national identity. Its legal personality would be in the Latin American country. It might not be subjected automatically to the antiforeign discrimination that was being practiced. However, incorporation in Latin America hardly guarantees the company protection against antiforeign discrimination.

In terms of the incidence of home-country taxes, this would seem at first glance to be the most desirable type of organization. The profits of the subsidiary would not be subject to the United States corporate income tax unless they were actually transferred back to the parent company in the home country.[3] As a rule, the profits of the subsidiary, unless transferred, would be subject only to the generally low tax rates of the Latin American country.

Subsidiaries incorporated in Latin America need not be wholly owned by the parent company. There are various possibilities:

The subsidiary may be wholly owned by the parent. In this case, it would be reasonably clear that the entire value of the subsidiary would be considered foreign investment.

The possibility also exists that the subsidiary may be something less than wholly owned by the parent company. In some cases, the law of the Latin American country may require that the subsidiary be at least 51 percent owned by local citizens. In fact, such a provision has been in the Mexican Constitution for many years. But, until recently, it seems only to have been used when the government thought it appropriate as a political measure. Recently, however, in Mexico, effort has been initiated to implement the provision at least so far as the foreign-owned mining companies are concerned. The program is called Mexicanization.

The term joint enterprise is generally applied to the case where there is mixed home-country and debtor-country ownership. In general, this is probably the best of the forms that foreign investment may take. The joint enterprise avoids some of the stigma attached to foreign companies. It also offers the best possibility for making a meaningful transfer of technical knowledge from the developed country to the underdeveloped country (The role of the joint enterprise is discussed somewhat more in Chapter Twelve.) [4]

TAXES: (1) *Individual.* Under United States tax law, the individual United States citizen, living abroad, can avoid the United States income tax if, during 18 consecutive months, he is abroad at least 510 full days.[5]

---

[3] The United States government has been considering the possibility of making certain subsidiaries, especially in Europe, pay the United States tax on profits even though such profits may not actually be transferred to the United States. But the chance that such changes will be applied to companies operating in Latin America seems slight.

[4] *See also,* Wolfgang Friedmann, *Joint International Business Ventures* (New York, Columbia University Press, 1961).

[5] Suggested changes in the law would probably not apply to United States citizens working in Latin America.

If the individual cannot avoid entirely the United States income tax by this means, there are other ways of reducing the impact. For example, the income tax which the United States citizen pays to a foreign government may be deducted from his United States income tax obligation in computing the burden of the United States tax. Thus, if the initial computation of his United States income tax obligation indicated that he owed $5,000 of tax against his income (foreign plus domestic) and if he had already paid an income tax of $3,000 to some Latin American government, the ultimate obligation to the United States would be only $2,000.

(2) *Corporate.* The United States income tax law, applicable to corporations, is the same as in the case of persons insofar as the credit for taxes paid to foreign governments is concerned. Income taxes paid to foreign governments are deductible from the United States tax liability before computing the actual amount of tax payable to the United States government.

It may be worth noting what this would mean in the case of a Latin American country applying the so-called 50-50 formula to the profits of a United States corporation. (This has been common in connection with oil companies.) After the United States corporation had paid half of its profits to the Latin American government, it would owe 2 percent of its profits to the United States government, assuming the United States to be taxing corporate profits at a 52 percent rate; it would owe nothing under the new United States tax rate of 48 percent.

For the tax year 1961, 4,740 United States corporations with a net income of $23 billion claimed a foreign tax credit of $1,223 million. Their income tax, payable to the United States, in the absence of the foreign tax credit, would have been $10,993 million.[6]

In general the foregoing comments would apply to a corporation operating a branch in Latin America. In the case of a United States corporation operating through a subsidiary, incorporated in Latin America, the United States income tax would not apply unless the profits made by the subsidiary in Latin America were actually transferred to the parent company in the United States. This is probably the strongest single argument for incorporating a subsidiary in Latin America.[7]

[6] United States Treasury Department, *Statistics of Income, Corporation Income Taxes, 1960–61* (Washington, 1963).

[7] On this point also suggested changes in the law would probably not apply to United States companies operating in Latin America.

In the general case, a subsidiary operating in the United States would be taxed in the ordinary manner. Then in addition, after it transferred some of its profits as dividends to the parent company, the parent company would be entitled to claim an 85 percent credit against those dividends. The parent company would be obligated to pay the 52 percent (or 48 percent or whatever it may be) rate against only the remaining 15 percent. However, dividends received from a subsidiary incorporated in Latin America would be taxed at the full rate. This would be an argument for not incorporating a subsidiary in Latin America.

The possibility of establishing a Western Hemisphere Trade Corporation modifies the foregoing possibilities. A Western Hemisphere Trade Corporation is (a) incorporated in the United States, being a subsidiary of some parent incorporated in the United States, (b) "all of whose business" is conducted within the Western Hemisphere, (c) but "95 percent or more of the gross income" is from sources outside of the United States (d) and "90 percent or more of its gross income [is] from the active conduct of a trade or business." [8] Such a corporation, if appropriately identified, enjoys a special deduction from taxable income which is the proportion of taxable income indicated by the following fraction: 14 as numerator and the sum of the normal and surtax rates as denominator. Thus, if taxable income in the ordinary course of events had been computed to be $1 million and the sum of the normal and surtax rates is 48 percent, 14/48 of $1 million would be $292,000 and $1 million less $292,000 would leave $708,000 of income subject to United States taxes. In this manner, a substantial tax advantage is given to that rather odd organization, a subsidiary incorporated in the United States which does almost all of its business outside of the United States but within the Western Hemisphere.

For the tax year 1961, 682 corporations filed returns as Western Hemisphere Trade Corporations. They listed total assets of $40 billion and net income of $1,953 million. After they took their Western Hemisphere Trade Corporation and other credits, however, their income subject to tax was $1,353 million. The potential income tax obligation resulting was for $695 million. Against this amount, a foreign tax credit of $507 million was claimed, resulting in an actual tax payment to the United States by Western Hemisphere Trade Corporations of well under

[8] *United States Code,* 1958 ed., 5, Title 26, Sec. 921, 4454.

$200 million. This is a tax rate of about 10 percent, instead of the ostensible 52 percent or 48 percent.

All of these tax subtleties add up to some odd, perhaps unfortunate, results. The whole mix of rules does not encourage the corporation to transfer profits to the United States, Latin American mythology on this point notwithstanding. Rather, it creates a tendency for the corporation to try to make its profits appear on the books as belonging to one of its subsidiaries which is operating in the jurisdiction with the lowest tax rates. This may mean profit transfer out of the Latin American country all right, but to the Bahamas, Switzerland, or Panama, rather than to the United States.

It has frequently been argued, especially by potential foreign investors, that the debtor countries should lure investment with special tax concessions. But such effort is to little purpose to the extent that the United States tax law is framed so as to tax away the tax reduction. If the United States taxes 22 percent when the Latin American government taxes 30 percent, and 12 percent when the Latin American government taxes 40 percent, a Latin American government is silly to reduce its tax to 30 percent in the hope that the lower tax rate will attract United States investment. The stultifying effect of this set of relations has been somewhat reduced by the possibility that, if a Latin American government reduces its income tax to encourage a United States investor, the United States government may not take up the slack. Such a dispensation was applied by the United States, for example, to the United Fruit Company investment in Costa Rica in 1958. (This is an example of the so-called tax-sparing treaty.) But dispensations such as this have apparently not been used very extensively. And the general situation is that it does not matter too much what the tax rate of the Latin American country may be; the foreign investor will end up with a composite tax burden equal to the United States tax rate. This is true because, in general, the rates of the Latin American corporate income taxes run under 48 percent. There are exceptions to this rule, however. Uruguay has a tax structure that seems to work out to give a tax higher than 48 percent.

It is frequently argued that the double taxation that is involved in paying income taxes both to a Latin American government and to the United States government is inherently unfair. The presumption seems to be that taxing the same thing twice makes for a double burden. It should be clear that this is not the basic nature of the impact of the tax pattern in the case of the United States corporation operating in Latin America. The tax burden, as a rule, adds up to the same figure in the case of the double taxation as it would if the Latin American government levied no tax at all. One may object, and perhaps properly object, to the increased amount of paper work that is involved in all of these circumlocutions. But that is a rather different sort of objection.

During much of the postwar period in the United States, it has seemed to be something approaching official policy to use tax incentives to encourage investment in the Latin American countries. Such policy has been defended as being a bonus to the investors and a favor to the underdeveloped countries. Whether it is really desirable policy, however, remains debatable. In any event, it does not seem to be the intent of the Administration in Washington to have recently proposed increases in the taxes on foreign investments apply to Latin America. The increases are aimed at the developed countries, such as those of western Europe.

PERCENT OF FOREIGNERS ON PAYROLL. The best jobs in many of the foreign-owned companies in Latin America have been held by foreigners. This irritates the Latin Americans; and to deal with the problem, it has become standard procedure to discriminate against foreign investors by requiring that some certain percentage of the number of employees should be local citizens. Typical percentages have been in the 80 to 95 percent range.

Alternatively, it has sometimes been provided that some such percentage of the payroll be paid to local citizens. This modification would help to force the employment of local citizens at relatively high levels in the corporate structure. Or it may be provided, as is done in Argentina, that a foreigner cannot be hired at all for a job if there is a qualified local citizen available.

Foreign corporations have fallen in line with this policy in part because it is the law, in part because native labor is cheap. In fact, of the various types of so-called antiforeign legislation enacted in Latin America, this is probably the type to which the foreign corporations, after initial complaints, have objected least. United States citizens object no more to hiring cheap labor in the Venezuelan oil fields than they do to the hiring of cheap, Mexican *bracero* labor in the Rio Grande Valley of Texas.

But, assuming that technological backwardness is one of the chief barriers to the economic development of Latin America, such provisions may have some undesirable features from the viewpoint of the Latin American countries themselves. The Latin American workers may gain knowledge by association with their North American counterparts. To the extent that there are relatively few such counterparts, the amount of such transfer of knowledge is reduced.

To make matters worse, the foreign investors have usually cooperated in attempts to observe this sort of legislation. The result has been that, to use Argentina as an example, well under 1 percent of the employees of foreign-owned companies are actually foreigners.

This is very odd in a setting where the Latin American countries really have need of as many foreign technicians as they can get and where they should hope the foreign technicians would stay as long as possible. The policy of the Latin American governments might better be to induce the foreign technicians to stay permanently and take out citizenship.

DISCRIMINATORY TAXES. The rule to which Latin American governments generally claim they are conforming is that taxes should not discriminate against foreign investors on the ground that they are foreign investors. Nevertheless, there are occasional examples of outright discrimination, and it is quite common for a Latin American government to identify some characteristic that actually describes only the foreign-owned companies and to tax on that basis. For example, in Chile the tax rate applicable to mining companies with over 200 employees has been higher than the tax rate applied to smaller companies. The smaller companies are more likely to be locally owned; the larger companies, foreign owned.

If the discrimination is against the foreigner, merely because he is a foreigner, that would seem undesirable. And yet in a world where discrimination is rampant, this may be one of the relatively less obnoxious manifestations. The United States income tax discriminates against foreign investments in the United States. It seems to place a burden of some 57 percent on earned profits being remitted to nonresident stockholders—as compared with the ordinary 52 percent rate.

For one thing, it is probably desirable that, in many cases, foreign investors migrate with their investments and take out citizenship in the country in which they are making the investments. The discriminatory tax would help to encourage this rather desirable action.

INTERNATIONAL INCORPORATION. There is something a bit anomalous about a corporation, "an artificial being, invisible, intangible and existing only in contemplation of law," [9] operating in a country other than the one which has chartered its existence. Also, since the international activities of these institutions have generated much of the international political friction of the past century or two, their *raison d'être* is a matter of some legitimate concern. Several years ago Eugene Staley suggested the international incorporation of businesses making international investments.[10] From the viewpoint of the corporations, this could have the advantage of freeing them from some of the stigma of being foreign. It also would permit some more rational taxing procedures. Such corporations might be taxed on all of their profits by an international agency. The agency might then operate on the basis of some agreed-upon formula for dividing the tax money among the countries in which the company operates. The formula might well give relatively large rebates to relatively poor countries and provide some much-needed revenue to the United Nations.

Desirable as such institutional changes might be, there has been relatively little discussion couched in such terms since World War II. The poor countries want to tax directly; and the foreign investors want to be able to run to their foreign offices for support.

Ownership of Minerals

At the present time in Latin America, three possibilities exist as to the ownership of minerals in the ground. They may be the property of (1) the surface owner or of (2) the state; (3) or the situation may be mixed. For example, in pre-Castro Cuba the state owned most minerals and granted concessions for their exploitation, but rights to some minerals were possessed by the surface owner. In most cases,

---

[9] Chief Justice Marshall in *Dartmouth College vs. Woodward*, 1819.
[10] Eugene Staley, *War and the Private Investor* (Garden City, Doubleday, Doran, 1935), p. 504–9.

however, the state claims ownership of the valuable minerals (the precious metals, the industrially useful metals, and oil), and the right to exploit is obtained by concession from the state.

The types of concessions under which mining companies operate in Latin America are fairly uniform from country to country. First, the concessionaire obtains an exploratory (*cateo*) concession for some such period as two years. During this period, the concessionaire determines whether the property is really worth developing. He can take ore out; and the government, to encourage the development of mining, grants him substantial tax exemptions.

If the property proves valuable, a working (exploitation) concession is then obtained, and the concessionaire becomes liable for ordinary taxes. He is also frequently required, thereafter, to keep the work of exploitation going continuously on pain of forfeiture. In Latin America the law frequently places emphasis on the social desirability of having an enterprise in continuous operation. By contrast, in the United States, the much greater belief in the importance of private property rights means that an owner of an enterprise should be able to shut down his operations whenever he wishes for as long as he wishes.

A third type of concession (*de beneficio*) must be obtained to establish a smelter or refinery.

Under the concession sort of title, the concessionaire's claim to the land is less secure than if he held it in fee simple. For example, a concession can be summarily cancelled for nonpayment of taxes or for letting the property lie idle for a time. On the other hand, the process for the taking over of private property, even in the case of nonpayment of taxes, is generally more complicated.

As an alternative to the development of mineral production by private concessionaires (foreign or domestic), the government may administer the production directly through a state agency. Thus the Mexican government has administered the national oil industry through Petróleos Mexicanos since it expropriated the private (mostly foreign) companies in 1938.[11] However, much of the Venezuelan oil industry continues in the hands of foreign concessionaires. Two of the chief companies are Creole, a subsidiary of Standard of New Jersey, and Royal Dutch Shell.

---

[11] Antonio J. Bermúdez, *The Mexican National Petroleum Industry* (Stanford, California, Institute of Hispanic American and Luso-Brazilian Studies, 1963).

It is also possible that the government nominally operate the properties but actually contract out certain important aspects of the operation to private companies. In both Mexico and Argentina, in recent years, there has been such contracting out of significant segments of the operations to foreign companies.

The foreign-owned mining companies, such as Anaconda producing at Chuquicamata in Chile and Cerro de Pasco operating in Peru, are generally operating under concessions from the governments concerned. By contrast, in 1952 Bolivia nationalized the private Patiño, Hochschild, and Aramayo tin-mining interests.

CHAPTER FOUR

MARKET BEHAVIOR: PRIVATE PRACTICES

The present chapter inquires into the theories and practices which influence the pricing methods and production and marketing decisions of private businessmen in Latin America.

Remote Areas

NONCOMMERCIAL. Much of Latin America is far removed from organized, commercial markets. Money is scarce in much of the rural area, where transactions frequently involve outright barter. But resistance to use of paper money in such areas has not proved as tenacious as some anthropologists were forecasting three or four decades ago.

In the remote areas much giving and accepting of goods and services occurs without a strict *quid pro quo*. It may be traditional that his neighbors help an individual build his house or clear his field; in exchange, he will help them when they have a similar sort of work to do. Under such conditions, an exact exchange for value received may never be given, and no effort is made to determine whether or not it has been. In fact, the failure to be concerned about obtaining a strict *quid pro quo* is an important characteristic of primitive cultures, as well as being a characteristic of intrafamily relations in a capitalistic culture.

Another possibility may be that, if a man sells something (say an egg) to his neighbor, he charges a small, token price that is much lower than the market price. But if he sells such an article to an outsider, he may ask ten or twenty times more. The contrary practice of generosity to outsiders may also prevail. In either case there is apparently little relationship between value and price. Customary or institutionalized procedures, which are not primarily concerned with problems of value, would seem to be the important factors affecting price.[1]

But increasingly, even in the remote areas, the price is influenced by the price set in some market where the forces of demand and supply may have been a factor—or at least where some of the forces of the type that operate out in the "great world of business" may have been a factor. (We do not argue here the question as to whether these forces are precisely equivalent to what the economist calls pure competition.)

COMMERCIAL. Perhaps the most famous example of commercial production and marketing originating in the remote areas of Latin America was the gathering of rubber in the upper Amazon valley fifty years ago. The unhappy conditions prevailing in that commerce have been vividly described by José Eustacio Rivera in *La Vorágine*. The rubber gatherers were effectively at the mercy of the middlemen in the river towns, the individuals who grubstaked them for their forays into the jungle to gather the sap of the Hevea brasiliensis. The art of pure exploitation seems to have been developed to a high degree of perfection in that setting of half a century ago. And the manufacturing enterprises in the United States and western Europe, which bought the product, seem to have condoned, if they did not positively encourage, the methods of the middlemen.

Such production and marketing arrangements are not entirely ancient history in Latin America. In fact, the exploitation of raw commodity gatherers by brokers and middlemen is probably still common in the back country of nine tenths of Latin America. Examples of industries where conditions are still not greatly changed by comparison with those prevailing in the rubber industry of the turn of the century include: yerba mate gathering in the Paraná valley; diamond hunting in the hinterland of Bahia; chicle gathering in British Honduras, Guatemala, and southern Mexico; and the gathering of carnauba wax in the northeast of Brazil.

MINING. Mineral production in Latin America is characterized by (1) a high degree of concentration in terms of the location of the

---

[1] Robert Redfield, *The Folk Culture of Yucatan* (Chicago, University of Chicago Press, 1941), p. 157.

deposits, (2) dominance of the industry by a limited number of companies (3) which are chiefly foreign (Anaconda Copper, Cerro de Pasco, American Smelting and Refining), (4) a measure of government intervention involving (a) participation as an operator in some cases and (b) the provision of credit to small-scale, private operators. (5) Important mining centers are likely to be far removed from the population centers of the country. Consequently the mineral economy is likely not to be well integrated with the national economy. And the technical knowledge of the foreign geologists and engineers is not likely to spill over in any important degree to the benefit of the rest of the economy.

(6) Finally, the mining companies are likely to participate in international price-setting and production-control arrangements, which may be either written agreements or merely tacit understandings. Since these arrangements are generally private, it is difficult for the outsider, at any given time, to know just what arrangements are in effect. And in fact, perhaps, at the given time the understandings (if any) may not be formalized in written agreements. But they may be, nonetheless, influential if they involve institutionalized understandings as to what is appropriate behavior.[2]

Middlemen and Marketing

It is difficult to do justice briefly to the role of middlemen in Latin American marketing.

A very wide spread between the price paid to the primary producer and the price paid by the consumer seems to exist commonly in Latin America. On this point Fernando Zamora has commented:

It is no less startling that a simple analysis of the difference between the price to the farmer and the ultimate retail sale price reveals a discrepancy so marked as to constitute a distinguishing characteristic of the economies of underdeveloped countries.[3]

Sometimes this is a result of the manner in which the farmer hypothecates his prospective crop at planting time to the middleman in order

---

[2] For an indication of what may be involved, *see*, United States, Federal Trade Commission, *Report of the Federal Trade Commission on the Copper Industry* (Washington, Government Printing Office, 1947). There are similar reports on other industries, petroleum for example. The copper report has considerable information on the situation in Chile.

[3] *Revista de Economía*, January, 1952, p. 23.

to obtain the wherewithal to buy seed and other supplies. To some extent, the price difference is the result of straight price spread. And the middleman is aided in profiting from this spread by the poor transportation facilities, which make it difficult to bring supplementary supplies into a high-priced market. He may also be aided by official and bank connivance. Commercial banks seem frequently to be willing to lend generously to middlemen in the marketing process, even when the lending is for the purpose of financing market-cornering operations. But they would not dream of supporting the individual farmer with the same generosity. Chronic inflation provides a favorable environment for such activities, as does the prevalence of oligopoly. On this latter point, the Economic Commission for Latin America has pointed out:

In many cases the wholesale trade is in the hands of a few enterprises, and the lack of competition tends to encourage excessive profit margins and high retail prices in combination with relatively low prices for the producer.[4]

The farmer is thus at a disadvantage when he markets his staples through middlemen. He is also at a disadvantage when he tries to market his perishables directly. He frequently must cut his prices drastically to sell the goods before they spoil. As Adolfo López Michelson has been fond of pointing out in his political campaigning in Colombia: "At 2 o'clock in the afternoon, rural Colombia begins to cut prices in the markets. Yucca goes down, meat goes down, corn goes down. The farmer cannot have anything left by nightfall. But the women who sell beer or cloth or cigarettes do not cut their prices. Industrial Colombia can wait. It can sell tonight—or next week." [5]

The improvement in marketing and distribution procedures is one of the major problems facing Latin America. It is a problem in terms of the viability of the marketing machinery and in terms of implications for economic development. (The problem is discussed further in Chapter Eighteen, Industrial Priorities.)

Low-Volume–High-Unit-Profit (LV-HUP)

In Latin America there exists little of the viewpoint that large volume and low profit rates may combine to make for large total profits.

---

[4] *Economic Bulletin for Latin America,* October, 1962, p. 233.
[5] New York *Times,* March 5, 1964, p. 4.

On the contrary, the businessman's basic attitude seems almost to involve a desire to maximize unit profits. At all events, the result seems to be that the Latin American businessman (in the market sector outside of agriculture) will stay out of an activity unless he anticipates making between 20 percent and 40 percent on his investment. This relation compares with a situation where profits typically run in the 10 percent to 15 percent range in industry and commerce in the United States.

An important consideration in connection with low-volume–high-unit-profit methods is the prevalent belief that high profit rates are more likely to be realized in a setting of small-scale operations and high markups. This is an institutional attitude which is not necessarily rational. But it seems to be present, and it is an important resistance inhibiting the development of Latin America.

Foreign Companies

Much has been made of the overshadowing importance of foreign companies in relation to the Latin American economies. However, historically, they have not played a particularly important role in Latin American production for domestic consumption (or merchandising). Their principal role for many years was in producing mineral raw materials for export. Increasingly, however, of late years foreign companies have been manufacturing in Latin America for the domestic market. And they have played a role in retailing. United States drug companies have come to play an active role in the merchandising of pharmaceutical products.[6]

In the area of the department store type of operation, the British-

---

[6] One United States drug company, McKesson and Robbins (which owns 50 percent of the stock of the Colombian Droguerías Aliadas), has been campaigning for the use of generic names, rather than patented trade names, in the labeling of drugs for sale in Colombia. McKesson and Robbins and the Colombian government have been resisted in this effort by the Colombian trade association, Asociación de Fabricantes de Drogas, eighteen of whose members are other United States drug companies operating in Colombia. Sale under the generic name should lower the price of drugs. The McKesson and Robbins board chairman, Herman C. Nolen, in describing the resistance to the generic-name proposal before the United States Senate Foreign Relations Committee, has been paraphrased as follows: "Retailers were urged to boycott the generic line; doctors received literature attacking its quality; medical journals were pressured to refuse McKesson advertising and to publish articles critical of generic drugs; some pharmaceutical companies cut off the supply of raw materials necessary for the generic program." See, *Hispanic American Report,* November, 1963, p. 890.

origin companies, Harrod's and Gath & Chávez in Buenos Aires, have played a role for several decades. But especially important in recent years has been the role of Sears Roebuck. Sears farms out much of its production to small-scale manufacturers in the Latin American countries where it operates. It then markets to a clientele which is largely upper middle class, in contrast to its lower-middle-class clientele in the United States. In spite of its relatively affluent customers, it is probably not too much of a mistake to say that it has a large-volume–low-unit-profit philosophy, at least by comparison with its Latin American-owned competitors. The example of Sears may be making a serious impression in Latin America. Also, the increasing numbers of United States-style supermarkets in the grocery-retailing field may be having a similar influence on Latin American marketing. At all events, in some of these areas, the foreign example may be serving as a salutary influence in Latin America.

Oligopoly

A Mexican Secretary of the Treasury, Antonio Ortiz Mena, said in 1963: "In a country in the process of development the assumptions of perfect competition are less well fulfilled than in industrialized countries."[7] An estimate published in 1957 indicated that 2 percent of the firms in Latin America accounted for 58 percent of the nonagricultural labor force.[8]

SIAM di Tella of Argentina advertises itself as "the most important manufacturing enterprise in Latin America." In 1961, it had gross sales of about $128 million (U.S.). The second most important firm owned by Latin Americans is said to be the Brazilian Industrias Reunidas F. Matarazzo, with gross sales of $100 million in 1961. These figures are relatively small by United States standards and are no particular gauge of the degree of monopolization in Latin American industry.

If obtainable, the most relevant data for appraising the role of oligopoly in the Latin American economies would be in terms of the share of the total industry, or total economy, occupied by one or a few firms. Relevant to such a comparison, Frank Brandenburg has indicated that

---

[7] *Trimestre Económico*, July, 1963, p. 451.
[8] *Latin American Business Highlights* (Chase Manhattan Bank), fourth quarter, 1957, p. 8.

some nine entrepreneur groups dominate the private Mexican economy.⁹

Apparently these nine (or so) groups each have their primary banking affiliation. Frequently the basic business connection of the leader of the group is, in fact, a bank.¹⁰ At any rate, each group has a relatively easy time in obtaining access to funds through its banking connections. The nine groups are also characterized by horizontal integration. For example, the Garza Sada group, beside controlling the Cuauhtémoc brewery, has interests in glass, steel, chemicals, finance, and insurance.

The horizontal integration of these dominant groups makes it difficult for outsiders (Mexicans who are not members of the ingroup) to establish a foothold in Mexican industry. The outsider is generally unable to obtain financing from the Mexican banking system, which is dominated by the nine. And he will find himself very vulnerable to price cutting or to cruder forms of political pressure and strong-arm tactics if he has tried to enter the industry in competition with the oligarchs.

There would seem to be every reason to believe that the situation is substantially the same over the whole of Latin America. Latin American business has been a better than average example of Adam Smith's dictum: "People of the same trade seldom meet together, even for merriment and diversion, but the conversation ends in a conspiracy against the public, or in some contrivance to raise prices." ¹¹ The result is monopoly-type pricing (LV-HUP), production curtailment, and high prices.

---

⁹ Frank Brandenburg, "A Contribution to the Theory of Entrepreneurship and Economic Development: The Case of Mexico," in *Inter-American Economic Affairs*, 16 (Winter, 1962), 3–23. The groups, some being identified with individuals and others with banks, are: Garza Sada, Banco Nacional de México (Legorreta), Banco de Comercio, Banco Comercial Mexicano, Carlos Trouyet, Raúl Bailleres, Aarón Sáenz, Elías Sourasky, and Sociedad Mexicana de Crédito Industrial. Four of these, Garza Sada, Banco Nacional, Carlos Trouyet, and Sociedad Mexicana de Crédito Industrial, are said to have sponsored over three hundred enterprises.

¹⁰ This association, if not identification, of the industrialists with the bankers contributes to the explanation of the high degree of debt financing (as distinct from equity financing) of Mexican industry, a situation which has been commented on by C. Patton Blair, "Nacional Financiera: Entrepreneurship in a Mixed Economy," in Raymond Vernon, ed., *Public Policy and Private Enterprise in Mexico* (Cambridge, Harvard University Press, 1964), p. 219. The lack of equity interest in corporations which, in terms of control, are closely held could be an explanation of a certain indifference on the part of the owners in the efficient operation of their enterprises.

¹¹ Adam Smith, *An Inquiry into the Nature and Causes of the Wealth of Nations* (London, printed for W. Strahan; and T. Cadell, in the Strand, 1776), I, 160.

One might guess that more goods would be produced in Latin America and the standard of living of the region would be higher if the Latin American businessman would think more in terms of how to adjust to competition and changing conditions and less in terms of how to avoid or neutralize competition.

But generally in Latin America in the circles of the professional economists, there is little discussion of the monopoly problem. There is little or no discussion of the extent of the problem and little effort to gather up-to-date information about the companies involved and the extent of their market control. Those who do write about the problem, Portnoy in Argentina, for example, do so on the basis of inadequate or obsolete data.[12] There is considerable instinctive popular indignation against monopolists and oligopolists. But the local ologopolists can generally succeed in diverting these sentiments against the foreigners when they tend to come to a head. It has, in fact, been pointed out that there is some tendency for the spirit of nationalism, which is currently rather strong in Latin America, to foster a sort of "tolerance toward the indigenous monopolies." [13]

An unfortunate result of the low-volume–high-unit-profit and oligopolistic character of the new Latin American industry seems to be a high-price, high-cost, relatively inefficient performance involving frequent examples of idle capacity.[14] And it is not strange that the products of such a set of institutional arrangements should have trouble competing on world markets, and even on their own markets.

Trade Associations

In almost all of the Latin American countries, producers and merchants are organized into two, or perhaps more, hierarchies of trade associations. The merchants are organized into a hierarchy of chambers of commerce (Cámaras de Comercio), culminating in a national cham-

---

[12] Leopoldo Portnoy, *La Realidad Argentina en el Siglo XX, II, Análisis Crítico de la Economía* (México, Fondo de Cultura Económica, 1961).

[13] For example, see the statement by Mario Henrique Simonsen, "The Role of Government and Free Enterprise," in Mildred Adams, ed., *Latin America: Evolution or Explosion?* (New York, Dodd, Mead, 1963), p. 138.

[14] The program of the Mexican Partido de la Revolución Institucional has said as much. *See, Trimestre Económico,* January, 1964, p. 146; as well as statements by David Felix in Albert O. Hirschman, ed., *Latin American Issues: Essays and Comments* (New York, Twentieth Century Fund, 1961), p. 90.

ber of commerce, called in Mexico: Confederación de Cámaras Nacionales de Comercio (CONCANACO). The manufacturing industries are organized into a hierarchy of chambers of industry or of industrialists (*cámaras de industriales*), working up to a national chamber of industry, which is called in Mexico: Confederación de Cámaras Industriales (CONCAMIN).

These national chambers are then likely to be associated with various international chambers. For the chambers of commerce, there are the Inter-American Council of Commerce and Production and the International Chamber of Commerce. For the industrialists there is the Asociación de Industriales de Latinoamérica.

There may, however, be trade associations in the other economic sectors, such as banking and agriculture. These associations may or may not be associated with the two basic hierarchies. Some Mexican examples may be mentioned: Asociación de Banqueros (banking), Cámara Nacional de la Industria de Transformación or CNIT (an organization of small enterprises in the manufacturing field, associated with CONCAMIN), Confederación Patronal de la República Mexicana (an employer organization oriented to the economic philosophy of the Catholic Church).[15]

In Latin America it is common for the law to prescribe that trade associations shall exist, to require that the individual business firms belong, to specify the organizational form of the association, to delimit the functions of the organization, and to specify its relationship to the government.[16] The trade associations are then (1) creatures of the law, (2) instruments facilitating private collusion among businessmen, (3) channels through which business may communicate its desires to the government, (4) channels through which the government may control the behavior of business, and (5) vehicles for development planning in cooperation with the government. At one extreme, the law may grant to trade associations, once formed, autonomous powers in policing trade practices and methods of competition. Such procedure was specified in

---

[15] Sanford Mosk, *Industrial Revolution in Mexico* (Berkeley, University of California Press, 1950); and Raymond Vernon, *The Dilemma of Mexico's Development* (Cambridge, Harvard University Press, 1963), esp. p. 75.

[16] With regard to the impact of the compulsory membership provision, it may be noted that in Mexico, for example, companies capitalized for less than 500 pesos, a very small sum, have been excused from the compulsory membership provision.

Article 256 of the Cuban Constitution of 1940. The trade association may be the instrument the government uses in relaying its instructions on business practices to the businessmen. The government may be obligated to consult with the appropriate business groups before implementing measures, such as tariff rate changes. Law or custom may decree that much of economic planning shall take the form of consultation between the appropriate trade associations and the appropriate government bureaus. This is an important aspect of the French planning arrangement that has been highly regarded in some quarters in recent years. The Mexican Law of Manufacturing Industries (1941), for example, specified that trade associations be consulted before the benefits provided in the law could be granted to a new industry. This procedure was intended to make sure that the new industry would not be a source of "disloyal competition" for existing industries.

In many of the Latin American countries, including the most important, Mexico, Argentina, Brazil, the purpose of the government seems to be to institutionalize the interrelations of business, government, and labor.

Alfonso Cardoso, a high official of the Mexican CNIT has written:

The exercise of economic control by the government ought to be done in association with those directly interested in the productive process—in order to balance order and liberty—and implementing the democratic principle of the participation of private citizens in governmental activity and thus avoiding the mistakes that result from the lack of knowledge or information necessary in decision making.[17]

An example of the use of the trade association as an instrument for facilitating collusion is found in the case of the Peruvian fishing industry. As the process was described in *Fortune* magazine, Luis Banchero Rossi, a major figure in the recent development of the Peruvian fishing industry, succeeded by 1961 in getting most of the industry into the Consorcio Pesquero del Perú.[18] He then, as the representative of the Peruvian Consorcio, succeeded in talking the International Fish Meal Exporters' Organization into agreeing to an international system of export quotas. The system subsequently succeeded in increasing the price of fish meal

---

[17] Alfonso Cardoso, *Experiencias en Economía* (México, EDIAPSA, 1953), p. 48.
[18] *Fortune,* March, 1964, p. 62.

from $55 a ton to about $90 a ton. The agreement has been endorsed by the Peruvian government.[19]

In Latin America, the relationship between the government and industry is colored by the fact that certain people frequently play a dual role as government officials and as industrialists; and they are frequently playing both roles at the same time.[20] In Mexico, former president Miguel Alemán is one of the leading businessmen of the country; Antonio Ruiz Galindo is a leading industrialist who has been in and out of high place in the government . . . and so on.

In Latin America, the relations of the government with the trade associations are in a state of flux. The relations vary a great deal from country to country. And, no doubt, the relative influence of businessmen and of government representatives when they get together varies a good deal depending on the personalities involved. Also there is considerable variation in the comprehensiveness of trade association organization. Nevertheless, there seems ground for generalizing that this relationship is becoming one of the most important institutional forces in Latin America. And its existence provides some of the basis for arguing that the politico-economic system evolving in Latin America has in it elements justifying comparison with the corporate state.[21]

---

[19] *Foreign Agriculture,* April 20, 1964, p. 14.
[20] Vernon, *The Dilemma of Mexico's Development,* pp. 149, 153.
[21] This comparison is discussed in Chapter Two, Evolution of Economic Systems since 1860.

CHAPTER FIVE

MARKET BEHAVIOR: GOVERNMENT REGULATION

General Attitude

There is a strange contradiction in the popular attitude in Latin America with regard to the government regulation of private business. It would be difficult to find a region in the world where the general population has a more deep-seated contempt for bureaucrats. But also, the people of the region seem to consider it appropriate that there should be substantial government regulation of the economy, planning for the economy, plus actual government ownership and operation of business. The acceptance of government regulation is general; the belief that it is appropriate is general; but the belief that it is inherently ineffective and graft-ridden is also general.

Governments in Latin America, since colonial times at least, have had a close connection with business operation. To put it one way, they have been consistently more paternalistic than has been the case in the Anglo-Saxon countries.

It has been part of the tradition for Latin American governments to be willing (1) to operate business themselves; and they have never hesitated because of theoretical inhibitions (2) to interfere with private business when they thought it desirable. There is no tradition to the effect that private enterprise *should* be free from public interference, such as has become a fetish in the United States.

Antitrust

DOMESTIC ANTITRUST LEGISLATION. The enforcement of competition, in the belief that, if real competition prevails, many of the country's economic ills would be automatically solved, has been a method by which the government of the United States has attempted to regulate business. One could scarcely expect Latin American law, with its Roman rather than common law origin, to be precisely similar to United States law in such a field. Under the circumstances, the amazing feature of the situation may well be the degree of similarity.

Already in colonial times, the Spanish law in force in Latin America characterized as illegal such practices as attempting to "corner" or monopolize the market for a particular commodity. And this sort of condemnation has generally remained in the laws.

Along this line, the constitution which Peru adopted in 1933, Title II, Chapter 1, Article 16, prohibited "industrial and commercial monopolies and cornering the market. . . . The law alone may establish state monopolies and *estancos* if in the national interest." And Article 28 of the Mexican Constitution of 1917 runs:

> There shall be in the United Mexican States no monopolies, restraints of trade of any kind . . . ;
> Consequently, the law shall severely punish and the authorities shall diligently prosecute any monopoly or concentration in the hands of one or a few, of articles of prime necessity, that has as its object the obtaining of an increase in prices;
> Also any act or measure restraining or tending to restrain free competition in production, industry, commerce, or public services;
> Any agreement or combination of any kind made by producers, industrialists, merchants, or carriers, or by those engaged in any other service, for the purpose of restraining competition among themselves and obliging consumers to pay exorbitant prices;
> And, in general, whatever constitutes an undue, exclusive advantage in favor of one or more specific persons to the injury of the public in general or of any social class.

A few of the Latin American countries have enacted legislation to implement such constitutional provisions. Argentina enacted such legislation in the 1920s and attempted to apply it to the foreign meat-packers. But in general in Latin America, there has been little legislation implementing the antitrust provisions of the constitutions and less effort to enforce such legislation when it does exist. Prosecution of important businessmen for efforts to monopolize industries, such as may be done by the Antitrust Division of the Department of Justice in the United States, is virtually unknown in Latin America. However, in isolated cases, there may be prosecution of unimportant businessmen for particular market-cornering or price-gouging efforts. But even that seems to be rather rare. The Brazilian example may be cited:

In Brazil an agreement among businessmen designed to prevent or reduce competition may be considered a criminal offense if it is managed "for the purpose of obtaining an arbitrary increase in profits."[1] the Pan American Union paraphrases the Brazilian law as follows:

> To destroy goods in order to effect an increase in price, to stop production in consideration of compensation "for giving up competition," to withhold goods so as to dominate the market and produce an increase in prices, to sell merchandise below cost for the purpose of avoiding competition, to spread rumors or to effect fictitious deals so as to cause a rise or drop in price, to give false information in prospectuses, to serve on the board of more than one company for the purpose of preventing or reducing competition, to manage banks, insurance companies and other similar enterprises in a careless or fraudulent manner and unfaithfully to report accounts so as to hide profits, are offenses punishable by imprisonment of from two to ten years.[2]

But there seems to have been relatively little prosecution and less conviction in Brazil under these legal precepts. The Pan American Union report has cited a few examples. In one such case: "An agreement between the handlers of coffee in Santos and based upon a schedule of rates approved by the Coffee Exchange was held not to be arbitrary."[3] The report goes on to say: "Agreements to divide territory would not be considered an arbitrary increase in profits because the increase would not depend exclusively upon the will of one of the parties."[4]

On the whole, far more ingenuity has been shown in finding grounds for permitting monopoly than has been shown in preventing it. For example, various Mexican laws have permitted monopoly at least under the following loosely defined conditions: (1) if technical improvement is supposed to result; (2) if monopolization may ultimately permit price reduction (3) or lower costs; (4) if rationalization of the production or distribution processes (why rationalization should raise prices is not clear) will not raise prices unduly; (5) if "ruinous" competition will be

---

[1] Pan American Union, *A Statement of the Laws of Brazil in Matters Affecting Business* (3rd ed., Washington, 1961), pp. 173–74.
[2] *Ibid.*
[3] *Ibid.*
[4] *Ibid.*

eliminated; (6) if the existence of a new industry results; (7) if desirable enterprises, which are tending to disappear, will be preserved; (8) if desirable classification and quality norms and rules of ethics may possibly result; (9) if exports may be encouraged by the monopolization; (10) or if any one of a miscellaneous collection of desirable results may occur without prices being thereby increased to the prejudice of the public interest. It would seem that bureaucrats, in deciding what practices to allow entrepreneurs to get away with, can find in such a set of rules grounds for permitting about anything they want to permit. The effect would seem to approximate the rule of bureaucratic whim rather than the rule of law.

At all events, much of Latin America has antitrust legislation very similar in form (if not in manner of implementation) to that in the United States. And yet, in Latin America as in the United States, there seems to be little confidence that, if competition were attained, it could function effectively as a regulator of the economy. The antitrust laws then are not considered the solution to the problems of collusion and monopoly. In fact, there is little concern to prevent collusive practices in Latin America. Rather, the laws give the government the power to proceed in emergencies against speculators exploiting the poor, not the leverage for dealing with industrial magnates. And, in fact, the governments frequently encourage monopoly and sponsor the imposition of restrictive practices on industry, doing so either through the instrumentality of the trade associations or by direct mandate.

An Argentine writer has summarized the Latin American attitude toward competition as follows:

Finally, managerial efficiency is seriously impaired by lack of competition in industry. Generally, Argentines do not feel the kind of antagonism toward monopolies and cartels conspicuous in U. S. public opinion. Their opposition to trusts in general is the consequence of, and applies only to, the exploitation of industry by foreign interests and their power in world markets; only rarely does it stem from profound convictions in the free-enterprise system. There is therefore a high degree of concentration of ownership in privately controlled industries.[5]

UNITED STATES LAW. It is reasonably obvious that antitrust laws should apply within the countries that enact them if the law itself is not

[5] Tomás Roberto Fillol, *Social Factors in Economic Development: The Argentine Case* (Cambridge, M.I.T. Press, 1961), p. 59.

to be a farce. What may not appear quite so obvious is that the United States antitrust legislation can affect internal legal arrangements and economic conditions within Latin American countries. This is true in spite of the fact that indignation has occasionally been expressed in certain quarters both in the United States and in Latin America in connection with the possibility that domestic United States law may have such effects. It sounds like an abridgment of that sacred-cow sovereignty.

The antitrust prosecution of the United Fruit Company in the United States is an example of what is possible along this line. The case was ruled upon in the federal court in New Orleans in 1958, the decision taking the form of a consent decree.[6] The United Fruit Company did not admit that it had done the things of which it was charged; but it promised not to do them in the future; and, in order to get the government off its back, it agreed to quite a few more concessions. It agreed to take positive initiative in creating a competitor in the banana business. This competitor was to be capable of importing nine million stems of bananas a year into the United States. United Fruit would provide the competitor with "assets, including liquid assets, producing banana land, ships and other essential accessory assets."[7] The company had been charged with the possession of a degree of monopoly power which permitted it to fix the price of bananas sold in the United States. To frustrate this behavior, it was provided that United Fruit could not act as the agent of other companies importing bananas into the United States. The company was prohibited from pressuring anyone to accept bananas in greater quantity, of lower quality, or at above-market prices, using as leverage the threat of not selling to him in the future. The company was forbidden from agreeing to restrict the production, purchase, transport, or sale of bananas in or to the United States market. Also, the United Fruit Company was required to divest itself of its controlling interest in the International Railways of Central America, a line serving Guatemala and El Salvador out of Puerto Barrios. At the moment of writing, it still remains unclear how effective the implementation of parts of this consent decree will be. United Fruit has until 1966 to implement several of the changes. But one thing is clear: the United States court

---

[6] New York *Times*, February 5, 1958, p. 1.
[7] *Ibid.*

has ordered the company to do things that, if done, will have an impact both legal and economic within Guatemala and El Salvador.[8]

Maximum or Ceiling Prices (Protecting the Consumer)

The standard of living in Latin America remains desperately low. Prices to primary producers are low. Prices to ultimate consumers are high. Middlemen profit from the price spread. Price levels rise rapidly in many Latin American countries. Wages also rise; but the wage share of national income is low by comparison with developed countries and does not seem to be increasing. In the effort to protect the consumers from price exploitation, various things have been done.

In some of the Latin American countries, fairly general laws give a government agency some discretion in controlling prices. Examples of such agencies are: the Superintendencia de Abastecimientos y Precios in Chile and the Comissão Federal de Abastecimento e Preços in Brazil.

(1) Sometimes the price-setting power covers a substantial range of commodities. (2) In other cases, it is limited to a few necessities. (3) Such laws are likely to apply even ineffectively only in the large cities. They are virtually meaningless in the countryside. (4) In other cases, laws may not provide for price setting, but merely prohibit price increases.

(5) An alternative approach to the problem of protecting the consumer is to establish a governmentally owned chain of stores (in Mexico called CONASUPO) to sell masa and beans to the poor at reasonable prices. In this effort, CONASUPO operates some motorized "supermarkets" to serve the poor districts of Mexico City.

In its issue of November 4, 1963, *Foreign Agriculture* discussed an effort by the Brazilian government to set the maximum price for slaughter cattle at the slaughterhouse at 4,200 cruzeiros per 15 kilos (21 cents per pound at the official rate of exchange). Movie admission prices are officially set in Mexico at four pesos or less (depending on the quality of the theater). Similar efforts have been legion in Latin America.

---

[8] In November, 1963, the United Fruit Company entered another *nolo contendere* plea in an antitrust suit in a federal court in Los Angeles and was fined $4,000. Charges of unfair competition by United Fruit toward Standard Fruit and Steamship Company and the Ecuadorian Fruit Import Corporation were involved. See, *Hispanic American Report*, October, 1963, pp. 755–56, and January, 1964, p. 1045.

Several things may be said by way of evaluation of these methods. (1) The regulatory machinery, where it exists, is inadequate to do an effective job. The identity of the agencies administering the price controls is frequently changed. This is one of the areas of public administration where the inadequacy of the original agency in performing its job is likely to lead to a proliferation of agencies and compounded confusion in the day-to-day administration of the program. Also, controls will be hurriedly implemented in one place in response to a crisis which has generated some public indignation, especially if it is an election year. Then, with the passage of time or the completion of the election, administration will be allowed to loiter.

(2) But the system does work to establish a price gap between the basic necessities (tortillas, beans, and so on) and the slightly better items.[9] The poor devil in the lower classes in Latin America may be able to obtain the basic necessities at extremely low prices, provided the government store has not run short or the price control is effective. But, if by some happy turn of events, he succeeds in raising his income modestly, he may find it difficult to improve his level of living in the same modest degree that his money income is increased. Rather, he finds that the price gap between the basic necessities and the next-better classification of goods is such that the improvement in his ostensible salary nets him very little by way of improved standard of living.

There are other undesirable results connected with the effort to keep the prices of the bare necessities extremely low while other prices are allowed to behave pretty much as they choose. (3) The policy is conducive to production curtailment in the area of necessities. The farmer would prefer to produce the more-or-less luxury goods that command the higher prices and forget about the basic necessities. So, production of the basic crops lags, as it has in Latin America generally.[10]

A similar lag occurs in construction of low-cost housing. The obligatory rents are set extremely low on the inferior housing already in existence; and as a result, profit-minded builders are not stimulated to activity in providing housing for low-income and middle-income groups.

---

[9] *Economic Bulletin for Latin America,* VII (October, 1962), 233.
[10] Roberto de Oliveira Campos, "Inflación y Crecimiento Equilibrado," in *Trimestre Económico,* XXVII (January, 1960), 94.

Attempts to keep low the prices of necessities in Latin America have ostensibly been well intentioned; but, in fact, they have rather generally missed the target. It might be better if the Latin American governments would envisage their primary target as combating middleman profiteering. Or, in any event, price setting should be used only occasionally as an emergency measure, not chronically. Like a lot of patent medicines and other nostrums, the method loses its efficacy when practiced all the time.

Price Floors (Protecting Producers)

Various measures have been attempted to aid Latin American producers in obtaining higher and more profitable prices for their output. Government agencies with such functions have proliferated.

Thus, in Argentina there exist or have existed the Junta Reguladora de la Producción Agrícola (agricultural crops in general), the Comisión Reguladora de la Producción y Comercio de la Yerba Mate (mate), the Junta Nacional de Carnes (meat), and the Junta Nacional de Granos (grain). Argentina indeed seems to have agencies charged with the regulation of most aspects of the economy.

In Brazil the constitution establishing the "New Order" in 1937 set up a hierarchy of "corporations" to control all phases of the economic life. With the overthrow of Vargas and the establishment of a new constitution in 1946, the Brazilian economy abandoned its formal commitment to the corporate state. But virtually all of the institutions of the corporate state which had become going concerns remained in existence. The Conselho Nacional do Petroleo has jurisdiction over the petroleum industry, the Instituto Brasileiro do Café has supervisory power over the coffee industry; the same is true of the Instituto do Açúcar e do Alcool as far as sugar and alcohol are concerned, of the Instituto Rio Grandense do Arroz for rice, of the Instituto do Cacau de Baia for cacao, of the Instituto Nacional do Mate (mate), and of the Instituto Nacional do Sal (salt).

The proliferation of such agencies is everywhere in evidence in Latin America. In fact, it comes close to being the general rule that there are, in each country, government agencies responsible for the regulation of each industry. Generally, the agencies seem to have as their chief concern making the industry profitable; but the protection of consumer interest in more goods at lower prices may also be ostensibly a matter of concern; that is to say, some agencies are ostensibly concerned with both producer and consumer interest.

(a) One of the standard procedures has been to guarantee a minimum price for the output of some crops some of the time. CONASUPO does this sort of thing in Mexico some of the time for some crops. Venezuelan law as early as 1944 authorized the Comisión Nacional de Abastecimiento to perform such a role. As a more specific example, it might be mentioned that in 1963 Argentina was guaranteeing to the producers of sunflower seed a price of 1,100 pesos per 100 kilograms, and to the producers of peanuts a price of 1,350 pesos per 100 kilograms.[11] Generally, there is considerable administrative discretion as to the identity of crops covered. The programs of some governments in this area have involved quite general coverage of basic crops. The programs of other governments are little more than token systems, or systems benefiting isolated crops sporadically. A good deal of politics can go into decision making in this area and probably does.

(b) Other measures, intended to have similar impact, include production limitation and marketing quotas, subsidies, and the providing of easy credit facilities. Argentina has at times paid subsidies to yerba mate growers; and it has provided easy credit facilities in efforts to expand cotton production. Such efforts in relation to particular crops have tended to be sporadic. But they have been extremely common in the sense that something like this is going on all the time in connection with various crops in various countries.

(c) The providing of storage facilities, silos to store corn in El Salvador, for example, has been a procedure permitting farmers in some cases to get out from under the pressure to sell their crops immediately after harvest at very low prices to the middlemen. The Argentine government operates grain elevators, and so on.

On the whole, the institutions intended to protect producers have come and gone in a confusing sequence of events. And generally the price support efforts have been engaged in on a very ad hoc basis in response to immediate pressures. Price support systems are not the result of any well-thought-out philosophy as to what prices ought to be.

The efforts to keep some prices down to protect consumer interest and some prices up to protect producers have resulted in a distortion of the

---

[11] *Foreign Agriculture*, October 7, 1963.

price patterns in the Latin American countries which has become one of the principal structural problems inhibiting Latin American economic development.[12] This statement is not intended as an allegation that there should be no thoughtful government attempt to influence prices. But, if correct, it does mean that most of the efforts up to now leave a good deal to be desired in terms of rationality in serving the public interest. (A procedure will be described at the conclusion of Chapter Six, Raw Commodity Control Schemes, that may satisfactorily deal with the chief problems.)

ARGENTINE BEEF. A brief history of Argentine beef may serve as an example of the evolution over the years of the problems of one industry.

In the first half of the nineteenth century, Argentina exported considerable quantities of jerked beef to the slave markets of the world, especially to the slave markets of Brazil and the United States. Then in the 1870s, high-quality frozen beef first began to be exported.

During the late nineteenth century, British companies or joint British-Argentine companies controlled the meat packing in Argentina and also dominated the international trade. But shortly after 1900, the big United States packers, Swift, Armour, and Morris, began to interest themselves in Argentina. Their technical superiority and financial resources permitted them to pay premium prices to Argentine *estancieros* for beef. They thus ingratiated themselves with that politically powerful group and obtained a foothold in the meat-packing industry in spite of the opposition of the British and even though the direction of the export trade continued to be from Argentina to England. In 1911 a major struggle occurred between the United States packers and the British. The United States packers, as a result of their ability to outbid the British for beef, succeeded in forcing the British producers to agree to a quota system describing how much the principal producers operating in Argentina would supply in the British market. The United States packers got 41.35 percent of the market; the British, 40.15 percent; and the Argentines, 18.50 percent. This was the same type of quota and market-sharing approach that the Chicago packers were also applying at that time in the United States. The United States packers had performed the remarkable feat of obtaining (as a result of technological superiority) dominance in

---

[12] *Economic Bulletin for Latin America,* VII (October, 1962), 233.

an industry in which they had no natural role either as providers of raw material, as providers of labor, or as providers of market.

Argentine estancieros have been dissatisfied a good part of the time with their dependence on the foreign packers and with the prices paid for their beef. Shortly after the end of World War I, this difficulty came to a head in a series of Argentine laws on prices, buying practices, and government supervision of the industry.

One of the principal difficulties has always centered around the price paid by the packers to the cattlemen. In 1923 the Argentine government passed the Minimum Price Law providing for the setting up of a regulatory commission which proceeded to set some prices. The packers refused to buy at those prices. The estancieros, who did not sell any cattle for a time, suffered considerably. The operation of the law was consequently suspended. It was briefly revived in 1930. But the attempt to enforce the law at that time merely resulted in the loss of some of Argentina's European market to Australia.

Another act passed in 1923 also caused considerable furor. This was the Packers Control Act. It required all packers to register with the government, to submit periodic reports, and to open their books to the government inspectors. With the information thus gained, the government might be able to determine just how high a price the packers could afford to pay the estancieros and stay in business. The packers did not want the government to have such information. As a result of their resistance, the law was not enforced for several years. Then, as a result of court action in 1934 holding the Packers Control Act to be constitutional, enforcement was attempted again. The United States companies decided to comply with the law and opened their books, but the Anglo, the big British packinghouse, balked and attempted to smuggle its records out of the country in twenty-one cases labeled corned beef. The records were seized and the resultant popular reaction against the Anglo sufficiently strengthened the government in its position so that there was not much question thereafter as to its right or power to inspect the packers' books if it desired.

Early in the 1930s the government set up two organizations designed to protect the Argentine cattle raisers against the monopoly power of the foreign packers and against the falling prices of the early depression years. One organization was the Junta Nacional de Carnes, which regulated prices, and the other was the Corporación Argentina de Productores de Carnes (CAP), which was eventually to operate a packinghouse. That these efforts were not more energetically pushed was probably due to the fact that the large estancieros (who controlled the government) and the foreign packers worked out a mutual understanding that gave relatively favorable prices to the large estancieros while sacrificing the interests of the small-scale ranchers.

During the 1930s the beef trade between Argentina and England was regulated by a series of agreements (such as the Roca-Runciman agreement of 1933). Britain was developing a system of imperial preference and the Argentine bargaining position was not good. World War II improved the Argentine bargaining position.

The demand for beef remained strong in the immediate postwar period. But the Perón government handled the matter so that the government, rather than the estancieros, obtained most of the profit. The Perón government also held down the price of beef within Argentina, to the benefit of the Argentine consumer. Estanciero discontent with those measures resulted in the limitation of production and a decline in the relative importance of the Argentine cattle industry on the world scene. Post-Perón governments have been somewhat more sympathetic to the cattlemen since 1955. But the Argentine cattle industry has experienced considerable difficulty in building the herds back. The domestic price of beef has risen considerably but remains low by comparison with beef prices in much of the rest of the world.

CHAPTER SIX

MARKET BEHAVIOR: INTERNATIONAL RAW COMMODITY CONTROL SCHEMES

This chapter is concerned with the marketing problems involved in connection with the chief Latin American exports. Since the special nature of these problems may be determined by the types of commodities involved, brief mention of the nature of the trade pattern may be appropriate at this point. (International trade patterns are discussed more at length in Chapter Nineteen.)

Trade Patterns

Latin American producers seem to experience special difficulties in consequence of the market behavior of typical Latin American exports by comparison with the market behavior of typical Latin American purchases.

Typical exports of Latin America are industrial raw materials, fibers, and primary foodstuffs: petroleum, copper, nitrates, silver, wheat, meat, sugar, and coffee. Such commodities in 1962 represented 91 percent of Latin American exports. The stereotype that Latin America is chiefly an importer of manufactured goods also seems to hold—however, not so clearly. In 1962 imports of industrial raw materials (including fuels) and food and fibers were 20 percent of the total Latin American imports.

Imports of manufactured goods (Standard International Trade Classification groups 5, 6, 7, 8) were 73 percent of total imports. But, of these manufactured goods imports, some 25 percent seem to have been intermediate or semiprocessed goods. Probably slightly under half of Latin American imports were finished manufactured goods.

Terms of Trade

CYCLICAL TERMS OF TRADE. The prices of Latin American exports seem to fluctuate more violently over the business cycle than do the prices of Latin American imports.[1] This phenomenon seems to derive from a general tendency for raw commodity prices to fluctuate more violently than do manufactured goods prices. And since Latin American exports are largely raw commodities and imports are largely manufactured goods, the indicated statistical relation tends to develop.

This tendency seems to be even more pronounced if one compares the prices of particular agricultural products with the prices of particular industrial products. Thus, if one graphs the fluctuations in the prices of coffee or sugar and compares them with the fluctuations in, say, the price of carbon steel in the United States, the coffee and sugar fluctuations are substantially more violent than is the case with the steel-price fluctuations. The steel price will be stable for long periods, while the coffee and sugar prices will be dancing around continually.[2]

---

[1] A fantastic amount of statistical work has been done on this relationship. The results are not completely unambiguous. But, on the whole, they would seem to justify the generalization. *See* my, *International Trade: Goods, People, and Ideas* (New York, Knopf, 1958), chap. 5.

[2] A similar phenomenon is observed domestically in the United States, where the available statistical evidence indicates that agricultural prices fluctuate more violently than do manufactured goods prices. In fact, there is some basis for alleging that the basic instability relation is between raw commodity prices and manufactured goods prices. This is a fairly important distinction. It would indicate that the relative instability of Latin American export prices is due to the fact that the region is primarily exporting raw commodities. However, there are other ways of looking at the matter. Some recent research indicates as an alternative that the influential relation is that internationally traded goods fluctuate more violently in price than do goods more generally consumed in the country where they are produced. More study needs to be given to these matters. *See,* Robert E. Lipsey, *Price and Quantity Trends in the Foreign Trade of the United States* (Princeton, Princeton University Press [for the National Bureau of Economic Research], 1963), chaps 1, 2. Someone interested in even more subtle ramifications of this sort of thing may be interested in looking at Joseph D. Coppock, *International Economic Instability* (New York, McGraw-Hill, 1962). Coppock indicates (p. 33) that, although the price fluctuations connected with primary

The fact that violent price fluctuations afflict Latin American exports should not necessarily be taken to mean that depressions strike Latin America with greater severity than they strike an industrialized country such as the United States. What is the criterion as to severity? In the United States the chief impact of depression is in terms of unemployment. Manufacturers are relatively successful in keeping prices from falling; but the price the developed country pays for the price stability is a severe cutback in production and, as a consequence, unemployment. Unemployment is a less important problem in Latin America, where chronic underemployment (not cyclical unemployment) is a more meaningful problem. But Latin America does suffer during the depression phase of the cycle because of the drastic drop in the prices received for her chief exports. However, such drops may not be the ultimate measure of hardship. There may well be more real suffering in Latin America, from time to time, as the result of sporadic crop failures in the area of subsistence agriculture than there is in consequence of bumper crops and low prices in connection with commercial agriculture.

At all events, the differences in the institutional arrangements in Latin America by comparison with the United States seem to indicate the existence of a considerable difference in the meaning of the business cycle for the two areas. However, as Latin America industrializes, the significance of this difference may be becoming less.

REASONS FOR SERIOUSNESS OF PROBLEM. Various factors, mostly institutional, but some not (such as the weather), seem to combine to occasion the result that raw commodity prices fluctuate more violently than do the prices of finished products.

Inelastic Demand. People tend to want about the same amount of food and clothing regardless of price and the demand for industrial raw materials is pretty much predetermined by the pace at which manufacturing is proceeding in the industrialized countries. These circumstances add up to relatively inelastic (insensitive to price changes) demand for raw commodities.

Inelastic Supply. At least in agriculture, the supply of the product is effectively dependent on the weather and on long-run forces. In ignorance

goods are more pronounced than those associated with manufactured goods, both the quantum and the total value of international trade in manufactured goods fluctuate more violently than they do in the case of primary goods.

as to what the price will be at harvesttime, the farmers tend to plant about as much one year as they planted the year before. And this tendency is accentuated in the case of the perennial crops such as coffee and sugar, where the size of the crop may be pretty much dependent on the weather and on the number of trees planted several years earlier.

Number of Producers. The circumstance that there is generally a large number of farmers cultivating any given agricultural crop means that it is relatively difficult for them to get together privately and reach agreement on crop restriction in an effort to raise the price. By contrast, in the typical manufacturing industry in a country like the United States, where most of the production may well be in the hands of three to eight firms, it is not only feasible but rather natural for them to reach some kind of understanding (not necessarily an overt agreement) about what is appropriate along the lines of production volume and pricing. In manufacturing, the producers can and do help themselves. In agriculture, this is rather more difficult because of the sheer number of producers.

Monoculture. Most of the Latin American countries specialize to a marked extent in the export either of one particular commodity or of a very limited group of commodities. Such economies have been called monocultures.

An extreme example of the monoculture situation is Venezuela, petroleum running over 90 percent of the exports of that country. For Brazil, 50 percent of that country's exports are coffee. The figure in the past has frequently run two thirds. Two thirds of Bolivia's exports are tin. Seventy to 80 percent of the exports of Guatemala, El Salvador, and Colombia are coffee. Half to two thirds of the exports of Chile are copper. Sixty percent of the exports of Honduras are bananas. Even in a case like Argentina, where, in 1959, 11 percent of the exports were beef and 13 percent were wheat, there exists a level of dependence on two commodities which is completely outside the frame of reference of a country such as the United States, where no single commodity would be 1 percent of the total.

Thus, many of the Latin American countries are dependent on one or a few commodities to a marked extent as their exports. And those commodities are generally in the raw commodity field where price fluctuations are pronounced relative to the fluctuations of manufactured goods prices.

When the price of the "single" commodity fluctuates, be it oil in

Venezuela or tin in Bolivia, the economy of the monocultural country is affected in a compounded manner. Cuba has had some periods of dazzling prosperity, for example, the "Dance of the Millions" in 1920, and some periods of abysmal depression and revolution, for example 1930–33, when the price of sugar was extremely low. In fact, the high price of sugar in 1963 seems to have been sufficient to make that a good year for Cuban sugar receipts in spite of a short crop.

However, this reservation should be made: From the domestic point of view, the economies of the Latin American countries are not as undiversified as they appear to be from the international point of view. And as time passes the economies are likely to become much more diversified. Substantial effort is now being expended to that end.

From the international point of view, however, these countries are still to a very pronounced extent dependent upon the caprice of the prices paid in the world market for a single raw material. It is a serious matter to be thus dependent upon the price changes of one or two commodities. A fall in prices poses difficult problems for the exporting country. If more commodities were included in the trade, fluctuations in price would tend in some degree to balance out so that the relative price stability of the group would serve to cushion the shock of individual fluctuations.

Small Countries in a World of Trade Barriers. The impact of such influences on the individual Latin American country is compounded by the fact that the countries are small. Smallness tends to create the monoculture situation. El Salvador is a coffee monoculture. But a country including El Salvador, the rest of Central America, Colombia, and Venezuela would not be a monoculture to anything like the same degree.

This issue of country size might be disregarded in a free-trade, free-communication world. But trade barriers combined with small size make the smallness an acute problem.

SECULAR TERMS OF TRADE. The claim, sometimes made, that the Latin American problem is rendered even worse by a tendency toward secular or long-term worsening in the terms of trade of the region seems not to be clearly established. The chief evidence which the Economic Commission for Latin America has advanced to justify such a contention has been that the British terms improved from the 1870s to World War II; and the Commission argued that surely the Latin American terms must have been behaving in a manner opposite from the British terms.[3] There are reasons for questioning that this proposition has been established. Much of the improvement in the British terms of trade during that period seems to have been a reflection of falling ocean freight rates, which were allowed for in the c.i.f. prices of British imports but not in the f.o.b. prices of British exports. Because of this method of handling ocean freight rates, the assumption that the movement of the Latin American terms is precisely opposite to the movement of the British terms seems dubious.

Another point is that the British terms seem to have worsened rather steadily from about 1800 to the 1860s and to have worsened from 1939 to 1952. Proof of the existence of a steady secular trend thus does not seem to be obtained from the British data.

Actually the position of the Economic Commission for Latin America is a good deal more sophisticated than the preceding comments may suggest. The Commission has argued that, in the developing countries, there has historically been a "tendency for industrial wages to appropriate the increase in productivity to the detriment of the primary activities."[4] From this argument it is thought to follow that the Latin American difficulties are a result of the fact that the region is not industrialized. Ergo, the Commission argues for industrialization.

At this point, however, it may be well not to draw the conclusion that concern for the Latin American terms of trade is uncalled for. There is pretty clearly a business-cycle-level problem of some kind and there may be a secular problem as well. In any event, it would not hurt the developed countries to cooperate in setting up machinery for dealing with the problem. If the problem exists, the machinery is there to deal with it; if the problem does not exist, no great harm has been done.

Historical Pattern

Off and on over the years there have been many international arrangements which have attempted to raise or support the prices of various raw

[3] United Nations, Department of Economic Affairs, *Relative Prices of Exports and Imports of Under-developed Countries* (Lake Success, New York, 1949), pp. 22–23.
[4] United Nations, *Towards a Dynamic Development Policy for Latin America* (New York, 1963), pp. 9, 83. It might be argued that the ECLA point would be better put if it ran to the effect that there is a tendency in developing countries for the factors of production (rent recipients and profit takers, as well as workers) to appropriate the increase in productivity.

materials in the production of which Latin America has had a significant interest: coffee, sugar, tin, copper, nitrate, henequen, wheat, cacao, and oil, for example.[5] Generally, the schemes involving the agricultural raw commodities such as coffee and sugar have involved agreements between governments. The copper schemes have generally involved the private companies as principals. The tin schemes, even though they have involved a metallic mineral, have generally been among governments.

There has been a certain consistency in the historical patterns in the evolution of many of these schemes. The scheme applicable to a particular commodity has generally first come into being as the result of low prices. The coverage of the original scheme has included a significant, but not dominating, percentage of production. Production restrictions have been set up and prices may rise as a consequence. But the chief beneficiaries have then been the producers who were not in the scheme and who continued to produce as much as they could. The scheme would then collapse. After a slight interval, a repetition of the low prices would force some of the producers (a larger group this time, but still less than 100 percent) into a new agreement. Again, the chief beneficiaries would be the outsiders, and so on.

Case Studies

COFFEE. Coffee is grown in many areas of Latin America. It comes from the highlands of Central America, from Colombia, from Venezuela. Those regions produce the so-called mild coffee. From Brazil, however, comes much of the coffee exports of the world, 39 percent in 1959, and the type grown is the so-called strong, or Brazil.

Coffee growing in Latin America is largely in the hands of the citizens of the countries involved. The individual Latin American, rather than the foreigner, has the chief stake as producer. For that reason, perhaps, the governments have taken an especial interest in the maintenance of a high price for the product.

Several characteristics of the coffee industry have exerted an influence on the economic impact of the control schemes.

---

[5] During the 1930s there was an extensive literature on international raw commodity control schemes. And the problem continues to be discussed a good deal in books and articles. One such book is, L. Baranyai and J. C. Mills, *International Commodity Agreements* (México, Centro de Estudios Monetarios Latinoamericanos, 1963).

(1) Coffee grows to advantage on fairly high, well-drained soil. The most suitable soil for this purpose has been the *terra-roxa* of São Paulo. In the older coffee-growing areas, the soil has well-nigh been worked to death.

(2) It takes new coffee trees several seasons to mature—six or seven years, in fact. This circumstance has occasioned some delayed reactions of a disconcerting nature. Trees planted during time of high prices have matured during times of low prices and made the prices yet lower.

(3) The demand for coffee appears to be fairly inelastic. At least the quantity consumed does not vary greatly over any short period of time as a result of fairly substantial price changes. Thus, very substantial price increases have followed only moderately short crops. And violent price decreases are likely to follow bumper crops.

São Paulo was the leading coffee-producing state in Brazil after the turn of the century. It was to the government of this state that the growers first turned following a large crop and low prices in 1905. This first valorization scheme was financed by a tax on coffee exports, and the proceeds from the tax were then used to support the coffee price.

In 1908 another bumper crop led to another valorization attempt, in connection with which the financing was somewhat different. The state of São Paulo borrowed abroad the funds necessary to finance the withholding of large stocks from the market. Coffee held off the market under this scheme was all sold profitably by 1918, and the foreign lenders were paid off.

Whether by accident or as a result of the merits of the schemes themselves (probably the former), those early control schemes seemed successful; and this fact made it likely that much the same procedure would be put into effect when difficulties arose again. This occurred in 1925.

At that time a permanent law for the "defense of coffee" was enacted by the government of the state of São Paulo. And the policy which had earlier been resorted to "as the necessity arose" became the permanent policy of the government of the state. Under this plan, all coffee had to pass through government warehouses. The state made advances to planters after their coffee had been deposited in the warehouse. Much of the funds necessary to finance the rather complicated credit operations involved were borrowed from abroad, but other funds were obtained from a transportation tax on coffee moved from the interior. The credits extended to the planters were perhaps too liberal; the scheme was perhaps a bit too successful at first in raising the price. The result was an overexpansion of the industry.

The reckoning came in 1929–30. Trees planted during the period of supported prices following 1925 began to mature. Foreign countries had also expanded production to take advantage of the prices the Brazilian controls were making possible. The price collapsed and then continued to drop as the trees insisted on continuing to mature.

Partly, no doubt, because of the disturbances in the coffee districts, 1930 was a period of political unrest in the country. Getulio Vargas took over the government of Brazil by force. This man, who ruled Brazil steadily from that time until 1946, was from the state of Rio Grande do Sul and not from the coffee country. It was obvious to him that something needed to be done about the coffee problem, but because of his origin, his motive was not primarily to make things easy for the *paulistas* of São Paulo.

During 1931–32 the federal government took the coffee valorization out of the hands of the state of São Paulo and began to deal with the problem on a national basis. The Departamento Nacional do Café was set up in 1933. A federal export tax on coffee was established, the receipts designed to provide funds for the support operations. It seemed necessary to destroy harvested coffee as well as to stop planting new trees because of the amount of productive capacity already in existence; a prohibitive tax was placed on new planting. In addition, a so-called sacrifice quota plan was adopted. Under this arrangement, the growers had to deliver a certain percentage of their crop to the government at prices below those prevailing in the market. This coffee was destroyed. From the beginning of coffee destruction until the cessation in 1944, 78,000,000 bags were burned. This is not a small figure. The total coffee exports of Latin America in 1939 were only 25,000,000 bags.

By these methods Brazil atempted to work out alone a problem which affected an industry that also existed in many other countries. By 1938 it had become obvious to Brazil that a control scheme, in which restriction of Brazilian supply was the principal measure, merely amounted to turning the coffee industry over to rival producing countries. Brazil, therefore, desired to have all producers committed to the control schemes.

In 1940 an agreement was finally consummated which virtually accomplished this. The Inter-American Coffee Agreement of that year included the major producers and the United States—fifteen countries in all—and established a pattern of national quotas applicable to the shares of each country in the international coffee trade. But World War II made the scheme largely meaningless.

Following World War II, the price of coffee was high for a decade. And it was only after price drops from the 1954 peaks became marked (about 1957) that the pressure for a revived coffee agreement became strong. During the next few years, there were several agreements which were abortive, chiefly because of the abstinence of the African producers. But by 1962 the pressure had become strong enough to induce the African producers to join in the comprehensive International Coffee Agreement of 1962.

This agreement was formulated in the general setting of the precepts for governing raw commodity control schemes which had been included in the 1949 Havana charter for an International Trade Organization. The votes in the governing board were equally divided among producing and consuming countries. The membership included most of the producing and consuming countries of the world (58, or so, countries). The agreement speaks of the desirability of establishing equitable prices. But there is no formula for identifying an equitable price, unless one believes that a commitment not to let prices go below 1962 levels qualifies as a formula. The substance of the control arrangements involved the fixing of annual export quotas. This involved the old base-year quota technique. The council would review the market situation and decide whether total marketings should be increased or decreased. Then the exporting countries would be assigned shares of the new quotas which would correspond with their percentage shares of the base-year quotas.

TIN. Malaysia and Indonesia have the largest deposits of tin in the world. Bolivia has the only deposits of real importance in the Western Hemisphere.

In Bolivia the principal companies used to be (1) Patiño, (2) Hochschild, and (3) Aramayo.

The years of World War I were characterized by large production and high prices. But following the end of the war the situation changed to one of surpluses; the price of tin dropped from a high of 87 cents a pound to 30 cents in 1921.

Several efforts (cartels) were made to control the production and price of tin during the 1920s. This was in spite of the fact that the industry was quite profitable during most of that period, and there was considerable new investment. But after the start of the depression in 1929, the industry found itself with large capacity for production, with surpluses, and with falling prices. The price dropped from 45 cents a pound in 1929 to 24 cents a pound in 1931. Private efforts sponsored by Patiño and the Tin Producers Association attempted to implement output restrictions. But the group proved unsuccessful in raising the price.

The governments of Malaya, Nigeria, the Netherlands Indies, and Bolivia (later joined by Siam) reached an agreement on March 1, 1931, for restricting output. This scheme involved 90 percent of the world's production of tin and was essentially an agreement among producers—omitting consumers. The approach was of the base-year quota type. The International Tin Committee set total quotas for the industry at levels intended (according to Article I of the agreement) to secure a fair and reasonable equilibrium between production and consumption with the view of preventing rapid and severe oscillations of price. Shares of the total were allotted to individual countries to correspond with market shares in the base year. The International Tin Committee was dissolved by mutual agreement on December 31, 1946, after having been dormant during World War II.

A new international agreement to regulate the tin industry was negotiated in 1953 and went into effect about three years later. The heart of the new tin arrangement was a buffer stock. The buffer stock is managed by the International Tin Council, with headquarters in London, which buys and sells tin in an effort to regulate the price. The manager is required to sell tin when the price goes over the ceiling and to buy when the price falls below the support level. In 1958 the ceiling price was £880 a ton; the support price was £640. But this range has been varied from time to time. At market prices between the ceiling and the support level, varying degrees of discretion are allowed in deciding whether to buy or to sell.

The Council was empowered to set export quotas for the producing countries when the buffer stock ran over 10,000 tons of metal. It was also conjectured that the buffer stock should not be allowed to run over 25,000 tons.

PETROLEUM. Venezuela is one of the major petroleum producers on the world scene. Mexico, Colombia, Trinidad, and Argentina produce respectable quantities. The chief producers in Venezuela have been Standard of New Jersey and Shell, the most influential members of the international petroleum community. They have dominated an international petroleum cartel which seems to have come into existence about 1928. The marketing arrangements dominated by those companies tied the price of Venezuelan crude at Venezuelan ports to an East Coast United States price which, at one time at least, was determined somewhat as follows: the Gulf Coast price plus tranportation to New York determined the New York price. The price at ports in Venezuela was the New York price minus transport cost from Venezuela. The Middle East price was determined in substantially the same manner relative to the New York price as was the Venezuelan, the Middle East price being the New York price minus transport cost from the Middle East.

The Venezuelan government has an interest in keeping the price at Venezuelan ports high. This is true because much of the Venezuelan tax revenue is geared to a tax on oil company profits. The higher the Venezuelan export price, the higher those profits will be. (And the system thus has also been tied to keeping the United States Gulf Coast export price high.) In recent years the Venezuelan government has made a major effort to keep this pattern of prices high. In trying to accomplish this result, the Venezuelan government has sponsored the Organization of Petroleum Exporting Countries. The chief members of this conspiracy against the gasoline buyers of the world are Venezuela, Saudi Arabia, Kuwait, and a few other similarly situated countries. The organization is working to raise the price of petroleum. But it also gears its appeal to moral considerations. A high price for crude could, it is said, support Venezuela, a poor and underdeveloped country, in a substantial development program.

To support its control efforts, the government of Venezuela has recruited the assistance of members of the Texas Railroad Commission to advise on measures for restricting the production of petroleum. The Texas Railroad Commission is quite expert in matters of this sort. The government of Venezuela has also created a government-owned Venezuelan Petroleum Corporation to handle directly some of the petroleum production of the country.

One or two things about these petroleum control arrangements are worth noting. Only in part is conflict of interest between the international companies and the governments involved. Both the companies and the governments have an interest in keeping the price of crude high. On the other hand, of course, the threat of expropriation or confiscation would produce a real conflict-of-interest situation.

SUGAR. Many of the institutional arrangements that were the heart of the pre-Castro International Sugar Agreement of 1953 have been destroyed. And Cuba and sugar have become much more a political than an economic issue. Consequently, it seems desirable, at the most, to include only a few comments about the sugar situation.

Some features of the system that has emerged are the following. (1) The United States has not been quite willing to turn the Cuban import quotas over to Cuba's competitors on a permanent basis. She wants to have the privilege of restoring them to Cuba as leverage in overthrowing Castro and helping a new government to get on its feet. Thus, in certain important respects, United States sugar policy is marking time. (2) The international sugar agreement is dormant. (3) The British situation is complicated by the independence of various of the former colonies, and by ambiguities in the relations between the former British colonies and the former colonies of members of the European Economic Community. Especially at stake is free access for cane sugar to the market of the European Economic Community. (4) Much of the Cuban sugar crop has been sold to the Soviet Union, but the size of the Cuban crop has been falling and a disastrous hurricane in the fall of 1963 made matters worse. Small crops, however, mean high prices, and the crop of 1963 was a substantial foreign exchange earner for Cuba. The Soviet Union has been trying to persuade Cuba to make a major effort to expand sugar production, but the Castro government would rather have help in expanding manufacturing. (5) The base-year quota system, with all its faults, is dormant but probably not dead.

A Typical Scheme

Typically, the raw commodity control scheme has provided for international agreement on total export quotas for all member-producing countries.

The controlling agency has set each year a total quota for the world, which has been a reflection of price considerations and of some guesses as to likely demand. Quotas have been assigned to the individual nations in such a way as to reflect the percentage of the total that the country in question provided in some earlier base year. Superimposed on these relations may be a production control scheme (generally also tied to base-year quotas) applying to the producers within each country.

A common adjunct, or alternative, to these arrangements is the stockpile or buffer stock. A national government, or an international agency, may buy up some of the crop when the price is low and plan to sell off some of the holdings when the price is high.

An important criticism of such arrangements is the stagnating effect of base-year quotas. They tend to freeze production into a mold. They make it difficult, if not impossible, for new, more efficient producers to enter an industry. After all, their base-year quota is zero. Improvement in production methods is consequently inhibited, and the region or company with the ability to produce at low cost may find itself at an effective disadvantage in expanding production.

Another difficulty with raw commodity control schemes has been the lack of a satisfactory theory for identifying a reasonable price.

I.T.O.

The proposed International Trade Organization Charter of 1949 took cognizance of the difficulties of raw commodity producers and proposed to approve raw commodity control schemes under certain circumstances, although in general it condemned international cartel arrangements. But certain characteristics were suggested for such schemes in an effort to protect consumer interest. For example, it was provided that, in the controlling bodies regulating the schemes, countries representing consumer interest should have a vote as large as that granted to countries representing producer interest.

However, the proposed charter failed to provide a meaningful principle to serve as a guide in determining what the core of a raw commodity control scheme should be. How to identify reasonable quotas and reasonable prices remained unanswered questions.

In spite of the fact that the International Trade Organization charter was not ratified, most of the postwar raw commodity control arrangements have ostensibly followed the rules suggested by that charter.

Model Scheme

A principle is needed. It may be constructive to suggest a guiding principle even though there is, by no means, general agreement among the authorities as to its desirability.

The general principle might be the proposition that in any given year raw commodity producers should be guaranteed a price at least as high as some percentage (perhaps 95 percent) of the price of the preceding year. Actual market prices would be permitted to fluctuate at will, subject to the so-called laws of supply and demand. Then the producer would be paid a subsidy amounting to the difference between the price on the market at the time of the sale and the 95 percent that he was guaranteed. The use of the market price instead of the actual sale price would protect against fraudulent underinvoicing of prices. This would be true because the producer would not get the difference between the actual sale price and 95 percent, but rather the difference between the market price prevailing on the day of the sale and 95 percent.

Such a scheme would permit long-run decline in the price of commodities in circumstances where such long-run decline is appropriate. The important good that it would accomplish would be to decrease the amplitude of price fluctuations in the short- and middle-run.

A device for capturing bonanza profits might be an ad valorem export tax, with rates rising as export prices rose.

It might be better if a control scheme of the sort recommended were administered by an international agency and the subsidies paid in foreign exchange. This would help deal with the problem of instability in foreign exchange earnings. However, the scheme could be administered by the governments of each of the countries concerned. The necessary financial resources to pay local producers from local sources are obtainable, given certain institutional changes. What is in short supply in the typical Latin American country is not the local paper money.

Such an arrangement would not necessarily solve the balance of payments difficulties of the countries concerned.[6] But balance of payments difficulties may rise for other reasons than export price fluctuations. It may be better to separate the balance of payments problem from the raw

[6] International Monetary Fund, *Compensatory Financing of Export Fluctuations* (Washington, 1963).

commodity pricing problem. To deal with the foreign exchange problem it might be desirable to set up a scheme guaranteeing each country against violent fluctuation in its foreign exchange earnings. Some features of the scheme might be similar to the percentage formula suggested above for determining the amount of the subsidy to the raw commodity producers. It is about time that an international organization such as the International Monetary Fund was given the power to do this sort of thing.

CHAPTER SEVEN

MARKET BEHAVIOR: GOVERNMENT BUSINESS AND PUBLIC UTILITIES

Business may be owned and/or operated by private enterprise. And the private enterprise may be subject to varying degrees of government regulation. It may be owned and/or operated by the government. And ownership and/or operation may involve a mixture of governmental and private roles. Commonly, that nebulous area of activity called public utilities (which comes close to being the phenomenon called infrastructure in economic development jargon) is in the twilight zone where any one of these ownership or operational forms may prevail.

Government Business

GOVERNMENT-SPONSORED MONOPOLY. It is nothing new in Latin America for the government to decide that a certain business should be operated as a monopoly. The exploitation of salt deposits or the marketing of salt at wholesale or retail has historically been a government monopoly, at least in Colombia, Peru, Ecuador, and Venezuela, and no doubt in many other Latin American countries as well. In Peru, salt, tobacco, denatured alcohol, explosives, matches, guano, and playing cards have also been handled as government monopolies. Emerald mining has been a governmental monopoly in Colombia. In Guatemala the government has maintained a monopoly for years in connection with tobacco, matches, and ammunition.

Farmed Out. In some cases these monopolies have been assigned (farmed out) to private concessionaires who operate the business as a monopoly but may lose the privilege if prices or methods do not accord with the desires of the government. In many cases, such grants have been made to favored politicians of the ingroup. Such grants have probably been revoked less often for breach of contract than because a succeeding government has wanted to turn the monopoly over to its own group of friends.

No doubt the result has frequently been profitable for the concession holders. But the important economic effects have probably been low volume, high prices, and inefficient operation, the effects one would expect from unregulated private monopoly.

Government Operated. Monopolies established by law may be owned and operated by the government. The mail is an example of this in almost all countries. A more specifically Latin American example is the oil company, Petróleos Mexicanos, in Mexico. In Peru the government operates the guano monopoly through the Compañía Administradora del Guano.

The distinction between farmed-out and government-operated monopolies is probably not worth belaboring on the assumption that, once adopted, a particular organizational form is thereafter consistently used. Some of these industries have been farmed out one year and operated by the government the next.

The chief difference between the two possibilities is that the concessionaire is in a position to extort monopoly profits and pocket them, whereas, in the case of government operation, the manager is paid a salary and the profits go to the government. But things are likely not to be this simple. The concession agreement may call for some form of profit sharing with the government. And the hired manager may have some arrangement (legal or otherwise) which would permit him to pocket a share of the profit.

Consequently, pricing policy may involve questions of more real significance than does ownership form. Is the monopoly (whether farmed out or government operated) required to maintain large volume and low prices in the public interest or is it permitted to operate on a low-volume and high-price basis? It is not the government ownership that determines whether an enterprise will be operated in the public interest; it is the pricing and production policy. For purposes of comparison, the role of the government-sponsored monopoly following a low-volume and high-price policy is equivalent to the role of the private monopoly permitted freely to pursue profit-maximization policies. Also, if basic necessities are involved, in the case of the government-sponsored monopoly, the operation has the effect of a regressive tax—even though the government pockets the profit.

The effect of monopoly (whether government operated or privately operated) historically has frequently been close to the effect of a regressive tax. And this has been especially characteristic of the Latin American scene. However, this is not necessarily the case, and in the last decade or two there have been some better-motivated efforts to use legal monopolies to encourage industrialization and to try to make more goods available at lower prices to the citizenry.

In such arrangements the degree of autonomy of the management in relation to government control becomes an interesting question. A government-owned and -operated monopoly can become the instrument of a powerful manager who acts with little or no effective government control. The manager may profit personally to considerable degree from his position. In so doing, he may make the agency a dynamic affair. He may negotiate international contracts with little or no control by the foreign office. He may not conform to the provisions of the national economic plan—if there is a plan. He may be a law unto himself. There are all sorts of interesting possibilities. It may be useful to cite a non-Latin American example of this sort of thing: the late head of the Italian government oil agency, Enrico Mattei. Another possibility is that management cannot or will not effectively run the agency: the Argentine State Railroads is an example.

GOVERNMENT IN COMPETITION WITH PRIVATE BUSINESS. Frequently Latin American governments have engaged in business activities without attempting to operate as monopolies. They have sometimes done so on the assumption that the prices and practices of private business would be more responsible if there were this measure of government competition. The beginnings of government competition with private enterprise in the public utility field have frequently been for reasons of this sort.

They have also entered an industry because the private companies were, in the opinion of the government, not producing enough. Electric power production has been an example in several Latin American countries, such as Mexico.

In some cases the governments have acquired, more or less automatically, the properties of some failing enterprise. Marginal mines, those at Pachuca in Mexico, for example, have been a case in point. In other cases, the government has gone into a line of business in order to cut itself in on a good thing. The Argentine government-owned meat-packing plant, CAP, is an example, as is the new Venezuelan government-owned oil company.

Perhaps one of the oddest arrangements of all is the case where the government owns and finances an enterprise and then farms out the operation to private enterprise (even foreign private enterprise). This has been the case with several of the new luxury hotels in Latin America, the Tequendama in Bogotá and the Tamanaco in Caracas. The hotel-operating subsidiary of Pan American World Airways, of all things, has been the instrument used in several of these cases. In Trujillo's day in the Dominican Republic, there were some fifteen hotels which were owned by the government, the operation being farmed out to private enterprise.

Such operations are a sort of travesty on the generally stated view that it is capital which is in critical shortage in Latin America. One is reminded of the extensive subsidies given by the Latin American governments to the foreign railroad builders of the nineteenth century. Is what Latin America really lacks capital, or is it something else? The something else might be technology (including effective management methods) and financial institutions adequate for channeling capital funds to the promoters in a position to put them to work constructively. (These questions are discussed in chapters Twelve, Fourteen, and Twenty-three.

MIXED COMPANIES. Many of the major industrial developments in Latin America in recent years have taken the form of mixed companies —companies jointly publicly and privately owned. This is the legal form of the Altos Hornos steel mill at Monclova in Mexico; it is the form of the SOMISA steel mill at San Nicolás in Argentina and of many other of the new and expensive forays into heavy industry in Latin America.

In the mixed company case, the government generally takes the entrepreneurial risk, does the initial planning, and then shares management and profits with private interests. The government may start out with and retain ownership of the majority control. But it has been rather common for the government, even though it starts off with majority control, to express intent to sell out the majority control to private interests.

In some cases, it has proceeded to do this. Examples have been the procedure of the Colombian Instituto de Fomento Industrial in the cases of coal mining, chemicals, paper, cement, rubber, and steel.[1] For example, in the case of the steel mill Acerías Paz del Río, which was set up in 1947 largely as a result of government initiative, by 1963 the Colombian government had sold off 80 percent of the stock to private interests and seemed to be intent on selling off the balance.[2] In other cases, the government has talked about divesting itself of control without actually implementing its stated intention. The Corporación de Fomento de la Producción in Chile has talked much of selling out its controlling interest in the enterprises it has promoted.

The mythology of free private enterprise is that profits are a reward for risk taking, or innovation, or putting up capital, or something of the sort. Since private enterprise has not generally played this role to any significant extent in the case of the mixed corporations, the question may be asked as to its proper role as a recipient of profits after it takes over control. Should it be allowed to make as much as it can after control has passed to its hands from the government? One might suppose that this would be a circumstance where profits should be subject to regulation, somewhat in the manner of public utilities. But the Latin American countries do not seem to have done much planning as to the basic principles to be applied in such cases in determining what an appropriate profit rate would be.

FOREIGN ATTITUDE. Off and on over the years, many United States government officials have counseled the Latin American governments

[1] *Overseas Business Reports* (United States Department of Commerce), OBR 63–107 (August, 1963), p. 4. For a discussion of activities along this line in Mexico, *see*, Calvin P. Blair, "Nacional Financiera: Entrepreneurship in a Mixed Economy," in Raymond Vernon, ed., *Public Policy and Private Enterprise in Mexico* (Cambridge, Harvard University Press, 1964), pp. 191–240.

[2] International Bank for Reconstruction and Development, *Eighteenth Annual Report, 1962–63*, p. 32.

against owning or operating business establishments. The United States has sometimes threatened to withhold loans from nationalized industries. During the 1950s, for example, Secretary of State Dulles warned Brazil that we disapproved of the government-owned oil industry of that country and would give it no financial support. In early 1963, a report of a committee headed by former General Lucius Clay recommended against loans to government-owned enterprises.

Although it is within the prerogatives of the United States government to lend to whom it chooses, it might nevertheless be good judgment not to clutter the record with examples of the use of the lending power to try to prevent the government operation of business in the underdeveloped countries. This is especially true since, in many Latin American countries, the knowledge that the United States is opposed to government ownership becomes a powerful argument in favor of government ownership.

United States Secretaries of Commerce ought to have a string tied around their fingers to remind them that part of their duty is not to sell the institution of free private enterprise to the Aztecs or their descendants.

EXTENT OF SOCIALIZATION. There is a good deal of government ownership in Latin America. The oil industry is nationalized in Mexico, Brazil, and Chile. There are also national government oil companies in most of the countries where private enterprise continues to play a role: Argentina, Venezuela, and Colombia. Most of the railroads of Latin America are now nationally owned. Many other public utilities have also been nationalized in the last decade or two. The chief foreign public utility companies (American and Foreign Power, Canadian Light, Sofina, and International Telephone and Telegraph) have been losing large segments of their holdings as the result of expropriation, confiscation, expiration of concessions, and so on. National governments have been the owners of various of the new manufacturing establishments, especially in the heavy industry field. The largest steel mills are owned by the governments of Argentina, Brazil, and Mexico. And governments own an assortment of other enterprises as well.

But from this the conclusion should not be drawn that Latin America is relatively more socialistic than is the United States. An accurate comparison of the degrees of socialization in the two regions would involve a compilation of data that would include municipally owned public utilities in the United States, and so on. A comprehensive comparison of this sort has not been made (but should be). Bits of relevant argument include some of the following:

It may be alleged as a tentative conclusion that the United States is at least as socialistic as Latin America because government enterprise represents about as large a percentage of the total economy in the United States as it does in Latin America. (But a theoretically satisfactory statistical demonstration on this point has not been made.)

A contrary argument might be to the effect that in Latin America the idea of government ownership is respected. It has been common in popular thought to accept the idea that socialization is a respectable form of organization and not an epithet. This has been true at least since the presidency of Batlle y Ordóñez in Uruguay in the decade before World War I.[3] Meanwhile, in the United States the idea is institutionalized (in spite of the post office) that government ownership is anathema.

In spite of these attitudes with regard to ownership forms, in the United States the federal government employee is generally held in considerable respect; but, in Latin America, the government employee is held in considerable contempt—on the ground that he is not conscientious, cooperative, or honest.

Other features of Latin American business organization are probably more worth worrying about than the degree of socialization. It is common for high government officials to have private business interests on the side. And close ties between public officials and private interests are a usual situation.[4] Also, government officials may manipulate government enterprise so as to make private profit therefrom.

The framing of the argument as though the important choice was between private enterprise and socialism is to miss the really important issues. Effective production, courteous service, lack of red tape, these things are desirable. And in some cases, better results are obtained by private operation; and, in other cases, better results are obtained by government ownership.

[3] Simon G. Hanson, *Utopia in Uruguay* (New York, Oxford University Press, 1938), p. 24.
[4] Raymond Vernon, *The Dilemma of Mexico's Development* (Cambridge, Harvard University Press, 1963), pp. 149, 153.

Public Utilities

Public utilities (or infrastructure) may be looked on as a special case of the problem of government versus private operation. What are chiefly involved are certain infrastructure-type industries such as electric power, water, transportation, and communication. Companies operating in these fields are likely to have special problems such as decreasing costs, or other characteristics leading rather naturally to monopolization. But it is futile to try to define a public utility in terms of those cost characteristics. It is better to leave the definition in terms of a rather general identification of the industries usually discussed as though they were public utilities. Such a definition leaves out the steel industry as well as such infrastructure items as highways, housing, and education.

RAILROADS. Much of the Latin American railway system was built by foreign investors in the period before World War I. As was the case in the United States, the railroad builders of Latin America did not generally make money from railroading. The railroads lost money. But considerable profit was made from the land grants.

The railroads in Latin America have faced major problems. One has been the topography of the routes traversed. Building railroads through the mountain walls of the Andes and Sierra Madres has been expensive. Numerous switches, sidings, and rack rails (cog railways) have been necessary. The Latin American railroads are a long distance from the plants where steel rails, passenger cars, freight cars, and locomotives are made. It is difficult to obtain replacements. World War II did not improve this situation. Latin American railways were able to obtain very little equipment between 1940 and 1946. As a result, the war's end found them even more run down than formerly.

Beginning with the acquisition by the Mexican government of a controlling interest in the National Railways of Mexico shortly after 1900, the railroads of Latin America have been progressively nationalized. The chief step in this march was taken by the Perón government in Argentina in buying the British-owned railroads in that country in 1947.

OCEAN TRANSPORT. A varied assortment of steamship lines provides more or less regular service between Latin America and the rest of the world. Some lines are owned in Latin America, some are not. The more important ones are not.

Examples of government-owned lines include Lloyd Brasileiro (Brazil), the Flota Mercante Gran Colombiana (Colombia and Ecuador), and Chilean, Argentine, and Mexican lines. Even Paraguay has incurred the expense of an ocean-going fleet.

Several of the countries, Panama and Honduras, for example, ostensibly have quite large privately owned fleets. But mostly this is because certain United States companies (e.g., the Standard Oil Company of New Jersey) find it expedient to assign many of their ships to foreign registry.

The chief United States lines serving Latin America are Moore-McCormack, Delta, Grace, and United Fruit. Both Grace and United Fruit combine their shipping interests with extensive activity in Latin American agriculture: United Fruit in bananas in Central America and Ecuador; Grace in plantations along the west coast of South America.

It sounded reasonable two or three decades ago, when Latin Americans complained about the rate gouging to which they were subjected by the foreign shipping companies, to agree with them that a way around this difficulty was for them to develop their own shipping lines.[5] This has been done by several of them. But the national shipping lines have generally proceeded to join the freight-rate conferences in partnership with the foreign shipping companies. And everybody proceeds to price gouge the shippers, with no obvious gain to the Latin American economies, if one discounts the profit gain of the Latin American shipowners. (If the government participates, one can view the result as a regressive tax.) An example of this sort of thing was brought to light in the fall of 1963 as a result of efforts by a Norwegian shipping line to get a greater share of United States coffee imports from Brazil into Gulf ports. It was reported that the cargo-revenue pooling agreement in effect divided the trade (or rather, the revenue from the trade regardless of who actually carried the coffee) as follows:[6]

---

[5] For a discussion of the economics of Latin American ownership of ocean shipping lines, *see,* Claudio Escarpenter, *La Economía del Tráfico Marítimo Internacional de Cuba* (Havana, Editorial Echevarria, 1958).

[6] New York *Times,* November 12, 1963, p. 69; September 23, 1963, p. 49.

GOVERNMENT AND PUBLIC UTILITIES 103

Nopal Line (Norwegian, private)	19.41 %
Delta Line (United States, private)	53.06 %
Lloyd Brasileiro (Brazilian government)	19.41 %
ELMA (Argentine government)	8.12 %
	100.00 %

Apparently this four-company pooling agreement affecting Gulf Coast ports is merely part of a larger twelve-company pooling agreement which also includes United States North Atlantic ports. In its complaint against the pact, before the United States Federal Maritime Commission, Nopal alleged that it had been forced into the pooling agreement by a Brazilian government regulation confining coffee shipments solely to pool members. (Lloyd Brasileiro got its 19.41 percent of the revenue whether it actually carried 19.41 percent of the cargo or not.)

It might be a better tactic, and a service to consumers everywhere at the same time, if Latin America fought its major battle against the rate-setting practices of the shipping conferences—instead of trying to deal with the problem by setting up an extremely expensive ocean shipping industry to provide a service that can be obtained from foreign companies without any capital cost to Latin America.

URBAN TRANSPORTATION. In the early days urban transportation was dominated by the foreign-owned power companies. Increasingly it has been taken over by municipal governments or by cooperatives; and buses have generally taken the place of streetcars.

WATER. The prevailing situation in Latin American cities has been that impure water has been inadequately supplied by the municipalities. Private companies have generally not operated in the field.

ELECTRIC POWER. Beginning about 1900, installations were set up in a number of cities for the purpose of generating electric power from imported coal. The coal was cheap, being imported from England on ships whose owners were glad to have the coal as ballast on the trip south. The ships then returned to England with cargoes of wheat and beef.

In these early days, the electric power field in Latin America was dominated by a few foreign firms such as Electric Bond and Share

(American and Foreign Power) and Sofina, an "international" company operating out of Brussels and Panama.

In Latin America at the time of the original grants of franchises, provision was made for regulating the rates which the companies would charge and a time limit was set on the concession. It was generally provided that, at the end of the concession period, the property would be turned over to the government.[7]

These arrangements did not work very well. Until about 1930 the companies seem effectively to have escaped regulation and to have set whatever rates they chose. But, as Latin American governments became more effectively nationalistic during the 1930s, the situation changed. The companies were held to the rates permitted in the charters; and as time passed, those rates became more and more inappropriate due to inflation. But it proved difficult for the companies to get permission from the government for raising the rates. As foreigners operating in an extremely conspicuous position, the public utility companies have been vulnerable to antiforeign criticism. And public pressure against rate increases has been difficult for the government to resist. At all events rates were held down by government action so that, with the passage of the years, the profits on public utility investments apparently have been among the lowest of those made by foreign investors.

So, little new investment in public utilities was forthcoming; and the Latin American countries, as they talked more about economic development following World War II, found themselves short of power. To the extent that there has been a lag in Latin American industrialization in recent years, it has probably been due in significant degree to the combination of circumstances that inhibited public utility investment, following an early, impressive spurt of investment in that field fifty or sixty years ago.

Faced with assorted difficulties and popular antagonism, the foreign-owned public utilities seem to have decided that the thing to do is to cast in the sponge and liquidate their investments on terms as favorable as possible. Typically, the arrangements that are being worked out have

---

[7] Two significant works on the electric power industry in Latin America are: David F. Cavers and James R. Nelson, *Electric Power Regulation in Latin America* (Baltimore, Johns Hopkins Press [for the International Bank for Reconstruction and Development], 1959); and Miguel S. Wionszek, "Electric Power: The Uneasy Partnership," in Raymond Vernon, ed., *Public Policy and Private Enterprise in Mexico* (Cambridge, Harvard University Press, 1964).

required the public utility company to reinvest the funds it realizes in manufacturing or some similar local activity that is not quite as sensitive as a public utility. American and Foreign Power seems resigned to liquidating its investment in Brazil on these terms. And they were the terms, pretty much, under which American and Foreign Power and Mexican Light and Power (of Canada) have liquidated their investments in Mexico.

Some of these investments are being liquidated with a reasonably good grace, in some cases even according to the terms of the original concession agreements. In other cases, considerable animosity has been generated as a by-product of the liquidation, as, for example, in the state of Rio Grande do Sul in Brazil, where Leonel Brizola liquidated the local subsidiary of American and Foreign Power with as much fanfare and associated bitterness as he could muster. (A flamboyant nationalization of a foreign-owned public utility is frequently a good way to get ahead in Latin American politics.) The animosity, however, may also be a result of the recalcitrance of the foreign investor. And a combination of hardheadedness of both sides can really generate trouble.

Generally the expropriated companies have subsequently been operated by the government.[8] Nationalization has frequently been followed by efforts by the government to raise the rates to the levels that had been demanded by the private companies as a condition for continuing to operate. The Mexican Ministry of Industry and Commerce raised power rates in a pattern such as this in early 1962, following the nationalization of the properties of American and Foreign Power in 1960.[9]

EVALUATION. The unsatisfactory state of the investment in the public utility field is one of the chief influences holding back the industrialization of Latin America. Investment in this field has lagged since at least 1930. This is especially regrettable because of the importance of public utilities in forming the infrastructure to support much of the development in manufacturing. The foreign investors have soured on emphasis

---

[8] There are exceptions to this procedure. When the L. M. Ericcson (Sweden) and International Telephone and Telegraph (United States) investments in the telephone system of Mexico were liquidated, control passed to Teléfonos de México, a company controlled by the private Carlos Trouyet interests, although the government held a substantial amount of preferred stock (New York *Times*, September 7, 1963, p. 23).
[9] New York *Times*, January 19, 1962, p. 44.

in these fields. And domestic private investors in Latin America never have looked on public utilities with favor. The rates of return are not high enough. But also the capital costs run very high and the requirements in terms of technology are demanding.

Provision for financing in the public utility (infrastructure) area has become a major concern of the International Bank for Reconstruction and Development and other agencies concerned with stimulating development, but the public utility field remains a problem area.

PART THREE

WELFARE

CHAPTER EIGHT

LABOR MOVEMENT

The traditional device by which working people have attempted to use self-help measures to raise their level of living has been the labor union.[1]

Development of Movement

Latin American labor was treated roughly before 1910. (There was legal slavery in Brazil until 1888.) As a reaction to such treatment, militant underground unions, frequently anarcho-syndicalist in philosophy, were being formed by the late nineteenth century. The Flores Magón brothers were active in such activities in Mexico. Strikes were called at the Cananea mines in Sonora in 1906 and at the Río Blanco textile mill near Orizaba in 1907. Díaz supported the employers and put the strikers down with military force and bloodshed. This was a rather common type of procedure in other Latin American countries in those days.

Generally during the nineteenth century, legal codes in Latin America prohibited the worker from signing a contract with his employer. In colonial times, such provisions had protected the worker from signing an agreement he did not understand. But the provision later retarded the rise of the labor union movement, which has been predicated on the signing of collective contracts between employers and labor unions.

Even the mere formation of a labor union was quite generally illegal until well into the twentieth century. But, by 1910, the labor movement had gained headway in spite of these difficulties. Mutual unions, encour-

[1] Among the more significant books on the Latin American labor movement are: Robert Alexander, *Labor Relations in Argentina, Brazil, and Chile* (New York, McGraw-Hill, 1962); Marjorie Clark, *Organized Labor in Mexico* (Chapel Hill, University of North Carolina Press, 1934); Moisés Poblete Troncoso and Ben G. Burnett, *Rise of the Latin American Labor Movement* (New Haven, College and University Press. 1960).

aged by the Catholic Church, had been established in several countries, and more militant, underground unions were fairly common.

In Mexico in the 1910–20 decade, legislation favorable to labor union organization was adopted. And the legality of labor organizations was subsequently affirmed in most of the Latin American countries.

In Latin America, government influence over unions, once their right to exist was established, became more important than has been the case in the United States. The particular union which has been supported by the government has been not only the most important union, but virtually the only one worth mentioning. So it was with the CROM in Mexico under Obregón and Calles (1920–28), and with the CTM under Cárdenas (1934–40), and so it is today with the largest unions in most of the Latin American countries.

Workers now in Latin America, fairly generally, have the legal right to organize. There is some tendency, even, to push this concept into a duty to organize. (There would be a duty to organize in a genuinely corporate state.) But perhaps the matter is better put in a somewhat pragmatic manner by saying that the government frequently and overtly sponsors unions, with a leadership of the government's choosing, and thus sees that the unions come into being. And the subsequent pressures can be pretty strong to see to it that the worker joins the appropriate union.

In most countries a legal concept, called *personería gremial* in Argentina, gives a certain exclusive status to the labor union which is "most representative" of an industry. This union, once identified, has the right to represent the whole industry before the government and before the employers. It also has the privilege of collaborating with the government as an advisory technical agency.

In Latin America, then, the relation between the government and unions is fundamentally different from the United States situation. In the United States the unions have operated in substantial independence of government interference in such matters as the selection of officers. In Latin America, once the government has decided to deal with unions at all, it has proceeded to influence their internal organization and to use them for political ends. In consequence, unions have alternately been the fair-haired instruments of government or been vigorously suppressed (if the government found the latter procedure expedient).

Current Organization

INTERNATIONAL ORGANIZATIONS. The Pan American Federation of Labor (Confederación Obrera Pan Americana, or COPA), organized in 1918 with the support of Samuel Gompers and the American Federation of Labor, was perhaps the first example of an international labor movement including various nationwide organizations such as CROM of Mexico.

Following the decline of COPA, the next significant international organization was a joint effort of the CTM (the successor to CROM as the chief national union in Mexico) and the CIO in the late thirties. The new organization was called the CTAL (Confederación de Trabajadores de América Latina) and the dominant figure was the Mexican Vicente Lombardo Toledano.

In the post-World War II period, Latin American national unions have belonged to three different international organizations.

(1) One has been the International Confederation of Free Trade Unions with headquarters in Brussels. This is the international organization with which the AFL-CIO of the United States has been affiliated. The Latin American regional organization which is affiliated with the ICFTU is the Organización Regional Interamericana de Trabajo (ORIT). Individuals are not members of the ORIT itself; rather, they are members of national unions recognizing some degree of affiliation (sometimes rather nebulous) with the ORIT. The General Secretary of the ORIT in 1963 was Arturo Jáuregui Hurtado.

(2) A second international organization, with headquarters also in Brussels, has been the World Federation of Trade Unions. It has been, more or less, Communist or Russian dominated or influenced. During much of the postwar period the regional organization in Latin America affiliated with the WFTU was the Confederación de Trabajadores de América Latina (CTAL). But efforts seem to be in progress on the part of the WFTU to substitute a new regional affiliate for the CTAL.

(3) A third regional organization is the Confederación Latinoamericana de Sindicalistas Cristianos (CLASC). It was founded at a 1954 conference in Santiago, Chile. This regional organization is affiliated with the Confédération Internationale des Syndicats Chrétiens, which dates back to a 1920 conference at The Hague. Ideologically, it adheres

to the principles of the papal bulls Rerum Novarum (1891) and Quadragesimo Anno (1931).

NATIONAL ORGANIZATIONS. The national labor organizations in Latin America have been involved in internal conflicts which have been partly ideological in nature, partly struggles for power. On the ideological side there have, of course, been involved the conflicts among (1) the Marxists (currently divided between the Stalinist-Chinese and the Russian-oriented wings); (2) the pragmatic unionists (oriented toward the methods used by the AFL-CIO in the United States and emphasizing material gains in wages, hours, and fringe benefits rather than emphasizing political action); and (3) the Catholic-oriented.

But frequently more important than the ideological struggle has been the struggle of personalities. The Latin American worker has been more attracted by the personality of some contestant for leadership than by his ideology. And the personal ties, *personalismo* in the relations between leaders and followers, can become extremely strong. There is personalismo involved not only in the relations of the union members to the leaders of the union, there is also personalismo involved in the relationship of the union to the various political leaders on the national scene.

In Argentina, the national organization has been the Confederación General del Trabajo. At present it is an uneasy fusion of pro-Perón and anti-Perón unions (the pro-Perón "62" group of unions and the anti-Perón "32" group).

In Mexico, the CTM (affiliated with the ORIT) remains the dominant union and Fidel Velázquez is the chief figure. To the left of the CTM is the AOCM (Alianza de Obreros y Campesinos de México). And to the right of it is a group of Catholic-oriented unions.

Similarly, in other Latin American countries there may be at least three organizations operating at the national level: (1) a Communist-oriented group of unions, (2) a group of unions officially recognized by the government, and (3) a group oriented to the Catholic position. But it is just as likely that there exists only one real national union and the three groups are struggling for power within the single "official" union. Of course, in each country, there are special local variations on these relations.

In general, the officially recognized union organization obtains certain perquisites. Its leaders will be the official channel by which the government consults with the labor movements; also, they will be part of the government-management-labor triumvirate that is institutionalized in many American countries as a major political force. It is important to the union to have these channels of communication.

Occasionally, dynamic individuals, such as Lombardo Toledano in Mexico, gain control of the labor movement, dominate it for a time, and have sufficient prestige so that the government must treat them with respect. More often, however, the labor unions have been junior partners in the government-management-labor triumvirates. They have gotten some fairly attractive crumbs only when the government, on the basis of political considerations, desired to be pro-labor. The labor movement has not generally been strong enough to demand significant concessions as a matter of right.

It is a result of these circumstances that it is not possible accurately to identify specific national unions in terms of their affiliation with the major international unions and then count heads and say how much of the Latin American labor movement is associated with the ICFTU, how much with the WFTU, and how much with the Confédération Internationale des Syndicats Chrétiens.

HIERARCHY. The basic organization in the union hierarchy is the *sindicato,* the organization at the level of the individual plant. The sindicatos are generally organized either functionally or geographically into *federaciones*. The federaciones will then be organized into a *confederación nacional* of the federaciones (or sindicatos) in a particular industry. There will also be a national confederación of the industrial confederaciones, including much, if not all, of the labor union movement of the country.

This is much too simplified a description. The organization is complicated by the occasional existence of competing hierarchies affiliated with the ORIT or the CTAL or the CLASC. In Brazil there are two hierarchies of organizations, one of which grew out of the efforts of the Vargas regime in the 1930s to form a corporate state; the other grew up out of other efforts to form a national labor union movement. All in all, the structure is not uniform from country to country, but the variations are not especially geared to the craft-union, industrial-union distinction that has been important in the history of the labor movement in the United States.

The laws of many of the Latin American countries provide for the obligatory existence of the sindicato-federación-confederación structure mentioned above. And those laws establish the legal rights and duties of the unions. Much of the struggle among Marxists, Catholics, and others, then, takes place within a framework involving such a hierarchy of legally recognized unions. And for tactical reasons, it is desirable for the competing groups to be in the officially recognized organization—more perquisites being obtained that way. But there also exists the possibility of a nonconformist hierarchy in addition. Which international organization the national confederación affiliates with constitutes a running battle in most of the Latin American countries, except perhaps currently in Cuba. And delegations from the officially recognized confederaciones may attend the international conferences of first one and then another of the international organizations.

Membership Size

It is probably worthwhile to try to say something about the membership size of the Latin American labor movement, in spite of the statistical difficulties involved. It has been estimated that there are about 12.5 million organized union members in Latin America.[2] About 2.5 million of these are in Argentina, 2.5 million in Brazil, 2 million in Mexico, 1.5 million in Cuba, and 1.5 million in Venezuela. These five countries thus account for about 80 percent of the labor union movement of Latin America in terms of numbers. A well-informed observer, Robert Alexander, has, however, estimated the Mexican, Venezuelan, Cuban, and Brazilian figures to be substantially smaller than those given above and has indicated a belief that total, genuine membership in the Latin American labor movement is nearer to 6.5 million.[3] The organized labor movement in the United States, an area with slightly less population than Latin America, has about 18 million members. In spite of its smaller membership, the Latin American union membership probably represents as high a percentage of the industrial labor force as is the case in the United States.

[2] *Statistical Abstract of Latin America, 1962* (UCLA), p. 4.
[3] Mildred Adams, ed., *Latin America: Evolution or Explosion?* (New York, Dodd, Mead, 1963), p. 180.

Procedures

COLLECTIVE BARGAINING. In the United States, collective bargaining is the approved means for working out disputes between employers and workers. And in what is considered the standard working of the process, the government is not involved as a third party. By contrast, in Latin America labor disputes are much less likely to be settled by direct negotiations between employers and workers discussing the issue of wages and working conditions. In Latin America, it is much more likely to be the case that the government dictates the terms of settlement in a process that frequently does not involve the employers and workers as effective participants in the bargaining process.

STRIKES. In the pre-1910 Mexico of Porfirio Díaz, the government was quite ready to take the employer's side and suppress strikes, with force if necessary, and the same was generally true throughout Latin America. Things began to change in Mexico with the Revolution of 1910, and they began to change over much of the rest of Latin America at about the same time. Article 123 of the Mexican Constitution of 1917 specifically permits strikes, the Board of Conciliation and Arbitration having the power to declare particular strikes legal or illegal. The instructions under which the Board operates are to the effect that strikes are to be declared legal if they are designed (1) to bring about equilibrium among the factors of production, (2) to force the employer to abide by his contract, (3) to obtain more satisfactory conditions on the expiration of the contract force, or (4) to aid some other labor group engaged in a legal strike. (5) Strikes must be voted by a majority of the employees affected.[4] The right to strike as a technique for gaining ends is now quite generally admitted in Latin America, but the strike is more likely to be successful if the government backs it than in the contrary case.

In fact, Latin American strikes are rather likely to have a political motive, to be intended to influence elections or political trends. One-day general strikes as gestures indicating how labor feels about public issues are rather common occurrences. And the completeness of the shutdown

---

[4] Pan American Union, *A Statement of the Laws of Mexico in Matters Affecting Business* (Washington, 1961), p. 121.

involved is frequently taken, especially by foreign newspaper correspondents, as a gauge of how the political winds are blowing. Be that as it may, such activities may have very little to do with wages and working conditions.

MEDIATION AND ARBITRATION. In Latin America neither collective bargaining nor strikes have served as effective devices for dealing with labor's pragmatic problems: wages and working conditions. Most Latin American countries now have provision for conciliation, mediation, or arbitration under various circumstances, which are generally laboriously spelled out in the laws. And such procedures have been used in a rather orderly way in such countries as Mexico, Venezuela, and Brazil. In other countries, the procedures may be used more or less at the whim of the executive branch.

Considerable legal specialization is involved in acquiring a serviceable working knowledge of these procedures. But some mention of the manner in which the process works in Mexico may help at least to indicate some of the problems that are involved.

The Boards of Conciliation and Arbitration in Mexico are composed of an equal number of representatives of capital and labor and of a government representative who possesses the balance of power. Arbitration is compulsory if one of the parties to the dispute so requests. If the employer refuses to submit to arbitration or to accept the award, the Board may declare that the labor contract between the employer and his employees is terminated; and the employer then becomes liable for the payment of discharge wages covering three months' pay to his employees. If the workers refuse to abide by the decision of the Board, the labor contract may also be declared terminated. Thus, while the Board cannot render a legally binding decision, its decisions are backed by certain sanctions which tend to make employers, and workers as well, think twice before disregarding them. To the extent that the government is directly responsible for the decisions of the Board (since its representative wields the balance of power), it is only natural that the force of the government is likely to be used to sanction those decisions. That force is not to be taken lightly in Mexico. In 1938 the government expropriated the properties of the major foreign oil companies following their refusal to abide by a Board decision which had been confirmed by the Supreme Court. But the side which the government will support varies from time to time depending on whether the government at the moment is prolabor or probusiness or pro-not-rocking-the-boat!

Compulsory arbitration of all disputes is not the general rule in Latin America. However, compulsory arbitration of particular issues may be provided for in individual collective contracts, and the governments have provided for compulsory arbitration in certain cases. Argentina, for example, has provided for compulsory arbitration in the case of disputes involving essential public services.

Extensive government influence in the settling of labor disputes has been part of the story since governments began to sponsor unions. Increasingly, that influence takes the form of more decisive government action in controlling arbitral decisions in labor disputes. This trend accords with the generally paternalistic attitude of Latin American governments.

COLLECTIVE CONTRACTS. The collective contract is an agreement between the union and the employer, setting out the conditions under which the laborers shall work. It generally includes provisions on wages, hours, safety precautions, vacations, hiring and firing procedures, and so on.

Two specific provisions of the Mexican law on collective contracts are worth mentioning. The first of these provisions is that a collective contract, regardless of its ostensible duration, is subject to revision every two years if either capital or labor so desires. If the parties fail to reach agreement among themselves, provision is made for the procedure called "economic conflict" to be followed before a Board of Conciliation and Arbitration. The Board can investigate the economic status of the company or industry, determine its real ability to pay, and prescribe changes in the collective contract in accordance with its findings. This procedure places the whole collective contract-negotiating procedure rather closely under the supervision of the state. In 1937, the "economic conflict" procedure was invoked by the unions in the dispute with the oil companies which led to expropriation the following year.

Another notable element in the Mexican law is the power of the government to establish what has been called "contract law." The Labor Code of 1931 provided that, when the collective contract has been entered into by two thirds of the employers and workers belonging to a specific branch of industry in a specific region, it may be made obligatory on all employers and workers in the same branch of the industry in the same region if the President of Mexico shall so provide by decree. This provision gave the national government rather extensive powers with regard to generalizing collective contracts to employers and workers who had not specifically agreed to them. (A similar procedure is applied in Argentina and other countries.)

In general, then, the laws of the Latin American countries provide that the signing of collective contracts shall be the normal procedure in employer-employee relations, determination of the specific provisions being left to the participants in a setting where the parties are generally heavily subject to government influence.

DISCHARGE. Increasingly, the Latin American laws protect the worker from arbitrary discharge. Notice before discharge and additional pay at the time of discharge are now generally required. A common provision is that three months' pay must be given at the time of discharge—even if the company is laying off all labor and planning to go out of business.

Ostensibly, the worker is better protected now than formerly against arbitrary action by his employer. However, over much of Latin America this protection is sporadic and unreliable. It is not easy for the individual worker, especially away from the capital city, to press his claim for such protection against an employer who has political connections.

RIGHT TO A JOB. Latin American labor laws have covered basic theoretical issues which have been avoided in United States legislation. An example of this has been the inclusion in some of the laws of the provision that the individual worker has a right to a job. The Brazilian law, for example, has such a provision. But for such provisions to have much meaning, someone must have an obligation to give him, not only a job, but also a reasonably good job.

Problems

REVOLUTIONARY ACTION VERSUS PRAGMATIC ACTION. Are Latin American labor unions in the future likely to be a force working toward gradual improvement in the welfare of the workers or are they likely to be a force tending to precipitate revolutionary change? The

United States press rather tends to give the impression that the Latin American unions are Communist-infiltrated agents of the devil working for revolutionary change and the establishment of Communist regimes in Latin America.

Celso Furtado, in speculating about the future role of unions, has hazarded the guess that the rural landless, for example, in Brazil the Peasant Leagues of Francisco Julião, are more likely to be the instruments of violent change than are the labor unions in manufacturing. According to Furtado, it is already obvious to the urban labor unions that they have much to gain in terms of real standard of living by a policy of gradualism. They can see possibilities for significant improvement in their own welfare as employers yield on wage, hour, and fringe benefit demands. They are not likely to forfeit these possibilities for the cause of violent revolution. On the other hand, the rural landless are confronted with a rigid, resistant class structure, bitterly fighting even minor changes. To them the only alternative seems to be cataclysmic disruption of the system. This is the reason the Northeast of Brazil is such a powder keg.[5]

Still, in many parts of Latin America, the labor unions in mining and manufacturing seem to have considerable propensity for serving as direct-action political intruments. Riots in Bogotá in January, 1963, were a reminder of this possibility.[6] And the behavior of the Federación Sindical de Trabajadores Mineros de Bolivia (FSTMB), led by Juan Lechín Oquendo, continues to indicate potential in the same direction.

Whether in the future the labor unions of Latin America are going to be essentially pragmatic or essentially political and revolutionary is one of the really important questions in the Latin American field. The assumption by the United States press that Latin American unions are essentially committed to Communism does not help with intelligent discussion of such an issue.

EFFECT OF NATIONALIZATION ON THE ROLE OF UNIONS. Another pending problem involves the relation of unions to nationalized industries. In the past in Latin America, labor unions have been in the

---

[5] Celso Furtado, "Brazil: What Kind of Revolution?" in *Foreign Affairs,* 41 (April, 1963), 526–35, esp. p. 533.
[6] *Hispanic American Report,* March, 1963, p. 56.

forefront in the struggle against private entrepreneurs, and particularly against private, foreign entrepreneurs. In the process they have been strong proponents of expropriation or nationalization. Of course, they would have preferred that the expropriated properties be turned over to them to run. But several experiments along this line have proven rather abortive failures in Latin America: the railroads in Mexico following expropriation in 1937, for example. Failing to establish themselves as the new managing group, the unions, nevertheless, up to now have remained strong advocates of nationalization as over against private entrepreneurship. But will they really like such nationalization after they have seen something more of the implications? The question may be brought to a head on occasions when labor unions attempt to strike against nationalized industries. Examples have already occurred. There was, for instance, a strike by the airline pilots of Aerovías Nacionales de Colombia (AVIANCA) in the fall of 1963. AVIANCA is jointly owned by the Colombian government and by Pan American World Airways. The government declared the strike illegal.[7] Other recent strikes against nationalized plants have involved, in Venezuela, Siderúrgica del Orinoco and the Colombian Empresa Colombiana de Petróleos.

The continuing conflict between labor and management in the nationalized tin mines of Bolivia has been bitter. The government-owned Corporación Minera de Bolivia (COMIBOL) has found it difficult to fight the unions on issues such as payroll padding and the subsidized, low prices of the company commissaries, which have been a significant financial drain on the Bolivian treasury as well as an example of substantial favoritism to the miners in contrast to the undernourished balance of the Bolivian population. The union, for its part, seems to view its role as largely political and to be little concerned to play a role calculated to improve the relative efficiency of the Bolivian tin-mining industry. The union remains, apparently, influenced by strong pro-Communist sympathies. There are contradictory attitudes present in the union approach. One might expect a union that is dissatisfied with its status under nationalization to develop anti-Communist views.

In general in Latin America, the governments have been the effective arbiters of labor disputes. But can they continue to play this role in a setting where they are also playing the role of employer? The unions have some rethinking to do with regard to their attitude toward the role

[7] *Hispanic American Report,* January, 1964, p. 1078; October, 1963, p. 800.

of government in a society which is substantially nationalized. Study as to what is actually involved in the role of labor unions in the Soviet Union may well be in order—followed by some speculation as to whether that is really what labor wants.

CHAPTER NINE

WAGES AND SECURITY

The first major social security enactments in Latin America were during the World War I period. At that time Uruguay put into effect a social security system with substantial coverage. The Mexican Constitution of 1917 provided for a general system of social security. And Chile established such a system in the early 1920s. Subsequently, most of the Latin American countries have provided by law for social security systems.[1]

Hours

The eight-hour day and the 48-hour week are now generally endorsed in the social legislation in the area. The first country to enact specific legal provisions to this effect was Uruguay in 1915.

It is impossible to go into detail with regard to the variations in the laws. But a few considerations may be noted. For the most part, the laws do not give complete coverage to all workers. In practice, agriculture has been unaffected even in those countries where the law ostensibly applies to the hours of work of agricultural laborers. But for the most part, agriculture is not even formally covered in the laws. Household service also has been almost unaffected. But in manufacturing, the 47- or 48-hour week seems to be something like the norm.[2]

Wages

MINIMUM WAGE LAWS. The early legislation on wages was designed primarily to protect agricultural labor against wage payments in kind

---

[1] Summaries of the social security legislation of the various Latin American countries are to be found in the following series: Pan American Union, *A Statement of the Laws of Mexico in Matters Affecting Business* (Washington, 1961). There are similar publications for virtually all of the Latin American countries.
[2] *Yearbook of Labour Statistics, 1963*, pp. 280–85.

and against the requirement that the peon make his purchases in the hacienda store (*tienda de raya*). Such practices limited his freedom of choice and were the means by which debt peonage was imposed. Laws ostensibly giving protection against this sort of thing were passed in Brazil in 1904, in Peru in 1916, in Mexico in 1917, and so on. But the passage of the laws has not necessarily accomplished the intended protection. Debt peonage (*yanaconazgo*) still seems to be not uncommon in Peru.

Of late years, all the Latin American countries have also adopted minimum wage laws. There is considerable variation in the nature of these laws. In Uruguay the law, after it was extended to cover agricultural labor in 1946, was among the broadest in Latin America. In several countries (Chile, Ecuador, Brazil, Uruguay, Guatemala, Cuba, the Dominican Republic, and Bolivia) the minimum wage varies from industry to industry, the rate usually depending upon government decisions as to the ability of different industries to pay. In Argentina, Cuba, Mexico, Peru, Nicaragua, Guatemala, and Brazil, the minimum may vary from region to region. It may also vary between city and country and in various combinations of these possibilities.

In most countries provisions for raising the *minima* with the passage of time have been more or less formalized. Generally, this can be done by executive decree. It does not require congressional action as it does in the United States.

In Brazil, for example, the minimum in Rio de Janeiro in 1962 was 21,000 cruzeiros a month (something like $40). As a result of inflation and other pressures, the figure had been raised to 42,000 by 1964. And in 1964, fourteen different minima were in effect (or ineffective) in the hinterland.

In Mexico in 1964 the minima varied from 32 pesos a day (12 pesos to the U. S. dollar) for urban labor in Northern Baja California to 8 pesos a day for rural labor in Guerrero. It was 21.5 pesos a day in the Federal District.[3]

The provisions in the Cuban sugar industry before Castro were a rather special case. The wage in the cane fields and in the sugar mills was planned to fluctuate with the international price of sugar. The law was intended to ensure to the Cuban workers a share of the exceptional profits made from high sugar prices in bonanza years. The procedure

[3] *Hispanic American Report*, March, 1964, p. 18; April, 1964, p. 179.

also carried the potential for sharp wage reductions when the price of sugar plummeted, as it frequently did.

ACTUAL WAGE RATES. Legal minimum wage rates may not give much clue as to what the wages actually paid may be. Some data on these matters have been compiled by the International Labour Office (see Table 1). Various (not entirely justified) manipulations of the ILO data indicate these comparisons in hourly wage rates in manufacturing in 1962.

Table 1

HOURLY WAGE RATES IN MANUFACTURING, 1962

	Local currency	Dollars
Argentina	44.7 pesos	0.33
Brazil (1959)	35.23 cruzeiros	0.18
Colombia	2.14 pesos	0.19
Mexico	4.82 pesos	0.38
United States		2.39

Source: *Yearbook of Labour Statistics, 1963*, pp. 325–28.

The margin of error in these comparisons is probably such that they do not prove much as to the differences among the various Latin American countries. The foreign exchange rate method of conversion leaves a good deal to be desired, especially in conversions of this type.[4] As a rough generalization, the purchasing power of the Latin American salaries is probably 30 to 50 percent higher than the foreign exchange rate method of conversion indicates. Even so, the wage rate in Latin America is significantly lower than in the United States.

In agriculture, the difference is greater. The day labor average in the United States in 1962 was about $6.90 a day; in Mexico it was about 10.9 pesos (87 cents) a day. And the wages in agriculture are much lower than in manufacturing in both the United States and Latin America. No wonder the Mexican farm laborer is desperate to come as a *bracero* to the United States—in spite of the wage discrimination to which he will be subjected.

Perhaps the most meaningful international comparison that could be

[4] "A Measurement of Price Levels and the Purchasing Power of Currencies in Latin America, 1960–62," in *Economic Bulletin for Latin America,* VIII (October, 1963), 195–236.

made would involve identifying certain skills in various manufacturing processes and comparing the wage rates for the same skill in various countries. A comparison of somewhat this sort, which still does not quite get down to the level of specific skills, indicated that in 1958 the average wage in Brazil's auto industry was 50 cruzeiros an hour (about 35 cents). This figure compared with an average wage of $2.65 an hour in the United States.

Also, within a given Latin American country, the pay for comparable skills is higher in the exclaves dominated by foreign corporations than it is in industries controlled by domestic entrepreneurs. The differences seem to be great. And they are much greater than the cost of living difference between countries or between the exclaves and the purely domestic economy.

One of the politically sensitive sore spots is wage rates involving equivalent skills. The machinist working for a national employer gets less than when working for a foreign investor. And the foreign machinist, working for a foreign investor, gets more than the native machinist working for a foreign investor. And since, in addition, the wage rates for equivalent skills are lower in Latin America than in the United States, it is possible to work up considerable righteous indignation about these relations. One spot where action has been taken has been in an effort to force foreign investors to pay to nationals wages comparable to those paid to labor brought by the foreign investor from the home country. But such procedure leaves another inequity, the inequity involving the difference in the wages paid by the native entrepreneur and by the foreign investor.

No doubt these wage-level differences should be narrowed. But what would be the best procedure for going about this? Perhaps something is to be said for trying to force domestic entrepreneurs to pay higher wages. Perhaps, at the same time, they could be helped in their competition with the foreign investors by means of a production subsidy.

Such an approach would have the additional advantage of increasing local effective demand to the considerable benefit of the local producers. Here may be one of those vicious circles that the economic development economists are fond of talking about, but one about which something can be done. It just conceivably may be that low wages in domestically owned industry (and low wages in agriculture as well) are a cause of the economic disadvantage of domestically owned industry relative to foreign-owned industry—and of agriculture relative to industry. In the past, domestically owned industry and agriculture have justified their low wages on the ground that they have to exploit their labor in this way or they could not compete at all with the more efficient foreign-owned industry (or agriculture could not compete with industry). But the low wages mean that these sectors attract the least efficient labor and their disadvantage relative to foreign-owned industry (or industry in general) is perpetuated. Also, the low, total purchasing power of the sector plays a role in perpetuating the disadvantage. Just possibly the spot to cut into this vicious circle is by the payment of higher wages within the disadvantaged sectors. The resultant greater efficiency within the sector and, ultimately, greater purchasing power by the sector are the developments which can change the economic-power relations among the sectors.

It may well be that minimum wages should be uniform across the board and that it is a mistake to perpetuate interindustry or interregion wage differences in the minimum wage legislation. And especially it may be no long-run service to the industry or region which is thus encouraged to continue to pay relatively low wages.

Female and Child Labor

The legislation generally requires special consideration for women under certain circumstances. It probably calls for time off and special hospital facilities for maternity. Such provisions are generally fairly meaningful in the larger cities and virtually meaningless in the smaller towns and in the countryside.

The laws also generally prohibit child labor at ages below, say, 12 or 14. Whether any child has ever been diverted by such laws from selling lottery tickets or newspapers or shining shoes is doubtful. But perhaps they do give some protection that is meaningful against certain types of factory work. Whether the factory work thus prevented is really more objectionable than the work that is actually done might be a debatable matter.

Workmen's Compensation

Broadly, Latin American law has reflected an increasing concern for establishing some insurance plan to provide compensation to the worker in the case of industrial accident or occupational disease. In such plans the obligation to take out the insurance is generally placed on the employer. Argentina had a law of this sort as early as 1915. Since that time almost all the Latin American countries have enacted similar legislation.

Workmen's compensation laws differ as to professional groups and risks covered. They also differ markedly in the adequacy of ostensible compensation. But it is possible to generalize on one point: The worker is not generously protected. Compensation for industrial accidents and occupational diseases is consistently inadequate for the maintenance of a decent standard of living on the part of the ill or injured. However, the problem will not be solved merely by raising the ostensible benefits provided by the workmen's compensation laws. The difficulty will not be met satisfactorily until the per capita productivity of the Latin American countries has been raised materially.

Old-Age Pensions (Jubilación)

The Uruguayan old-age pension system, first adopted in 1919, provided that, at the relatively low age of 60, or upon total incapacity, the individual would receive a pension. The necessary funds were obtained by taxes on the employer, on real estate, and on such consumption articles as playing cards and alcohol. At first, the system was noncontributory, in the sense that the worker himself did not make periodic contributions to the fund. In the Uruguayan and other systems, the workers now generally contribute to the funds, as do the employers and frequently the government. Virtually all countries now have such systems.

In general, the so-called social security laws proper cover invalidity, old age, death, and unemployment. But they also may cover maternity, sickness, and even industrial accidents and occupational diseases; or these latter problems may be handled in separate legislation. Much of the Latin American population is now nominally covered. Coverage in the Mexican social security program, for example, reached 5.5 million people in 1960. In Argentina the basic pension rate is about 82 percent of the salary at the time of retirement.

The retirement age at which one becomes qualified for old-age pensions under many Latin American laws is substantially earlier than is the case in the United States. Under various circumstances people of 45 or 50 years of age may be entitled to old-age benefits. For example, retirement after 20–23 years of service is the rule in Argentina. It has been said that in Argentina, out of a population of 21 million, there are 4.5 million retired persons qualified for old-age benefits.[5]

A similar situation exists in Uruguay where the 1963 report of the Comisión de Inversiones y Desarrollo Económico indicated that retired people constituted 30.2 percent of the total population. In Uruguay private employment has been increasing "at a rate of 0.9 per cent a year, government employment at 2.6 per cent, and the retirement lists at 5.9 per cent." [6]

No wonder the accumulated resources in the social security funds (especially after being depleted in current governmental expenditures) are frequently not adequate to meet claims. Too much has been promised.

Medicare

In the United States the social security system does not provide for medical care or hospitalization in case of illness. There are exceptions, of course. Members of the armed forces, members of Congress, and certain members of the Executive Branch have the benefit of socialized medicine.

In Latin America the ostensible medicare protection is far more comprehensive than is the case in the United States. Chile, Brazil, Peru, Colombia, Venezuela, and Mexico have systems which, on paper, seem to promise quite complete medical protection. In Argentina the coverage is quite complete for substantial segments of the population, those in "covered employments," and virtually nonexistent for the rest of the population. But even in a country such as Chile, where the coverage is nominally quite general on paper, in fact, the facilities are inadequate and overcrowded. And frequently, the person who might benefit from the facilities finds it physically impossible to get to them.

Hospitalization or medical care is frequently provided to the workers and their families through facilities associated with the company, industry, or government agency for which the individual is working. This association is frequently formalized in terms of membership in the vari-

---

[5] *Hispanic American Report,* May, 1963, p. 293; September, 1963, p. 725.
[6] *Ibid.*

ous institutes into which the system may be broken down, workers in different industries being in different institutes. This has been the arrangement in Brazil. In Argentina coverage is available for the most part only as a result of the fact that one is working for a government agency or a company which has organized hospitalization and medical care. If the individual does not have the proper employment association, he may not have access to medical care regardless of what the law may say about the generality of the system.

The Latin American systems are not to be condemned because the facilities are frequently inadequate and the doctors, orderlies, and nurses are underpaid and because in many cases the worker has no effective way to get to the medical service to which he is presumably entitled. There is likely to be a straight transportation problem. In other cases he is victimized with fantastic intervals of waiting for attention, cursory examination when he finally sees a doctor, and poor quarters and food when he gets into a hospital. But to damn these conditions implies that the worker had a better alternative before the systems were established or would have a better deal if he went to see a private doctor. The latter argument savors of Marie Antoinette's remark that the peasants who did not have bread ought to eat cake.

Unemployment

Unemployment insurance is not a major feature of social security plans in Latin America, unlike the United States situation. Perhaps this is because unemployment in Latin America has not been the acute indicator of depression that it has been in the United States. The Latin American problem in this area is better called underemployment than unemployment. And the problem of underemployment is not adequately dealt with by unemployment insurance plans. It is true that job tenure has been precarious and markedly dependent on the whim of the employer. But large blocs of the population have not been thrown out of their jobs overnight in the manner that rocks a developed country when depression strikes.

Nevertheless, unemployment insurance does appear as a feature of some of the programs, the Mexican, for instance; and as industrialization progresses it will be an increasingly appropriate measure.

More common, however, is the provision for discharge pay. The employer may be required to pay, perhaps, three months' pay at the time of discharging a worker. Such programs may deal more effectively with the erratic and personalized nature of the Latin American hiring and firing process than would a comprehensive system of unemployment insurance. But there are difficulties. Peculiar pressures are put on the firm that is losing money and is considering going out of business. It is kind of like kicking a fellow when he is down to make the almost bankrupt employer pay three months' discharge wage to all his workers before he can go out of business.

Aside from the special problems posed in the going-out-of-business case, there is a good deal to be said for the discharge-pay approach in contrast to the unemployment insurance approach. For one thing, the discharge-pay approach puts more pressure on the employer to make an effort to maintain his level of operations.

Aguinaldo

A Christmas bonus of one month's salary is common in Latin American industry, but it is by no means universal. In Spanish it is called an *aguinaldo*.

Profit Sharing

Proposals for profit sharing have been popular in Latin America; Chile in 1931 was probably the first to enact legislation providing that employees should share in business profits (up to 10 percent of the total amount of such profits) although the Mexican Constitution of 1917 had envisaged the possibility.

Some provision for profit sharing is also present in the laws of Argentina, Brazil, Bolivia, Ecuador, and Venezuela. But the effective coverage of such laws is far from general.

About 1962 the Mexican government began to plan the implementation of the profit-sharing plans envisaged in the Constitution of 1917. The plan, which went into effect in April, 1964, called for profit sharing by all foreign companies and most Mexican-owned firms (about 80 percent of Mexican business concerns in all). Coverage initially included about 4 million workers. One estimate indicated that workers would share in about 14 percent of after-tax profits.[7]

[7] New York *Times,* December 13, 1963, p. 7; Houston *Post,* December 30, 1963, Section 3, p. 11.

Exceptions to the profit-sharing provisions in Mexico include certain small businesses, new industries, extractive industries during the exploration phase of their activities, industries producing goods not previously produced in Mexico, and various government-endorsed companies devoted to social improvement. (I am unaware of the rationale for this latter provision.)

Coverage and Adequacy

President Manuel Prado said in an address to the Peruvian Congress in 1941: "Peru has the great privilege of possessing social legislation as advanced as any in America. No country on this continent surpasses it in the fulfillment of the postulates of true social justice." The implementation of social legislation was a joke in Peru in 1941; it is still a joke. Perhaps the situation is not quite so bad in Mexico, Brazil, Chile, and Argentina as it has been in Peru; nevertheless, in an important sense, the Peruvian situation is symbolic of the Latin American situation in general. A former president of Chile, Carlos Dávila, once said in speaking of the social legislation of Chile, where the system is far more effective than is the case in Peru: "One is inclined to recall the poet who talked of the sense of frustration felt by the people in contemplating the magnitude of their rights in principle in contrast to the insignificance of their rights in fact." [8]

The facilities which are supposed to exist do exist to some extent in the large cities. But they are overcrowded and inadequately manned. It is probably unavoidable at present in Latin America that skilled medical doctors should be in short supply. However, with all the underemployment in Latin America, there is no reason there cannot be a sufficient number of orderlies, attendants, and trainee nurses. Yet even in this area the programs are understaffed and the personnel is desperately underpaid. By contrast with the cities, there is in general not even a pretense that the facilities exist in the smaller towns and in the countryside.

Perhaps part of the trouble has been as a result of the fact that the social security codes came, not as the result of effective pressure from below, but as the result of largesse from above. What was given in many

[8] George M. McBride, *Chile, Land and Society* (New York, American Geographic Society, 1936), p. xviii.

of the Latin American countries as largesse, could also be effectively denied at the whim of the rulers after they were entrenched in power. Or perhaps one could better say: Frequently the revolutionary leaders, after they have secured their power position, have not been particularly interested in implementing the social legislation whose espousal helped them in obtaining power. And the implementation of an effective social security program is a difficult task, requiring conscientious dedication to the work over many years. This dedication has been largely missing in the political leadership in many of the Latin American countries.

The social security legislation has been enforced fairly effectively against foreign-owned companies and virtually not at all against local businessmen with political connections. The fact that foreign companies comply better with the social security codes and the minimum wage laws probably does not reflect any particular altruism on their part. They are in a spot where they virtually have to behave this way.

The fact that many of the Latin American countries already have, and have had for many years, on the books attractive-looking social security legislation, raises a question about the Alliance for Progress approach. As is known, the Alliance for Progress has been recommending that the Latin American legislatures enact new laws providing for significant, even revolutionary, social and economic changes. The ground rules of the Alliance for Progress are then supposed to be that the passage of such legislation entitles the complying country to foreign aid under the Alliance. If laws on the statute books which sound like substantial social security programs are the qualification, most Latin American countries should qualify automatically or can qualify by reenacting the same old laws. One of the mysteries is why Latin American upper classes have resisted so vigorously the enactment of such legislation as the Alliance for Progress calls for. Mostly, all they would need to do to qualify under the Alliance is to reenact some laws that have actually been on the books for a long time, the enforcement of which they have been successfully postponing.

To return to the main point, until national productivity and real national product are increased substantially, much of the welfare legislation in Latin America is going to remain hope and expectation rather than reality. A lot remains to be done before these systems will really do the job they are supposed to do. And in some of the countries, the smaller and poorer countries, the basic facilities do not exist at all.

CHAPTER TEN

LEVEL OF LIVING, INCOME, AND PRODUCTION PATTERNS

In this chapter, data, largely statistical, are presented in an effort to measure Latin American welfare.[1]

Health

Health and sanitary conditions in Latin America are good by comparison with Asia and Africa. They are miserable by comparison with the United States and western Europe. It is difficult to describe the situation more precisely with words or statistics. Seeing it and smelling it can give only impressions. A few bits of miscellaneous information may help to indicate the setting.

The median age in South America is about 21 years. In the United States it is about 30 years. In the United States, deaths of infants under one year of age per thousand live births number about 25. In Mexico, the figure is 70; in Argentina, 61; in Brazil, 170.[2] Life expectancy at birth in the United States is about 70 years. In Mexico the figure is 39

---

[1] Sources which are generally useful for statistical data on Latin America include: *International Financial Statistics* (a monthly published by the International Monetary Fund); *Monthly Bulletin of Statistics* (published by the United Nations); *Statistical Abstract of Latin America* (a publication of the Center of Latin American Studies, University of California at Los Angeles); *Statistical Bulletin for Latin America* (published at irregular intervals by the Economic Commission for Latin America); *Statistical Yearbook* (United Nations); *Yearbook of Labour Statistics* (International Labour Office). A publication summarizing much of the sort of information covered in this chapter is: United Nations, Economic Commission for Latin America, *El Desarrollo Económico de América Latina en la Postguerra* (New York, 1963).

[2] *Statistical Abstract of Latin America, 1963*, pp. 17, 19.

years; in Argentina, 59; in Brazil, 42. Life expectancy at birth is some 15 years greater in the United States than it is in Latin America. Tuberculosis, pneumonia, dysentery and gastritis (*diarrhoea*), malaria and various parasitic diseases are the killers in Latin America. The death rate from cancer and heart disease is relatively low by comparison with the United States. People do not live long enough to have the privilege of dying from these rich man's diseases.

In the United States (circa 1962), there were 740 people per medical doctor. The Latin American average was 1,900 people per doctor, and in Haiti the figure was 11,000 per doctor.[3]

Food Consumption

Food consumption averages, per capita, for several Latin American countries are given in Table 2. The Food and Agriculture Organization

Table 2

Country	Year	Calories per day	Meat (pounds per year)
Argentina	1959	2,950	201
Brazil	1957	2,680	64
Mexico	1958	2,440	53
Peru	1959	2,050	37
Venezuela	1960	2,490	55
United States	1960	3,120	209
India	1960	1,990	

Source: *Statistical Abstract of the United States.*

is of the opinion that a per capita caloric intake of 2,550–2,650 represents a minimum level.[4] Many of the Latin American countries average an intake below the FAO minimum.

Lack of food on the grocer's shelf is sometimes taken as a sign that an economy is in trouble. This has been the case, for example, in terms of the manner in which the United States press has handled Cuba. It

---

[3] United States, Agency for International Development, *Proposed Mutual Defense and Development Programs, FY 1965* (Washington, 1964), p. 208.

[4] Food and Agriculture Organization, *Proposals for a World Food Board and World Food Survey,* p. 37.

has been assumed that the fact that food is scarce in the shops means that the people have suffered a decline in the standard of living under Castro. Actually the food shortage in the shops might mean something else. It might mean that an increase in the purchasing power of the poor has cleared the shops; it might be a reflection of effective efforts to keep prices down; it might also be a result of the prevalence of black-marketeering.

Housing

Living in a grass-roofed rancho invites snakes and spiders as house guests. Living in an adobe hut with a tin roof in the middle of a hot, arid plain, without running water or sanitary facilities, also means something in terms of standard of living. But these circumstances are rather difficult to evaluate quantitatively.

Quantification may, however, reveal certain aspects of the housing problem. In 1960 there were said to be 6,409,000 dwellings in Mexico.[5] Only 2,069,000 of the dwellings had running water. One-room dwellings represented 53 percent of the total. And of the one-room dwellings, 27 percent housed seven people or more, and 55 percent housed between three and six people. Two-room dwellings constituted 29 percent of the total number of dwellings. And, of the two-room dwellings, 38 percent housed seven people or more, and 51 percent housed between three and six people.

There is a statistic called the "density of habitation" that is a rather interesting guide to standard of living. It has been estimated that in the United States there are about 0.7 persons per room in dwellings intended for habitation. In Argentina the figure is 2.2 persons per room. In Guatemala the figure is 3.1 persons per room (not per bedroom either).[6]

As for the sewerage: Only about 40 percent of urban Managua, Nicaragua, has any, according to the Inter-American Development Bank. And you can imagine what the statistics would be for the smaller towns of Nicaragua and for all tropical and rural America if they were to be had.

---

[5] *Review of the Economic Situation of Mexico* (Banco Nacional de México), March, 1964, p. 3. The data are from a study by the Instituto Nacional de la Vivienda.

[6] United Nations, *Statistical Yearbook, 1962*, pp. 610–21.

Literacy

At least half the adult population of Latin America is illiterate. In the United States 2.5 percent of the population over ten years of age is illiterate. In Mexico the figure is 43 percent; in Argentina, 13 percent; in Brazil, 51 percent; in Guatemala, 70 percent.

In the United States about 8 percent of the population has completed four years of college. Only for Chile in Latin America is the figure over 2 percent; and it is 1/10 of 1 percent for Haiti.

Population Growth Rate

Efforts to raise the standard of living in an area such as Latin America are conditioned in two ways by the population growth. A sparsely populated area may be able to use its resources to better advantage if it can obtain a population increase. This may well be the situation for substantial areas of interior South America. On the other hand, fantastic population growth rates in areas which are already densely populated and poverty stricken may be little more than tragic. This would seem to be the situation in Haiti.

In recent years world population and United States population seem to have been growing at about the same rate: 1.8 percent a year. For Latin America the growth rate seems to be about 2.8 percent; and some countries are growing at a rate higher than 3 percent a year (for example, Brazil, Venezuela, and Mexico).

In spite of this explosive population growth, Latin America remains one of the relatively underpopulated areas. The region has only some 7.1 percent of the population of the world (225 million in 1962) occupying 15.2 percent of the land area.

The Latin American population increase seems to be more the result of falling death rates than rising birth rates.[7] This should mean that, once the average population age has risen somewhat, the rate of population increase will fall.

[7] United Nations, *El Desarrollo Económico de América Latina en la Postguerra* (New York, 1963), p. 81.

Production

Latin America accounts for something like 4.2 percent of the non-Communist industrial production of the world; her population is about 12.2 percent of the world's non-Communist population (circa 1960). This relation (4.2 percent to 12.2 percent) may be about as handy a single measure as there is for gauging the degree of Latin American underdevelopment.

In the slightly more restricted manufacturing setting, as late as 1958, Latin America had only 3.7 percent of the manufacturing of the non-Communist world, 5.3 percent of the light manufacturing, and 2.7 percent of the heavy industry. This rather modest amount of manufacturing (value added in manufacturing) was divided among the principal Latin American participants as indicated in Table 3. The presence of two

Table 3

SHARES OF VALUE ADDED IN MANUFACTURING

	Percent
Argentina	21.6
Brazil	23.6
Mexico	20.6
Venezuela	6.3
The 9 Latin American Free Trade Association countries	81.1
Latin American total	100.0

Source: *Statistical Yearbook, 1962* (United Nations), p. 70.

thirds of all Latin American manufacturing in Argentina, Brazil, and Mexico is rather strong evidence of the relative importance of those countries on the Latin American scene, if one were not already convinced.

During the last few years there has not been agreement among the experts as to whether Latin American economic development has been lagging or progressing at a respectable rate. The Economic Commission for Latin America, for example, has expressed alarm concerning the slow pace of development.

And yet, one who had done nothing more than observe the amount of construction going on in various of the capitals of Latin America might say: "How can there be any doubt but that this region is growing apace?" There are some isolated voices defending the proposition that the region is growing at a respectable rate. Claude Zarka has condemned the "economic development pessimists" in strong language, some of which translates loosely as follows: "These authors, perhaps, live at the dawn of spectacular economic development. They see only stagnant economies struggling without real hope." [8]

It is not easy to assemble statistical data to resolve the question. For one thing, there is not general agreement as to the best criterion for judging economic development. Should it be the index number describing industrial production or the index number covering only manufacturing production? Should it be national income, or gross national product, or gross domestic product? Should these concepts be converted to a real per capita basis? Or do all of these objective, materialistic measures lack something unless allowance can be made for subjective elements of welfare such as peace of mind, culture, courtesy, and freedom of action?

Despite these elements of uncertainty, it is probably useful to present some statistical data, pro and con, dealing with the evidence as to the recent pace of development in Latin America. Index numbers describing the trend in industrial production (manufacturing, mining, and power) are shown in Table 4. Index number series describing manufacturing

Table 4

INDUSTRIAL PRODUCTION
(Index numbers: 1958 = 100)

	1938	1948	1958	1962	1963
Latin America	34	57	100	126	128
Argentina	51	84	100	95	87
Brazil	24	42	100	149	153
Mexico	44	57	100	129	140
United States	33	73	100	126	133
World (except Communist bloc)	44	62	100	130	137
USSR	18	27	100	146	158

Source: Various United Nations publications, including especially the *Statistical Yearbook* and the *Monthly Bulletin of Statistics*.

[8] Claude Zarka, "Inégalités Economiques entre Nations Tendent-elles a Croître?" *Revue Economique,* September, 1962, p. 750. Eastin Nelson has expressed similar views.

alone do not look greatly different from these industrial production series.

Such figures hardly seem to support the thesis of an alarming lag in Latin American development. In fact, they look like an annual growth rate averaging over 5 percent since 1948 and over 4 percent since 1958. Allowing for a population growth rate of about 2.8 percent a year, this would make a per capita (industrial production) growth rate of about 2.2 percent a year (1.2 percent since 1958). Latin America might well like to do better, but this record is not bad, except for the Argentine performance.

By contrast with industry, the performance in agriculture has been clearly unimpressive. Per capita agricultural (including livestock) production in Latin America seems to be at about the same level as during the middle 1930s. Production increase has been offset by population increase.[9] However, in this respect the Latin American history is not greatly different from the history of the United States and of the rest of the world in general.

When one recalls that there have been positive efforts to cut back agricultural production in connection with important commodities such as coffee and sugar, the significance of the lag in agricultural production may not represent the frustration of efforts to expand production. In Argentina in particular, however, this may not be true. Lag in agricultural and cattle production in that country may well be part of the evidence of a significant failure in its development efforts.

The economics of agriculture remains a special problem about which a good deal more needs to be said. But the last word is not necessarily that Latin America is condemned to a secular decline in the importance of her agriculture relative to the rest of the world. (See the discussion of comparative cost in Chapter Twenty, Trade and Development.)

Per Capita Income: International Comparison

One of the most popular comparisons involves an effort to convert the per capita income of various countries into dollars. And yet this is one

---

[9] *Foreign Agriculture*, January 14, 1963; *Statistical Bulletin for Latin America*, March, 1964, p. 109; Food and Agriculture Organization, *Production Yearbook* (various years).

of the most dubious of the comparisons. It is, however, probably worth looking at a comparison set up in these terms, as shown in Table 5, in

Table 5

PER CAPITA INCOME IN U.S. DOLLARS, CIRCA 1960

	Uncorrected	Corrected
Argentina	533	799
Brazil	268	375
Haiti	99	149
Mexico	298	415
Venezuela	645	645
20 Latin American countries	307	421
United States	2,400	2,400

Source: United States, *Economic Policy and Progress in South America* (Washington, 1962), p. 120; various United Nations statistical publications; "A Measurement of Price Levels and the Purchasing Power of Currencies in Latin America—1960–62," in *Economic Bulletin for Latin America*, VIII (October, 1963), 195–236. In this case, the correction for differences in the purchasing power of money is that suggested by P. N. Rosenstein-Rodan, "International Aid for Underdeveloped Countries," in *Review of Economics and Statistics*, XLIII (May, 1961), 107–38.

order to try to interpret its degree of usefulness. The uncorrected figures are obtained by estimating gross national product, dividing by the population, and translating to dollars at par or prevailing rates of exchange. The corrected figures are obtained by making an additional allowance for estimated differences in the purchasing power of money and are due to Rosenstein-Rodan.

Total national income figures for 1960 that would correspond to these per capita figures would be:

	Uncorrected	Corrected
Latin America	$ 60 billion	$ 84 billion
United States	414 billion	414 billion

The attempt to compare per capita incomes presents difficulties.[10] The per capita estimates need to be stated in a common denominator. The United States dollar is a handy common denominator. But the use of

[10] Harry Stark, *Infirmities of Per Capita National Income Estimates . . .* (Miami, 1961).

the dollar in this role means that income figures need to be converted from the national currencies to dollars at some rate of exchange. (1) If either the International Monetary Fund par rate of exchange is used for this purpose, as is generally the case, or if some other prevailing rate is used, there may be difficulty due to the fact that it does not accurately reflect the comparative purchasing powers of the currencies. (2) Large segments of the Latin American economies are less effectively integrated into the monetary economy than is the case in the United States. Consequently, there is a larger potential margin of error as efforts are made (or not made) to allow for the nonmonetary items. There may well be significant underestimate of Latin American real income because of this factor. (3) Even in the monetized sector of the economies, there may be significant underestimate of income because the wealthy keep their own estimates low in order to escape taxes. (4) Difference in consumption habits means that a comparison of money income is not necessarily a very accurate guide to the satisfaction gotten from spending real income. Uncertainty as to the welfare implications of money income is injected, for example, by the difficulty of making proper allowance for expenditures on heating in cold countries and on air conditioning in hot countries. (5) The operation of the law of diminishing returns (declining satisfaction per unit of consumption as increasing amounts are consumed) probably means that the real satisfaction derived from having "twice as high" an income is actually not "double" in any meaningful use of the word "double." So, the high incomes are not, relatively, as much higher as they seem. (6) An additional intractable problem involves the difficulty of allowing for varying degrees of inequality in the distribution of income. And income is much more unequally distributed in Latin America than is the case in the United States.

It may be noted that one estimate assigns the highest per capita income in Latin America to Venezuela, the other estimate assigns it to Argentina (a country whose current growth rate is very low).

The high figure of $645 for Venezuela requires additional comment. It needs to be corrected by several factors. One of these factors has already been mentioned. The price level, given the foreign exchange rate, is high in Venezuela by comparison with most Latin American countries (although perhaps relatively not as much higher as it was ten or fifteen years ago). Also, the computation of per capita income is made by dividing the population of the country into a figure for gross domestic product which, to be a more accurate guide to the level of living of Venezuelans in Venezuela, needs to be corrected by the subtraction out of (7) profits remitted to foreign investors, (8) salaries remitted home by foreigners working in Venezuela, (9) net outflow of capital (in years when there is a net outflow). These corrections would seem to justify cutting the estimate of per capita income in Venezuela accruing to Venezuelans by approximately half—perhaps to about $350, a correction of a different sort than that allowed for by Rosenstein-Rodan. Even after these changes are made, Venezuelan income would still seem high by comparison with quite a few Latin American countries. However, much of the income is concentrated in Caracas and in the oil camps. The balance of the Venezuelan economy has an extremely low level of living, a level of living comparable with Venezuela's Caribbean neighbors.

The last three factors are especially important in the Venezuelan case, but they are also operative in several of the other countries; and they will be of considerable importance in the cases where the export balance of trade is large.

(10) A last difficulty that should be mentioned is the professional weakness of the statistics-gathering agencies in the Latin American countries.

Despite all of these if's, and's, and but's, it is obvious to the observer that the welfare of the mass of the population in the Latin American countries is substantially below that of the mass of the population in the United States. And the per capita income estimates in dollars are possibly some kind of a rough, but very rough, guide to the magnitude of these differences and to the differences among the Latin American countries.

Structure of Employment

In Latin America only 35 percent of the population (1960) is reported as being economically active.[11] This figure compares to 41 percent in the United States and 46 percent in the United Kingdom. This relation is important. It reflects the inordinately high percentage of the Latin American population which is very young. And it indicates the

[11] United Nations, *El Desarrollo* . . . , p. 83.

extremely heavy burden placed on the relatively small percentage of the Latin American population which is economically active.

Table 6 indicates both the structure of employment and the nature of income distribution by sector shares.

Table 6

SECTOR SHARES OF EMPLOYMENT AND PRODUCT, 1960

	Latin America		United States	
	Employment in sector as percent of total employment	*Product of sector as percent of G.D.P.*	*Employment in sector as percent of total employment*	*Product of sector as percent of G.D.P.*
Agriculture	47.0	21.8	11.6	4.2
Mining	1.0	5.0	1.2	1.3
Manufacturing	14.6	21.9	27.3	29.3
Construction	4.9	3.6	4.7	5.3
Services	32.5	47.7	55.2	59.9
Gross domestic product or employment	100.0	100.0	100.0	100.0

Source: The table has been compiled from various sources, including especially: United Nations, *El Desarrollo Económico de América Latina en la Postguerra* (New York, 1963), pp. 28–32; *Economic Bulletin for Latin America*, VII (October, 1962), 224; *Statistical Bulletin for Latin America*, I (March, 1964), 14; and the *Survey of Current Business*.

AGRICULTURE. Some 47 percent of the economically active population of Latin America is in agriculture. The range in these percentages seems to be from a high of 85 percent in Haiti to a low of 25 percent in Argentina. The relationship suggests a statistical correlation that may be unexpected to some. The agricultural country par excellence, which is also the country with the highest level of living in Latin America, is the country with the lowest percentage of the economically active in agriculture. The poorest country is the country with the highest percentage of the economically active in agriculture. There is a remarkable consistency about this inverse correlation up and down the scale.

Unfortunately, this correlation reveals little about the cause and effect interrelations involved in the connection between standard of living and percentage of the population in agriculture. It is not necessarily an argument for forcing people out of agriculture if there is no place for them to go. And it is not necessarily an argument for industrialization if the new manufacturing plants fail to absorb a substantial labor force. Actually, additional capital outlay in agriculture might conceivably be the most appropriate policy for dealing with the problem in the first instance. (There will be more discussion of problems of this type in Part Four.)

THE SERVICES. One may be superficially impressed by the number of beggars in Latin America, by the number of people selling lottery tickets, by the number of people engaged in retailing, by the number of household servants; and he may conclude that a high percentage of the population in the service industries is also a characteristic of underdevelopment. But this conclusion would seem not to be justified. The United States has a larger percentage of the working population (over half) in the services than does Latin America. One needs to be a bit more specific in identifying the particular unproductive services in which substantial numbers of Latin Americans are underemployed. All too many are engaged in the services mentioned above. It does not follow from this that there is a high proportion in the services generally.

Two or three household servants, such as would be a major (and very expensive) luxury in the high-standard-of-living United States, are commonplace in the Latin American home, where a fantastic amount of time is spent on minding children, washing, cooking, and cleaning (especially cleaning on hands and knees with a dirty rag and a bucket, or hitting clothing with a rock by a creek). Even extremely poor families may well have a servant (perhaps an even poorer relation from the country). Oscar Lewis comments on this phenomenon in *The Children of Sanchez*.

"The services" is an ambiguous term. The United States has a far larger proportion of the labor force in the services than does Latin America. As here used, the terms "services" and "commerce" are catch-alls for some lottery-ticket selling, household servants, movie attendants, as well as retail clerking, working for transportation facilities, wholesaling, paper shuffling for banks, even clerking for the government in its service agencies.

Some of this activity is most useful and productive (the activity of the retail clerk, the transportation worker, and the bank teller). Some of it is an underemployed excuse for work (the sale of lottery tickets and much of the supremely inefficient work of the household servant). It would help in understanding the role of the services in industrialization if the productive services could be identifiably separated from the unproductive services. But this seems virtually impossible, at least in the current state of the statistics on the services.

The proportion of clerical work in the labor force expands substantially as a country develops and the standard of living rises. In fact, the expansion in the clerical sector more than offsets the contraction in the household servant (and lottery-ticket selling) sectors. The development of a substantial reservoir of competent, female secretarial help has made a major contribution to production in the industrialized countries. This is an area where Latin America has fallen notably behind. A large proportion of those working for the government are performing clerical functions. Omnipresent and all important is the repairman.

In spite of the household servants and the shoeshine boys, the service sector, on the whole, does not seem to be exploited. In 1960 it accounted for only 32.5 percent of the economically active and received 48 percent of the gross domestic product. This is pretty good. In fact the relation is worth some additional study—to check its accuracy and, if accurate, to explain it.

MANUFACTURING. The percentage of the economically active population in manufacturing was quite low, 14 percent. But even in the United States under 30 percent of the economically active are in manufacturing. The Latin American percentage in manufacturing will no doubt rise; but it is doubtful that it will come to overshadow the percentage in the services.

In fact the lag in the growth of employment in manufacturing is one of the more alarming features of present circumstances in Latin America. Manufacturing is not absorbing the population that is flocking to the cities. They are being forced into unskilled personal services.[12] Manufacturing is supposed to be the dynamic, high-income sector of a

---

[12] United Nations, *Towards a Dynamic Development Policy for Latin America* (New York, 1963), p. 52.

developing economy. It is bad news for Latin America to the extent that the manufacturing sector fails to provide opportunity to a substantial percentage of the citizenry.

CHANGE IN SHARES. The statistical evidence to support the supposition that increase in employment in manufacturing is not a really dynamic growth sector is shown in Table 7. Employment in manufacturing

Table 7

RELATIVE GROWTH RATES OF EMPLOYMENT AND PRODUCT
BY SECTORS IN LATIN AMERICA
(Average Annual Percentage Rates)

	Employment (*1945–1960*)	Gross Real Domestic Product (*1945/49–1956/61*)
Agriculture	1.3	3.5
Mining	1.2	6.9
Manufacturing	2.8	5.9
Construction	6.2	4.8
Services	4.1	4.7 (est.)
Total (average)	2.6	4.8

Source: United Nations, *El Desarrollo* . . . , pp. 25, 31. See Table 12.

seems to be growing at a rate only barely faster than the average. Most of the increase in the labor force is going into construction and the services. That these tendencies do not correspond to the allegations of the theory of competition is indicated by the fact that the high growth rates in gross domestic product are in manufacturing and mining.

Income Distribution: Sector Shares

In both rich and poor countries agriculture contributes a smaller percentage to the gross domestic product than is represented by the percentage of the economically active in agriculture.

In Haiti the 85 percent of the population in agriculture gets perhaps 73 percent of the gross domestic product; in Argentina the 25 percent of the economically active in agriculture gets 20 percent of the gross domestic product; and in Venezuela the 41 percent of the population in agriculture gets an extremely low 6 percent of the gross domestic product. Even in the United States, the 12 percent of the population in agriculture receives only 4 or 5 percent of the product.

In the United States and in Latin America, agriculture seems to be at a bargaining disadvantage in relation to the other sectors of the economy in staking its claim to an income share.

The share of income going to people in the services, 48 percent, is rather respectable considering that only 32.5 percent of the population is in the services. Again, this relationship suggests that something more is involved in the services than the activities of household servants, lottery-ticket sellers, and shoeshine boys.

Productivity of Sectors

Attempt is made in Table 8 to estimate the relative productivity of

Table 8

LATIN AMERICAN LABOR PRODUCTIVITY, 1960

	Product per economically active person (in dollars)	Productivity of each sector in relation to average productivity
Agriculture	406	46
Mining	4,400	503
Manufacturing	1,320	151
Construction	646	74
Services	1,280	146
Averages (weighted)	876	100

Source: Same as for Table 6.

the different sectors of the Latin American economy in 1960. The procedure used in compiling the table involves some very rough modifications of the estimates made by the Economic Commission for Latin America for 1950. The productivity indexes, based on an average of 100, are merely a reflection of the same differences (they involve the same ratios) that are reflected in the estimates of product per economically active person. The high estimate for mining and the low estimate for construction are worth wondering about.

If competitive adjustments worked according to the mythology of the theory of competition, of course, long ago much more of the population should have moved out of agriculture.

Explanation as to why this change has not occurred is largely in terms of the institutional rigidities that will be discussed in the next chapter.

Income Distribution: Factor Shares

About 1959 or 1960, at a rough estimate, the percentage of national income going to wages and salaries in Latin America was between 50 and 55 percent.[13] The estimate for Argentina was 50.7 percent; for Brazil was 47.2 percent; and for Venezuela was 63.1 percent. By comparison, the share of national income going to wages and salaries in the United States is estimated to be some 71 percent.

Figures such as these would involve as a corollary that, in Latin America, a much higher proportion of national income goes to interest, rent, and profits than is the case in the United States.

They also involve another corollary. Wages and salaries seem to be a relatively small fraction of production costs in Latin America. Emilio Mújica has estimated that in Mexico they represented 10 or 15 percent of costs of production.[14]

Income Distribution: Degree of Inequality

Some rough, but probably roughly accurate, estimates of the degree of inequality in income distribution in Latin America have been made and are shown in Table 9. According to these figures, the wealthiest 5 percent of the Latin American population receives 33 percent of all the personal income in the region. By contrast, in the United States, the wealthiest 5 percent, in 1961, was estimated to have received 19.6 percent of personal income in the country. Also, by contrast, the poorest 50 percent of the United States population is estimated to receive some 22 percent of the total personal income.[15]

---

[13] Economic Commission for Latin America, *Boletín Económico de América Latina, Suplemento Estadístico*, December, 1962, pp. 6–45; *see also*, Leopoldo Portnoy, *Análisis Crítico de la Economía Argentina* (Buenos Aires, Fondo de Cultura Económica, 1961), pp. 53, 110.

[14] Emilio Mújica, "Los Salarios en la Industria," in *Revista de Economía*, September, 1952, p. 283. This relation can stand some more study.

[15] *Statistical Abstract, 1963*, pp. 336–37.

Table 9
PRESUMED INCOME DISTRIBUTION IN LATIN AMERICA, CIRCA 1956–1960

Categories	Proportion of population in category	Proportion of total personal income received by category
I. Poorest	50	16
II. Next to poorest	45	51
III. Next to richest	3	14
IV. Richest	2	19
Total	100	100

Source: United Nations, *El Desarrollo* . . . , p. 68.

It seems pretty clear that income is more unequally distributed in Latin America than is the case in the United States. The region is poor and difficulties are compounded by the circumstance that such wealth as there is happens to be very unequally distributed. And an authoritative voice, that of Raúl Prebisch, alleges that the degree of inequality in income distribution in Latin America is increasing.[16]

The importance of this possibility may justify citing some additional comments. Celso Furtado has written with regard to Brazil that in recent years the real wage level in that country has remained practically stationary. And, in particular, he has said that there has been no observable improvement in the condition of rural labor.[17] Also, with regard particularly to Brazil, Robert Alexander has written: "The Brazilian workers are to a very large degree paying for their country's industrialization; their real wages are kept down to provide the large profits characteristic of the Brazilian economy, most of which are to a large degree ploughed back into its further development." [18] And Mrs. Ifigenia de Navarrete has made a quite sophisticated (statistically) study of Mexico indicating increased inequality in that country during the period 1950 to 1957.[19]

---

[16] Raúl Prebisch, "Producir y Vivir Depende de Latinoamérica," in *Combate*, III (January, 1961), 25.

[17] Celso Furtado, *Desenvolvimento e Subdesenvolvimento* (Rio de Janeiro, Fundo de Cultura, 1961), p. 264; Celso Furtado, "Brazil: What Kind of Revolution?" in *Foreign Affair*, 41 (April, 1963), 526–35.

[18] Robert J. Alexander, *Labor Relations in Argentina, Brazil, and Chile* (New York, McGraw-Hill, 1962), p. 134.

[19] Ifigenia M. de Navarrete, *La Distribución del Ingreso y el Desarrollo Económico de México* (México, Instituto de Investigaciones Económicas, Escuela Nacional de Economía, 1960), p. 95.

Mario Henrique Simonsen has written: "This destruction of the salary scale of the middle class is one of the most serious consequences of chronic inflation." [20]

If increase in the inequality in income distribution is going on in Latin America, this is important. It seems generally agreed that the rise of a substantial middle class in Latin America would be a stabilizing influence as well as being evidence that the general welfare is really improving. Increasing disparity in income distribution casts doubts as to whether the rise in gross national product is as meaningful for the population as a whole as it might be.

Another argument for less inequality in income distribution is to reduce the power of the wealthy in corrupting governments. Its upper class is the great cross that Latin America bears. Peter Nehemkis said in a recent Congressional hearing:

> I am also bound in all candor to say to you that the majority of Latin America's business elite (whose true interests are not tied to the preservation of the status quo) have been astonishingly shortsighted. With few notable exceptions, they have not shown any sense of noblesse oblige; any pronounced willingness to accept public responsibilities; or to furnish progressive leadership; or to exert an enlightened leverage on their governments.[21]

(Whether the business community in the United States has, in recent years, shown much noblesse oblige is a question it may be discreet to skip.)

Cardinal Câmara of Rio de Janeiro is reported to have said that "the selfishness of many rich people of Latin America and their blindness is a much more serious and urgent problem than Communism itself."

General Evaluation

By way of general evaluation of the state of economic development in Latin America, the following things may be said:

(1) The over-all rate of growth is respectable but not as rapid as might be desired.

---

[20] Mario Henrique Simonsen, "The Role of Government and Free Enterprise," in Mildred Adams, ed., *Latin America; Evolution or Explosion?* (New York, Dodd, Mead, 1963), p. 128.

[21] United States Congress, Joint Economic Committee, *Economic Developments in South America* (Washington, 1962), p. 53.

LIVING, INCOME, PRODUCTION PATTERNS 151

(2) Average real per capita income is low, but not as low as in South Asia and much of Africa.
(3) There is major inequality, as among individuals, in the distribution of income; and the degree of inequality may be increasing.
(4) Some countries (Mexico, Brazil) have been growing much more rapidly than others (Argentina, Chile, Paraguay).
(5) Agricultural production has lagged in relation to industrial production, but not relative to the agricultural production of the rest of the world. Mexican agricultural production has risen quite respectably.

PART FOUR

ECONOMIC DEVELOPMENT

CHAPTER ELEVEN

BASIS FOR INDUSTRIALIZATION: INSTITUTIONS

Feasibility Considerations

PRECONDITIONS. There is a sense in which it is unimportant to worry as to whether a region has or has not a basis for development or industrialization. The job of each region is to use what resources it has as effectively as it can (or as effectively as it wants to).

Prior lack of capital, skilled labor, purchasing power, or natural resources is no argument against such effort. Capital, skilled labor, and purchasing power are not present anywhere before the event of industrialization. They generate as economic development goes on.

Lack of technical knowledge, purchasing power, entrepreneurship, or capital before the inception of the development process are certainly not evidence of inability to industrialize. The stock of all of those things grows as development progresses. The presently industrialized countries did not have generous stores before they began to industrialize. Of course these statements do not deny that nurturing the expansion in the stocks of these items may be an important part of the development process.

Possession, or lack of it, of the fourth factor of production, land or natural resources, plays a somewhat different role. It is desirable to have a large stock of natural resources. But lack of a generous stock is no argument against doing as well as possible with such resources as are available.

In addition to the question of the adequacy of the resource base for industrialization, the question of the feasibility of development may be argued in terms of the presence or lack of the necessary motivation for making the process evolve.

PRIMUM MOBILE (PROFIT MOTIVE). W. W. Rostow has centered his theorizing about economic development on the concept of the takeoff into self-sustained growth.[1] His chief concern has been to identify the stimuli that will occasion takeoff. Similarly, Albert Hirschman began his work on economic development with a discussion of the search for the *primum mobile* that is supposed to get the process going. Joseph Schumpeter seems not to have had any doubt that it was appropriate to orient his theory of economic development to the profit motive as the driving force.[2]

A word about the profit motive as a possible *primum mobile* in connection with Latin American economic development may be appropriate at this time.

It is part of the mythology (and mythology can be a powerful force) of free private enterprise in the United States that attractive profit rates are necessary to call out the best in the businessman. If investment is lagging, the cure is higher profit rates. But this concept turns out to be not as unambiguous as it might be. There is no rational way of identifying just how high the profit rate needs to be to accomplish these miracles. Maybe it just needs to be higher than it was last week, without any regard to how low it was last week. In fact it may well be that the profit rate is a highly psychological proposition. If you think you can get a higher profit rate by wailing about it, then you wail; and it is true that investment does not occur until the higher rate is forthcoming (or until hope of getting it by griping is lost). But in a somewhat different setting the businessman might have been quite willing to engage in the same investment on the strength of profit-rate expectations half as high. After all, businessmen have twenty-four hours in their day just like everybody else; and they will not necessarily sit on their hands because profit rate expectations are 8 percent instead of 12 percent.

---

[1] W. W. Rostow, *The Stages of Economic Growth* (Cambridge, England, University Press, 1960); Albert O. Hirschman, *The Strategy of Economic Development* (New Haven, Yale University Press, 1958), p. 1.

[2] *Theory of Economic Development* (Cambridge, Harvard University Press, 1934). The first German edition was in 1911.

There has been so much talk in the United States to the effect that profit rates need to be raised to stimulate investment and save the economy that this attitude has carried over into study of the Latin American scene. One expert on Latin America, Tom E. Davis of the University of Chicago, has gone to considerable effort to prove that the rate of return on investment (including capital gains) received by shareholders of Chilean common stock has run 2 percent by comparison with 5 percent in similar situations in the United States.[3] Davis has then said that the low profit rate in Chile is "the chief deterrent to private investment, or at least an often neglected deterrent." And he implied that what was true for Chile was probably true for Latin America as a whole.

He is probably just wrong if he believes the profit rate in manufacturing in Latin America is low. And he is further wrong if he thinks artificial devices for raising average profit rates in Latin America are the nostrum for the Latin American ailment.[4]

Profit rates in the industrializing sectors in Latin America have generally been quite high. Intuitive evidence for recent years can be observed in terms of the relatively large amount of luxury residence construction (and luxury apartment-house construction) in the larger Latin American cities. A considerable number of people are doing awfully well. This suggests that, whatever is holding back Latin American industrialization, it is not the lack of the bait of large profits in the industrializing sectors.

In Latin America in the past relatively high profit rates in manufacturing have simply not attracted investment in manufacturing. Institutional factors have worked for other results. The social status attached to landholding has stimulated investment in land even though profit rates there have been relatively low. The political security obtained from foreign bank deposits has encouraged their accumulation, even at purely nominal interest rates. The desire for security in the hereafter has motivated generous contributions to the church. But the idea that a slightly higher profit rate in manufacturing is what it will take to stimulate industrialization in Latin America seems not to be supported by the historical evidence on Latin American profit rates. If high profit expec-

[3] United States Congress, Joint Economic Committee (Hearings), *Economic Developments in South America* (Washington, Government Printing Office, 1962), p. 7.
[4] I have worried a good deal with the comparison of profit rates. See my, *International Trade: Goods, People, and Ideas* (New York, Knopf, 1958), chap. 29.

tations necessarily called forth growth, Latin American manufacturing should have grown apace long before now.

In economic development literature, from time to time, items other than attractive profit expectations have been identified as the prime movers behind economic development (or some particular spurt of economic development). A spurt in exports may be identified as a prime mover (the case of Brazil after World War II according to Furtado) or a spurt in foreign investment (the case of Argentina before World War I). Or an improvement in costs relative to costs in other countries may be so identified. A spurt in demand may also be so identified.[5]

The reader may identify, in the effort to find a *primum mobile* that will consistently explain spurts in development, a logical exercise somewhat like the chicken and egg sequence. A better rule might be that any disturbance which cuts into a circular flow at any stage in the flow may lead to permanent and continuing change.

However, it should be noted that effort to identify a *primum mobile* that is consistently responsible for development spurts is a quite different thing from analyzing a particular spurt in terms of an effort to identify particular circumstances that may have given it emphasis. The latter effort may be extremely useful for acquiring understanding of a particular country or process.

The institutional theory, which is emphasized later in this chapter, has a far different manner of explanation as to the conditions that motivate the growth process.

Modern Development Theories

In the days before the recent rash of economic development theories, it was common to write off a country's prospects for development on the basis of lack of resources or lack of effective demand or some such thing. The economic development theories of more recent years have not been this naïve, but they have still concerned themselves with the preconditions for growth or with the effort to identify a *primum mobile* that might get the process going or keep it going.

There was Schumpeter's profit-motive-motivated innovator of World

[5] W. Beckerman, "Projecting Europe's Growth," in *Economic Journal*, LXXII (December, 1962); Celso Furtado, *Formaçao Econômica do Brasil* (Rio de Janeiro, Fundo de Cultura, 1959), pp. 227–248; Raymond Vernon, *The Dilemma of Mexico's Development* (Cambridge, Harvard University Press, 1963), p. 84.

War I vintage. There was Rostow's preconditions for a takeoff into self-sustained growth. There is the idea that the underdeveloped countries are generally caught in a sort of vicious circle of poverty and low productivity (Myrdal) and that they need to implement a big push in all sectors of the economy (balanced growth) if they are going to break out of the vicious circle (Nurkse, Rosenstein-Rodan). There has been the idea that growth will proceed more effectively if it is unbalanced. This idea has been reflected in the poles-of-development concept of François Perroux, and in the agglomeration effects and unbalanced growth concepts of Hirschman, Singer, and, much earlier, of Alvin Hansen. Hansen emphasized canals, railroads, and the automobile as having led the various historical spurts of United States economic development. Whether these modern-day innovations have added much to Alfred Marshall's concept of external economies is an issue that need not detain us here.

There is also another theory which has not been much used by the economic development theorists or practitioners, but which would seem to have considerable explanatory power. This theory, on which much of the following discussion leans, is the institutional theory of Thorstein Veblen and of Clarence Ayres.

Institutional Theory

The institutional theory was summarized in Chapter One somewhat as follows. Economic progress is conditioned by:

(1) The static resistance to change, and especially to the assimilation of new technology, which exists because of the institutional organization of society;
(2) The dynamic forces inherent in the process of accumulation of technical knowledge;
(3) The appropriateness of the available raw material resources to the state of technical knowledge.

The accumulation of technical knowledge is the great dynamic force in economic progress. To say that the accumulation of technical knowledge is a dynamic force is to say that it goes on as a continuous process because of its own inner logic. It does not need to be motivated by outside forces such as the profit motive. One bit of new knowledge leads to another. But the tempo of assimilation of the new technology by the economy is controlled by the flexibility of the institutional order prevailing in that economy. Some institutional orders are more resistant to the assimilation of new technical knowledge than are others. The understanding as to why one institutional order or one society is more resistant to the assimilation of new technology than is another provides the basic explanation as to why some countries are developing more rapidly than are others.

One might say that the chief economic development planning problem is to create the institutional conditions which will permit technical knowledge to be assimilated. For the most part this involves the weakening of some already existing institutional arrangements. As for the technical knowledge itself, it may be generated internally or it may be obtained from abroad. The immigration of technical knowledge can make a major contribution to development in the Latin American countries. But for this to happen the institutional orders in the Latin American countries must permit the reception and use of the knowledge. "The rapid assimilation of technology entails new patterns of living and new attitudes of mind." [6]

The assimilation of technical knowledge, in two societies where the institutional resistances are of about the same obduracy, will have greater impact in increasing production and welfare in the society endowed with those raw materials particularly appropriate to the given state of technical knowledge. For example, after technology has developed methods for making aluminum out of bauxite, bauxite mining will occur at places where there happen to be bauxite deposits. It cannot occur at other places and it will not occur before the advance of technology has created the demand for bauxite.[7] Also, in a certain state of technology (the present state), the manufacture of alumina from bauxite occurs in the neighborhood of major water-power facilities.

In the remainder of this chapter a few institutional barriers to development will be identified. This is, however, not an effort at an exhaustive list. Other institutional barriers are identified elsewhere in the book with

---

[6] United Nations, *Towards a Dynamic Development Policy for Latin America* (New York, 1963), p. 17; *see also,* Joan Robinson, *Economic Philosophy* (Chicago, Aldine, 1962), chap. V.

[7] Implicit here is Erich Zimmermann's distinction between resources and neutral stuff. *See, World Resources and Industries* (revised ed., New York, Harper, 1951), chap. 1.

fair frequency. The following chapter discusses the role of technology and the role of raw materials in development.

Institutional Barriers

LANDOWNERS. Historically the landowning class has been the most powerful force on the Latin American scene. As a class they have had a vested interest in the preservation of the institution of private property and in the preservation of certain special privileges, both social and economic. For example, their political power position has permitted them to resist taxation effectively. And in general, land taxes in Latin America have been low and remain low. Also the landowning group has wanted a peon-type labor supply effectively tied to the land by some such institutional arrangement as debt servitude.

As a by-product of the social status going with land ownership there has been a tendency for the economic value of land to be "comparatively low in relation to its market value." [8] Once a major disparity of this sort exists in a country's pricing pattern, it is extremely difficult for competition to work to ensure anything like the best or most efficient use of resources. The resultant inefficiency in the use of resources has been immediately apparent in the inefficient use of land itself. The landowner, primarily interested in the social-status implications of land ownership, has not been especially interested in the efficient use of land.[9]

David Felix has pointed out that the providing of cheap food to support workers in industry has required technical improvement and additional investment in agriculture. But the *latifundistas* have been interested neither in technical improvement nor in additional investment. Output per capita has remained almost stationary, employment opportunities in agriculture have remained poor, people have migrated to the cities, food prices have soared. This is the sort of thing that is currently called a structural problem by many economic development economists.

In recent years the relative power position of the landowning class in Latin America has probably declined somewhat. But the landowners

---

[8] United Nations, *Towards a Dynamic Development Policy for Latin America* (New York, 1963), p. 43.

[9] Luiz Carlos Bresser Pereira, "Problemas da Agricultura Brasileira e suas Causas," in *Journal of Inter-American Studies*, VI (January, 1964), 43–55, and esp. p. 51; *see also* the statement by David Felix in Albert O. Hirschman, *Latin American Issues: Essays and Comments* (New York, The Twentieth Century Fund, 1961), p. 86.

are still a force to be reckoned with, even in Mexico, a country that has been actively trying to deflate their importance for fifty years.

DICTATORSHIP. It would take more space than can be devoted to the subject in this book to argue out the question as to whether dictatorship or democracy is likely to be more inhibitory in frustrating development. Both are institutions. But one particular black mark should be mentioned against dictatorship. It tends to drive away the technically competent or to make them reluctant to return. It has been observed that young people, trained under technical exchange programs, who should in the normal course of events return to their countries to help with economic growth, are frequently reluctant to return. And, often, they cite as the reason for their reluctance their fear of the dictator.

ARMY. Historically the army has been an important institution on the Latin American scene. It might be accurate to say that over the past hundred and fifty years Latin America has been ruled by a kind of accommodation arrangement between the landowners and the army. Of late years the importance of the army has been inflated in some important respects by the increased sophistication of the military equipment that it possesses. Much of this equipment has been provided by the United States, ostensibly to build up the Latin American armies so that they can fight off the Russians. The actual result of thus building up the equipment position of the armies has been to make it almost impossible for any third force in the Latin American countries to stage a successful revolution. If the army is unhappy with a regime, it can be overthrown. If any other groups are unhappy, that is just too bad.

This makes it rather important to try to determine what the armies stand for, ideologically speaking, in Latin America. Mostly, in the past, the armies have been rather unimaginative defenders of the status quo in the economic and social areas. However, immediately after a military coup it has now become institutionalized procedure for the leaders (1) to promise free elections as soon as things settle down, (2) to make some strong statements endorsing economic development and improvement in the standard of living, and (3) to put the leaders of the political opposition in jail or to expatriate them. Some military leaders, once in power, may continue to make efforts to help the poor a major part of their program. But the nature of their upbringing prevents them from being effective, imaginative implementers of economic development. And the circumstances of the power struggle in which they are engaged are likely to require their chief attention to the detriment of effective work on development.

But mostly the regimes that follow military coups very shortly lose any especial interest in effectively working for the general welfare. Their chief concern becomes how to keep the lid on—and how to latch onto some foreign aid funds.

CATHOLICISM. R. H. Tawney has attributed much of the difference in development in the Protestant and Catholic countries to differences in certain of the economic practices which are by-products of the two religions.[10] An example would be the difference in attitudes toward saving. The Catholic disapproval of the taking of interest allegedly inhibited saving in Catholic countries before the Industrial Revolution. The Protestant glorification of saving as a virtue (combined with approval of the taking of interest) facilitated the accumulation of capital in the countries of northern Europe and the United States. (This point may have been important in explaining the inception of the Industrial Revolution, whether or not it is particularly important as an influence on the economic growth of the 1960s. The Keynesian argument, that autonomous investment may draw out saving whether or not individuals make a positive decision to save a high proportion of income, suggests alternative arguments.)

Also it has been argued that there has been a tendency for the Catholic Church to resist the use of the scientific method in research, and the assimilation of the knowledge derived from such research. This attitude has presumably been a result of the commitment to the inductive method of logic to which the Catholic Church has been oriented since the days of St. Thomas Aquinas. The syllogistic logic (thesis, antithesis, synthesis) says that one knows final truth by assumption, and one can then apply deductive logic to the solution of particular problems. This sort of thinking creates difficulties in the way of the use of the scientific method in research. Consequently the Catholic culture has been reluctant to accept the results of scientific, inductive research. I believe that it was

[10] *Religion and the Rise of Capitalism* (London, Murray, 1926).

Ortega y Gasset who said that Spanish scientists resisted Einstein's theory of relativity not so much because they considered it inaccurate as because they considered it a personal affront.

The Church remains a powerful influence in Latin America. But its influence is complex. The Church espouses what is in some respects a coherent body of economic doctrines. (This body of doctrines was discussed in Chapter Two). Nevertheless differences in emphasis and interpretation make it possible for some segments of the Church community to be among the most reactionary elements in society, the Sinarquistas in Mexico for example; and, at the same time, other elements in the Church community may be leaders in the effort to introduce social and economic reform. Despite these differences, the Church as a coherent institution remains a force to be reckoned with. For example, after being a bulwark of the Perón regime for many years, the Church played a significant role in his overthrow in 1955.

It should probably be added at this point that the role of the Catholic Church in Latin America at the present time in inhibiting change may not be much more effective than the role of some of the Protestant churches in the United States. And certainly scholars in Latin American universities, even though they may be Catholic, have considerable freedom to use the scientific method in their research; and many do so.

BUREAUCRACY. Historically the Latin American bureaucracy has been an underpaid, paper-shuffling dead hand.[11] Unable to be constructive, in considerable measure because of his lack of status, the low-level bureaucrat has reacted by being surly and uncooperative in his dealings with the public.

Public administration is in need of substantial shaking up. The Economic Commission for Latin America has commented:

> If Latin American private enterprise is lagging behind the requirements of development it is not surprising that the same is true of public administration. Its organization is a survival from times past, with additions and adjustments, but without basic changes. . . .
>
> There is a background of inertia, of perpetuation of inefficiency, which is preventing the public administration in Latin America from adapting itself to the requirements of economic development, except in a few special cases. This applies to simple as well as to complicated functions, and the

---

[11] Frequently the salaries are "unbelievably low." *See,* United Nations, *Towards a Dynamic Development Policy for Latin America,* p. 57.

result is apparent in the needless trammelling of economic activity—in fact of all activities that bear any relation to the State—and in every imaginable kind of inefficient and time-consuming procedure.[12]

However, in recent years there have been some significant changes in this regard. Influential bureaucrats, sometimes now called *técnicos,* have been playing a role of increasing importance in running the governments and in shaping the economic development programs.

In Latin America, as elsewhere, there is a tendency for a government, when it is confronted with an urgent problem, to set up a new agency to deal with it. Such an agency will almost never be abolished; but when the same problem recurs a few years later, yet another agency will be established to deal with it. This is done, with some justification, because the old agency has probably become stagnant and set in its ways, if not positively corrupt; and it has failed to solve the problem. At this juncture, however, the role of the old agency becomes the frustration of the work of the new agency.

Albert Hirschman has described the working of this process from the 1870s to date in the Northeast of Brazil.[13] The general pattern involved creating a new agency to deal with the problems created by each successive major drought. Some of these agencies have been an Inspetoria of Works against Droughts, DNOCS, São Francisco Valley Commission, São Francisco Hydroelectric Company, the Bank of the Northeast of Brazil, and SUDENE. Most of these agencies continue to exist. One of the more interesting parts of the Hirschman description deals with the efforts of DNOCS to frustrate the establishment of SUDENE in 1958.

Old agencies, unlike old generals, neither die nor wither away. They retain a major power to resist progress, even after they cease to play a constructive role themselves.

LACK OF ENTREPRENEURSHIP. Everett Hagen and others have embarked on a campaign of glorification of the businessman-entrepreneur-innovator in an effort to explain how to accelerate development.[14] But one might well ask whether the system of free private enterprise (complete with competition and substantial absence of government interference—as described in United States mythology if not United States practice) is what the Latin American countries need. We in the United

---
[12] United Nations, *Towards a Dynamic . . .* , pp. 56–57.
[13] *Journeys Toward Progress* (New York, The Twentieth Century Fund, 1963).
[14] *On the Theory of Social Change* (Homewood, Ill., Dorsey, 1962).

States have a proneness for thinking that the poor countries should copy our successful behavior. In fact, the attempt to sell United States institutions, especially the institution of private enterprise, is standard United States operating procedure in connection with foreign aid programs. Every now and then an Under Secretary of Commerce feels it his duty to make a statement something like this to an underdeveloped country audience:

> Free enterprise promotes economic progress. . . . The principles of dynamic capitalism which have made our free-enterprise system so eminently successful will be equally effective in creating a progressive and dynamic world economy if the world is willing to give it half a chance.[15]

Whether what Latin America needs is some John Jacob Astors, John D. Rockefeller, Srs., and Jay Goulds is not certain.

It was argued in Chapter One that, to be viable, the institutional system of a country needs to be homegrown. For people to accept with a good grace certain ways of doing things, they need to have the feeling that those ways are their own idea. The United States might be well advised to leave up to the less-developed countries themselves the decision as to how much free private enterprise they want. Beyond this, the fact that laissez-faire, free private enterprise worked well in the United States in the nineteenth century, if it did, would hardly be compelling evidence that it would work well in Latin America in the last half of the twentieth century.

Hagen has said something fairly correct, if hardly novel, in alleging that ostracized groups may be more receptive to new methods than are the dominant social groups in a society; and he has said that successful entrepreneur-innovators are more likely to come from ostracized groups. Many of the successful businessmen in Latin America are Armenians, Syrians, Greeks, and Italians—not to forget the Hindus. The role of the ostracized group may be fitted into the institutional theory as part of the picture. Such groups are less bound by institutional fetters. But the Hagen argument can hardly make much claim to being a major independent theory of development.

The necessity for innovation in connection with the development process does not establish the necessity that the innovator be profit-motivated. Probably the circumstances that will call forth innovation are much better explained, as the institutional theory does it, in terms

[15] Walter Williams, in *Foreign Commerce Weekly,* March 21, 1955, p. 17.

of the absence of institutional barriers to the acceptance and application of new technical knowledge. The trouble with Hagen's approach is that one man's food is frequently another man's poison. A *norteamericano* might innovate in response to the lure of profits where a Latin American idealist in the tradition of Rodó would not deign to do so. Even the ostracized, but ambitious, individual in Latin America will frequently be culturally constrained to try to realize his ambitions in the Latin American way by obtaining land rather than by going into manufacturing. Jorge Amado, in *Gabriela,* indicates that the continuing goal of his Syrian hero is to become a cacao plantation owner.

One of the best potential sources for developing a substantial group of entrepreneurs is the artisan group. Latin America is blessed with hundreds of thousands if not millions of artisans. They sell in the front of the store. They manufacture, with one or two employees plus various members of the family, in the back of the store. The artisan has a certain amount of experience with the problems involved in handling a labor force. He has some conception of what is involved in organizing a production process. He has some conception of the problems involved in merchandising. Yet he is generally quite poor. He does not have the social status required for borrowing at the bank. Many artisans would be far better credit risks than certain socially acceptable bums with grandiose ideas, who happen to be kinsmen of the oligarchs and who do have access to credit. The banks should show positive initiative in facilitating large numbers of artisans to expand their activities.

Sears Roebuck has rendered a service in Latin America by searching out people such as this, giving them contracts to supply Sears with certain items, and giving them financial and planning assistance into the bargain. If Latin American banks would do this sort of thing on a far larger scale, it conceivably could make a major contribution to the industrialization of Latin America and do it at a level where it would count with some speed.

The Brazilian economist Alexandre Kafka has pointed out that Latin Americans already have marked proclivities for entrepreneurship and innovation. He wrote: "There is a general sensitivity to, and preparedness to act on, economic incentives, which is evident not only in the more advanced urban centers but also in the hinterland." [16]

---

[16] Howard S. Ellis and Henry C. Wallich, eds., *Economic Development for Latin America* (New York, St Martin's Press, 1961), p. 8.

An example of the transfer of an entrepreneurship-type cultural trait that should "better have stayed at home" might be cited. Foreign students are encouraged to come to the United States to study and acquire technical knowledge of one kind and another so that they can go home and contribute to the development of their own country. One thing that many such students study in the United States is business administration, including courses in marketing that explain about commodity speculation. Also they learn that profit making is respectable procedure—and that anything within the letter of the law goes. Then they go home and make their almighty fortunes in commodity speculation or in foreign exchange speculation. Their foreign study has been useful to them but not of much use to their country.

It seems likely that, in spite of Hagen's concern, the entrepreneurs can look after themselves. In any event the United States had better let the Latin Americans decide for themselves how much desire they have for free private enterprise.

DECENTRALIZATION AND DELEGATION OF RESPONSIBILITY. The marked centralization that characterizes the governments of Latin America may facilitate the preparation and implementation of comprehensive development plans. But on the other hand it may inhibit many people from showing an initiative in putting new ideas into effect of their own volition, which would be very helpful in furthering development.

A situation of rather similar type exists within the firm. The role of the Latin American businessman (or government bureau chief) in relation to the making of minor day-to-day decisions within his enterprise is involved.

The point may be illustrated in connection with the role of the secretary. It is common knowledge that so far as many going concerns in the United States are concerned, the secretary (generally female in gender) holds the operation together while the boss is off wheeling and dealing or playing golf. The effective female secretary has been one of the major United States contributions to the world of industry and business. Meanwhile the Latin American executive has an (institutionally conditioned) reluctance to entrust his underlings with the power to do anything in his absence. He has to see everything, decide everything, sign everything. And, in many cases, he is busy doing other things; and a lot of seeing, deciding, and signing does not occur. On top of that, his attitude toward the female secretary is not calculated to encourage her to effective work. Although the Latin American male, when it comes to social events, may be a far more courteous gentleman in his relation to the ladies than is his North American counterpart, he has some tendency to treat female secretaries like dirt, to pile drudgery-type work on them without any conception of the amount of work involved, and without granting any decision-making discretion.

Some of the really significant development problems are connected with the internal organization of the production process. The Economic Commission for Latin America has said:

> Production equipment is often misguidedly used, with the result that its performance is inferior to that registered even in countries with medium industrial yields, not to mention those where productivity is high. Several factors combine to determine this situation: the organization of the factory and the system of distribution of labour, defective raw materials, inadequate supervision, careless treatment of machinery and plant. All these problems can be solved. That is, they can be solved provided private enterprise does not confine its efforts to the initial functions of promotion. It must also be indefatigable in its endeavours to increase yields and reduce costs.[17]

THE SPANISH LANGUAGE. Not enough is said in the discussion of economic development about the disadvantage of speaking a language in which very little of the technically important work of the world has been written. The Latin American technician is under the handicap that most of the knowledge he needs is available only in other languages. The Spanish and Portuguese languages are, in a way, institutional barriers to development.

Like Latin America, the world as a whole is working under an unnecessary language handicap, occasioned by the proliferation of languages and the difficulty of communicating among people who speak different languages. The computer, capable of translating at great speed (and with little accuracy), offers the deceptive possibility of retaining the proliferation of languages and yet having material from other languages readily available. This is a real make-work, feather-bedding-type solution of the language problem. The machine translation encourages the translation of fantastic amounts of relatively worthless material. A major librarian's headache is in the making. But the worst disservice done by the possibility of machine translation is to permit us to avoid

[17] United Nations, *Towards a Dynamic* . . . , p. 47.

facing up to the serious implications of the multiplicity of languages. The machine cannot solve the problem of ordinary man-to-man communication between people who speak different languages. Each traveler cannot carry along with him a $3 million machine to permit him to "ask directions" of the local citizens he meets on the street, or to help him order food in a restaurant, or to help him discuss a problem with another scientist, or to help a technical-assistance expert give counsel to those he is supposed to teach.

The people of the underdeveloped countries, who are the chief sufferers from the multiplicity of languages, could advocate a genuinely worthwhile, non-nit-picking cause (for a change) in the United Nations by spearheading a drive for one language.

Let me, with some misgiving, suggest a possible procedure. Attempt should be made to identify some one language as the language which would be the next language that anyone thinking of studying an additional language would study. After this has been done, the United Nations would strongly recommend the passage of laws in all nations requiring that the second (or next) language anyone learns should be this particular language. Some such step as this would surely have to be the first step in attempting to establish one language.

Of course the decision as to what this second language should be poses some ticklish political and social problems. A possible procedure for resolving the problem might be as follows. First there should be a vote as to whether the second language should be Esperanto or some language in use. If the vote is for Esperanto, that settles the matter. If the vote is for a language in use, a list of all the potential candidates should be assembled. It would be hoped the process of selection could be simplified by the willingness of the representatives of some languages not to press their cases. But the collection of reasonably strong candidates could still well contain fifteen or twenty names. It should be clearly understood by all the proponents of the various candidate languages that, if their language is selected, it will be reworked by a committee of scholars in the interest of simplification. For example, the Spanish-speaking people would agree that, if Spanish were selected, the grammar, spelling, etc., of Spanish could be reworked by a committee of scholars —which could well decide the inflection of verbs in Spanish is unnecessary, that some of the procedures for forming the plural should be simplified, and so on.

After the panel of candidate languages is assembled, the United Nations General Assembly might vote on them (either by a one-nation, one-vote procedure, or perhaps by a procedure that would increase the vote of the more populous countries). Whichever procedure is adopted, there could be a vote as to which language was preferred. The language getting the least votes would be dropped from the polling. Another vote might be held in another month and a second language dropped. Over a period of a year or eighteen months this process could work the vote down to one language.

It would then become the obligation of the individual governments to enact laws providing that the next foreign language anyone learns should be the selected language.

It is more than high time something like this was done.

General Comment

Other institutional barriers include banking practice, work rules established in collective contracts, the low pay of foremen and plant superintendents, the too-small size of many of the countries, and so on.

It is important not to put the wrong interpretation on the preceding comments about institutional barriers. The argument is not intended to lead to the conclusion that institutions should be abolished; institutions are with us to stay. And it is most desirable that this should be the case. A world without institutions would be a world without order or organization. The moral is that man should be the master of his institutions, not the other way around.

CHAPTER TWELVE

BASIS FOR INDUSTRIALIZATION: TECHNOLOGY AND RESOURCES

Technology

The Veblen-Ayres theory of economic progress says that technology is a dynamic, cumulative force. The chief problem in economic development is the assimilation of new technical knowledge against the resistance of established and static institutions.

TECHNICAL SKILL. It is frequently said that the native populations are not possessed of either the mental attitude necessary for an easy transition to a machine economy or of the technical knowledge to use the machine with enough efficiency so that its product can rival in price the product of the older industrialized centers. The argument is in a sense correct at present. But, as an alleged proof that Latin America cannot develop, it rests on the assumption that the "egg came before the hen." Workers in general have acquired technical skill as industrialization has progressed. The worker did not already possess technical knowledge, full-blown, at the time (whenever that may have been) when the use of the machine began.

There are assorted problems of institutional adjustment as the worker moves from subsistence agriculture to industry. The nature of this aspect of the problem is indicated by Robert Alexander.[1] Using Chile as an example, one difficulty seems to be that, as a peon on the agricultural estates, the laborer was used to paternalism. And he feels a need for continued paternalism when he moves to the city and becomes an industrial worker. In fact as a more general principle, the circumstances under which paternalism is shed may be a significant explanation for the amount of personal irresponsibility shown by workers in early phases of the transition from the farm to industry. This adjustment is one of the Latin American institutional problems.

INTERNATIONAL MOVEMENT OF TECHNOLOGY. The spread of technical knowledge from one country to another (and the failure of the spread and assimilation of such knowledge because of institutional resistance) is probably much more important in explaining economic development and the lack of it than is any other international factor. Various examples of the role of the spread of technical knowledge may be cited.

The establishment of sugar growing in the Caribbean area in the seventeenth century has been explained by the transfer to that area by the Dutch of knowledge acquired by them previously in other areas such as their East Indian colonies and the Northeast of Brazil, which they partially occupied between 1624 and 1654.

The technological decadence of Spain during the colonial period (relative to England) probably prejudiced the development of Latin America relative to the development of the United States. Spain was short on knowledge to transfer and the Laws of the Indies inhibited the transfer of such knowledge as she had. This circumstance provides much of the explanation as to why the Latin America of the nineteenth century was lagging relative to the United States.

The development of copper mining at the great Chuquicamata deposit in northern Chile was dependent upon the introduction of a method developed by Jackling in Utah for processing low-grade porphyry ores.

The development of the plantation rubber industry in the Far East depended upon the smuggling of *Hevea brasiliensis* seeds out of Brazil by H. A. Wickham shortly before the turn of the century.

But isolated examples of the international movement of technical

[1] *Labor Relations in Argentina, Brazil, and Chile* (New York, McGraw-Hill, 1962), pp. 327–37.

knowledge fail to indicate the general impact of the process. To make matters worse, there is no monetary measure, or other handy yardstick, for describing the phenomenon. Nevertheless, it is an all-pervasive, all-important process.

Foreign Investment. Technical knowledge can move by itself. It can also be transferred as a by-product of foreign investment. Has it been to any important degree? This is perhaps the chief question in determining whether foreign investments can play a significantly useful role in furthering economic development.

Erich Zimmermann has indicated one frequent characteristic of the foreign investment of the past that would tend to cast a doubt on the efficacy of this process in contributing to the long-run growth of the pool of technical knowledge in the underdeveloped country.[2] Zimmermann envisaged that foreign investments, especially in oil and mining, occurred in a setting that might be called an exclave (or depending on how you look at it, an enclave), a geographical area apart from the rest of the economy. The copper-mining area around Chuquicamata, Chile, or the oil-producing area around Lake Maracaibo in Venezuela (with refineries off on the Dutch-owned islands of Curaçao and Aruba) would be examples. Such foreign investments have been in but not of the economy of the debtor country. They involved little real contact between the foreign-owned industry and the rest of the economy. Where this has been the case little of the technical knowledge of the foreign engineers and geologists has rubbed off on the people of the underdeveloped country.

A group of experts from the International Monetary Fund has commented with regard to the role of the foreign banana companies in Honduras that their "highly capitalistic" and "large-scale investment" has not seemed "to influence, in and of itself, to any significant degree the total economy of Honduras."[3]

Ragnar Nurkse observed the possibility that foreign investors may not be "eager to impart technical and managerial knowledge to the local population."[4] He indicated that this was in considerable measure due

---

[2] Erich Zimmermann, *World Resources and Industries* (rev. ed., New York, Harper, 1951), pp. 129–130.

[3] Javier Márquez, *et al., Estudio Sobre la Economía de Honduras* (Tegucigalpa, Banco Central de Honduras, 1950), p. 7.

[4] Ragnar Nurkse, *Problems of Capital Formation in Underdeveloped Countries* (Oxford, Basil Blackwell, 1953), p. 88.

to a suspicion that the trained labor would then go off to work for someone else.

Jack N. Behrman, whose job as Assistant Secretary of Commerce might have made him a strong apologist for foreign investors, has said that United States business has failed to send its best men into the foreign field.[5] The second-rate people who are sent abroad are paid relatively well, more than they would get at home. And they are not interested in training local people to substitute for themselves. Yet, a locally trained man, once trained, could do the work just as well for a fraction of the amount it costs to have a relatively inefficient United States expert on the job.

In connection with its Latin American investments, United States ownership generally insists on having almost exclusive control at the planning, management, and policy-making levels. So, on the basis of this sort of a picture also, the amount of technical knowledge contributed by the foreign investment process has tended not to be what it might have been in a slightly different institutional setting.

These conditions provide part of the explanation of the economic stagnation (in the face of foreign investments) of many countries during the nineteenth and early twentieth centuries. Mining and railroads were the chief objects of international investment in the nineteenth century, and neither of them seems to have transferred much technology. The foreign investments in oil also tend to have rather limited usefulness in spreading technical knowledge. The increased emphasis in recent years on manufacturing may offer more prospect for diffusing technical knowledge in volume. On the whole, foreign investment has not been a distinguished spreader of technical knowledge. Nevertheless, foreign investment and foreign investors might operate as important vehicles for spreading technical knowledge if they really desired to do so.

The licensing of manufacturing processes (and the providing of technicians instructed to make a conscientious effort to try to transmit the relevant technical knowledge) is a method by which foreign investment proper (with some of its unfortunate side effects) could be avoided and the underdeveloped country could get important knowledge. From the viewpoint of the licensing company, a steady return beginning promptly, little capital investment, and little managerial energy are involved. The

[5] Raymond F. Mikesell, ed., *U.S. Private and Government Investment Abroad* (Eugene, Ore., University of Oregon Books, 1962), p. 115.

device has not been much used, however. Apparently United States companies have not been particularly interested in training foreign licensees. There are problems of policing quality (the good name of a product is involved). A dangerous competitor might be built up. Also United States antitrust laws create some problems if the licensor tries to protect himself by agreements providing for exclusive marketing territories.

Foreign investment involving joint participation by foreign and domestic capital in new manufacturing plants (joint enterprise) is also a channel through which foreign investment might make a contribution to the facilitation of the spread of technical knowledge. Joint ventures potentially provide an institutional setting conducive to the exchange of knowledge. The stake of Westinghouse in the Industria Eléctrica de México is an example of a joint venture.

There are several problems, however. The domestic participant may conceive that he has done his share by providing the right political connections, and he may be something of a parasite so far as the actual conduct of the company business is concerned. In his influence on company policy, he may prefer high and stable dividends to finance conspicuous consumption. The foreign investor might prefer to plow back dividends and take advantage of the capital gains provisions of the United States tax law. The domestic participant may want to impregnate the company with nepotism. The Madison Avenue orientation of the foreign investor may cause him to want to use high-pressure selling techniques that are distasteful in the Latin American environment.

United States companies with foreign, direct investments are rather generally opposed to joint ownership. They have argued that the local citizens participating in ownership are likely to have a get-rich-quick attitude; they are likely to have a low standard of ethics; they are likely to want to deal with the government by offering bribes; and worst of all, if the government in power changes, they are likely to lose their "in" and be a liability rather than an asset to the company.

Despite their advantages, but perhaps because of some of the incompatibilities they reveal, joint ventures get little support either from the Latin American governments or from foreign investors. Lincoln Gordon pointed out that one of the basic Brazilian government regulations controlling and presumably encouraging foreign investment (a so-called

Instruction 113) was not being applied effectively to joint ventures, an example of Brazilian governmental misgivings about the device.[6]

There may be some truth in these arguments. But there is something wrong with the conclusion. If the foreign investor had picked his associates in the first place because of competence, reliability, and promise, instead of because of political connections, a lot of the unfortunate results would not have followed.

The joint venture is a device that merits a good deal more experimental use. To the extent that foreign investment can play a useful role in development, it is the joint venture that offers the best prospects.

Hiring. For the most part, however, technical skills are gotten a lot more cheaply by going out and hiring the technicians than by paying the additional charges that foreign investment demands for its services as intermediary. Between 1920 and 1940 the Soviet Union hired a very substantial number of technicians and engineers in the United States. They probably made a not inconsiderable contribution to the amazing Russian industrial development which followed. And they were a lot cheaper than foreign investment. Much the same sort of thing can be said concerning the Japanese industrialization of the late nineteenth and early twentieth centuries. The chief difference would be that the Japanese went abroad and picked up the technical knowledge for themselves—rather than hiring it to come to them.

But there seem to be human inconsistencies and equivocations in connection with implementation of the direct transmittal of technical knowledge. One almost gets the impression at times that the underdeveloped countries do not want help of this type. They would rather have the money instead. Presumably this attitude is in part a result of what has been called "the income redistribution effect of foreign investments and foreign aid." The monetary aid may represent a real gain for the people through whose hands the money passes, whether or not the country is any better off as result of the aid. The same possibilities for siphoning off some of the gain do not exist in the case of straight technical assistance.

But even in situations where technical assistance is emphasized, frustration frequently occurs. For example, in spite of all the talk in Argen-

---

[6] Lincoln Gordon, *United States Manufacturing Investment in Brazil* (Boston, Harvard University, 1962), p. 44.

tina and by Argentine spokesmen about the desirability of foreign investments and about the desirability of obtaining technical knowledge from abroad, there exists in the actual human relations a very substantial reluctance to accept and assimilate quickly and effectively the proffered help. The technician, brought to the country at considerable expense on the initiative of private enterprise, is frequently kept in a state of semi-isolation. The proprietors of the enterprise that has hired him to give technical aid on a given project may be overly concerned to prevent him from acquiring much knowledge of the details of the operation of the business. Perhaps they fear that he may use such knowledge to supplant them in control of the enterprise or to form his own enterprise to compete with them later. The net result may be that they try to milk the technician of key bits of desirable knowledge without permitting the technician really to know what the problem is. Thus the procedure which might provide the most satisfactory alternative to foreign investments is frequently not used in an effective way.

When the initiative is governmental the situation is frequently just as bad if not worse. The one- to three-year tours of duty that have characterized technical assistance in the past are something like the worst of all possible worlds. The inexperienced technician, who is more or less trained on the job (such as the Peace Corps member), is just about ready to start making a significant contribution when his two years are up. The middle-level technicians on one- to three-year tours of duty under technical assistance programs have done much worthwhile work. But the procedures used with regard to them have too commonly also resulted in a major waste of effort. The expense involved in moving the family and household effects of such people for tours of duty of this length skyrockets cost. Then, too, the type of middle-aged man who will take two years off from his regular career is likely to be a maladjusted individual who will bungle his assignment. Better planning by the Agency for International Development and the Alliance for Progress should make it possible to use better people on six- to ten-week assignments (college faculty on summer assignments, *real* experts on two-week assignments, and so on), avoid the expense of moving the families, get a lot more work out of them in a short period of time, and generally contribute more to economic development than has been accomplished with the longer tours of duty that have been customary in the past.

But what mainly matters is not that some foreigner stands ready to provide the crucial pearl of wisdom when needed. What matters is the effective assimilation and use of the knowledge on the part of the people of the underdeveloped countries themselves. They need to make the acquisition of technical knowledge something of a religion—as the Japanese did after 1868. Removing the barriers to assimilation of knowledge is largely up to the people of the underdeveloped countries themselves. The process can be accelerated very little by increased foreign investments, especially if the foreign investor is himself not straining to impart technical knowledge. But this is not too important. Most of the world's technical knowledge is reasonably available to people with a modicum of determination to acquire it.

But how interested are the Latin Americans in acquiring technical knowledge and what do they envisage is involved in the process? Occasionally in the Latin American writing of recent years the overriding importance of the acquiring of additional technical competence has been appreciated. But when the Latin American speaks of how this knowledge is to be acquired he may say: "Give it to us. . . ." The language in Spanish may be: *"Los países industriales deberían . . . facilitar a América Latina el acceso a. . . ."* For the Latin American to assume that after the North American extends the technical knowledge on a platter all else follows as a matter of course seems to involve a bit of wishful thinking.

There seems to be an absence of clear conception as to what is involved in assimilating technical knowledge and this absence was noticeable in 1962 at the United Nations Conference on the Application of Science and Technology for the Benefit of Less-Developed Areas. The problem is the mastering of the knowledge, making the knowledge one's own, adapting it to local conditions, improving on it. The formal availability of the knowledge is of little worth in a setting where the institutional order resists receiving it.

But neither do the developed countries seem to be prepared to provide technical knowledge in an unstinting way. One might mention an effort to assemble discarded textbooks that had been used in the public schools of Texas and which were about to be condemned, many of the books being in excellent condition. The idea was to send the books to Latin American schools. It was literally a case of sending to Latin America books which would otherwise have been destroyed. But it was found that this could not be done. The textbook companies had provided in the small type in their contract with the state that the discarded books had to be destroyed. After all, the companies might be deprived of a sale sometime, somewhere in Latin America, if a million books were sent free to that part of the world.

By contrast with some of the pessimistic remarks that have been made up to now, a method that offers serious possibilities for efficacy in the international transmission of technical cooperation has been developed by Dr. Morris Asimow of the University of California at Los Angeles for helping with development in the state of Ceará in northeastern Brazil. Several graduate students from U.C.L.A., in the summer of 1962, working with a group of Brazilian students, surveyed the possibilities for establishing new manufacturing plants in the state of Ceará. They developed a $2 million program for capitalizing the new enterprises. Specifically, they worked out provision for financing chiefly from Brazilian sources. The sale of stock on the installment plan to the business and professional people of Ceará was involved. The heart of the plan was the creation of five new, small factories producing sewing machines, radios and motors, pressed wood cement, ceramic products, and corn products. Some seventy students at U.C.L.A. in collaboration with a group of students from Brazil then worked out detailed plans for the design of the factories. The method seems to involve a happy combination of youthful enthusiasm and idealism on the part of young people from both countries, substantial local financial self-help, and competent technical supervision. But also the approach provides for private imagination in terms of how and what to innovate. The results will be worth watching.

MIGRATION. John Stuart Mill wrote a century ago in his *Principles of Political Economy:*

It is hardly possible to overrate the value, in the present low state of human improvement, of placing human beings in contact with persons dissimilar to themselves, and with modes of thought and action unlike those with which they are familiar. . . . Such communication has always been, and is peculiarly in the present age, one of the primary sources of progress.[7]

We know, even without having comprehensive national income statistics at our disposal, that real per capita income in the last century and a

---

[7] John Stuart Mill, *Principles of Political Economy* (new impression of the sixth ed., London, Longmans, Green, and Co., 1904), p. 352.

half has risen very substantially in the United States, Canada, Australia, New Zealand, South Africa, Argentina, Uruguay, and Chile. It has risen much less markedly, and is still obviously much lower, in the tropical countries. The first group of countries differs from the second in at least two respects. The first group consists generally of Temperate Zone countries. The second significant difference has been in migration patterns. Generally the first group of countries received an extensive immigration of people with a considerable technical background. The countries of the tropics have not received a significant immigration of this sort.

The countries of both groups have been debtors during most of the last century and a half. It is probably roughly accurate to say that foreign investment has been equally active in the two types of regions. Even qualitatively, there has been considerable similarity in the foreign investment patterns. During the nineteenth century, railroads, public utilities, and mining represented important investments in both types of countries. Consequently it seems not unreasonable to allege that foreign investments do not explain the difference between these two types of regions in the rates of economic growth.

Although climate may well be a significant part of the explanation of the difference, climate has probably chiefly operated through its role as a determinant of the migration patterns. The important point is that the standard of living has risen significantly in countries that have both received migration and received foreign investment. It has not risen in countries that have received foreign investment alone. (Air conditioning may well be the technical development that will permit the tropics to overcome their immigration handicap.)

A few examples of the importance of the migration of people with technical knowledge in contributing to the economic development of the countries to which they go may help to establish the point. The expulsion of the Jews from Spain in 1492 must have been an important factor in explaining the subsequent technological stagnation of Spain. The Revocation of the Edict of Nantes in France in 1685 and the consequent migration of many Huguenots from France to the Low Countries and England seem to have made a significant contribution to the development (especially of the textile industry) of the Low Countries and of England.

Celso Furtado has explained the failure of a steel industry to develop in Brazil at the time it began to develop in the United States in the eighteenth century in the following terms: Brazil had as much need for iron products such as horseshoes as did the Thirteen Colonies. Iron ore and charcoal were as available in Brazil as in North America. But what Brazil lacked was immigrants with a background of experience in iron metallurgy. Furtado's explanation of this was that England had a steel industry and Portugal did not.[8]

Using Argentina, Brazil, and Chile as his particular examples, Robert Alexander has said that historically a large proportion of the new industries in those countries has been established by migrant artisans.[9] Then migration was virtually cut off in the 1930s. That source for the effective and imaginative inception of new industries was lost. It should be noted that this source of technicians (except for occasional highly publicized and generally unimplemented offers to receive groups of technically trained refugees) has been cut off by the action of the underdeveloped countries themselves.

For the presently underdeveloped countries to participate in the gain from migration some changes need to be made. The laws of the underdeveloped countries are replete with discrimination against the foreigner. He may be forbidden from occupying this or that type of job. He may have to serve an apprenticeship all over again. He will probably have to pass a professional-qualification examination all over again.[10] And the examiners may not be particularly sympathetic to his passing. Difficulties of this sort plague both the technicians and the professional men: doctors, engineers, and so on, who, with the desire to help, go to work in the underdeveloped countries.

The individualized screening of the would-be permanent immigrant makes for difficulty. The person trying to obtain a permanent entry visa may be made to wait months under conditions in which he has no idea as to what is going on or how long the wait may continue. After he finally gets into the country where he desires to work, his administrative troubles are far from over. He is likely to be required to report at regular intervals to the police. He is liable to be deported rather summarily.

---

[8] Celso Furtado, *Formaçao Econômica do Brasil* (Rio de Janeiro, Fundo de Cultura, 1959), p. 97.

[9] Alexander, *Labor Relations in* . . . , pp. 52, 157, 247.

[10] Pan American Union, *A Statement of the Laws of Argentina in Matters Affecting Business* (3d ed., Washington, 1963), pp. 304–5.

Petty administrative harassment is the order of the day. Neighbors may suggest he is not really wanted. Laborers and labor unions in the underdeveloped countries are apprehensive of what the presence of the foreign technician means to them in terms of jobs. They may believe that, if only the foreign technician would go home, there would be a good-paying job for a local citizen.

However, the difficulties of the foreigner in fitting into the local community may also be due to his own predilection for living off to himself in rather exclusive foreign colonies. Nevertheless, the underdeveloped countries could help the cause of their own development by eliminating laws and practices discriminating against foreign technicians. Beyond this, they could well genuinely encourage the foreigners to become permanent residents and to take out citizenship. They pay little more than lip service to this sort of behavior now.

Unfortunately the net movement of technicians may actually be out from Latin America rather than in. There is a significant migration of the technically competent from Latin America to the United States. A similar point has been made by Charles V. Kidd: "The migration of substantial numbers of scientists from less developed countries is in a sense a national catastrophe." [11] And the New York *Times* of April 14, 1963, spoke of the number of newly trained technicians in Argentina trying to get export visas to come to the United States.

The United States, which needs them least, has gotten more gain from technical immigration in the period since the the end of World War II than have all the underdeveloped countries put together. In the 1952 to 1961 decade the United States received about 600,000 immigrants in the professional, technical, or skilled categories. During this period more than 30,000 qualified engineers came in. (Parenthetically, United States universities graduate about 35,000 engineers a year.) With a bit larger welcome mat out, the underdeveloped countries could attract many of these people.

Certain writers have indicated the existence of a superfluity of well-educated people in underdeveloped countries, a phenomenon which, if it exists, would seem to be contradictory to much of the preceding argument. Frank Brandenburg has written of Mexico: "Education and

---

[11] United States, *Science, Technology, and Development, vol. IX, Scientific and Technological Policy, Planning, and Organization* (Washington, 1963), p. 21.

technology are not in short supply; on the contrary, there appears to be an over supply of competent technicians and administrators." [12] Further evidence of the abundance of technicians in Mexico is alleged to be the existence of unemployment among them and their migration from Mexico to Central America and the United States. What is the meaning of this observed phenomenon that educated people often find difficulty in obtaining work in underdeveloped countries? Does it mean that there is no pressing need for more educated people? Surely not. It means that educated people alone, especially people educated in the classics and law, are not enough. The institutional setting must permit them to utilize their skills and knowledge. Nevertheless an increase in the sheer number of educated people is an important, dynamic force, in spite of the temporary unemployment of some educated people.

One of the best things the United States could do to facilitate economic development elsewhere would be to encourage young engineering and business administration graduates (who should have studied one foreign language in the course of their college education) to go abroad, planning to live in some foreign country, with the thought that they would probably stay there all of their lives, became a part of the local community, and take out local citizenship. But the Latin American countries need to be willing to receive them in a manner calculated to make them feel they are welcome.

Incidentally there is no presumption that the pattern of development that will evolve in Latin America will call for just the population distribution that exists at present within the region. Maybe it will be appropriate for a lot of Haitians to migrate to Mexico and Argentina, just as it is appropriate that there be a significant population shift from countryside to urbanized manufacturing center.

Certain areas (the upper Amazon valley, Patagonia, and Haiti) may lag in terms of number of factories to the square mile relative to other areas of Latin America. But this is no grounds for sentencing people born in the upper Amazon valley, Haiti, or Patagonia to the necessity of living there permanently and suffering a relatively lower standard of living in consequence. One of the little-mentioned but important institu-

---

[12] Frank Brandenburg, "A Contribution to the Theory of Entrepreneurship and Economic Development: the Case of Mexico," in *Inter-American Economic Affairs*, 16 (Winter, 1962), 18, 21.

tional barriers to the economic development of the region is the reluctance of the various Latin American countries themselves to permit free intra-area population movement.

EDUCATION OF THE NATIVE-BORN. Of course in the long run, the technical education of native-born people must completely overshadow in importance the international migration of skilled people in terms of numbers of people involved.

The process has two aspects: (1) study in the great universities of the world by students from the underdeveloped countries, and (2) the improvement of the educational systems in the underdeveloped countries.

Assistance to the youth of the Latin American countries to study abroad should be an important means for transferring technical knowledge. And it surely is. However, there are certain problems. The students frequently make frantic efforts to remain in the United States and in western Europe after they have finished their education. By way of explanation of the tendency of underdeveloped-country students to try to stay in the countries where they have studied, it may be said that there are other reasons than merely a desire for the soft life. Frequently the thought of returning to a dictatorship and trying to work conscientiously for the welfare of the country when the rulers of the country are chiefly engaged either in political adventures or are busily feathering their own nests is not a very appealing prospect.

The improvement in the educational systems of the Latin American countries is, of course, in the long run even more important than foreign study. One-semester teaching assignments by professors from the United States and western Europe can play only a minor role in this process. But it would make much more of a contribution if the Latin American universities would actually hire on permanent assignments young (and eager) graduates of developed-country universities.

The Latin American universities need to develop competent, permanent faculties, whose chief commitment is to education, and who are not quarter-time teachers on pay scales fit for day laborers. Also the teaching staffs need to be freed from the continual coercion and threat of punitive action on the part of student political groups, groups frequently more concerned with making the university a battleground in the Cold

War than with acquiring the knowledge that may help their country to stand on its own feet in substantial independence of both the United States and the Soviet Union.

Per capita expenditure on education runs from a low of one dollar per head per year in Haiti up to $7 in Argentina, $10 in Chile, and $35 in Venezuela. By contrast the United States spends $92 per capita per year on education.[13]

TECHNOLOGY AND AGRICULTURE. As was indicated in Chapter Ten, there has been a lag in the growth of agricultural production in Latin America in recent years. This may be due in some degree, as is claimed by the Economic Commission for Latin America, to the fact that, as technology progresses, raw materials have represented a falling fraction of the value of the finished product. But it may also be due in some significant degree to the limited technical improvement in Latin American agriculture in recent decades. There has been a major improvement in the technology of agriculture in the United States during the last few years (improvement in equipment, fertilizers, insecticides, seeds, land-use methods, farm administration, and so on). The improvement has been sufficiently pronounced to raise the question as to whether in international markets the comparative advantage of the United States may be in agricultural rather than in industrial products.

Latin American agriculture, especially Argentine agriculture, seems to have fallen behind in this race to assimilate technology into agriculture. Perhaps in part this has been due to overzealous effort to use raw commodity control schemes as the solution for the problems of agriculture.

There are agricultural experiment stations, such as that of the Inter-American Institute of Agricultural Sciences at Turrialba, Costa Rica, which represent a modest beginning in efforts to take advantage of the fantastic possibilities for improving the technology of tropical agriculture. And the Mexican government, in recent years, has shown awareness that land redistribution is not enough as a solution to the agricultural problem. A good deal of the international technical assistance of recent years has been in the field of agriculture. But there is a fertile field for additional work. And, interestingly, a good deal of the useful exchange may

---

[13] Center of Latin American Studies (U.C.L.A.), *Statistical Abstract of Latin America, 1962,* p. 28.

Resources

The third element in the model of the institutional theory was the appropriateness of the available raw material resources to the state of the technical knowledge.

In one way of looking at the matter, Latin America has been a wealthy region. First and last, over a billion dollars worth of silver has been taken out of the mines around Potosí in Bolivia. Mexico, Peru, and Bolivia are among the legendary mining countries of the world. In more recent decades the copper of northern Chile, the petroleum of Lake Maracaibo in Venezuela, and the iron ore of the Caroní River valley in eastern Venezuela and of the state of Minas Gerais in Brazil have shown that Latin American mineral resources are still significant. The region has also been the supplier of some of the chief commercial-agriculture products of the world: Brazilian coffee, Cuban sugar, Argentine wheat and beef, Central American bananas. And there is no particular reason to doubt that the region will have its share of the raw materials which the technical discoveries of the future will make important.

Of course one cannot know now with any exactness which raw materials will be the most important in the years to come. At any given time the material that makes up the earth is, in the conception of Erich Zimmermann, either neutral stuff (useless, at least in terms of the technical knowledge of the moment) or resource (currently valuable in terms of the industrial processes being used).

At any given period in the process of economic development, planning decisions can take into account only currently known processes and currently known resources. But new technical discoveries are continually making things that were neutral stuff into resources. Also new deposits of already valuable minerals are continually being discovered. Either of these two developments can alter the resource picture in a country and change the desirable industrial emphasis.

Use of current knowledge of resource availability is important in planning. But long-run, rigid plans should not be drawn up which assume technical knowledge and resources to be fixed and which then project development trends into the distant future on the basis of those assumptions. Rather the course is to utilize as effectively as possible such resources as the region has and to be thoughtful in discovering new resources and in adjusting to new methods.

Conclusion

Mass migration of technicians can transfer knowledge. The international movement of scholars on a major scale can transfer knowledge. The genuine will to assimilate knowledge can accomplish miracles. But the "making available" by one country of its sum of technical knowledge to another country (in a setting where static institutions ensure that nothing more happens) is going to accomplish very little.

The forces of technology have sufficient power to implement a significant industrialization and development in Latin America if the institutional barriers can be reasonably relaxed.

CHAPTER THIRTEEN

PLANNING

There were various, largely abortive, efforts to plan the development of manufacturing in Latin America during the nineteenth century. Protagonists of development during those times were Lucas Alamán in Mexico during the Santa Anna period, Limantour during the Díaz period, the Baron de Mauá in the mid-part of the nineteenth century in Brazil, and Alberdi in Argentina at about the same time. In spite of these forerunners it seems to be now customary to visualize the effort to plan economic development as a characteristic of the period since the end of World War II.

Economic development in Latin America is by now a much-advocated goal, if not a fetish. Given the recognition of the goal, it is not surprising that plans to realize it should be established and that a group of professional planners should appear on the scene.

First, a word may be said about the planning profession and its methods. The economics profession is now providing specialists who present themselves as economic development experts, no special certification being required. It is probably desirable to have a few economic development planners who have the world as their oyster. Such people have a useful, general perspective. And suggestions made in plans such as theirs, which are based on the knowledge the planner has acquired in many countries, can be valuable whether or not the plan is used as a whole.

But the best plan ever conceived is not going to be implemented effectively if the planner leaves for home on the first flight after the plan is submitted and if implementation is left to the gods and the local políticos. And yet frequently that is the only thing the planner can do with a good grace. The local politicians may well not want him hanging around. And since he has other fish to fry he is glad to leave.

Relatively few planners can play the grand role, however. Needed in much greater numbers are dedicated individuals who will live with particular countries or regions all of their professional careers. Such people need a composite sort of education such as our highly specialized university departments do not now give. They need a substantial amount of engineering, a substantial amount of foreign language, and a substantial amount of social science, especially economics. They simply cannot afford the five-year undergraduate programs in engineering (allowing almost no electives outside of engineering) that characterize most United States engineering degrees today. And they do not have much need for the price theory they pick up in many economics programs. They need some administrative competence such as may be acquired in some judiciously selected courses in business administration or public administration but is more probably picked up by a very few people in the school of hard knocks. They need some accounting, and some statistics, and a course on resources, such as Erich Zimmermann used to give.

Chiefly, of course, such economic development experts should be nationals of the country where the project is going on. But the universities of Latin America are generally unequipped to provide graduates of this type. And cooperation between Latin American and developed-country universities can make a contribution in developing appropriate programs, both in Latin America and in North America.

Also migrant technicians and economic development specialists from the United States, western Europe, and the Soviet Union can make a contribution (at least they can make one if they do not let their home-country politics interfere with their work). But to make an important contribution they need to live with a particular development project for a long period of years, if not for a professional lifetime. Especially since the politicians, who come and go, cannot provide real continuity in the implementation of plans, the providing of continuity becomes an important part of the role of the development specialist.

Planning Agencies

Plans may be drawn up at various levels of government (or by private enterprise) to cover various dimensions of geographical area and various periods of time. The chief levels at which plans may be drawn up would seem to be (1) the region within the nation, (2) the nation, (3) the bloc of several nations, such as Central America or Latin America, and (4) the world level. Also (5) the United States, or other outside nations, may participate in the planning of underdeveloped countries. There may be planning for the individual business firm or governmental unit. The annual budget of a governmental unit may be looked on as an annual plan; and most corporations plan ahead for their next production period.

The agencies at the various planning levels may combine a planning role with a plan-implementation role. The relative importance of the two activities varies considerably from agency to agency and country to country.

SUBNATIONAL REGIONAL AGENCIES. In a few cases there have been important organizations set up to plan for specific geographical regions. In Mexico the Papaloapan River valley in the southern part of the state of Vera Cruz is being planned as a unit. In Brazil the Superintendency for the Development of the Northeast (SUDENE) is trying to plan for and implement plans for the development of the poor and drought-plagued region back from Recife, Natal, and Bahia. In Colombia there is the Corporación de los Valles del Magdalena y del Sinú, which is responsible for much of Colombia's northern lowland. In Argentina there is the Instituto de Desarrollo del Valle Inferior del Río Negro, planning for the lower valley of the Río Negro.

Of course individual state and provincial governments are also, potentially if not actually, planning agencies of this type. But historically in Latin America they have not played a major role in development planning.

NATIONAL AGENCIES. Generally at the national level there are planning committees, perhaps called National Economic Councils, that are a combination of various cabinet ministers plus perhaps the heads of the central bank and one or two other agencies concerned with development. This organization may or may not be effective. Questions of personality are involved. The president of the country may pretty much go his own way (in which case there is probably no plan in a documentary sense) or there may be some particular cabinet minister who effectively dominates the planning process (as for example, from time to time, Alsogaray in Argentina).

Mexico has, since 1934, made use of a series of Six Year Plans, which have been prepared by the Partido de la Revolución Institucional as political platforms in connection with presidential elections. Many of the economic development economists have not been prepared to admit that the early Six Year Plans really constituted national planning in a professional sense. A planning bureau was set up in 1961 in the Office of the President, which is intended to plan in a professional and continuing manner. Most Latin American governments also have a Ministry of Economics, or of Development, or some such thing, which will play some role in development planning and in the implementation of development planning.

Then, since money is an important intermediary in the whole process, the various central banks will participate in activities connected with economic development. Also numerous special-purpose banks and development corporations have been set up. Such agencies include Nacional Financiera in Mexico and institutions called development (or *fomento*) corporations in many of the Latin American countries. Chile has perhaps the most famous fomento corporation in Latin America (Corporación de Fomento de la Producción).

The establishment of numerous governmental or government-sponsored banks and institutes to do development lending on a large scale is a fairly recent development. Most of the countries have such agencies now. Peru has a Banco Industrial. Chile has had an Instituto de Crédito Industrial. Venezuela has a Banco Industrial. Argentina has the Banco de la Nación and the Banco de Crédito Industrial Argentino.

In several Latin American countries the effort to coordinate the work of the domestic agency concerned with economic development with the contribution of foreign technicians has led to the organization of entities called *servicios* within a Latin American governmental department. The 1960 *Report* of the Mutual Security program (United States) defined a servicio as follows:

A servicio is a partnership arrangement between the aid-receiving government and ICA [AID] whereby an organization is created within a ministry of the host government (public health, agriculture, and so forth) to carry out projects mutually planned and agreed upon by ICA [AID] and host country personnel in a particular field. It is a joint operation to which each partner contributes skills and funds.[1]

The servicio approach has had the advantage of putting the foreign technicians to work side by side with their local counterparts. This should provide a setting that is conducive to technical interchange. And there would seem to be rather strong reason for believing that this is one of the more constructive approaches to the foreign aid problem. However, this approach seems to be in the process of deemphasis.[2]

MULTINATION REGIONAL AGENCIES. In Middle America there is an Organization of Central American States. It has as subsidiary agencies a Central American Free Trade Association and a Central American Bank for Economic Integration. These agencies implement, among other things, a General Treaty of Central American Economic Integration (1960). Guatemala, El Salvador, Honduras, Nicaragua, and Costa Rica (but not Panama) were members in 1964.

The basis for yet another framework of economic development planning agencies in Latin America seems, also, to have been established in the Treaty of Montevideo of 1960 establishing the Latin American Free Trade Association. The clauses in the Treaty that provide for the principle of complementarity create the possibility that the administrative branch of LAFTA, which has headquarters in Montevideo, may establish its own planning machinery to try to determine which nations will specialize in the expansion of which branches of production.

LAFTA is set up to be a hemisphere-wide organization, but at present (1964) only has some nine members—albeit the nine include the most important countries of the region.

INTER-AMERICAN LEVEL. At the hemisphere level there is an assortment of organizations, some associated with the Organization of American States and the Pan American Union, others associated with the United Nations.

Organization of American States. The Pan American Union, the secretariat of the OAS, contains both a Department of Economic and Social

---

[1] United States, Mutual Security Agency, *Report, 1960* (Washington, 1961), p. 36.
[2] John P. Powelson, *Latin America: Today's Economic and Social Revolution* (New York, McGraw-Hill, 1963), p. 229.

Affairs and a Department of Technical Cooperation. Also in the OAS framework is the Inter-American Economic and Social Council, a high-level consultative group to which has been delegated much of the responsibility for supervising the planning to be done under the Alliance for Progress—such of the responsibility as the United States government has been willing to delegate. However, whether the OAS could do an effective job even if it had more authority is open to question. It is not well known for the efficacy of its operations.

Inter-American Development Bank. Another inter-American agency, ostensibly affiliated with the OAS but actually more or less autonomous, is the Inter-American Development Bank (IDB), located in Washington and headed by a Chilean, Felipe Herrera. It helps with development planning in the various Latin American countries, and makes three different types of loans. (1) It can make loans to support projects that are likely to be reasonably profitable. Such loans will be comparable in risk, maturity, and interest rate to ordinary commercial lending. (2) Low-interest-rate loans to finance infrastructure may be handled by the Bank's Fund for Special Operations. Maturities might be of the order of forty or fifty years and interest rates be 1 or 2 percent. (3) Also, in 1961, the United States government turned over to the so-called Social Progress Trust Fund (to be administered by the Bank) a sum of $394 million to be used for low-interest-rate loans to support infrastructure and social overhead operations involving (a) land settlement and improved land use, (b) low-income housing, (c) community water and sanitation facilities, and (d) education. The Bank has, so far as an outsider can judge, proceeded energetically with efforts to use these funds effectively.

Economic Commission for Latin America. Also at the inter-American level is the Economic Commission for Latin America, a United Nations agency with headquarters in Santiago, Chile, which was headed for many years by an Argentine, Raúl Prebisch, and has been headed since 1963 by José Antonio Mayobre of Venezuela. This Commission has been an industrious and imaginative force on the Latin American scene since the late 1940s.

Latin American Institute for Economic and Social Planning. In July of 1962, under the joint sponsorship of the Economic Commission for Latin America, the Inter-American Development Bank, and the United Nations Special Fund, there was established a Latin American Institute for Economic and Social Planning, also in Santiago. It is to specialize in the training of development planners and in the formulation of planning techniques.

WORLD-LEVEL AND UNITED STATES AGENCIES. It is impossible to do justice here to the lengthy catalog of agencies associated with the United Nations and the United States government, which have had something to do with the planning of Latin American economic development.

The Plan

What is a plan, actually? The answer is not as unambiguous as might be desirable, either as to what goes into a plan or as to what should go into one. (1) Is it merely a description, a prediction, of what is going to happen in any event? (2) Is it a description of that which it would be nice to have happen, containing no sanctions, except an appeal to sweet reason, to cause it to happen? (3) Is it a program for private enterprise that a government will try to enforce by various indirect coercions? (4) Is it a set of principles describing the policy tools to use in the event any one of various possible difficulties arises? (5) Is it an indication as to what the government plans to do about social overhead, infrastructure, and socialized enterprise, without regard to the role of private enterprise? (6) Is it a blueprint for a whole economy (public sector plus private sector) backed by a whole range of measures to ensure its implementation? (7) Is it the brainstorm of an economic planner, which will be appropriately filed?

Is it something drafted by nongovernmental experts, by governmental experts, by cooperative action by government and private enterprise, or by a university professor who has temporarily abandoned his classes? Or is it some permutation or combination of these possibilities?

The climate for implementation will probably be more propitious if the plan is in some important sense the joint work of the government, of business, of labor, and of the general public. (Such cooperation seems to have worked well in France in recent years.) In Latin America the role of trade associations and labor unions is formalized in such a way that those organizations are readily available for consultation. But a substantial measure of the will to compromise is necessary on all sides if such cooperation is to work. Whether there is much "will to compromise" in Latin America is by no means clear. Nor is it clear that arrangements to bring private enterprise and labor into consultation with the government can necessarily be counted on to safeguard the consumer and public interest in more goods at lower prices.

The Economic Commission for Latin America has been one of the foremost exponents of development planning of a comprehensive and obligatory type. And presumably this will be the orientation of the Latin American Institute for Economic and Social Planning. The basic reference on the position of ECLA with regard to planning procedures is *An Introduction to the Technique of Programming,* which was prepared by ECLA and published in 1955. The position has been elaborated with considerable care in subsequent publications.[3]

PLANNING MODELS. *Macrovariable Model.* It may be worthwhile to present a hypothetical growth model for Latin America using the basic macroeconomic relations that have been used by the Economic Commission for Latin America. As a starting point, the desirability of a 5 percent per annum growth rate (real gross domestic product) may be assumed. This is the basic target of the United Nations Development Decade, and it was used by Raúl Prebisch and his planning group in preparing for the United Nations Conference on Trade and Development in the spring of 1964. The figure is quite close to the 2.5 percent increase in real *per capita* income assumed to be desirable in Alliance for Progress planning (since population is growing at about 2.8 percent per year). The model worked out by the Prebisch group described the situation for all of the underdeveloped, or developing, countries.[4] To illustrate what this sort of model would mean for Latin America alone, it may not do too great violence to the model (which is a very rough thing anyway) to recompute it for Latin America, assuming that the same structural relations apply to Latin America as apply to underdeveloped countries generally.

The rough estimate is made that Latin American gross domestic

[3] United Nations, Economic Commission for Latin America, *Analyses and Projections of Economic Development, I, An Introduction to the Technique of Programming* (New York, 1955); *see also,* United Nations, Economic Commission for Latin America, *Economic Development Planning and International Co-operation* (Santiago, Chile, 1961).
[4] United Nations, *World Economic Survey, 1962, 1, The Developing Countries in World Trade* (New York, 1963), pp. 5–9.

product was $60 billion in 1959 and, assuming the 5 percent growth rate, ought to be $102.6 billion in 1970 (at 1959 prices); so:

	1959	1970
1. Gross domestic product	$60	102.6

Next, it is assumed that the ratio of capital to GDP needs to correspond with the ratio that prevailed between 1950–59. As a result of these relations, gross domestic fixed capital formation becomes:

2. Gross domestic fixed capital formation	9.4	17.4

It is, then, assumed that imports are a constant percentage of GDP, and exports are a constant percentage of the GDP of the rest of the world. And the rest of the world is only growing at a rate of 3.7 percent per year. Consequently the following trade patterns would prevail:

3. Commodity imports	7.0	13.7
4. Commodity exports	6.7	9.7
5. Payments for investment income and other services (net)	1.3	2.7

These relations leave an international balance of payments gap (rows 3 and 5 minus row 4) of:

6. Gap on current account	1.6	6.7

In 1959, $1.6 billion of foreign investment filled the gap. In 1970, $6.7 billion will be needed.

Too much weight should not be given to the individual figures. The original United Nations model has been modified and simplified almost beyond recognition. And the allegation that Latin American gross domestic product in 1959 was $60 billion is rather arbitrary, although roughly within the realm of possibility. But the model should serve the purpose of indicating how the macroeconomic variables are assumed to interact on each other in rather constant predictable manners.

One cannot judge before 1970 the accuracy of these projections. He can speculate that their accuracy may not be great but also believe that exercises of this sort have some degree of usefulness. If the exercise does nothing more than suggest better analytical methods, it is not entirely a waste of time. But some measure of check on the accuracy of a model of this type may be made by looking at a set of estimates made in 1950.[5] It was assumed to be desirable to raise real per capita income by 2 percent annually. It was assumed that the population of Latin America would grow at a rate of 2.25 percent per year. Some assumptions about capital/output ratios permitted an estimate of annual new capital requirements in industry and agriculture of $2,540 million. Domestic voluntary saving in Latin America was estimated to run about $1,990 million a year. (The procedure in the 1950 model was not quite the same as in the 1962 model.) Using this figure, a residual, to be provided by foreign investment, was estimated at $550 million.

We have some information as to how far off some of these estimates were. For example, Latin American population has grown at a rate of about 2.8 percent per year. So the estimate of population growth was off by 0.55 percentage points, or about 24 percent. Note, in addition, the considerable difference between the 1950 and the 1962 estimates of capital requirements and of the size of the gap to be filled by foreign investment.

The insertion of foreign investment into such models as a residual creates various problems. (It will be alleged in Chapter Fifteen that there are grounds for not handling foreign investment in this way.)

Also it should be noted that it is a quite different thing (1) to assume a particular growth rate as a starting point and then to make all the rest of the model conform (2) from testing several different possible growth rates in order to see which growth rate can be implemented. Surely the latter is better procedure. And yet it has been rather common to start the analytical process with the arbitrary assumption as to the desirable rate of growth.

Several of the economic development plans that have been drawn up in recent years are roughly of the same sort as the plans described above. This is, for example, true of Mexico's Plan for Immediate Action, 1963–65 and of that country's Long-Term Plan, 1965–70. In the Mexican plans, the residual assigned to foreign investment seems to be about 10 percent.[6]

The foregoing planning techniques are oriented primarily to the manipulation of national income variables and hinge on the assumption of a constant capital coefficient (capital/output ratio). Other planning tech-

---

[5] United Nations, *Measures for the Economic Development of Underdeveloped Countries* (New York, 1951), p. 76.

[6] *Review of the Economic Situation of Mexico* (Banco Nacional de México), February, 1963, pp. 5–9.

PLANNING   199

niques exist and have been used extensively by the Economic Commission for Latin America and by various Latin American governments: input-output matrices, linear programming, and so on.

Input-Output Matrix Model. The Economic Commission for Latin America has been encouraging the various national governments to make use of input-output matrices as a planning technique.

Input-output matrices can be set up to describe the relative proportions of different resources (inputs) needed in producing goods. Generally this is done in a setting where the state of technology is assumed as given and the current state of relative resource prices is also given. The input-output tables have many columns and rows for each of the industries or sectors of the economy. The figures included in the boxes (column-row intersections) estimate the inputs that a given industry receives from some other industry or, looked at the other way around, describe how the output of a given industry is distributed to some other industry.

An example of a matrix is given in Table 10. Columns 11, 12 and

Table 10

Industry producing	Industry purchasing	
	11. Petroleum and coal	12. Rubber products
11. Petroleum and coal	4,829	12
12. Rubber products	1	41

Source: Division of Interindustry Economics of the Bureau of Labor Statistics.

rows 11, 12 are taken from the "Interindustry Flow of Goods and Services by Industry of Origin and Destination, 1947." Data are for the United States and in millions of dollars. One of the things the table says is that in 1947 the rubber products industry purchased $12 million of materials from the petroleum and coal industries and the petroleum and coal industries purchased $4,829 million from themselves.

If the planner assumes that the technology of the rubber products industry (or of any industry) requires a constant percentage of petroleum and coal per unit of output, it would be said that the industry has constant technical coefficients. On such assumptions all sorts of projections into the distant future can be made describing the various quantities of outputs of other industries that will be used as inputs by given industries, as different industries develop—perhaps at different rates. But much of the usefulness for long-run planning goes out of the input-output models if the technical coefficients are not constants. And since changing technology is an important feature of long-run growth, the assumption that they are constant would seem to be dubious.

This is not to say that input-output models are useless. Once some priorities have been assigned to different industries, they can be used as a check on whether the development plan is making full use of the available resources. And, in connection with day-to-day decision making, it can be useful for the official to have an input-output matrix in front of him. He can visualize his economy better.[7]

Linear Programming. Linear programming is a decision-making process that works somewhat as follows. If the planner has certain pieces of information (perhaps as to various elements of cost and as to resource availability) and knows what he wants to maximize (perhaps profits or national income), linear programming provides a mathematical method for describing the desirable productive process.[8]

If linear programming had a real usefulness in economic development planning, it would be in connection with the assigning of priorities to economic development projects. But actually the priority problems seem, at least at present, to be a little too complicated and a little too subjective for linear programming to handle usefully without the assistance of human judgment.

Linear programming is a technique for decision making that has some important usefulness at the level involved in the determination of the quantity of a product to be produced in a given plant during the next production period. If the costs of raw materials and of labor are known or assumed and if the selling price can be assumed with reasonable accuracy (and similar bits of information are predetermined) for the individual firm, it is possible to use linear programming techniques to determine such things as the most profitable level of production. By

---

[7] Underdeveloped countries are a long way from having statistical data adequate for preparing the tables. But some of the raw material is increasingly available. *See,* for example, "Projection of Demand for Industrial Equipment," in *Industrialization and Productivity,* Bulletin 7, 1964, pp. 7–24.

[8] H. H. Liebhafsky, *The Nature of Price Theory* (Homewood, Illinois, Dorsey Press, 1963), chap. 17.

and large such information is not predetermined for a whole nation and the usefulness of linear programming as a technique for planning the nation's development is correspondingly limited.

THE PLANNING PROBLEM. A conception of planning as appropriately involving a rather meticulous government effort to plan the economy down to small details seems to be more accepted in Latin America than in the United States. And to the extent that development planners sell this bill of goods in Latin America, they are selling some merchandise abroad that they could not sell at home. Why is it that the land of Don Quixote has an affinity for the comprehensive, compulsory plan? It might be said that the Germans do not need a plan to regiment an economy and that the Latins cannot regiment an economy with a plan. (This may be more of a compliment to the Latins than to the Germans.)

Although it is difficult and probably undesirable to implement long-run development plans with precision this does not necessarily mean that it is a complete waste of effort to draw them up. But if one insists on drawing them up and also insists on looking on such plans as action plans, then it is necessary, as a matter of good administration, to clarify and radically modify the procedures generally used. It is procedurally impossible to draw up a ten-year plan (using the best input-output and linear programming procedures) that will accurately describe either what will happen or what should happen over the next ten years. For example, in estimating the future size of the market, a good deal more may be involved than just projecting the existing trend. There is the important uncertainty as to whether access to foreign markets will be freer. (How effective will the Latin American Free Trade Association be five years from now?) Rational solution is not helped by assuming a closed economy, even though such an assumption might make the planner's job easier.

Perhaps the plan can be (and even should be) fairly definite in terms of what it says about the first year of the ten-year period—at least so far as the public sector of the economy is concerned. What is said about the private sector should probably be visualized as persuasive, rather than obligatory. But the role of the planning for the other nine years in the original plan should be considered as being useful only because some rough general and tentative perspective about the future is desirable. Then toward the end of the first year a new ten-year plan might be elaborated (covering through the eleventh year from the inception of the procedure). Using computers, such reformulation of plans could become a fairly routine operation. And significant policy changes could be incorporated each year. But again, only the first year of the new plan would be thought of as an action plan in any meaningful sense. And so on.

What appropriately should go into an economic development plan to make it useful rather than an impossible strait jacket?

There need to be some rather general judgments about emphasis. These are not readily quantifiable as exact sums of money. And thus they do not fit the conception of a plan embraced by many planners. Nevertheless they involve the sort of thing which is discussed in the remainder of this book.

Also some of the most important aspects of planning consist of having a kit of tools (changes in government fiscal policy, changes in monetary policy, changes in antitrust policy, changes in other things) and having an idea as to the appropriate direction to manipulate a particular tool when a particular problem arises. A conception as to the appropriate direction in which to use a policy tool is a type of decision that needs to be coordinated with the decisions other governments are making in dealing with the ever-changing array of problems with which they are confronted. There does need to be international coordination of the policy pattern.[9]

The use of a kit of policy tools of this sort to meet problems as they arise is not what most economic development planners mean by planning. But just possibly the planners are wrong in assuming that the comprehensive, binding plan is the ideal plan. Maybe the essence of planning is the reservoir of tools and knowledge that permits adequate confrontation of problems as they arise plus the ability to decide what to do next, for example, which industry to establish next and where—the complementarity problem juxtaposed with the optimum use of resources problem.

UNPROGRAMMED PLANNING. Some of the chief elements to be taken into account in the sort of "unprogrammed economic development encouragement" which is recommended here may be the following:

[9] I have tried to elaborate the meaning of such a policy pattern in the last chapter of my *International Trade: Goods, People, and Ideas* (New York, Knopf, 1958), chap. 36.

(1) Resource allocation or reallocation is the primary problem. The assumption should be that all resources should be used with reasonable efficacy. (This is not necessarily the "efficiency" of modern price theory.) And there will be substantial emphasis on increasing productivity as a major worthwhile effort. Actually, of course, so far as resource allocation is concerned, how most of a country's resources will be used has been predetermined by how they were used last year. So, planning in terms of resource allocation can concentrate on the changes in resource allocation that it is desirable to make currently. It can concentrate on drawing productive resources from the least productive occupations and attempting to apply them in sectors that have more potential, without illusion that a perfect theoretical optimum is about to be realized.

What is involved is the "more effective" mobilization of the "least effectively used" resources. In Latin America this means having a Minister of Economics or a Minister of Fomento with a knack for taking large numbers of the underemployed of the large cities and putting them to work doing something at least slightly more productive than the things they have been doing. It means bank financial support for private businessmen who will put people to work at slightly higher real salaries and doing slightly more productive things than they have been doing. The Minister of Economics, the banker, and the businessman need to develop an experienced eye for identifying underemployed resources and the potential for more effective use. As a starter, there is little reason a Latin American city should have dirt or filth in the streets, or uncollected garbage. Given the state of the manpower situation, all that this particular improvement in the level of living requires is a modest investment in brooms and scoops and the use of some army mobile equipment that is being underutilized anyway. Tegucigalpa, Honduras, could do itself considerable good very easily.

The knack for mobilizing available resources is important. This means the local leaders must be able to see a locally available stock of building material or some other resource that can be readily and inexpensively used as the base for the more productive use of manpower.

Not only is much local resource that might be used in production allowed to remain idle, but also there are all too many examples of resources which in past decades have been used productively but which have fallen into disuse. Latin America has abdicated its primacy in many lines of production. Brazilian rubber and Ecuadorean quinine and cacao are examples. It has let industries with prospects for expansion languish. The handicrafts of all the countries from Mexico to Chile, Argentine beef, and Brazilian coffee are examples. The methods the Latin Americans have chosen to use in such matters as the efforts to protect the price of coffee have generally been at the expense of the share of the market of the most efficient producer, which is to say Brazil.

In addition to concentrating on the mechanics of moving resources to more effective uses, the plan should do the following things:

(2) It should contain provisions for the implementation of the assimilation of new technical knowledge;

(3) There should be suggestions as to methods for removing or circumventing obvious institutional barriers to development;

(4) There should be consideration as to how the mobility of people, intellectual knowledge, and goods can be increased; and

(5) Measures for increasing productivity (as distinct from measures for increasing production) should be handled as though they were serious, top-priority problems.

(6) The complementarity question involves the decision as to which region or country will develop which industry. This is a touchy and difficult subject in Latin America, where some twenty independent countries are talking about coordinating their development efforts. But surely, if complementarity were really to be planned, a group decision would have to be made as to which countries would get which industries before any development occurred. But these are the 1960s; a lot of industries have already been set up in a lot of countries; and it is rather difficult to turn the clock back. On top of that, several countries are hurrying to establish certain industries so that, when the time comes for the group decisions on complementarity, they can say that they already have such and such an industry as a *fait accompli*. (To single out only one example among many, Peru is currently, 1964, busy doing this with an automobile industry in a setting where there are probably already too many different automobile-manufacturing firms in Latin America.)

Price theory has some explanations as to how decisions on complementarity are made. But in the oligopolistic real world, the Latin American countries are not going to leave decision making in this area entirely to the impersonal forces of a nonexistent, competitive market. Nevertheless, unless the really important complementarity questions are going to be predetermined by a series of faits accomplis (as many of them have already been, the Latin American countries need to get together with some speed to determine the rules that will determine which country can establish which industry next.

That this is the actual intent of at least some of the Latin American countries is indicated by the following statement from the program of the Mexican Partido de la Revolución Institucional:

> We should conceive of the Latin American economy as a planned economy. It would be inconsistent to practise duplication and waste of resources. The basic meaning of the Free Trade Zone is to procure a complementary interchange which favors a harmonious industrial development for the region.[10]

(7) Rather than a lot of ten-year development plans, what Latin America needs is a set of several hundred industry studies, one study to the industry. The study should contain the basic information the planner needs to apply to his local conditions in deciding whether or not to establish a particular industry. The studies should describe the basic nature of the industry, the cost patterns involved in the alternative production processes, the relation between raw material cost and value added, the importance of being close to raw materials in relation to the importance of being close to the market, identification of the optimum plant size and discussion of the "inefficiency cost" of a plant size other than the optimum, labor and capital requirements per unit of output, needs in terms of skilled labor and special purpose machinery, what to look for in determining whether a particular industry is appropriate in a particular region.

Considering the large number of feasibility studies that have been made in recent years concerning the appropriateness of establishing particular new companies in particular places, it is amazing that such studies generally start from scratch and determine and identify *de novo* the crucial variables to take into account.

The United Nations, with its publication *Industrialization and Productivity,* has tried to deal with the problem of providing the sort of basic data on the industry which planners need. But we are here dealing with a massive and important problem, and it is about time some order was brought out of the chaos that is the methodology of the "industry study."

[10] *Trimestre Económico,* January, 1964, p. 147.

The Agency for International Development could make a really useful contribution to development by sponsoring a series of several hundred industry studies, each of which would contain the array of information mentioned above. Perhaps if such information were available it would be a little less likely that countries in planning development would insist on planning for industries (a) for which they have to import most of the raw materials, (b) for which a plant of optimum size is not feasible in the near future, and (c) which do not fill an immediate level-of-living need.[11]

The Alliance for Progress

Various people and nations have tried to capture sponsorship of (and perhaps also credit for) Latin American industrialization, and they have wanted to call the program by their chosen names. President Kubitschek of Brazil took an initiative in the late 1950s and called the program Operation Pan America. (When the Kennedy administration took over sponsorship in 1961, it chose to use the term Alliance for Progress.)

Operation Pan America was a proposal made in 1958 by the government of Brazil for planning, or at least consulting about, economic development in the Americas, which used the Organization of American States as the instrument. A series of conferences, culminating in one in Bogotá in the fall of 1960, discussed these plans. The result of the latter conference was the Act of Bogotá recommending "Measures for Social Improvement and Economic Development within the Framework of Operation Pan America." The chief financial measure taken at that time was an agreement by the Eisenhower Administration to put a substantial sum of money into a Special Inter-American Fund for Social Development to be administered in large part by the Inter-American Development Bank. Measures for land reform, improved housing, education, and public health, as well as tax reform, were envisaged. Following the Bay of Pigs episode in the spring of 1961, the Kennedy Administration put some $500 million into this dormant Fund; and the Inter-American Development Bank has been proceeding with the use of the $394 million

---

[11] As Central America plans its economic development many of the industries under consideration seem to have various of these objectionable features. *See,* United Nations, *Posibilidades de Desarrollo Industrial Integrado en Centroamérica* (New York, 1963).

which went specifically into its Social Progress Trust Fund. (Of the balance of the $500 million, $100 million was turned over to the Agency for International Development and $6 million was turned over to the Organization of American States.)

But even before this implementation of Operation Pan America, the Kennedy Administration was calling its Latin American program the Alliance for Progress and had taken over, as its own, the ideas for internal social and economic reform (land reform, tax reform, and so on). The Alliance for Progress became an inter-American program, as distinct from a purely United States program, by its adoption at a conference in Punta del Este, Uruguay, in August of 1961.

FINANCING. The Alliance for Progress, as set up at Punta del Este, involved a general commitment to social and economic reform on the part of the Latin American countries plus a commitment (the term commitment may be too strong) on their part to contribute some $80 billion to their own development over the following ten years. For its part the United States seems to have promised that foreign resources to the extent of $20 billion would be provided during the same ten-year period. It is hard to be sure how much has been effectively formalized in terms of the shares of the $20 billion. But apparently, of the $2 billion a year of foreign resources to be provided, the breakdown was supposed to be as follows:

	Million dollars
United States government	$1,100
United States private investors	300
International agencies	300
European public and private investment	300

That there was no one at Punta del Este authorized to commit the international agencies or the European public and private investors seems not to have been a major issue at the time.

The drafters of the program left vague the extent to which the program merely incorporated what was already going on and the extent to which it was a genuinely expanded program. For example, in 1960 United States (public and private) aid and new investment totaled $931 million by comparison with the $1.4 billion envisaged for the Alliance. And in

1957 (to pick an atypical year) private United States investment alone in Latin America was about $1.4 billion. Thus, whether these figures were to be brought up to the indicated levels or whether the whole $2 billion was to be additional by comparison with what had been was not a trivial question.

It seems that aid in the amounts tentatively called for has not actually been provided, even if one subscribes to the more conservative of the two possibilities. According to the Department of Commerce, United States government net foreign assistance to Latin America (including grants and credits but excluding military supplies and services) amounted to $700 million in 1961 and to $600 million in 1962. It is a bit difficult to look at the foreign aid legislation itself and combine its provisions with the actions of agencies such as the Export-Import Bank and tell how much United States aid to Latin America is properly attributable to the Alliance. It seems that accounts are not specifically kept describing the performance of the Alliance as such. Maybe no one really wants to keep them.

What about the contribution the Latin American countries themselves are supposed to be putting into the program? No specific figure seems to have been stated in the Punta del Este Charter. But it has been frequently said in the press that the over-all ten-year program was conceived as a $100 billion operation. If there is tentative agreement of this sort it would mean $80 billion (or $8 billion a year) of domestic self-help to correspond with the $20 billion of foreign aid. But the ambiguities here are as great as those involved in interpreting the foreign commitment.

One might make a case that the Latin American countries have all along been contributing more than $8 billion a year. The macro model presented earlier in the chapter estimated $9.4 billion in 1959. So, if $8 billion a year is envisaged as the amount that Latin American countries are going to put into economic development during the decade of the sixties, that commitment seems to be met automatically. But this is mere conjecture. What the Declaration formally says is merely that the Latin American countries are to "devote a steadily increasing share of their own resources to economic and social development," and each country is to "formulate a comprehensive and well-conceived national program for the development of its own economy." And this brings us to the connection of the Alliance for Progress with planning.

PLANNING. Specifically, what of these national programs? The Charter says that each country "should formulate, if possible within the next eighteen months, long-term development programs." The plans were then to be submitted to a subcommittee of "nine wise men" appointed by the Organization of American States and the Inter-American Development Bank, and operating under the Inter-American Economic and Social Council. Presumably an accepted plan would then be the basis for the receipt of Alliance for Progress aid during a decade that may or may not have started in August of 1961, and even though nobody in particular had an obligation to provide all the funds which the country was authorized to receive. The approval of the plan might be looked on as something similar to the granting of a hunting license.

There have been delays in the submission of the plans. By the end of 1963, two years after the Punta del Este conference, only Chile, Colombia, Venezuela, Honduras, Mexico, Ecuador, and Bolivia had actually submitted plans.

There have been various difficulties. A country wants to ask for as much foreign aid as it can get away with, while having its domestic policy strait-jacketed as little as possible. It needs to contract for some social reform, but how much? It will probably prefer to step on the institutional toes that will complain the least. Thus it is not really strange that many countries are lagging in preparing their plans. They want to be sure which way and how strongly various winds are blowing.

Some of the Latin American countries want to avoid preparing the plans at all if they can get by without. The first thing Fernando Belaúnde Terry did after being inaugurated as President of Peru in July, 1963, was to call for "a sense of urgency" in the Alliance for Progress. He then alleged that there may not be time for "detailed studies" before the "financial rescue operations" are needed. He said: "When a ship is sinking, it sends out an SOS and it is necessary to come to its aid." [12] How good the sinking ship analogy is might be questioned. But, whether good or not, it seems to be inconsistent with the planning approach endorsed by the Alliance for Progress.

A good deal is involved in the preparation of these plans. What standards should apply?

We might use the Chilean Ten-Year Plan as a whipping boy. The "nine wise men" appointed Flavian Levine and Felipe Pazos (the former

---

[12] The Houston *Post,* July 29, 1963.

a Chilean and the latter a former Cuban central banker) to evaluate the plan. One might wonder at the propriety of having a Chilean judge the Chilean plan if questions of complementarity and priority are involved. At any rate the two referees endorsed the plan, and it consequently became the officially accepted vehicle for describing the pattern of Alliance for Progress operations in relation to Chile—as of October, 1962. The Plan called for $10 billion to be devoted to Chilean development in the succeeding ten years. This was a nice round number, which was never regurgitated by a computer mulling over an input-output matrix; $10 billion over ten years makes $1 billion a year. Almost in keeping (but shading it a little), it was provided that Chile should carry a little less than 80 percent of the cost and foreign aid a little more than 20 percent—$253 million a year during the 1963–65 period and $200 million a year thereafter. It would be silly to ask less than the norm.

But one might ask the additional question, how does $2,159 million of foreign aid for Chile during the ten years fit in with the $20 billion for all Latin America in ten years. Chile has a higher standard of living than most of Latin America. Should that entitle her to more or less than the average amount of aid?

The Charter said:

Similarly, presently existing differences in income levels among the Latin American countries will be reduced by accelerating the development of the relatively less developed countries and granting them maximum priority in the distribution of resources and in international cooperation in general. In evaluating the degree of relative development, account will be taken not only of average levels of real income and gross product per capita, but also of indices of infant mortality, illiteracy, and per capita daily caloric intake.[13]

Chile's population of perhaps 7,627,000 would seem to be slightly under 4 percent of a Latin American population of 200 million. For Chile to claim over 10 percent of the total Alliance for Progress foreign aid funds would seem to be a bit excessive, in view of Chile's relatively high standard of living. For the "nine wise men" to permit Chile to stake a claim to over 10 percent of the foreign aid would seem to indicate

---

[13] Pan American Union, *Alliance for Progress, Official Documents Emanating from the Special Meeting of the Inter-American Economic and Social Council at the Ministerial Level* (Washington, 1961), p. 10.

that the integrating agency did not feel authorized to evaluate one country's plan in terms of the total picture. Odd!

The plans of other countries have followed the Chilean precedent and called for more than proportional shares of the amount of foreign aid that ostensibly would be available.

The effects of this behavior, however, were not to exhaust a meager kitty before its time. There was no kitty. But as a precedent for hemisphere-wide planning, the operation left a good deal to be desired.

REFORM. In addition to preparing acceptable development plans as a basis for receiving Alliance for Progress aid, the Latin American countries were supposed to adopt substantial programs of social and economic reform. They might revise their tax structure to make it more progressive or proceed with a vigorous land reform. In the appraisal of these reforms somewhat the same problems arose as came up in evaluating the development plans. Who was to decide whether the reform program was adequate, an inter-American agency or the United States government?

MODIFICATION. It seems to have been the feeling of dissatisfaction with these arrangements that led in 1963 to the establishment of a new agency with general supervisory powers over the Alliance for Progress. This was the Inter-American Committee for the Alliance for Progress of which a Colombian, Carlos Sanz de Santamaría, became the head. It is difficult to tell whether the important difficulties have been resolved. The Latin Americans hoped that the new Inter-American Committee for the Alliance for Progress would become the effective vehicle for making decisions. It may be that all the Latin Americans got was a new organization with the same old circumscribed powers. The chief thing the Alliance for Progress seems to have called up is a group of right-wing and military revolutions as a consequence of the efforts of the oligarchy to defend the status quo.

An additional complication was introduced into an already complicated picture in the spring of 1964 by the nature of the foreign aid request which the Washington administration presented to Congress. Two thirds of the requested $3.4 billion of foreign aid was to go to six countries, two of them (Chile and Colombia) being Latin American. It was indicated that the grounds for selecting them were that they had been outstanding in planning and in implementing internal adjustments to make maximum use of available aid. This modified approach to foreign aid might be called the showpiece approach.

There is a good deal to be said for rewarding effective performance. But for this approach to command respect, the criteria used in judging performance need to be unambiguous, reasonable, and objective. The criteria that would single Chile and Colombia out for favored treatment are, so far as this writer is aware, ambiguous and fuzzy. It might as well have been argued that Chile, already a high-standard-of-living country (relative to the rest of Latin America) and being plagued by inflation (as evidence of poor planning), should have been barred from aid. The inclusion of both Pakistan and India in the group of six countries to receive two thirds of the total aid (the other two being Nigeria and Turkey) smells mightily of pure politics rather than of objective economic-performance criteria.

A good deal more thought needs to be given to the implications of objective criteria for assigning shares of foreign aid.[14]

General Comment

Highly centralized, detailed planning, even if desirable, requires a good deal more information and raw statistical data than any of the Latin American countries currently have at their disposal. The plans the region is trying to gestate at the behest of the Alliance for Progress are too detailed and comprehensive.

What is really needed in the planning models are some basic decisions as to which countries will specialize in which industries (the complementarity question), agreement on a few general principles to control long-run behavior and assure policy coordination, plus careful appraisal and reappraisal every year as to specifically what will be done next. Despite all the talk about planning in general and complementarity in particular, there has been no orderly effort to assign areas of specialization to the different countries.

[14] The author has speculated on this problem in "Foreign Aid," *Inter-American Economic Affairs,* 16 (Spring, 1963), pp. 21–30.

CHAPTER FOURTEEN

CAPITAL FORMATION: DOMESTIC

Robert Redfield has described a process by which capital funds have been stored in certain Indian cultures.[1] In the Indian communities of Quintana Roo and Chan Kom, wealth has been stored in the form of gold chains worn by the women. In terms of saving-investment relations this manifestation might be said to mean that real saving (or the potential for real saving) was dissipated in the production of a form of "real" capital that was incapable of reproducing further goods.

It has been true that the Indians of the New World have in general accumulated little capital goods on their own initiative. The irrigation systems of the Incas in Peru and the floating gardens of Xochimilco near Mexico City might be considered exceptions to this statement. But this failure to accumulate capital might be better visualized as a consequence of technological backwardness than as a consequence of lack of saving potential.

The conquest of Latin America by a relatively small number of Spaniards and Portuguese was possible because Europe was technically more advanced than was Indian America, at least with regard to militarily useful equipment. Spain and Portugal did bring a certain amount of machinery (not a great deal) and some technical knowledge to the New World. To the extent that they brought these things, they brought the actual capital that served as the basis for the development of the mining industry in the New World. But the conquerors were more interested in exploiting than in improving technical knowledge or increasing the quan-

[1] *The Folk Culture of Yucatan* (Chicago, University of Chicago Press, 1941), p. 165.

tity of capital goods. The amount of actual capital equipment used in exploiting the mines in the New World was kept at a minimum, and the techniques used in those mines, although they were quite advanced in the fifteenth century when originally introduced, were obsolete relative to British techniques in the seventeenth and eighteenth centuries.

In the use of available technical knowledge, the mining industry in Latin America fell behind the rest of the world during the latter part of the colonial period, and the accumulation of capital goods did not keep pace with the accelerated tempo of accumulation in western Europe, especially in England.

In view of the fact that, under capitalism, the accumulation or creation of capital funds is necessary before capital goods can be made available for production, it becomes appropriate to inquire where such capital funds as did exist in colonial Latin America came from. For the most part, during the colonial period, neither capital funds nor capital goods came from Spain or Portugal. In fact the net movement of funds was in the opposite direction. The wealth of gold and silver mined in the New World furnished not only most of the "funds" used in the New World but also "funds" for export to Europe.

Funds for the development of mining and for the meager amount of industrialization that developed in Latin America in the colonial period were generated in Latin America. And the equipment for the most part was made in the New World—using such technical knowledge as the Spaniards had brought with them.

When the gachupines left the New World to return to Spain in the early part of the nineteenth century they took most of the available liquid funds along with them. Independence, therefore, found Latin America endowed with little capital equipment worth having, with little internal liquid capital or funds, and with no status at all in the international money markets. Such funds as were available were largely in the possession of the Catholic Church and to a lesser extent in the possession of the landowners. And both of those groups were interested in using such resources as they had to acquire additional land. And as the society repeatedly used such liquid funds as it had to buy land (or mortgages), the market value of land rose above its economic value.

This preference for land (over manufacturing facilities) seems to have been due primarily to institutional (status and social) considerations and not, as John Maynard Keynes alleged, to "a high interest-rate on mortgages." [2]

Basic Sources of Capital Funds

DOMESTIC PRIVATE SAVING. *Individual.* In the literature on economic development, over and over, one finds statements such as this by the Banco Nacional de México: "Mexico's internal savings are insufficient for its capital needs: she must recur to foreign capital." [3] Such an allegation ought to suggest at least two questions. Is domestic saving really deficient in the underdeveloped countries? And the second question would be: Can foreign capital effectively fill the deficiency if there is a deficiency? Up to now, the generally accepted view has been that domestic savings are the difficulty and that foreign investment can fill the gap. It may well be that both the pessimism and the optimism have been misplaced.

There is increasing evidence that lack of the potential for domestic saving has not been the factor holding back development in the Latin American countries. There is considerable reason to believe that significant amounts of actual or potential domestic savings in the underdeveloped countries have gone (1) into land and mortgages, (2) into the construction of imposing public buildings and churches, (3) into foreign balances, and (4) into the expense of rearing people who do not live very long. Also, (5) there has been a good deal of ostentatious spending and living which could have provided savings.

Contrary to what was just said, it has been argued that the use of funds to buy land cannot actually absorb saving because the funds continue to exist in the possession of the seller of the land, and the analysis needs to be pursued to determine how he and subsequent owners of the funds use them. The land purchase was merely an intermediary in a process rather than being the final resting place of the saved funds.

It is probably true that in a general-equilibrium world, where money is neutral in terms of real effects, investment in land could not absorb real saving. But in a dynamic world where money is not necessarily

[2] *The General Theory of Employment, Interest and Money* (New York, Harcourt, Brace, 1936), p. 241.
[3] *Review of the Economic Situation in Mexico* (Banco Nacional de México), October, 1961, p. 5.

neutral in terms of real effects and where the use of money is conditioned by the institutionalized peculiarities of the people through whose hands money passes, it may be that the manner in which money is spent, perhaps on land, actually does inhibit its spending on some unemployed resources which might have been put to work on capital creation but instead are allowed to remain idle.[4] Bidding up the price of land may be an alternative to potential real saving and capital formation.

We are dealing with an ongoing process and not with a general-equilibrium-type situation. Money is held and then spent, held and then spent, in a process that takes time. And, to the extent that this process is going on in a society where there is an institutionalized tendency for all of the participants to prefer land ownership to investment in manufacturing, the result is an increase in the price of land relative to other prices, accompanied by no corresponding necessity that the money will find its way into the purchase of real capital.

Similar questions exist in terms of whether the placing of one's idle funds in foreign balances absorbs real savings. But in a dynamic, imperfect, and institution-ridden world, the possibility that it does surely exists.

Some quite responsible people have argued that there is adequate, actual (or potential) saving in Latin America and indicated that the real problem is misdirection in the use of saving. In the list are Alexandre Kafka, Frank Fetter, and Albert Hirschman.[5] And the Economic Commission for Latin America itself has argued that middle-class saving in Latin America is significant in amount.[6]

It is pretty clearly established that almost all of the private, voluntary

---

[4] For a discussion of the proposition that the role of money is not necessarily neutral, see, John G. Gurley and Edward S. Shaw, *Money in a Theory of Finance* (Washington, The Brookings Institution, 1960).

[5] Alexandre Kafka, "The Theoretical Interpretation of Latin American Development," in Howard S. Ellis, ed., *Economic Development for Latin America* (New York, St Martin's Press, 1961), p. 8; Frank W. Fetter, "The Need for Postwar Foreign Lending," in *American Economic Review, Papers and Proceedings,* 33 (March, 1943), 343; Albert O. Hirschman, *The Strategy of Economic Development* (New Haven, Yale University Press, 1958), p. 37; Hla Myint, "An Interpretation of Economic Backwardness," in *Oxford Economic Papers,* 6 (June, 1954), 132–63; Hans W. Singer, "Problems of Under-developed Countries," in Leon H. Dupriez, ed., *Economic Progress* (Louvain, Institut de Recherches Economiques et Sociales, 1955), p. 191. Singer was especially concerned about the losses involved in rearing a population that does not live very long.

[6] *Comercio Exterior,* September, 1963, p. 683.

saving that is done in any country is done by a quite small proportion of the wealthier people. And it stands to reason that a region with the extreme inequality in income distribution that Latin America possesses, and with a small, extremely wealthy element in the population, has a very respectable saving potential. Also, pyramid building in both Egypt and Mexico demonstrated a potential for grinding some capital formation out of people living on the very borderlines of subsistence.

In Latin America, probably, the trouble has chiefly been with the nature of the saving and expenditure behavior patterns rather than with the actual lack of the potential for saving. Those patterns of behavior are institutions—and examples of institutional barriers to development.

Corporate. Corporations (or other businesses) may plow back profits into plant expansion rather than distributing them as dividends to the stockholders or profits to the owners. In fact, this is an extremely important source for the monetary savings that finance industrial investment in the United States. In the United States, where corporate ownership is largely divorced from the control of corporate policy, the professional managers, who control corporate decision making, may have a personal interest in corporate expansion as distinct from an interest in the payment of maximum dividends. (They will then have the satisfaction of managing growing corporations.) A similar force is not at work to such a degree encouraging the growth of Latin American corporations. The Latin American corporation is more likely to be managed by its owners. As managers, they are perhaps more likely than their North American counterparts to distribute dividends to themselves in order to engage in conspicuous consumption or in order to save in the ways that are popular in Latin America (by investment in property, by building up foreign balances, or by contribution to the church).

The Banco Nacional de México has estimated that in Mexico about $1.00 is reinvested out of every $4.72 of business profit.[7] In the United States about half of profits seems to be reinvested by the average corporation and half distributed as dividends. Some of the Latin American industrial giants, such as Matarazzo in Brazil, have financed their own growth by plowing back profits. But this seems not to have been the pattern of Latin American industry in general. Business financing with instruments of debt, such as bonds and borrowing from banks, is em-

[7] *Review of the Economic Situation in Mexico,* April, 1958, p. 5.

phasized in Latin America; equity financing is relatively less popular.[8]

Maybe it is just as well that plowing back profits is not a pronounced practice in Latin America. Plowed-back profits have a significant weakness as a source of funds for financing economic development. They will not facilitate the appearance of new entrepreneurs.

Financial Intermediaries. (1) *Insurance.* Insurance, in the United States and western Europe, has been a significant device for mobilizing private saving and for feeding it into the investment channels selected by the insurance companies. But much of the appeal goes out of trying to save through voluntary private insurance channels in economies that are characterized by erratic and chronic inflation. It is of course possible to word insurance policies so that they contain some corrective for the impact of inflation. But this is a rather awkward procedure; and, at any event, it has not been done to a significant degree in Latin America, although there has been talk about it.

In countries where the private insurance companies are obligated to invest their funds within the country, this requirement, of itself, is likely to be discouraging to the expansion of insurance-type operations. In Latin American countries where the law permits the insurance company to invest its excess funds in the United States or in other foreign countries, the insurance companies, which take advantage of this dispensation to invest abroad, may avoid some of the adverse effects of inflation, but in so doing they fail to play a significant role in channeling funds into investment within the Latin American countries.

The role of social security overlaps the role of insurance. Both the social security programs and the insurance companies serve as important middlemen in the process of transferring saved funds to other uses that may include the creation of capital. In addition, of course, both the social security funds and the insurance premiums may ultimately be used in paying benefits to the insured.

Social security procedures raise several questions (questions to which the answers are by no means given in an entirely satisfactory manner in the United States). Is it desirable to tax the poor to raise a considerable part of the funds that will in fact be used in the investment programs of

---

[8] Calvin P. Blair, "Nacional Financiera: Entrepreneurship in a Mixed Economy," in Raymond Vernon, ed., *Public Policy and Private Enterprise in Mexico* (Cambridge, Harvard University Press, 1964), p. 219.

the governments? Might it not be better to finance the social security payments, when they come due, out of current tax revenue and finance public investment with the use of progressive taxes?

(2) *Securities and Financieras.* Investment banks and securities exchanges are standard devices for mobilizing private savings for investment and for facilitating the subsequent resale of the securities.

But the investment banking procedure for handling the marketing of new issues of securities has not been extensively developed in Latin America. Perhaps this is due to the historical predilection for land and foreign balances and to a continuing preference on the part of the industrialists themselves for the close-holding of corporations. At any rate, security marketing in Latin America does not reach the general market that is reached by the investment bankers in the United States. And stocks, the type of security that avoids some of the adverse implications of inflation, are not a popular investment in the region.

Several of the Latin American countries have securities exchanges of sorts: Mexico, Colombia, Brazil, Argentina, and so on. But these exchanges do not do much business. (The exchange is likely to help make the rent money by side operations, such as running the foreign exchange auction for the monetary authorities.) And in general the securities of Latin American corporations are not sold freely through the exchanges. This is probably in part because the countries are too small, and the securities traded are limited to those of the corporations of that country. A securities market, to attract a significant volume of trading, has to offer a wider range of choice to the customers than is available on the typical Latin American exchange.

To fill the void existing because of the underdevelopment of investment banking and securities exchange facilities, an alternative institution, the *financiera,* has been developed in Latin America. The financiera may buy the stocks and bonds of individual business enterprises and then sell its own securities to the public. Financieras may be either public or private. The financiera procedure deals with the difficulty connected with the lack of familiarity on the part of the investing public with the individual business enterprise. A pooling of risks results. However, the difficulty involved in marketing the financiera bonds in economies institutionally oriented to appreciate real property ownership still remains. And financing development out of personal savings through institutions such as the financieras is probably going to remain a marginal operation as long as inflation remains a chronic characteristic of the Latin American economies.

It may be worth noting a modification of the bond instrument which has been used (for example, by financieras in Mexico) to facilitate bond sales. The issuing agency agrees to repurchase the bond on demand from the bondholder. But this procedure does not really provide assured long-term financing and may turn out to be an expensive way to raise money because of the high interest rate.

All of this adds up to unsatisfactory local arrangements for mobilizing savings through private channels; but it also adds up to the suspicion that much could be done by way of mobilizing private, domestic saving if some institutional adjustments were changed. In spite of its weaknesses, the financiera is evidence of a willingness to experiment with new institutional arrangements.

(3) *Special-Purpose Banks.* Many Latin American governments have elevated the special-purpose bank to an important role in the mobilizing of capital funds. Frequently such institutions have been established by the governments: Nacional Financiera in Mexico, the Banco de la Nación Argentina and the Banco Industrial de la República Argentina, the Banco Nacional de Desenvolvimento Econômico in Brazil, the Corporación de Fomento de la Producción in Chile, and so on.[9]

These banks may serve as intermediaries in an assortment of possible saving-investment channels. They may borrow abroad and supervise the allocation of the borrowed fund among local activities. They may serve as the channel through which government funds or central bank funds move to individual investment projects. And, like the private financieras, they may float their own security issues to raise private funds to lend to particular projects.

In some respects the situation created by the activities of a special-purpose bank such as Nacional Financiera in Mexico would be comparable to a situation in New York involving a United States government agency as the principal investment banker.

(4) *Commercial Banks.* To a limited extent commercial banks serve as an intermediary through which private, voluntary savings are transferred to people who will use them in the purchase of capital. But to a much more important extent the role of the commercial bank involves

[9] *Ibid.,* pp. 191–240.

the creation of funds against fractional reserves. These funds may then be used in the purchase of capital without the necessity of prior, voluntary, personal saving. And to the extent that this latter operation reflects an autonomous impact of banks in the investment process, such activities are better discussed elsewhere than under the heading of private saving.

GOVERNMENT SAVING. The government may be the vehicle by which resources are mobilized to create new capital without the necessity for prior, private, voluntary saving.

(1) Fiat money might be the instrument; but, in general, more sophisticated tools are preferred. The government may finance the purchase of real capital (2) by tax and spend policies in the setting of a balanced budget, or (3) in the setting of an unbalanced budget by selling bonds (a) to the public or (b) to the banks and, perhaps, permitting the banks to use the bonds as reserves behind an expansion of the currency.

COMMERCIAL BANKS. Banks may create funds against fractional reserves which an investor may then use to buy equipment. The supply which can be obtained from this source is unlimited in a monetary sense. The government can print bonds and sell them to the banks. The government then has the money (bank notes) which the banks have paid for the bonds. Meanwhile the banks can use the bond certificates as the reserve behind new bank-note issues or other types of credit extension. At a subsequent time the banks could even use the new bank notes as the funds with which to purchase yet another bond issue from the government. It is true that virtually all of the Latin American countries can extend the amount of available credit in this way. And, in addition, the banks on the basis of fractional reserves can create a considerable amount of credit without government participation in issuing bonds. It follows that the amount of capital funds which may be raised is potentially unlimited, although, at a given time and place, the amount is limited by rules, laws, and institutionalized norms of behavior.

But it does not follow that the raising of capital funds in this way will immediately bring about the endowment of Latin America with unlimited amounts of capital goods. The net result of the whole operation may be merely to raise the price level, if the loaned funds are not effectively used.

The creation of capital funds by banks against fractional reserves represents a form of forced saving. This is true in the sense that the funds give the businessmen, who borrow the money from the banks, the buying power necessary to bid certain of the real resources of the country away from the rest of the citizenry. In the more favorable case, it gives him the power to buy and put to work resources that would otherwise be idle. (The special role of banks in the saving-investment process is discussed more at length in Chapter Twenty-three.)

FOREIGN BORROWING. Borrowing abroad has been one of the most discussed and most controversial of the methods used in Latin America for mobilizing capital funds. It is discussed in Chapter Fifteen.

Nature of Investment-Saving Relation

Saving is supposed to provide the wherewithal to finance real capital accumulation. As an extension of this concept the idea seems to have become imbedded in the theoretical planning models of recent years that investment (or capital formation) has to be financed by prior, personal, voluntary savings.

Keynes surely showed that this need not be the case. The necessary equality between investment and saving involves a process by which the saving may be drawn out as the result of a train of events that may well begin with autonomous investment. Neither the size of investment nor the equality of saving and investment is necessarily dependent on prior saving. And certainly the financing of investment is not dependent on the further restrictions that the prior saving be private and voluntary.

In real-life terms what is involved is something like this. A dam or a machine is capital. The resource necessary to produce the machine or the dam is mainly human labor, raw materials, and equipment. If those real resources are available and if it has been decided that it is desirable to build a certain plant, it is silly to be deterred by lack of prior, voluntary, personal saving. A government may create (if need be out of whole cloth) the legal-tender funds necessary to pay the wages to the labor, or to buy the raw materials and equipment. Then, the labor is paid, the work is done, the dam is built, and the capital has been created. Where was the saving? We might say that the fact that a certain amount of the labor supply, raw material, and equipment available to the country was being used to provide capital goods (instead of consumer goods or instead of remaining idle) was the effective real saving. But, to try to visualize the saving as a monetary phenomenon, it may be helpful to add that the funds created to pay the labor represent legal-tender purchasing power added to the already existing stock of purchasing power in the country. People (other than those participating in the new investment project) may find out that their incomes will buy a bit smaller percentage of the total supply of goods available in the country than they would before. This reduction in relative purchasing power may be looked on as a kind of forced saving. But even for "this rest of the population" there may well be an increase in absolute purchasing power —if the economy is growing as a result of the investment.

Thus so far as the society as a whole is concerned, saving need not be a sacrifice in any important interpretation of the meaning of the word sacrifice. Rather, investment and saving are an interrelated process in which the use of the word saving tends to mislead as to the nature of what is going on.

Thinking along these lines indicates that, insofar as real capital is important, what matters is the real wherewithal to provide real capital. If the country has the labor, the technology, and the raw materials necessary for the production or providing of the capital (and the inclination to use them in the production of capital), there is no intelligent reason why it should be deterred from producing the capital merely because of lack of prior, voluntary, personal, monetary saving. Of course the country may effectively be deterred (at a specific time) from producing the capital by institutional inhibitions, or by unwillingness to reallocate resources, and by scarcity of resources in an absolute sense.

Joan Robinson has gone so far as to say: "The emphasis on saving is more misleading than helpful." [10] The point is important because of what it means with regard to the philosophy on income distribution that a man of good will may assume. If prior, voluntary, private saving were necessary to investment and if the wealthy did most of the voluntary, private saving, then substantial inequality in income distribution would contribute to saving, investment, and growth. This would be true because the wealthy really do save a larger proportion of their incomes than do the poor. That part of the mythology is correct. But, if prior personal saving is not a necessary preliminary to the process, then the argument for unequal distribution of income loses much of its force. The argument

[10] *Economic Philosophy* (Chicago, Aldine, 1962), p. 117.

against the progressive income tax (based on the proposition that it inhibits saving) also loses much of its force. And one is then justified in emphasizing the relative importance of mass purchasing power. And mass purchasing power will be greater if there is more equal income distribution and if the progressive income tax, or some other progressive tax, is effectively used.

Applicability of Keynesian Theory

The simple Keynesian model relates the propensity of people to spend (and save) to a determination of the effect of a given increase in investment on national income. Crucial to this analytical process is a determination of the proportion of a change in income or product that will be spent on consumption. See Table 11.

Table 11

MARGINAL PROPENSITY TO CONSUME IN THE 1950s

Argentina	0.76
Brazil	0.61
Chile	1.06
Colombia	0.71
Mexico	0.77
Peru	0.73
Venezuela	0.60
Weighted Latin American average (13 countries)	0.72
United States	0.64 (circa 0.9 if the ratio were consumption to disposable income)

Source: *Boletín Económica de América Latina, Suplemento Estadístico*, December, 1962. Computations based on constant pesos.

The data attempt to relate cumulative change in personal consumption to cumulative change in gross national product for a period of ten to twelve years (roughly 1950 to 1961). For example, during this period in Argentina the increase in personal consumption spending was 76 percent of the increase in gross national product. Computed on a year-to-year basis the marginal propensities fluctuate violently and are frequently perverse (the change in personal consumption having a sign opposite to that of change in gross national product). In one flukish situation the figure was 24.07.

There is some doubt as to whether the relation of personal consumption to gross national product is the most pertinent comparison. Perhaps it would be better to relate personal consumption to personal income (or disposable personal income). This latter comparison would give, in general, a far higher propensity to consume than 0.72 and a higher multiplier than 3.6. But the multiplier in this case would not be relevant for determining the effect of new investment on gross national product.

For purposes of decision making, it is a little difficult to be sure just what kind of a dynamic process we have hold of. The Latin American marginal propensity to consume of 0.72 by contrast with the United States propensity of 0.64 (giving multipliers of respectively 3.6 and 2.8) would indicate that in Latin America a given bit of new investment would have a greater effect in increasing national income than is the case in the United States.

The considerable differences between the marginal propensities to consume of Mexico (0.77) and Brazil (0.61)—two rapidly growing countries—and the similarity between the Mexican and Argentine (0.76) figures, Argentina being a stagnating country, indicate the necessity of considerable caution in the use of these relations in development planning.

The margin of error in the estimates of propensity to consume is extremely high. And there is very wide fluctuation in the figures from year to year and over the business cycle. In addition, the data is not available to support the claim that there is a substantial degree of constancy from one phase of the cycle to the corresponding phase of the next cycle.

Capital-to-Output Ratios

Despite the essential irrelevance of business-cycle theory of the Keynesian type to the problem of economic development, some of the influential theories of development have used Keynesian tools of analysis, such as the capital/output ratio. Roy Harrod has been a proponent of this approach.[11]

In the application of the national income theory variables to economic

[11] R. F. Harrod, *Towards a Dynamic Economics* (London, Macmillan, 1948).

development the capital/output ratio becomes crucial. There has been considerable discussion in the literature as to alternative components that might go into this ratio. Perhaps the most satisfactory of the concepts is the one which relates net fixed capital formation (public and private) to change in gross national product (i.e., change in capital stock to change in product). Net fixed capital formation is gross fixed capital formation minus depreciation. It is possible to assemble data in these terms for several of the Latin American countries for a ten- or eleven-year period roughly covering 1950 through 1960, as shown in

Table 12

CAPITAL COEFFICIENTS AND GROWTH RATES, CIRCA 1950–1960

	Capital coefficient (*capital/output ratio*)	Real GNP Growth rate (*percent*)
Latin America		
Argentina	8.14	1.3
Brazil	2.20	5.5
Chile	0.53	3.1
Colombia	2.02	4.7
Peru	1.13	2.5
Venezuela	3.19	6.6
Weighted average (11 countries)	2.4	3.3
United States	2.38	3.3

Source: Economic Commission for Latin America, *Boletín Económico de América Latina, Suplemento Estadístico*, VII (December, 1962), 6–45. The results differ rather markedly from those presented in United Nations, *El Desarrollo Económico de América Latina en la Postguerra* (New York, 1963), p. 33.

Table 12. The ostensible growth rates are biased down by the inclusion of Argentina and the exclusion of Mexico. (The reader is warned that the growth rate estimates of Table 7 differ.)

One may suspect that these data are not particularly accurate. But economic development planners have been interested in using capital coefficients in economic development planning. And it is therefore probably worth saying a bit about what this information indicates and fails to indicate.

First, let me allege that, if the capital coefficients for a given country are computed on a year-to-year basis, they vary in an erratic manner. A capital coefficient for the relationship between one year and the next is hardly worth computing.

The data here presented cover about half the Latin American countries and involve a period of ten years. The capital coefficients vary over a wide range; and at the extremes (oddly) are two of the countries which have been lagging in their growth: Argentina and Chile. Argentina apparently has an extremely high capital coefficient and Chile a very low one. This Argentine-Chilean contrast does not augur well for the proposition that the capital coefficient is likely to be about the same for two countries in much the same circumstances. And if one leaves Argentina in the data, an extremely poor correlation ($-.391$) is found between capital coefficients and growth rates. If one leaves Argentina out of the data, a rather better correlation ($+.65$) is found.

But, in the literature, it has generally been assumed that the correlation between capital coefficients and growth rates is negative. Thus the exclusion of Argentina, which gives a higher correlation, results in a relation with the wrong sign.

Despite the dubiety of the data, it is worth seeing what they look like in the Harrod model of economic development:

Perhaps the preceding capital coefficients may be alleged to average to a capital coefficient for Latin America as a whole of 2.4. And the annual growth rate in real gross national product in Latin America for the corresponding period of the 1950s may be alleged to have been 3.3 percent.

Harrod's basic formula (with international trade included) is:

$$GC = s - b$$

where:

(1) G is the increase in production (in a given period of time) stated as a percentage of total production.
(2) C is the so-called capital coefficient, or capital/output ratio.
(3) the fraction of production saved is "s".
(4) The balance of trade (the difference between exports and imports) stated as a percentage of production is "b".

If one assumes that for the analysis of economic development it should be assumed that the balance of trade is zero,[12] the Harrod equation for this group of countries becomes:

$$.033 \times 2.4 = .0792 + 0.$$

The equation says that during the 1950s this group of countries supported a growth rate of 3.3 percent a year by saving 7.92 percent of gross national product, in a setting where the capital coefficient was averaging 2.4. Such information, if accurate, would have a certain historical interest.

But it is quite another thing to allege that the capital/output ratio of 2.4 has significant usefulness for planning the economic development of the future. (The reader may recall that the capital coefficient was made to play such a role in the macro development model presented in Chapter Thirteen.) There is, for example, too much difference among the capital/output ratios of the different countries to justify applying this average with much confidence. Also there has been so much variation in the ratios of the individual countries over time that one should also be cautious in applying one country's historical ratio to its own future.

Investment Outlays

If the capital/output ratio were a constant (and if "s" and "b" in the Harrod equation were also constants), it would follow that it would be possible to predict the effect of a given bit of new investment on real production or income.

Using the same data that were used in estimating the capital coefficients, it would seem that in Latin America net fixed investment has been running about 9.8 percent of gross national product. (One may be philosophical about the difference between this figure and the savings percentage in the Harrod formula even though savings are supposed to equal investment.) In the United States it has been running about 7 percent.

The percentages in gross terms run higher but involve approximately the same relation between Latin America and the United States. In Latin America gross fixed capital formation as a percentage of gross national product has been averaging 19.2 percent, in the United States it has been averaging 16 percent.

[12] It will be argued in Chapter Fifteen that this is a legitimate assumption.

CAPITAL FORMATION: DOMESTIC

The figures for several of the eleven countries for which computations could be made are shown in Table 13.

Table 13

INVESTMENT-TO-GROSS-NATIONAL-PRODUCT RELATION, CIRCA 1950–1961

	Net fixed capital formation/GNP	Gross fixed capital formation/GNP
Argentina	0.10	0.22
Brazil	0.10	
Chile	0.015	0.10
Colombia	0.09	0.20
Peru	0.03	0.19
Venezuela	0.19	0.24
Weighted Latin American average (11 countries)	0.098	0.192
United States	0.07	0.16

Source: *Boletín Económico de América Latina, Suplemento Estadístico*, December, 1962. The reader may note that the figures in this table do not combine with the figures in the "Marginal Propensity to Consume" table to add up to a neat 100 percent. In fact there are some rather serious inconsistencies.

The data, as far as they go, indicate that Latin America is investing a slightly larger percentage of gross national product than is the United States. One should probably not put too much confidence in the precision of these figures. But they are probably accurate enough to indicate that Latin America has been making a respectable investment effort.

A Different Perspective

Perhaps for purposes of economic development planning it would be better to have a little different perspective on the role of investment than that provided by the Keynesian theory.

An alternative might be an attempt to estimate the amount of real resources which the country finds it possible to commit to development during the coming time period. Then the financial problem becomes the arrangement of the financial interplay that is necessary to put the real resources to work.

The knowledge that prior, voluntary, personal saving is not necessary as a preliminary to real capital formulation is important knowledge for understanding the long-run growth problem. This insight is provided by national income theory. However, it is doubtful that national income theory has much more than that to offer to long-run development planning. Keynesian theory was originally set up to deal with the business-cycle situation, not with the problems of economic development. The temptation to try to use Keynesian theory in substantially unmodified form as development theory is derived in part from the fact that the multiplier process ostensibly starts off with an increase in real investment, and what could be more important in facilitating economic development than an increase in real investment? But investment in the Keynesian model serves its useful purpose in increasing real income and employment only until such time as full employment or full use of resources has been achieved. This conception, putting idle resources to work by increasing investment, is essentially a short-run type of operation. Content-wise it has little to do with the long-run problems involved in discovering and using new resources and improved technology, changes which are of the essence in development.

Ambiguity might have been avoided if the Keynesian theory had been originally stated as a theory as to what the increase in the money supply can do in a setting of unemployed resources. If this were visualized as the real setting of Keynesian theory, some of the temptation to apply inappropriate concepts to economic development might have been avoided.

Saving, investment, and capital formation of course can contribute to the industrialization of Latin America. But it is easy to overemphasize their importance. This overemphasis is especially likely to happen in the economic development planning that assumes there is a constant relation between capital stock and output. Such planning misses the far more important point that improvement in technology and the use of new resources may well make a more significant contribution than is made by the lump of capital itself. At the very least, far from planning in terms of an investment of $5,000 or more per worker, as is frequently done, Latin America ought to consider as very suspect an investment that does not give at least one job for every $2,000 of investment.

CHAPTER FIFTEEN

CAPITAL FORMATION: FOREIGN RESOURCES

Historical Background

As a starting point in the discussion of foreign investments it may be useful to list the chief characteristics of the process during the period from Independence down to about 1937.[1]

(1) The lenders in western Europe and in the United States were generally private citizens, not governments. The borrowers in the Latin American countries were either private interests or governments.

(2) The investments occurred erratically. Spurts of investment would be followed by periods when virtually no investment would occur. For example a major spurt of British investment went to Argentina in the 1880s; there was very little investment in the 1890s; then another spurt followed during the decade before World War I.

(3) The ostensible face value of the investment was a significant overstatement of the gross real investment. Discounts to buyers on some of the early bond issues, such as those of Mexico floated in London in the 1820s, were close to 50 percent of the ostensible face value of the bonds. Debt service obligations to the creditors seem to have over-

[1] Some useful books on the background of foreign investments in Latin America include: Willy Feuerlein and Elizabeth Hannan, *Dollars in Latin America* (New York, Council on Foreign Relations, 1941); Leland H. Jenks, *Our Cuban Colony, a Study in Sugar* (New York, Vanguard, 1928); Charles D. Kepner and Jay Henry Soothill, *The Banana Empire* (New York, Vanguard, 1935); M. M. Knight, *Americans in Santo Domingo* (New York, Vanguard, 1928); Raymond F. Mikesell, *Foreign Investments in Latin America* (Washington, Pan American Union, 1955); J. Fred Rippy, *The Capitalists and Colombia* (New York, Vanguard, 1931); Edgar Turlington, *Mexico and her Foreign Creditors* (New York, Columbia University Press, 1930); and Max Winkler, *Investments of United States Capital in Latin America* (Boston, World Peace Foundation, 1929).

shadowed the value of the contribution being made by the new investment, in general, from the beginning of the process.

(4) Meddling in the internal politics of the borrowing country by the diplomats and businessmen of the creditor countries seems to have been standard procedure. Any history of nineteenth century Latin American politics will give innumerable examples—involving virtually every country from Mexico (through Nicaragua and Haiti and Venezuela) to Argentina and Chile. These activities have sometimes been called imperialism.

(5) Much of the investment (especially in the case of the bond issues rather than the direct investments) seems to have been used in ways that contributed little or nothing to the development of the country. The proceeds from bond issues were frequently used to pay off the army of a successful rebel or to finance an ornate nonfunctional monument (examples include the antecedents of the Monument to the Revolution in Mexico City and the capitol in Havana). Frequently the proceeds of the investment merely became an income supplement to the political insiders in the Latin American countries. To the extent this was true, the chief economic effect of the foreign investment was an income redistribution effect in the borrowing countries.

(6) Given this background it is not strange that defaults on bond issues and the confiscation (or expropriation) of direct investments were common occurrences. In fact it is roughly accurate to say that the typical Latin American country was in default on various bond issues more often than not. And during the 1930s, Latin America was in default on virtually all of its foreign bonded indebtedness. This is not to say that the bondholders necessarily lost money, even in the case of default. In fact such statistical studies as are available indicate that, overall, the bondholders made money. The defaults merely meant that, as a group, they did not net as much as they expected to net. And of course, individual bondholders did lose money.

Also direct investment, such as foreign-owned oil properties in Bolivia in 1937 and in Mexico in 1938, were occasionally taken away from foreign investors under circumstances that may or may not have involved "equitable" compensation.

By about 1937, the Nazi infiltration of Latin America seemed to indicate the desirability of an effort at conciliation with the Latin American countries, in spite of the fact that there was mass default at the time. The Roosevelt Administration seems first to have approached the Wall Street investment bankers in an effort to encourage them to sponsor a renewal of lending. The bankers proved unresponsive. The consequence was a major change in the nature of the lending process, at least a major change in the identity of the chief lender. The United States government, using the Export-Import Bank as its instrumentality, stepped into the field of foreign investment in a major manner. Where, before 1937, most foreign lending had been private, from that date onward the United States government played a major role in foreign lending and in international assistance.

The year 1937, little marked at the time, seems then, in perspective, to have been a significant watershed in the history of the foreign investment process.

Attitudes

Given the history of foreign investments and the current state of international political and economic relations, it is, perhaps, not strange that some complicated and inconsistent attitudes toward the desirability of foreign investments should have developed in both the debtor and the creditor countries.

For example, in Latin America, people (who have heard much about the high profits made by foreign investors, who do not appreciate foreign meddling and imperialism, and who have developed a nationalistic spirit) have developed an attitude antipathetic to foreign investments. But also people in Latin America visualize foreign investments and foreign aid as a powerful force which can accelerate economic development. And, strangely, the same people frequently have both views with regard to foreign investments at the same time.

In the creditor countries, some people, influenced by the past defaults and expropriations, are prone to condemn foreign investments. Others are attracted by the possibilities for making money from foreign investments (the legend of the Seven Cities of Cibola is not dead). Also foreign investments are viewed as devices for aiding development in a world which, it is thought, would be a healthier place to live in if the poor countries were better off. Also foreign aid may be a device for getting support against the Russians in the Cold War.

All in all it seems fair to say that the attitude toward foreign investments is ambivalent all around. And this ambivalence has led to some odd policies in both creditor and debtor countries.

IMPERIALISM. Emphasis on the struggle between debtor nations and creditor nations, viewed as nations with different interests, has been overdone. A far more important cleavage is that between consumers all over the world (who are benefited by the greatest possible production) and producers (who, in order to make greater profits, or higher wages, may curb the output of the machines or the output of labor).

Complaints against imperialism and exploitation need to identify what those phenomena consist of. A complaint against foreign investors on the ground that they have made excessive money profits runs into difficulty. Such statistical evidence as is available simply does not confirm the claim that foreign investors in general enjoy higher profit rates than are enjoyed by local businessmen in the debtor country in the same line of activity. Isolated examples of high profits are interesting, even occasionally sensational, but are hardly the basis for a general appraisal of the role of foreign investments.[2]

But even assuming the possibility of high money profits, what is the nature of the exploitation? Presumably international economic exploitation would have as its essence some net loss of goods. But to the extent that the creditor countries are busy taking measures (tariffs and otherwise) to reduce imports relative to exports, it hardly seems that creditor countries are especially interested in the net drainage of goods from the debtor countries. To the extent that the creditor country ends up with an import trade balance (and it will be argued below that this is generally the case), the creditor country accepts the import balance in spite of itself. (This should be obvious to anyone who has spent five minutes observing how nations act during tariff negotiations.)

It may well be that the meddling by the creditors in the domestic politics of the debtor countries, an offense against the sovereignty, dignity, and self-respect of the debtor country, has been a blacker mark against the creditors than economic exploitation per se.

Investments have given rise to many and bitter international incidents: the United States occupied Haiti in 1915—the reason, at least in large part, to protect property owned by United States citizens. The

[2] *New York Times,* October 23, 1963, p. 7. Excessive profits by foreign-owned drug companies in Brazil are the theme of this article.

Germans, British, and French threatened Venezuela in 1902, avowing a desire to be compensated for loss of property and other damage and a desire to have Venezuela pay her public debt obligations. Frequently on the ground of protecting the property of its nationals, the United States has justified armed interventions in Nicaragua, Haiti, the Dominican Republic, and Cuba. All the great powers of the world have done the same sort of thing to a greater or lesser extent, and the debtor countries have protected themselves as best they could. "Yanqui," British, and German imperialism have all been denounced in the debtor and industrially weak regions of the world.

LATIN AMERICAN REACTION. *Calvo Clause.* The Calvo Clause has been an instrument used by the Latin American countries in their effort to resist the influence of the capital-exporting countries. As embodied in Article 27 of the Mexican Constitution of 1917, the Clause read: "The State may grant the same right [to acquire ownership in lands, and so on] to foreigners, provided they agree before the Ministry of Foreign Affairs to consider themselves as nationals in respect to such property, and bind themselves not to invoke the protection of their governments in matters relating thereto; under penalty, in case of noncompliance, of forfeiture to the nation of property so acquired."

To illustrate how the Calvo Clause may operate, or rather fail to operate: the clause appeared on the shares of stock of the Aguila (the subsidiary of the Royal Dutch Shell in Mexico). But when expropriation took place in 1938, that fact did not deter the Shell from appealing to the British government for diplomatic support and obtaining it. England severed diplomatic relations with Mexico for several years over the issue.

Incoming Capital. The borrowing country frequently requires that the foreigner must obtain permission from the government before he can make an investment. But the criteria used in regulation vary substantially from country to country; they are frequently changed and operate more as a barrier to investment than as an orderly regulator of investment. In fact it might be said that the basic rule is that an ad hoc judgment is made in each case as to whether to permit a given bit of foreign investment. And there are really in existence no general criteria regulating the process in a predictable manner.

Withdrawal of Profits or Principal. Various Latin American countries have also established restrictions on the withdrawal of profits or of capital. Such restrictions are probably less prevalent in the 1960s than they were in the 1930s and during the immediate postwar period. Nevertheless new restrictions along this line are not infrequent. For example, in early 1964 a new set of Brazilian control regulations limited the legal remittance of profits abroad to 10 percent a year of the real foreign investment of a company in equipment and capital; and, by July, the Brazilian government was in the process of modifying the January changes.[3]

CREDITOR-COUNTRY REACTION. In some quarters in the creditor countries, the reaction to defaults and expropriation has been to abstain from new investment or to lend erratically. Also there has been, upon occasion, pressure for sending the Marines or for taking over the Customs, or for trade embargoes. And it has been standard practice to appeal for support to actual, or alleged, principles of international law such as "equality of treatment between foreigners and nationals," the existence of a "minimum standard of treatment," or the "requirement" that "compensation be prompt and equitable." Meddling in local politics and stirring up of revolution have also been possibilities.

Several of the foregoing measures are now out of fashion. In recent decades it has become more common and respectable to argue for the desirability of guarantees or tax advantages. In fact a limited number of treaties have been signed in which the United States government agrees with the debtor government to compensate the United States investors (under certain rather closely defined circumstances) in the event of default, confiscation, or inability to transfer funds internationally because of exchange controls.

Also investors have argued that either the United States government or the debtor government would do well to give them certain tax advantages. (Matters of this sort were discussed in Chapter Three.) Investors have cultivated some strong biases in terms of a belief that they should be granted special privileges, tax exemptions, and so on. It is only natural that they would try to get such privileges as they can. But it is rather common for them to mistake special privileges for a favorable investment climate. A dictator who will grant special privileges (Rojas Pinilla in Colombia, Trujillo in the Dominican Republic, or Pérez Jiménez in

[3] New York *Times,* January 18, 1964, p. 28; New York *Times,* July 16, 1964, p. 43.

Venezuela) may be regarded with more favor than is a reasonably democratic regime with a solid base in popular support which cannot, for political reasons, grant special privileges to the investors.

It would probably be a good idea if foreign investors would forget their perennial pleas for special privilege and if the politicians in the Latin American countries would stop trying to bribe the foreign investors with promises of special privileges. Even as notorious an antiforeign investor as João Goulart in Brazil was quite capable of pleading the special privilege case. He said in November, 1963: "Foreign capital that comes to join in the effort and in the sacrifice of the Brazilian people on its march towards economic emancipation will be welcome always and assured all manners of guarantees." [4]

Statistics

Table 14 serves to indicate the investment of the United States and its citizens in Latin America by comparison with the United States investment in the world at large.

Table 14

INTERNATIONAL INVESTMENT POSITION OF THE UNITED STATES

	As of end of 1962 (in millions of dollars)
U.S. investments abroad, total, world	80,126
U.S. investments in Latin America, total	15,305
Private	12,190
Long-term	10,251
Direct	8,472
Short-term	1,939
U.S. government credits and claims	3,115
Foreign assets and investments in U.S., total, world	47,368
Latin American assets and investments in U.S., total	4,146
Net U.S. investment in Latin America	11,159

Source: *Survey of Current Business*, August, 1963, p. 22.

As of June 30, 1963, total cumulative authorized credits to Latin America by the Export-Import Bank were $3,484 million, of which total $2,013 million were outstanding.

[4] Brazilian Embassy (Washington, D. C.), *Press Release*, No. 38, November 6, 1963.

Cumulative United States government foreign assistance to Latin America for the period since 1946 was, at the end of 1962, $3,927 million (of which $575 million were made available in 1962). Total United States government foreign assistance to all countries for the same period had cumulated to $91,536 million.

Investments and Development

GROWTH OF INVESTMENT. (1) *Via Balance of Trade*. Foreign investment is supposed to be an instrument by which an underdeveloped country can obtain from abroad the capital which it lacks. Or, to put the matter somewhat more loosely, it is an instrument that can make a net real resource contribution to the borrowing country. To the extent that foreign investment may also provide technicians (who are paid wages), pay taxes, or pay salaries to Latin American workers, these are additional contributions and not an inherent aspect of the investment, or capital, or resources transfer itself. The distinction may be clearer if the reader will recall the standard classification of the factors of production (land, labor, capital, and enterprise), of which capital is only one. Capital is therefore not entitled to claim credit for the total product.

The standard model of the foreign investment process has it that, during the period when the investment is being made, the flow of resources from the creditor country to the debtor country will manifest itself in an export balance of trade on the part of the creditor country and in an import balance of trade on the part of the debtor country. The real resource transfer that the foreign investment implements is manifested in these trade balances. Later, when debt service becomes substantial and the debts are being repaid, the debtor country will have the export balance and the creditor country the import balance.

This process might be schematized as involving the following relations:

Immature borrower:	Import balance of trade
Mature borrower:	Export balance of trade
Immature lender:	Export balance of trade
Mature lender:	Import balance of trade

For the process to justify substantial payment of debt service and principal repayment (and the corresponding debtor-country export balances for many years), it would seem that the first phase, when the debtor has the import balance, should be of substantial duration and involve a substantial transfer of capital or other resources from the creditor to the debtor.

The actual nature of this relationship as between debtor and creditor countries needs to be analyzed in the course of appraising whether foreign investment is particularly likely to make the contribution that justifies its existence. If, for example, there is a tendency for investment income received by foreign investors to rise, roughly, *pari passu* with the increase in investment, then foreign investment cannot be relied on to make a net reource (or capital) contribution at all as a dynamic proposition. Is it true that investment income tends to rise more or less in step with investment from the beginning of the investment process?

There is now a considerable reservoir of statistical information indicating enough probability that this is the case when countries of any size are involved so that development planners had better not continue to make an automatic assumption that gross, new international investment can be counted on to make an initial, significant resource contribution to the underdeveloped countries.

Some of the evidence should be mentioned. The chief growth of British foreign investments occurred in the period 1870 to 1914. It appears clearly established that during this period, and almost continually during this period, the nature of the relation between investment and income from investment was such that the foreign investment process, overall, was financing its own growth plus a net movement of resources *to* Britain and not *from* Britain.

Data for the United States indicate that, far from shifting over from an immature debtor to a mature debtor in 1873, the United States was a mature debtor (in the sense that net debt service leaving the country exceeded net investment entering the country) as a general pattern from the time statistics on the matter start to be available, which is about 1790. There were brief periods when new investment exceeded debt service in the 1830s and about 1870. But the existence of the prolonged period (1790 to 1873), which international economics texts describe as being a time when the United States enjoyed a consistent import trade balance financed by foreign investment, seems to be pure myth. The indebtedness grew all right, but the United States had an export balance on goods and services (debt service excluded) as a general rule during that period.[5]

Probably most people (who have had a thought on the subject) are under the impression that the period since World War II has been one in which there has been a significant resource contribution by the United States and other developed countries to Latin America as a result of the foreign investment process. Quite the contrary seems to be the actual case. The International Monetary Fund balance of payments data for the Latin American countries indicates that, for the countries as a group in the sixteen years 1946 through 1961, the foreign investment process (investment combined with debt service) financed a net outflow of resources from Latin America to the rest of the world in the amount of $4.2 billion. Net capital inflow into Latin America was $11.8 billion and net debt service transferred out was $16 billion for the period of years as a whole. Estimates of the size of Latin American balances in New York and in numbered bank accounts in Switzerland (and in similar caches) range from $5 billion to $25 billion. The magnitude of even the smaller sum is evidence that the wealthy of Latin America are not particularly committed to the underwriting of Latin American development. The sum is substantial; and if the surreptitious outflow of all such funds from Latin America could be allowed for, the net outflow of resources from Latin America, financed by the foreign investment process during the postwar period, would probably look substantially larger than it does.

If one adds foreign aid to the picture, the composite of the lending and the giving together has not financed a net flow of resource to Latin America since World War II. Actually net grants to the region for the period (grants received $1 billion, grants made $900 million) would seem to have been only about $100 million (according to the IMF data). If the foreign investment process financed a flow of resources

---

[5] Wendell Gordon, "The Contribution of Foreign Investments: A Case Study of United States Foreign Investment History," in *Inter-American Economic Affairs*, 14 (Spring, 1961), 35–56; Wendell Gordon, "Foreign Investments," in *University of Houston Business Review*, 9 (Fall, 1962), 1–69. For an example of continued use of the assumption that debt service in the early years of foreign investment can be assumed to be effectively nominal, *see*, R. F. Harrod, "Desirable International Movements of Capital in Relation to Growth of Borrowers and Lenders and Growth of Markets," in Roy Harrod and D. C. Hague, eds., *International Trade Theory in a Developing World* (New York, St Martin's Press, 1963), pp. 113–41, esp. p. 127.

from Latin America of $4.2 billion, it would seem that the investment process combined with the grant process financed a net drainage of resources of $4.1 billion.

Data taken from United States government sources (which in some important respects are quite different from the IMF figures) nevertheless indicate the same sort of relation as between the United States and Latin America. During the period 1946 through 1964, the United States (government plus private and long-term plus short-term investment) has invested $8.7 billion, net, in Latin America and taken out $13.6 billion, net, in debt service. Thus the foreign investment process has netted the United States something like $4.9 billion from Latin America. The United States Department of Commerce estimates some $3.5 billion of grant aid has been provided by this country to Latin America in the postwar period. (This figure may not be consistent with some of the IMF figures.) Even after allowance for grant aid is made, the Department of Commerce figures, which net the foreign investment process with the foreign aid process, still make the composite result indicate a net contribution by Latin America to the United States for the period of about $1.4 billion.

Undervaluation of exports is a common phenomenon in Latin America. It is practiced to avoid the governmental exchange controls, to reduce the burden of export tariffs, and for similar reasons. To the extent that this has gone on, it may well be that the foreign investment process has financed even more of an outflow from Latin America than is indicated by the above figures.

It might be added at this point that it seems clear that the 1920s, which were allegedly a period of major foreign investment in Latin America, also involved larger net debt-service payments than net new investment. In that period Latin America had a consistent export trade balance in the face of the increasing foreign investment. One might be tempted to speculate (we do not have the data) that there never has been a period of *significant duration* when the foreign investment process financed a net flow of resources to the region.

In the early independence period (from 1810 to 1830) there seems to have been a significant withdrawal of capital by the Spaniards, the gachupines, from Latin America. It has been estimated that this influence was strong enough to offset the new British investments coming into Latin America and meant that, during the early years of independence, the foreign investment process financed a net flow of resources out from Latin America.[6]

Even the foreign investment in railroads in the late nineteenth century seems not to have been the pure foreign contribution that it has sometimes been assumed to have been. Funds (or financial assistance) were obtained from several sources:

(*a*) *Direct foreign investment* in railroad stock and bonds. Contrary to general belief, however, not all the funds were obtained in this way, and it well may be true that most of them were not so obtained.

(*b*) *Government subsidy*. The separate governments consistently subsidized the railroads, using some such criterion as: "so many pesos to the mile." A substantial proportion of the capital was obtained from this source rather than from the foreign direct investor. It is true, however, that in many cases the government did not raise these sums by taxation, but by floating its own bond issues.

(*c*) *Tax exemptions*. By this means, the railroad companies were relieved of a substantial financial burden, especially in the early period of their operations.

(*d*) *Land grants*. Substantial land grants provided a strong inducement to enter the field. Indeed, in the early years in Argentina, much of the profit derived from railroading accrued from the sale or colonization of land grants.

(2) *Via Accretion*. We know that foreign investment in Latin America has grown. It has to have grown somehow for the net United States investment in Latin America now to be something over $11 billion. How could this growth have occurred without being implemented by a net wealth transfer from the United States to Latin America? The answer seems to be that it has generally occurred by a process that might be called accretion. The first "foreign investments" in the Americas involved the appropriation of wealth already in the Americas by the Spanish, Portuguese (and English)—by Cortés, Pizarro, and the owners of tobacco plantations in Virginia. In fact much of the foreign investment in the early periods apparently took the form of the appropriation of land by the Europeans. Subsequently the increment in the value of

---

[6] Francisco López Camara, "Las Contradicciones de la Economía Mexicana después de la Revolución de Independencia," in *Investigación Económica*, XXIII (Primer Trimestre, 1963), 189–222, esp. pp. 218–9.

the land over the years involved "an increase in foreign investment in Latin America." Of course in fact the process of foreign investment growth was more circuitous and less direct than this oversimplified scheme suggests. Individual foreign investors have transferred wealth to the debtor country. The movement of a drilling rig from the United States to Latin America by Standard of Jersey is an overt investment where the transfer of real capital is the tangible evidence of the additional investment. But the same year that the rig goes to Venezuela there may well be a compensating transfer of crude oil out of Venezuela. The oil may be sold in the United States. And a certain amount of the proceeds of the sale may be appropriated as profits in dollars in the United States by Standard of Jersey. In fact, these dollar profits, derived from the inflow of oil into the United States, may well exceed in value the cost of the drilling rig which was sent to Venezuela.

There is no point in arguing that foreign investment never corresponds with a resource transfer from the creditor to the debtor country. But there is some point in indicating that, as a basic relation among nations, the value of foreign investment seems not to increase as a result of a net transfer of wealth from the creditor to the debtor. Rather it tends to grow as a result of the increase in the value of the investment already there. The net investment of the nationals of one country in another country increases as a result of the plowing back of profits, as a result of the increase of land values, and so on.

It may seem strange that a loan could possibly be offset by debt service as large as the loan from the beginning of the lending process. But it should be remembered that we are not talking about individual loans but rather about relations between nations. We are talking about macro and not micro relations. And the matter is made more feasible by the tendency of borrowers (borrowing perhaps at 6 percent) at long term to hold much of their borrowings in short-term balances in the creditor countries at nominal (even zero) rates of interest for significant periods of time before they use the funds.

But a down-to-earth example may help even more in conceiving how this possibility can be. One of the major single blocs of foreign investment in recent years was an investment of about $1.5 billion in Venezuelan oil between 1956 and 1958. The immediate occasion for this spurt of investment was that the Pérez Jiménez government permitted the taking out of new concessions for the first time in many years. Much of the ostensible investment at that time took the form of a payment in dollar balances in the United States by the oil companies to the Venezuelan government for the new concessions. It would seem that large amounts of the funds found their way into the personal accounts of Pérez Jiménez and his henchmen in the United States, Switzerland, and elsewhere. That regime was overthrown in Venezuela shortly after. The leading figures of the regime went into exile. Much of the 1957 investment of the oil companies had its effective manifestation later as purchasing power in the hands of those exiles outside of Venezuela.

THE INCREASE IN REAL CAPITAL. Foreign investment may not contribute to an increase in the stocks of real capital in the debtor country. And real capital equipment may be obtained from abroad without the necessity for foreign investment as a counterpart. The proceeds from Brazilian coffee exports may be used to finance the purchase of capital equipment in the United States. Thus, at the level of international relations, the connection between foreign investment and the accumulation of capital equipment is far from necessary.

ALTERNATIVE CONTRIBUTIONS. To allege that foreign investment is neither a necessary nor a sufficient condition for acquiring capital equipment from abroad is not necessarily the same thing as alleging that foreign investment is useless.

The usefulness of foreign investment could be in the technology that it provides as a by-product rather than in the net resources it contributes. But it should be noted that in such a case capital investment is being justified on the basis of the contribution of a by-product of capital, a rather odd position for that most important of all productive resources to be in. (The role of capital in providing technology was discussed in Chapter Twelve.) In that chapter it was argued that there are better and cheaper ways of acquiring technology than as a by-product of the foreign investment process. However, it might be emphasized here that, even though foreign investment may facilitate the acquiring of capital in the underdeveloped country, if it is true that debt service grows in step with additional investment, the same amount of real net capital (and the same amount of technology consequently) could have been acquired by better development planning and a more judicious use of the country's export proceeds, without the incurring of any foreign investment.

In some of the analyses of foreign investment, much has been made of their contribution in terms of taxes, jobs provided, contribution to national income, and so forth.[7] But these same contributions to taxes, jobs, and income could have been made by the equivalent domestic investment. If foreign investment does not make a significant, net international-resource contribution to the economy of the debtor country, then what it is contributing is a means for by-passing local institutional difficulties rather than capital. And we are back with the point that the subsequent debt-service costs seem like a pretty high price to pay for getting around one's own institutional rigidities.

It has been alleged that the internal institutional adjustments that the Latin American country would need to make to finance the same amount of capital import with the proceeds from its own exports, without recourse to foreign investment, are not possible. The institutional resistances are too great. But maybe, on the contrary, this is just the point where the battle needs to be fought. The role of foreign investments is somewhat perverted from that visualized in the mythology, if it is necessary only because Latin America is institutionally incapable of mobilizing domestic saving and is incapable of the effective use of export proceeds to finance capital imports.

In spite of all that has already been said as to the ambiguity of the foreign investment contribution, let us assume that the possibility exists that foreign investment may make some kind of meaningful contribution to economic development. In such a case would it make the contribution to best advantage if the investment was of steady magnitude each year over many years or if the investment occurred as a short-lived spurt?

A predictable, consistent flow of foreign investment would seem to be the more desirable of the two possibilities in terms of facilitating continuing and intelligent economic development planning. On the other hand it might be argued that an isolated spurt of investment (or erratic investment) would be more likely to jolt a country out of an institutionally imposed lethargy.

There is considerable sentiment to the effect that such spurts may make a significant contribution to development. We cannot discuss here at any length the question as to whether the concepts of the "big push" and of the "takeoff" have validity. But something may well be said as to

[7] Samuel Pizer and Frederick Cutler, *U. S. Investments in the Latin American Economy* (Washington, Department of Commerce, Office of Business Economics, 1957).

the relation among those concepts, foreign investment, and Latin America. Latin America has seen several abortive big pushes, takeoffs, or spurts of industrialization in the last hundred and fifty years. For example, Argentina received major spurts of foreign investment in the 1880s and again just before World War I. Yet Argentina is currently the generally cited example of a country thoroughly frustrated in its development. The big push did not evolve into self-sustained growth.

It is probably also desirable at this point to grant the possibility that certain types of foreign investment may be much better than other types, and may even make a worthwhile contribution. Joint enterprises and international licensing of patents are arrangements that may fall in this category. (There was some further discussion of the merits of the joint enterprise possibility in Chapters Three and Twelve.)

At all events the development planner needs to take some long second looks at the foreign investment process before he leans very heavily on it in his development planning. He needs to double-check that the particular investment he is recommending will really provide net resources in a constructive way to the borrowing country.

THE FOREIGN-INVESTMENT TO TOTAL-INVESTMENT RATIO. For Mexico, in the time of Porfirio Díaz, there are some spotty data indicating that foreign investment may have contributed 53 percent of the investment funds in Mexico, while domestic saving was contributing only 47 percent. In the decade of the 1950s it seems that domestic saving may have contributed 88 percent and foreign investment only 12 percent.[8] Estimates from the same source indicate that, during the period 1939 to 1950, internal saving accounted for 92 percent of investment, and foreign investment for only 8 percent. This was a period of even more rapid growth in Mexico than the 1950s. A falling off in the proportion of foreign investment to total investment does not seem to have hurt Mexico particularly.

Celso Furtado has written: "The available data indicate that foreign investments represented in Brazil, in 1929, 23 percent of the reproducible capital in existence in the national territory, and that this proportion had fallen to 7.5 percent in 1950."[9] This would be more indication that

[8] *México: 50 Años de Revolución. Vol. I. La Economía* (México, Fondo de Cultura Económica, 1960), p. 524.
[9] Celso Furtado, *Desenvolvimento e Subdesenvolvimento* (Rio de Janeiro, Editôra Fundo de Cultura, 1961), pp. 110–11.

perhaps the importance of foreign investment in the development process has been overemphasized—since the 1950s was a period of rapid development in Brazil.

In recent years it has been rather common to say that the growth rate in Latin America slackened markedly about 1957 or 1958. In searching around for possible explanations, one may be struck by the fact that 1957 and 1958 were foreign investment peaks. It is no great credit to the development contribution of foreign investments if investment peaks are followed by stagnation in growth. And yet there is a respectable amount of evidence to the effect that this is fairly likely to happen. It happened in the United States about 1840 and in 1873. It happened in Argentina about 1890 with the Baring crisis.

Foreign Aid

If foreign investment has failed to help much with development, it is tempting to speculate that foreign aid, that is to say grants or gifts (or soft loans), might do better. Such arrangements, it would seem, should make it possible to provide a significant amount of real resource aid before being overshadowed by debt service.

And yet the case for a major, continuing amount of aid to help the underdeveloped countries is not as unambiguous as the Biblical injunction, "it is more blessed to give than to receive," would suggest. It well may be almost literally correct that there is a high inverse (not positive) correlation between the amount of per capita aid that countries have received since World War II and their rate of economic development. The Latin American country which has received the most aid on a per capita basis, Bolivia, has been characterized by frustration and stagnation. This is true despite the fact that the aid received has been substantial, and the United States has behaved in a responsible fashion so far as Bolivian internal politics have been concerned. Also Bolivia has had the benefit of more advice, per capita, from foreign economic development experts than any other three countries in Latin America. One wishes that a case so well and decently handled by so much expertness (including Carter Goodrich of Columbia University) could have been a successful showpiece. The Alliance for Progress has talked about making showpieces out of Colombia or Chile. Maybe they had better not; the case history of showpieces is not so good.

The implications of foreign aid as a new form of power politics are also serious. Philip Ray has remarked:

Indeed, it appears that our foreign aid has taken upon itself a kind of neodollar diplomacy. Thus we suspend aid in Peru, then restore it; flourish our fleet to help Bosch in the Dominican Republic, then go in with aid when he is seemingly secure, then deny it when he is overthrown; hesitatingly court Jagan in British Guiana with aid because, although a Communist, he was elected to his office; deny aid in Honduras when the junta is not to our liking; withdraw our aid in South Vietnam and then as suddenly restore it; first oppose and then submit to the Brazilian request for more Latin American authority over our Government aid programs; become discouraged with aid in Haiti while extolling its accomplishments of the moment in some other place.[10]

Various observers of the Latin American scene, including Albert Hirschman, have commented on the tendency on the part of the workers to let equipment, plant, and roads deteriorate and on "the inadequate care for existing capital in capital-poor countries." [11] Possibly it is because much of the capital equipment has been received ostensibly as largesse that the upkeep is poor.

Maybe, for better or worse, the identity of the country which develops more and faster is going to be determined internally in the Latin American countries themselves; and charity, however well meant or well received (and it is frequently neither), is not going to make much contribution. The pace of development is going to be controlled much more in terms of which countries get their armed forces and their oligarchies and their extremist movements under control and then proceed really to work effectively at the job of development.

This is no argument against aid in the event of catastrophes such as the Chilean earthquake of 1960. But, psychologically, what is involved in such cases is not even in the same frame of reference as aid for economic development. There is then a strong suspicion that economic development does not reliably result from foreign aid programs set up as charity.

This statement is not intended to deny the desirability of an orderly

---

[10] Testimony of Philip A. Ray, Chairman, International Bond and Share, in United States Congress, Joint Economic Committee (Hearings), *Private Investment in Latin America* (Washington, 1964), p. 21.

[11] Albert Hirschman, *Strategy of Economic Development* (New Haven, Yale University Press, 1958), p. 141.

CAPITAL FORMATION: FOREIGN RESOURCES

tax system, administered by an international agency, which might assign grants-in-aid back to individual countries.

Conclusion

Foreign investment is much overrated as a source of capital. And capital is much overrated with respect to its role in industrialization.

CHAPTER SIXTEEN

PRIORITIES AND COMPLEMENTARITY

The essence of planning should be (1) some tentative judgment about the broad pattern of development (not worrying too much about the details) plus (2) some carefully made decisions about what to do next.

Of course, at any given stage in the development process decisions must be made by somebody as to what industry to develop or expand next (the priority question) and where to locate the industry (the complementarity question); and these early decisions will have certain cumulative effects in making it more likely that the country will continue along one path or another. Certain major directions of movement, which it will be difficult to change, will be established. These early decisions are probably not acts which can be programmed with any confidence by input-output or linear programming methods. And they are not decisions that can be entrusted to the profit motive and the individual entrepreneur operating in his limited frame of reference. Where will the next great dam or highway be built? Shall the country build a steel mill, a plant to make sulphuric acid, another textile mill, expand food processing? Or is the country big enough to start down several routes at once? The country may be poorly advised—especially if it has less than fifty or seventy-five million people—to try to do very many of these things at once.

At least this is the way matters might look if there ever were a point in time when economic development began, if there ever were a takeoff from a situation which had involved no industrialization and a rigidly traditional set of institutional arrangements. Whether such a takeoff out of limbo (or a limbo that just barely has the proper preconditions) ever has occurred or ever could occur may be debatable. In any event this is not the nature of the choice before the Latin Americans as they pursue economic development and industrialization in a setting where a good deal of development has already occurred, in a setting where a good many of the basic decisions have already been made.

A discussion of development planning that assumes there is free choice in opting among the alternatives is unrealistic. And yet it is probably desirable to describe what the range of choice might be and then speculate with regard to the actual choice genuinely available.

Consumer Goods, Capital Goods, Infrastructure, and Social Overhead

Consumer goods directly provide for the wants and needs of people. Capital goods are an accumulation of goods devoted to the production of other goods. Infrastructure is the economic setting (transportation facilities, power, communication facilities) that needs to exist to make manufacturing of either consumer goods or capital goods feasible. Social overhead is the educational facilities, the health and sanitary facilities, the housing that need to exist to equip people to produce effectively.

The real planning problem is the assignment of emphasis among consumer goods, capital goods, infrastructure, and social overhead in a setting where the constraint should be visualized as the resources available (not the money available). Also within these four great categories priorities need to be assigned to various alternative possibilities. Then (and this is especially true of a region as large as Latin America) if a lot of waste and duplication is to be avoided, there is the problem of deciding which region or country shall specialize in which industries. This is the complementarity problem.

But this is not the beginning of the world, and in Latin America a lot of the decisions have already been made. The region already has considerable amounts of facilities for producing consumer goods and capital goods. It has some infrastructure and some social overhead. Also some countries are already producing some things and other countries other things. A good deal of the decision making in the complementarity area has already been done. And various countries are hastening to effect the establishment of various industries as faits accomplis before an effective

Latin American organization can be set up to control the complementarity pattern.

As matters stand, certain basic decisions on priorities and complementarity are crying to be made. And it may be much better if they are made in a process that involves some possibility of taking long-run perspective into account.

J. E. Meade has given a mountain-climbing example that is revealing in terms of what is involved: The goal is to climb the highest mountain in the range. One can stand off at a little distance and tell which mountain this is. He can then make some roughly accurate judgments about route. This is the position of the government planner trying to chart a rough course in the infrastructure area. By contrast the individual businessman operating in a setting of pure competition can look just a little way ahead. He is at the base of the mountain range, and he knows that he needs to climb up. He does climb up a step at a time (in terms of price theory he moves rationally by marginal increments). He improves his position or increases his elevation with each rational step until after a while he finds he has climbed the wrong mountain.

It might be added to this analogy that neither procedure may discover the pleasant valley halfway up the flank of one of the middle-sized peaks. A bit of purposeless wandering about has a place in the process. Trial and error is going to have to be the story in a lot of the decision making that determines which minor industries get established where. It is desirable to experiment with a lot of alternatives, and many of them will go sour. But a lot of industries that turn out to be very fine things would be missed if a lot of different people were not experimenting with a lot of different projects. It is in this area where the independent businessman has more to contribute than does the government planner.

In the material which follows an effort will be made, first, to identify some criteria that may be useful in assigning priorities and selecting complementarity patterns and, second, to indicate how these criteria might apply to some particular industries.

Priority Criteria

LEVEL OF LIVING VERSUS POWER. What actually is the motivation behind the effort at economic development in Latin America? Is it an effort to raise standard of living or an effort to increase the relative power of the region in the modern world? It can make a good deal of difference in the assigning of priorities. Much of the emphasis on heavy industry (especially the steel industry) can be justified only on the basis of power considerations, power considerations that the Latin American leadership would deny exist.

In fact, a sophisticated rationalization for emphasis on the steel industry has been built up on the basis of other considerations—how legitimately is debatable.

CONSUMER GOODS VERSUS CAPITAL GOODS. Various reasons have been given for placing extraordinary emphasis on the development of a capital goods industry.

(1) Historically the Latin American countries have been dissatisfied with the results of a system in which they have been especially dependent on the export of a few primary commodities to the industrialized countries. They feel that such a system makes them especially vulnerable to economic fluctuations off in the developed countries, which are beyond their control or influence.[1] Especially lamented may be the inability to purchase needed equipment or raw materials during a depression. These circumstances then become an argument for developing an integrated industry, that is to say a steel industry.

Strangely enough, however, the development of the core of heavy industry does not seem to remove this dependence on imports. The nature of the dependence may change without changing perceptibly the degree of dependence. This is especially likely to be true for a small Latin American country which may be able to set up a blast furnace but which cannot possibly set up the associated enterprises and raw material sources that are necessary to make basic industry a going concern, a truly integrated operation. It is rather likely that the isolated basic industry will prove extremely dependent on equipment and raw material imports, just as was the case with the nonintegrated economy producing consumer goods that preceded it. Raúl Prebisch has commented about this phenomenon: "It remains a paradox that industrialization, instead

---

[1] Aldo Ferrer, *La Economía Argentina—Las Etapas de su Desarrollo y Problemas Actuales* (México-Buenos Aires, Fondo de Cultura Económica, 1963), pp. 155–235.

of helping greatly to soften the internal impact of external fluctuations, is bringing us to a new and unknown type of external vulnerability." [2]

(2) Albert Hirschman has justified underdeveloped-country emphasis on a steel industry on the ground that the steel industry is characterized by high backward and forward linkage.[3] This is a way of saying that steel companies buy a lot from primary industries and sell a lot to industries engaged in final manufacture, such as the auto industry, and high backward and forward linkage is presumed to be a desirable characteristic for an industry to have. There is considerable reason to question whether such a study provides a very strong argument for emphasis on a steel industry in Argentina, Peru, Colombia, and in Central America. Backward linkage is not benefiting Argentina much, if the backward linkage consists chiefly in a considerable increase in the importation of iron ore and of coal. The forward linkage is not benefiting Colombia very much if the steel plant at Paz del Río is operating well under capacity.

(3) In addition, that model of expeditious development, the Soviet Union, has concentrated on heavy industry. Copying success is hard to criticize. And yet, the things the Latin American government, which is genuinely concerned with welfare, ought to look at in the Soviet Union are the low standard of living, the agricultural troubles, and the consumer goods production lag.

(4) In the areas where capital goods industries have developed they may have contributed some external economies, some conglomeration effects, to the benefit of the country as a whole. The presence of a basic steel industry undoubtedly facilitates the establishment of steel-using industries in the neighborhood. The providing of tin plate for the expansion of food canning could be a case in point.

The case history of Latin American steel industries up to now seems to provide a good example of what is wrong with the infant-industry argument for tariffs. The Chase Manhattan Bank has reported in a study that it has made of Latin American steel industries that "local production has not yielded significant savings to steel users." [4] In fact it is alleged that there has been a tendency to set the prices at which the

---

[2] Rafael Izquierdo, "Protectionism in Mexico," in Raymond Vernon, ed., *Public Policy and Private Enterprise in Mexico* (Cambridge, Harvard University Press, 1964), pp. 246–47.

[3] *The Strategy of Economic Development* (New Haven, Yale University Press, 1958), p. 108.

[4] *Latin-American Business Highlights,* December, 1956, p. 6.

locally made steel products are sold "at or near, the cost of imported products (including tariff)." [5] If the Latin American countries are going to insist on using infant-industry tariffs as a device for encouraging industrialization, they owe it to themselves to develop some methods for forcing the protected producers to operate in terms of large volume and low unit profits.

The exaggerated emphasis in Latin America on showpiece developments in heavy industry is the sort of thing that has been called by Hla Myint—in the tradition of Thorstein Veblen—conspicuous production. The steel-mill approach to economic development has much in common with the "trickle down" approach to raising the income of the poor by raising the income of the rich first and hoping that a little sifts through their fingers. The financial activities connected with the original building of the steel mill and the mill's productive activities after it is established figure largely in the national income accounts. Those activities inflate national income data without, of themselves, contributing much to consumer welfare.

To put the matter a little differently, the Latin American countries will be able to get by with much lower capital-to-output ratios if they deemphasize steel. This could mean substantially lower capital cost per unit of increase in welfare.

But what has just been said should not be interpreted as a clarion call for the dismantling of all the steel industries in Latin America and the abstention from any further steel-industry development. Certainly the countries that have already made the major effort involved in getting mills started are obligated to make some more major efforts to make the operations as efficient and effective as possible, although they may have to write off a good deal of the original capital investment to make the mills competitive with imports. And steel from Paz del Río may well be able to undersell imported steel in landlocked Bogotá as a permanent proposition. Similar special circumstances in other cases may help with working out a reasonably satisfactory solution for the difficulties of the plants-in-being. But, for the present, it would probably be a mistake for more Latin American countries to try to develop integrated steel mills. Central America should abstain from this gesture.

The steel industry is a good example of a situation where several countries (Argentina, Colombia, Peru) have jumped the gun on the

[5] *Ibid.*

establishment of a rational complementarity pattern by establishing their own steel mills with precipitation.

SPECIALIZATION VERSUS DIVERSIFICATION (THE ECONOMIES OF CONGLOMERATION). Specialization in a limited number of lines of activity is probably desirable, especially in the early phases of development in small countries, even though the country has equally good chance of success in any of a somewhat wider range of activities. A country that establishes a world-wide reputation for quality and efficacy in certain lines of activity will find that associated industries will be fighting to establish themselves in the favorable setting. The process will possess an internal dynamism that is absent when effort is made to develop too many lines of industry at once.

A slightly different aspect to the economies of conglomeration concept is the possibility that a particular major project, effectively and imaginatively pushed, may carry a lot of development along with it. Brasilia is such a project; so might be the Pan American Highway, if somebody would get behind that project and get the highway built.

Conglomeration may be visualized as either a function of geography or as a function of industrial specialization. In connection with the complementarity ideas of the Latin America Free Trade Association, the poorer countries have been afraid that conglomeration by regions would leave them to retrograde. Two rather different things may be said about this. One is that it may be well if there is some population shifting away from the rural areas to the industrial centers and from Haiti to Mexico and from Bolivia to Argentina.

The other point is that a small center (in a large, free trade area) may specialize to advantage on some particular manufactured product, a specialization such as has not in the past been possible because of the trade barriers and poor transportation facilities among the Latin American countries. The small center might have a quite high standard of living in consequence even though it is not the center of an industrial complex, and it may be a very pleasant place to live. (Small countries just cannot afford industrial complexes like the Ruhr or the North Central United States unless they have some significant resource endowments and some substantial international trading possibilities.) But small countries can make a pretty good thing of specialization (Swiss watches, Dutch cheese, quality textiles, and tin processing) if they want to. And various of the small Latin American countries, if they are just bound to maintain their political independence, could profit by some of these examples—meantime concentrating on productivity rather than on protectionism.

There are, however, limits to the economies of conglomeration and some of the industrial centers in Latin America may well have approached these limits. In Mexico in 1960, 51 percent of the value of manufacturing for the entire country was concentrated in the Federal District around Mexico City and in the states of Nuevo Leon and of Mexico. This contrasted with a concentration of 39 percent in those areas in 1950. Mexico could well deemphasize development in the Federal District, where there is a serious problem of water shortage, and concentrate especially on the development of the smaller industrial centers.

BALANCED VERSUS UNBALANCED GROWTH. A frequent point of argument among economic development planners has involved the question as to whether growth should be balanced or unbalanced. Balanced growth presumably means that the various sectors of the economy should develop *pari passu*. But it may mean something more: that many new industries need to develop at about the same time. The argument is that the increased purchasing power of all will provide a market for the products of all. This approach to the implementation of development might be called "the big push."[6] In contrast to the balanced growth, or big push, approach would be an emphasis on complementarity and the economies of conglomeration.

The critics of balanced growth, arguing against the desirability that all industries grow at equivalent pace, have been on firm ground. There may be a very salutary effect to be obtained from a spurting ahead of one industry or one population center. Such spurts may carry a lot of associated development along with them.

But there is another sense in which a type of balance is important. There needs to be a balance, not necessarily an equality, in the growth of (1) a group with engineering and scientific background, (2) a group with managerial and supervisory ability, (3) a group of independent entrepreneurs with reasonable access to domestic credit, (4) the size of

[6] Proponents of this approach have been P. N. Rosenstein-Rodan, Ragnar Nurkse, Tibor Scitovsky, and W. Arthur Lewis.

the market, (5) availability of materials, and (6) availability of equipment.

SKIPPING VERSUS REPETITION (AND THE TECHNOLOGICAL FRONTIER). Should the countries just starting economic development plan to skip some of the stages through which the already developed countries have gone? Or should they plan in terms of repeating the growth process through some kind of standardized model? A Mexican writer, Manuel Germán Parra, has defended the proposition that it is necessary to repeat all the standard stages.[7] Probably the popularity of W. W. Rostow's book, *The Stages of Economic Growth,* has done little to dissipate the notion that there is some preordained group of stages that needs to be gone through.

And yet, one of the advantages that the underdeveloped countries now have in this rat race is that they can profit from the errors of those who have gone before. And especially they can skip some of the stages through which the already developed countries have labored. It would be judicious for the underdeveloped countries to jump immediately to the frontiers of knowledge in some carefully selected areas. The country that is short of both water power and coal, such as Argentina, could become a pioneer in atomic-power development. (Or perhaps the recent spurt in petroleum production in Argentina has taken the edge off of that recommendation.) Cuba is a country lacking all three: water power, coal, and petroleum. That country might give thought to atomic power. And it might be an interesting proposition to put to the Russians—whether they were willing to make Cuba a showplace in the peaceful uses of atomic energy.

DOMESTIC RESOURCES. Also, so far as the new industries are concerned, there should be a hard core of domestic resource providing a major part of the raw materials going into the industry. Brazil is wealthy in a broad range of raw materials from bauxite through water power to iron ore. Why should it beat its brains out trying to develop an oil industry?

Further development of steel industries in Latin America should probably be limited to the countries with substantial iron-ore reserves. The countries with the especially large iron-ore reserves are Brazil and Vene-

---

[7] *La Industrialización de México* (México, 1954), p. 27.

zuela (and perhaps Mexico and Cuba). It should be reasonably low-cost to operate major steel industries in Brazil and Venezuela on the basis of imported coal. The United States has coal and needs iron ore. Transportation arrangements could bring coal south from Pennsylvania on the same ore ships that carry iron ore north to the United States. But the Brazilian and Venezuelan industries would need to be able to market freely over all Latin America—and be willing to draw labor freely also from the rest of the region.

In order to approximate efficient operation the single plant needs to produce more steel than many of the Latin American countries will be able to consume domestically in this century. And if all countries are going to play the steel-industry game they cannot all dispose of their surpluses by export.

One of the disappointing features of economic development planning in Latin America has been the lack of attention to the question of locally available raw materials as a criterion for identifying a worthwhile industry. For example in a recent study of possible new industries for Central America, the lack of availability of local raw materials was a characteristic of many of the industries under consideration.[8]

Latin America does have a great variety of resources crying for development. Included are some of the major water-power resources of the world on the eastern slopes of the Andes in Colombia, Ecuador, Peru and Bolivia. But beyond an obvious resource such as this lies a variety of plant, animal, and mineral resource, the potential of which has scarcely been estimated.

MANPOWER. Underemployed, unskilled manpower is a potential resource of Latin America—especially in the Caribbean area. But south and east Asia have an even richer endowment in underemployed, unskilled manpower. Consequently, Latin America, in searching for its best areas of emphasis, needs to walk a narrow line between a major commitment to the strictly labor intensive industries and emphasis on the capital intensive—capital also not being one of the chief major Latin American resources. In a three factor of production world, Latin America is relatively wealthy in raw materials, relatively lacking in labor and capital.

[8] United Nations, *Posibilidades de Desarrollo Industrial Integrado en Centroamérica* (New York, 1963).

However, the population growth rate in Latin America is extremely rapid. It is running 2.5 to 3.0 percent a year in most of the Latin American countries (Argentina being an exception). This means that the Latin American countries need to take the population utilization problem very seriously, even though life is not quite so cheap in Latin America as in Asia.

Thus there is no simple conclusion as to whether Latin America should emphasize capital-intensive or labor-intensive industries. But the planner needs to remember that Latin America has a rapidly growing reservoir of a type of labor supply that is highly proficient in work requiring care, attention to detail, and a feel for form and quality. But the labor supply does not have the educational background necessary for industries that require a substantial amount of education on the part of the labor force. The tendency of Latin American industrialists to turn out shoddy merchandise and not take advantage of the craftmanship instinct of the Latin American labor force is one of the things that has gone wrong in the recent evolution of Latin American economic development.

MAJOR IMPACT QUICKLY. In the Latin American countries, the thinking concerning the goals of economic development is a mixture of thinking in terms of power politics with thinking in terms of a desire for improvement in the welfare of the citizenry. There is much talk to the effect that in the "revolution of rising expectations" there needs to be a major and immediate improvement in the level of living if violent revolution is to be avoided. But there is not going to be quick improvement in the standard of living if primary emphasis is placed on political power considerations and on the steel industry. To raise quickly the standard of living, emphasis should be on the industries that would increase production considerably with relatively little capital expenditure, especially in the area of food, clothing, and shelter. And there are plenty of such industries with a growth potential in Latin America.

Especially in view of the phenomenal rate of population growth in Latin America, the availability of consumer goods needs to be taken seriously as a basic problem. The first Latin American country effectively to opt consciously for consumer goods industries in its development thinking (to the deemphasis of heavy industry) may surprise itself by the degree of success it has in increasing welfare. And, in the end, it may have occasion to be rather proud of itself for having the intestinal fortitude to disregard the political power and status considerations that have encouraged emphasis on steel.

Complementarity

The Treaty of Montevideo, establishing the Latin American Free Trade Association (1960), provided for effort to develop patterns of complementarity assigning primacy in one industry to one country and in another industry to another.

Article 16 says: "With a view to expediting the process of integration and complementarity . . . the Contracting Parties: (a) Shall endeavour to promote progressively closer co-ordination of the corresponding industrialization policies, and shall sponsor for this purpose agreements among representatives of the economic sectors concerned; and (b) May negotiate mutual agreements on complementarity by industrial sectors." In Article 17, it is added that: "Any Contracting Party concerned with the complementarity programmes shall be free to participate in the negotiation of these agreements. The results of these negotiations shall, in every case, be embodied in protocols which shall enter into force after the Contracting Parties have decided that they are consistent with the general principles and purposes of the present Treaty."

The Economic Commission for Latin America has also been concerned about planning in these terms. To many development planners it seems clear that, if there is to be any rational assignment of the primacy in the various industries among the various countries, the broad outlines of a complementarity pattern need to be established very early in the development process. And certainly it is true, assuming the establishment of a complementarity pattern to be desirable, that nothing is going to be accomplished by waiting till the various countries have already begun to develop certain industries and then telling them they should do something else.

Despite the general agreement that it is desirable for Latin America to develop a rational complementarity pattern, very little actually has been done along this line. The Alliance for Progress calls for each country to draw up a ten-year development plan. Common sense would seem to indicate that the first step in this process would be for the region as a whole to reach some tentative agreements as to which countries are going to specialize in which industries. Drawn up in such a setting, the national plans would then make better sense. But almost nothing of this sort has been done. There have been a few instances where associations have been formed for particular industries (the Latin American Association of Glass Producers, for example) with the apparent thought that the association would have some degree of responsibility for working out a complementarity pattern for that particular industry.

But the approach being used in the framework of the LAFTA seems to be that the initiative is taken by two or three countries which decide that it would be nice if one of them specialized in one thing and the other in something else and they traded. Then, to make this arrangement into a region-wide complementarity agreement, they have to induce the other countries to come in and agree to the primacy of the first two countries in the production of the particular articles involved. And this is where the hitch seems to be developing in the generalizing of the complementarity agreements. The other countries do not like to be confronted with these accomplished facts by the countries that took the original initiative. In fact the chances are extremely good that those early initiatives were taken in connection with just those important industries that everybody would like to have. So, the generalization of the incipient complementarity agreement hits a snag, as it has already, apparently, in the cases of motor vehicles, glass, petroleum products, and various wood and paper products.[9]

The implementation of complementarity agreements is, politically, a hot potato. Would Central America tolerate a pattern which said that it should not develop a steel industry? No one wants to give up the right to establish an automobile industry. But Brazil wishes some of the others would.

No over-all, coordinated pattern, however rough, has been drawn up. The individual countries are drawing up their ten-year development plans under the Alliance for Progress with very little regard for what their neighbors are doing.

If input-output matrices and linear programming were worth much in the field of development planning they would be the devices used in establishing complementarity patterns. But I believe that it is correct to say that these planning tools have not yet successfully been used in this sort of an effort. And it may well be in the nature of things that they cannot

[9] *Comercio Exterior,* April, 1964, p. 241.

be so used and should not be. The evolving technology that makes today's neutral stuff into tomorrow's resource is going to play havoc with the best-laid, long-run plans anyway. And we are back with the proposition that the real essence of planning is the ability to adjust to changing circumstances.

Let me suggest a pattern. (This is the sort of thing one really should not do, especially after the preceding remarks, but also because of the likelihood of being proven all wrong by time. Nevertheless, speculating in such terms may have some usefulness in understanding what is involved in the complementarity problem.)

Perhaps, for the present, Latin America should think in terms of six or eight major industrial complexes on the ground that (at least for now) that is as many as could hope to develop enough of a reputation as industrial centers to become real attractions for peripheral and supporting industries. There should only be two or three centers using a heavy steel industry as their center of gravity: the Minas Gerais-Guanabara region in Brazil and the lower Orinoco-Caroní valleys in Venezuela. There could well be industrial complexes oriented to heavy chemicals in the Lake Maracaibo region of Venezuela and in the Isthmus of Tehuantepec-Vera Cruz region of Mexico. There could be industrial complexes oriented to consumer durables and industrial equipment in Mexico, Argentina, and in the São Paulo region of Brazil. (In fact there already are.) Not ranking as major industrial complexes, but having significant textile, food-processing, and other light industries, would be such places as Santiago de Chile, Havana, Bogotá, Lima, and any place else that is capable of doing it. Middle-sized, basic steel industries already in being in Chile, Peru, and Colombia should certainly continue to do as best they can and be as efficient as they can. They are water under the bridge now and should be made the best of in terms of efforts at efficient operation.

The major industrial complexes will attract additional service and associated industries. Indeed they already are doing so. There will be forward linkages (assorted consumer goods industries will be created because the basic industries are there). There will be backward linkages (raw materials such as limestone will be produced for the industries such as steel). The development of a pool of skilled chemists in the heavy chemical industry could make skilled people available to move out laterally into related activities such as the drug and synthetic fiber industries. The technicians with machine-tool skills developed in one durable consumer goods industry can move laterally quite freely into other durable consumer goods industries—from automobile manufacturing, to farm-equipment manufacturing, to railroad equipment, to earth-moving equipment, and so on. The geologist, in the early days of the oil industry, rather easily shifted from metallic mineral and coal prospecting to oil prospecting.

As Hirschman has pointed out: "The investments of one period call forth complementary investments in the next period with a will and logic of their own." [10] Once the development process becomes truly dynamic, the ongoing process becomes the master of the plan or should. And the ten-year plan, too rigidly adhered to, becomes an institutional hindrance to development.

Perhaps it is desirable to acknowledge in concluding these comments on complementarity that, if the Latin Americans were to try to reach agreement on a complementarity pattern, there is strong likelihood that the conference would break up in substantial disagreement. Even though this should happen, the discussion could well have been useful in terms of indicating to some countries some things they would be poorly advised to try to do.

It is desirable to make the "next step" in any development program as intelligent a step as possible. It is desirable that all the Latin American countries not develop the same industries at once. But to an important extent, much of Latin America's complementarity pattern is already a fait accompli and much of the rest of it should not be made rigid.

Complementarity is desirable. It is the counterpart of specialization and of the gains in terms of lower costs that go with specialization. But it does seem likely that Latin America is not going to establish its complementarity pattern as the result of rational hemisphere-wide planning, although Raúl Prebisch is going to give the effort a good try. Rather, to a marked extent, the complementarity problem is going to establish itself (or already has) as a result of the basic nature of the forces at work. And in a world where it is probably just as well that we cannot read the future, it may be just as well that we cannot predetermine the future.

[10] *Strategy* . . . , p. 42.

CHAPTER SEVENTEEN

PRIORITIES: INFRASTRUCTURE AND SOCIAL OVERHEAD

There is no question as to the general necessity for infrastructure (public utilities, transport, and power), and for social overhead (education and health) in all countries. It does not matter what particular channels the subsequent industrialization is to follow. So, complementarity-type problems are not so much involved in this area. But there are questions as to what particular infrastructure and social-overhead facilities should be provided, where they should be set up, and how soon. These are priorities problems.

Pure competition and the free, private entrepreneur seem not to be able to provide much of the needed infrastructure in any sort of an orderly and reliable way. Or to put the matter a little differently, one of the chief arts that the modern industrialist needs to practice is the art of maneuvering government into making a significant contribution to his basic capital needs out of public funds and calling it infrastructure or social overhead. (This is an art highly developed in the United States by real estate promoters who would like for the city to pave the streets and provide the utilities.) In Latin America, on the contrary, the governments have been fairly successful in maneuvering foreign investors into supplying infrastructure in the form of roads, schools, power, and health facilities.

However, the nature of the *quid pro quo* gets a bit complicated. Latin American governments also have given major subsidies to foreign investors, as for example to the early railroad builders. And, on the other hand, even though foreign investors have provided a good deal of infrastructure, this has not necessarily meant a net flow of resources from the creditor country to the debtor country. It might rather mean in road building the use of the asphalt and heavy crudes being produced by the foreign oil company in the debtor country. Actually here, as in so many other situations, the foreign investment is not so much performing the role of providing capital internationally as it is substituting for an institutional failure on the part of the Latin American government. And naturally, the roads and schools and other facilities provided by the foreign investors tend to be in the neighborhood of the oil camps rather than in the population centers.

Priorities as between Infrastructure and Manufacturing

In a sense these are different worlds, and infrastructure has about the same relation to the capital goods industries that capital goods have to consumer goods. A certain amount of infrastructure provided early in the development process makes it possible for capital goods production to make more of a contribution, and to make it sooner, to welfare. However, there are questions of emphasis involved. An all-out, early, infrastructure effort, with little emphasis on consumer goods, could mean that the increase in consumer goods production lags for many years. By contrast, a modest emphasis on infrastructure in the beginning, combined with relatively more emphasis on consumer goods could have a much more significant effect more quickly on standard of living. Approximately these same remarks could be made with regard to the relation between capital goods and consumer goods industries.

In any event, it seems that a respectable amount of the early effort must go into transportation and power and irrigation and dams and schools and sanitation—even though some questions of emphasis remain, questions that can be resolved only by a subjective decision of the present generation as to its evaluation of immediate and future gains. However, in a setting of underemployed resources these questions may not be as crucial as planners sometimes assume. A lot of expansion can occur in one area without there being need for contraction in other areas. And the question is where to go ahead, not where to cut back.

Priorities among Infrastructure Projects

The economist may point out the importance of developing Latin American transportation if the region is to be able to take advantage of the possibilities of complementarity and specialization for lowering costs. He can say something about the power needs. But he has little to offer by way of objective criteria for passing fine judgments on the degree of emphasis to go to transportation, by comparison with power, by comparison with housing, by comparison with education, by comparison with health and sanitation. On the whole these tremendously important social questions involving degree of emphasis have to be answered by the society as a whole (it may be hoped by democratic or other reasonably enlightened means) on the basis of nonquantifiable evaluations.

In subsequent sections we shall discuss some of the problems involved in the expansion of various of the infrastructure and social-overhead sectors. But no real effort will be made to answer the question as to the relative degree of emphasis to go into one of these sectors by comparison with another. And input-output analysis and linear programming are hard put to give satisfactory answers to such questions.

Transportation

RAILROADS. The position of railroads in the transportation picture of the future is ambiguous. In the United States railroads as carriers of passengers are in a state of major decline. But as carriers of freight they continue important. In the Soviet Union they continue important as both carriers of freight and carriers of passengers. In Latin America, for various reasons, railroad transportation facilities are generally in an inefficient state. No real network exists linking the different regions of Latin America; so, the railroads have not played the role in long-distance transportation they might have played. Even as national transportation networks the railroads of Latin America have left a good deal to be desired. Brazil, for example, has no effective national network. But even so, the railroads that are already in existence should be put back on an efficient operating basis and a few connecting links could make the existing systems far more serviceable. The Argentine could strike a major blow for itself by straightening out its run-down, deficit-ridden railroads.

Railroads have been at a disadvantage relative to highways because commercial highway users such as truckers do not pay all costs, but effectively parasite on facilities provided by society in a way that the railroads cannot do.

Despite the assorted difficulties, Mexico has rather actively and apparently rather effectively in recent years continued a program of railway development. The completion of the rail connection between Mexico City and Yucatan, and between Ojinaga and Los Mochis are examples of such activity.

It would not take a whole lot of additional railroad building (although it would require some modification of gauges) to make it possible to travel from the United States to Buenos Aires. The thought is intriguing. Even though there were little through freight and few through passengers (and there might be more than one would think—it would be a nice trip), the amount of middle-distance hauling could increase substantially as a counterpart to the development of the Latin American Free Trade Association.

Nevertheless, probably the main emphasis in transportation should be (and no doubt will be) on highways and on air transport.

ROADS. Latin America has a sixth the road mileage of the United States in an area over twice as large, and of that road mileage a third is improved by comparison with two thirds in the United States.

The lack of hard-surfaced roads is one of the principal bottlenecks to the economic development of Latin America. Incidentally, improved highway facilities would create the possibility of a major tourist appeal on the thousands of miles of coast from Baja California to eastern Venezuela. Literally thousands of miles of this coast compare favorably with the Riviera. The sale or lease of lots (very small lots) along this ocean front, and for quite a ways inland, could provide a considerable amount of foreign exchange to aid in economic development. The laws prohibiting the ownership of land within 50 kilometers or so of the coast might have to be changed. But they are probably one of the more useless bits of antiforeign legislation on the books anyway. The foreigner owning an ocean-front lot in the region of Mazatlán is not going to be

INFRASTRUCTURE AND SOCIAL OVERHEAD

the crucial factor betraying the beachhead to the Japanese. (A renter could do that job just as well.)

At least since the first Pan American Conference met in Washington in 1889, there has been talk of building a Pan American Highway connecting all the American countries. The original project for a Pan American Highway provided that each country should bear the expense of the stretch of road through its territory. This policy was not getting the road built with sufficient speed down toward Panama. For that reason the United States in 1941 offered to carry two thirds of the cost to Panama—perhaps $20,000,000 in the Central American countries and $30,000,000 in Mexico.

The completion of the highway could give a real boost to Latin American development. And yet, the project continues to languish. The highway, in an unimproved sort of way, was pushed through to Panama in 1963. But if somebody does not get a move on, it will not be through to Bogotá, Colombia, or Quito, Ecuador, in this century. The through traffic movement that the completion of the highway would permit is important. Even more important might be the stimulation which the completion of the highway would give to the building of feeder roads. And the various Latin American countries ought to be able to build a lot of feeder roads without the help of a great deal of foreign investment. Big bulldozers and "cats" may expedite the building of four-lane highways with minimum grades. They are not so important for the building of feeder roads where much of the traffic is going to be by oxcart (or burro)—and the rest of the traffic had better slow down.

Incidentally (although one cannot prove such things) a good part of the explanation as to why Mexico is one of the few Latin American countries experiencing a respectable rate of growth may be due to the fact that transportation to and from the United States is relatively easy.

Maintenance does not necessarily require a lot of expensive equipment (although it should require the care of the equipment one already has). The Latin American highway system could be maintained much better than it has been with the expenditure of a modest amount of continuing, thoughtful effort in keeping chuckholes filled. And the labor force for this kind of work is readily available and in substantial quantities: the army. The officer corps could, to advantage, spend time on basic highway maintenance procedures and in supervising road work. The officers would then know the terrain better.

Improvement in the transportation system is an absolute imperative in the economic development of Latin America; and it is immediately necessary if the Alliance for Progress and the Latin American Free Trade Association are to amount to much. As a nucleus in the development of a transportation system in Latin America the interior communication system (not ocean transport) is the heart of the matter. And it would seem that a first step in the integration of the system would be the completion of an arrangement which would permit overland transportation connecting the extremes of Latin America. This is essential if there is to be any coherence in the region, even though few people make a direct nonstop trip from Tijuana to Ushuaia. Latin America needs to conquer itself.

AIRLINES. The DC-3 brought many rural regions of Latin America, especially in Central America and down through Colombia, Ecuador, and Peru, from the fourteenth century to the twentieth century in short order, as far as some aspects of their existence were concerned. The use of small, inexpensive, general purpose planes in a sparsely populated region as large as Latin America is a major transport contribution. Whether Latin America is using scarce resources very wisely by trying to operate intercontinental jets is not so clear.

OCEAN SHIPPING. Somewhat the same thing may be said about the efforts of several Latin American countries to operate ocean shipping lines.

Ocean-going ships are expensive, and poor countries can probably advance their welfare more effectively by spending their money differently. In ocean shipping, capital cost per sailor seems to be about $50,000.[1] This contrasts with capital costs per worker in the manufacturing area in the range between $5000 and $20,000. It would seem that on the whole the Latin American countries have better things to do with their capital than invest it in an ocean-going shipping industry. Why raise the capital/output ratio by expenditures of this sort, if that can be avoided? Especially Brazil should give priority to internal transport in preference to ocean shipping.

And yet as recently as August, 1962, a conference of Latin American

---

[1] Claudio Escarpenter, "Problemas Generales del Transporte en América Latina," in *Economía Latinoamericana,* I (November, 1963), 217.

transportation experts held in Montevideo came out for substantial development of ocean shipping facilities. Maybe the United States in the last century was accidentally lucky in being forced to develop transportation across the interior of the country because of the inconvenience of going around Cape Horn or of transshipping across the Isthmus of Panama. If Latin America were forced to develop transcontinental transport facilities because it could not use ocean shipping, it might be a good thing.

Dams and Power

Dam building has been a widely heralded and early emphasized element in the development of infrastructure. The threefold usefulness in providing power, flood control, and water for irrigation has contributed to the popularity of dam building.

It may nevertheless be true that, relatively speaking, too much of the early economic development effort in Latin America has gone into big dams in the wrong places. Big dams may owe some of their popularity to their size. Completion of one can occasion a major celebration. They are impressive showpieces; they do provide some power; they do provide some flood control; they may provide irrigation—although they have been a conspicuous failure in this respect in Brazil's Northeast. These things are all desirable. They are easy for a development planner to fit into a plan.

This is not an argument against the occasional desirability of big dams. It is an argument against a major amount of the early development effort going into big dams in the wrong places. A corresponding amount of effort on small dams could help a whole lot more people with their irrigation needs in a whole lot more area with a whole lot less canal building. And flood control may frequently be better handled by small dams nearer the headwaters than by large dams lower down the rivers.

Latin America has a major share of the water-power resources of the world: 12 to 15 percent. And the region has only 3 or 4 percent of the world's facilities for turning water power into electricity. Up to now, the rivers with the really fantastic potential have been largely neglected because of their geographical isolation. They are the rivers coming off the eastern slopes of the Andes in Ecuador, Colombia, Peru, and Bolivia. By contrast some of Mexico's dam building has been on rivers that have run short of water, such as the Nazas, causing great hardship in the Laguna area around Torreón.

Housing

Whether housing is properly capital goods or consumption goods is unclear. A good deal of the consumer-type satisfaction one gets out of life is obviously a result of having pleasant home surroundings. And housing is not exactly "goods used in the production of other goods," one of the definitions of capital. And yet, the statisticians commonly include residential construction in investment statistics. And it is difficult to get construction data that segregate housing, from housing projects that include stores, and from factory construction and investment in machinery.

And in an important sense adequate housing is (with education) an infra part of the infrastructure necessary for the support of human capital. That is to say, it is social overhead; and yet it is a sort of social overhead, unlike education, that may be called up by the profit motive.

Adequate housing is itself a significant element in standard of living. But housing in Latin America is generally wretched and may be getting worse.

In his 1963 address to the annual Mexican bankers' convention, Secretary of Hacienda, Antonio Ortiz Mena, said that "if the present tendency continues, [the housing shortage] within thirty years will be 4.5 million units, the shelter for over 20 million Mexicans." [2]

The population of Latin America has been growing at a rate of about 2.8 percent a year; but the population of urban areas has been growing at a rate of about 5 percent a year. This involves a major movement from the country to the city, especially to the one or two largest cities in each country. The residential housing problem in the Latin American cities is therefore particularly acute. William F. Butler, of the Chase Manhattan Bank, has calculated a basic need for 1.5 million new housing units in Latin America per year if Latin America is not to lose ground in terms of housing. Butler has estimated the cost of this program to be $3.75 to $4 billion a year. Latin American countries seem to be spending $2 to $3 billion a year now on residential construction.

Residential construction in Latin America now accounts for about

[2] *Trimestre Económico*, XXX (July, 1963), 449–50.

one fifth of gross capital formation (public and private). This is about the figure that has prevailed historically in the United States, and indicates that the Latin American relative effort in housing is respectable.

The International Basic Economy Corporation, a Rockefeller enterprise intended to help with the industrialization of Latin America by serving as a successful example of how to do things, has decided to go into the residential housing area in Latin America. In connection with announcing plans for the financing of this operation, Rodman Rockefeller made some estimates with regard to the savings potential in Latin America and how the IBEC intends to mobilize Latin American family saving to finance housing. One statement ran to the effect that: "Approximately 18 million urban families throughout Latin America are in a position to amortize a mortgage of a reasonable duration on a home of low cost." [3] Satisfactory mortgage institutions that might serve as the middlemen in Latin America in this sort of operation have not developed, he believes, in large measure because of the disorganizing effect of chronic inflation. IBEC plans to encourage house-mortgage financing by assisting the establishment of building-and-loan-type institutions and will try to avoid the inflation difficulty by adjusting interest and principal on both savings and mortgages on the basis of an index designed to correct for changes in both wages and prices.

The housing problem may be far less serious than sometimes considered when viewed in terms of cost and far more serious in terms of institutional adaptation. Leonard Currie, reporting to a Symposium on Latin American Housing conducted by the Chase Manhattan Bank in 1962, said: "The priority needs for these people, in terms of physical facilities, are: water supply, sewage disposal, access streets, electricity, play areas, schools, community centers for meetings and adult training, churches and clinics or dispensaries. . . ." [4] At the same symposium, T. Graydon Upton, executive vice president of the Inter-American Development Bank, declared: "In my opinion, frequently both Latin American planners and Americans set their sights far too high. A tremendous improvement over present conditions can be obtained by

---

[3] United States Senate, Committee on Banking and Currency, *Study of International Housing* (Washington, 1963), p. 106. Other material on the housing problem includes: "Housing in Latin America," in *Latin American Business Highlights* (Chase Manhattan Bank), 12 (Second Quarter, 1962), 9–11; Chase Manhattan Bank, *Housing in Latin America* (New York, 1962).

[4] Chase Manhattan Bank, *Housing in Latin America*, 7.

operating on a very modest scale . . . in many areas the emphasis must be on community facilities, water, and planning living space, rather than shelter per se."[5]

The multistoried, overarchitectured showpieces that have characterized some of the publicized housing efforts in Latin America have probably represented far more cost than need be per dwelling unit.

The housing programs might be built around the following elements:

(1) The governments should establish truly massive programs for providing access streets, concrete slabs, and water, sewerage, and electricity (or gas) at nominal cost to the poor.

(2) The construction of the houses on the concrete slabs should be left largely to the homeowners, with the proviso that the government needs to take vigorous action to break the sellers' market in low-cost building materials. Competent advisers need to be available in large numbers to counsel with the people. Experimentation in the building-material field ought to be a high priority item in manufacturing. Incidentally, so far as the house-building technology itself is concerned, a tremendous amount of housing (and factory-building construction) should be possible with the labor force and raw materials available, without major investment in construction equipment, and using fairly cheap building materials. Much is already being done in efforts of this sort. The CINVA-Ram device for making cheap bricks out of sandy clay and a small amount of cement is an example.[6] The process was developed by a Chilean, Raúl Ramírez, at the Inter-American Housing and Planning Center (of the Organization of American States) in Colombia.

(3) For middle-income housing the development of mortgage institutions is a possible device for handling the financing.

(4) Effective planning help needs to be given to ensure recreation areas (and the policing of recreation areas). Soldiers might be used in the policing of playgrounds in housing projects. The soldiers could organize games for the young and help with community recreation and social activities for the adults. This should help reduce the amount of hooliganism.

(5) The abolition of rent control should help to stimulate private

---

[5] *Ibid.*

[6] Donald S. Stroetzel, "Earth Bricks by the Millions," in *Americas*, April, 1964, pp. 5–9.

housing construction. What then would keep the landlord from charging high rents? The existence of the increased amount of housing would help. Improved, rapid urban transportation would help by giving the occupant a wider range of choice. In Argentina, and probably in several of the other countries as well, the problem, especially at the level of middle-class housing, has been rendered particularly serious by the rent control and other regulatory procedures that have made it unprofitable for private enterprise to build new housing for people at that income level.

Education

Education in law and the classics and the philosophy of Spinoza is not especially what Latin America needs. Reading, writing, arithmetic, civics, simple bookkeeping, and the skills of a trade are the hard core of the matter for the bulk of the population. And here the Peace Corps can play a role and is playing a role. The young college graduate (with some language knowledge and some engineering background, or the knowledge of a trade such as machinist or horticulturist) can substitute in some degree for the major lack of high-school-level teachers in Latin America. It is too bad the programs of engineering schools in United States universities cannot be a little less packed with five years of engineering courses—so that the engineering student would have a little time to take a foreign language and just a modicum of social science. Such a person would make the ideal Peace Corps member.

The school building itself should not be a major problem if the community is willing to divert a modest amount of effort to its construction. Historically, the proliferation of churches in Latin America indicates that this sort of building is well within the capabilities of the average Latin American community. The problem involves the institutional adjustment necessary in mobilizing the community for the effort.

Health and Sanitation

It might be argued that there is little point in emphasizing health, with the consequent multiplication of the population, until goods production is capable of looking after the increased population. But better health is an absolutely important characteristic of a higher standard of living.

Adequate water supply and sanitary facilities are necessary to health. Facilities such as these are being actively promoted by the Social Progress Trust Fund of the Inter-American Development Bank. Among possible areas of foreign aid emphasis, health and sanitation should have a high priority. And it might well result that the rate of population increase would fall in a healthier, better-off Latin America.

CHAPTER EIGHTEEN

INDUSTRIAL PRIORITIES

By 1930 there were textile plants of respectable size in many of the countries, especially Mexico, Brazil, Cuba, Chile, Argentina, and Colombia. Also, there was ore processing for export in Mexico and in the countries along the west coast of South America. (However, the mines and smelters were generally located far from the population centers and employed relatively few people; so, their impact on the economies was slight.) There were major meat-packing plants in Argentina and breweries here and there. Otherwise, manufacturing was largely limited to artisan-type production of consumer goods. Heavy industry was almost nonexistent, an exception being a steel mill established at Monterrey, Mexico, about the turn of the century.

Latin America has about 12.2 percent of the population of the world outside the Communist bloc. In 1958 the area had about 4.2 percent of the industry of the world and the following shares in various manufacturing sectors, as shown in Table 15.

Table 15

LATIN AMERICAN SHARES OF WORLD PRODUCTION

	Percent
All manufacturing	3.7
Light	5.3
Heavy	2.7
Food, beverage, tobacco	7.3
Textiles	6.6
Basic metals	3.4
Metal products	1.6

Source: United Nations, *Statistical Yearbook, 1962.*

Subsistence versus Commercial Agriculture

Subsistence agriculture provides a bare living, if that, to people who grub about with primitive tools, such as a wooden hoe and a forked stick, and live off their own meager product. In commercial agriculture, the farmer grows a crop for the market and, with the money he gets from selling his produce, buys on the market much of what he consumes.

Approximately half of the economically active population of Latin America is in agriculture. This half of the working force contributes less than a quarter of the total output. This is because most of the population in agriculture is in subsistence agriculture. This is where the extremely low incomes are. The country with the most highly developed commercial agriculture, Argentina, has a relatively small percentage (25 percent) of the labor force in agriculture.

Typical of the subsistence agriculture in Latin America are the *ejidos* of the central plateau of Mexico, where corn (for tortillas) and frijole beans are raised with generally backward methods involving very low yields per acre. The potatoes of upland Peru and Bolivia are another example, as is the yucca or manioc (or mandioca, or tapioca, or cassava, or Spanish bayonet) of much of the lowland area of tropical America. These crops are typically grown on small plots of land, called *milpas* in Mexico.

Subsistence agriculture carries with it various peripheral activities that in some sense set the tone for a particular culture. In Mexico there is the fermented drink, *pulque,* which is obtained from the maguey cactus. In the highlands of Peru and Bolivia there is the chewing of the coca leaf. (Cocaine is obtained from the coca leaf.) The laborious soaking of the poison out of the yucca is one of the chief activities of the tropics.

But on the world scene, foreigners are likely to identify various of the Latin American countries with their chief commercial crop. Indeed, the commercial crop frequently represents a half or more of the exports of the Latin American country. And the strength of the economy in international finance is closely tied to the prices obtained for these export crops. The standard examples are Brazilian, Colombian, and Guatemalan coffee, Argentine beef and wheat, Cuban sugar, the bananas of Central America and of Ecuador, the cacao of Brazil and Ecuador, the cotton of Mexico, Peru, Brazil, and Argentina.

Also, Latin America provides (or has provided) to the world markets some strategic and specialty items which have a rather unique importance, even though they may involve a relatively small proportion of the country's exports. Examples of this sort of thing are the carnauba wax of the Northeast of Brazil; the quebracho (for tanning leather) of the Paraguayan and Argentine Chaco; chicle (chewing gum) from the sapodilla tree of British Honduras, the Petén region of Guatemala, and southern Mexico; quinine from the cinchona bark of Ecuador; rubber, originally from the Hevea brasiliensis of Brazil; angostura bitters, originally from the lower Orinoco valley; yerba mate tea in southeastern South America.

Subsistence agriculture is relatively more important in the lives of people. Commercial agriculture is relatively more important in establishing the tone of Latin American commercial and financial relations with the outside world. Thus, the Latin American population is drastically affected by the sequence of drought and rainfall, crop failure and bumper crop—but in very different ways, depending on whether commercial or subsistence agriculture is involved.

Beyond a shadow of a doubt, the highest priority in Latin American development planning should be to get people out of subsistence agriculture and into commercial agriculture or industry or the more productive services.

Agriculture and Light Industry

The major Latin American industrialization emphasis ought to be in the area of consumer goods production and distribution, especially emphasizing new, novel, and frontier products in these areas.[1]

It has been rather common in the literature dealing with these matters to allege a dichotomy between manufacturing and agriculture and then to allege some peculiar merit in manufacturing that means that the fortunate souls working in that area receive a higher income than do the people working in agriculture. A better classification (for most purposes) would probably draw a line between (1) a complex of activities that gets consumer goods into the hands of people, on the one hand, and (2) heavy industry on the other.

---

[1] Lester R. Brown, "How Much Food the World Will Need by the Year 2000." in *Foreign Agriculture*, XI (February 10, 1964), 3–4, 16.

In this modified classification, the concept of the consumer goods industry would involve (1) raw commodity and agricultural production, (2) processing, (3) transportation, and (4) ultimate retail sale. It takes the composite of these operations to make a coherent productive process. Agriculture does not stand alone as a process apart from processing and ultimate sale of the consumer goods. To speak of agriculture as a branch of activity which should be deemphasized because people engaged in agriculture have a relatively low standard of living misses the main problem. Agriculture and raw commodity production are a necessary part of the productive process. It is true that people in agriculture enjoy a relatively low standard of living; and this should be a cause for concern. But the proper conclusion is not the abolition of agriculture. Agriculture needs to be fitted into a coherent pattern of consumer goods production that views the process involving everything from raw commodity production to the sale of the finished consumer goods as a whole. Appropriate institutional adjustments need to be made to assure that people in the agricultural phase are not at a standard-of-living disadvantage. (Suggestions as to possible institutional adjustments are made in Chapter Six.) It is hard to see how anyone can properly quarrel with the proposition that increased food and clothing, available at the consumer level, are a major element in raising the standard of living. In fact, combined with housing, food and clothing are the most part of the crass and material aspect of the standard of living.

To the extent that a country finds it possible to concentrate on such activities and omit heavy industry, it will be possible to raise standard of living a great deal faster with less capital expenditure. To the extent that a country has to divert energy to the creation of heavy industry, the improvement in the standard of living will be delayed; and the capital coefficient, or capital/output ratio, will necessarily be higher, making capital costs per unit of welfare improvement higher in the early part of the process, with consequent inhibiting effects on the effort to improve the standard of living.[2]

---

[2] Two arguments of contrary tone should be mentioned. It has been argued, for example, by Aldo Ferrer, *La Economía Argentina* (México-Buenos Aires, Fondo de Cultura Económica, 1963), p. 176, that heavy industry is needed to avoid a disastrous dependence on equipment imports such as may disorganize an economy largely dependent on light industry when business cycle fluctuations occasion a contraction in the capacity to import. There are various difficulties with this argument. It does not deal with the implications of the situation where the underdeveloped country is simply too small to support a reasonably low-cost

It is a mistake to differentiate agriculture from manufacturing on the ground that agriculture is based on the natural resource land and is not (or should not be) capital intensive and mechanized. Agriculture should be looked on as a mechanized segment of various consumer goods industries. Agriculture needs to be concentrated in areas where machinery can be used, where irrigation can be practiced successfully, or where the soil is fertile. Fertilizer production becomes a high priority item; and in the area of equipment manufacturing, farm machinery is to be emphasized in preference to airplane manufacturing and shipbuilding.

Plant hybridization offers possibilities for improving productivity. Of course, Henry Wallace's hybrid corn has been used in Mexico now for some years. The possibilities for improving the technology of agriculture are increasing rather than being exhausted. Hybrid sorghum is a hardy, inexpensive substitute for corn. Firms such as Asgrow already have the technical competence to be of real help to the Latin American countries in effecting agricultural improvements. But, as the experts at any agricultural experiment station will emphasize, these comments do not begin to scratch the surface of the possibilities. And there should be a lot more agricultural experiment stations plus more effective institutional procedures for getting the findings of the stations into use.

The point is sometimes made that when a businessman shows enterprise, especially in Latin America, and provides a new product in substantial quantities (say, chickens in an area where the diet has been deficient in protein), there is likely to be difficulty in finding marketing channels and buyers. How can this be? How can a region whose chief problem is low standard of living also have as a problem surpluses of consumer goods? The enigma is really worse than this because, on top of everything else, agricultural production has been lagging in Latin America. What is going on?

It is true that there is a real physical limit to the amount of beans, coffee, and sugar an individual wants to eat. But a lot of Latin Americans do not have all the beans, sugar, and coffee they would like—much less all the beefsteak. How can one explain a failure of effective

heavy industry. And it does not confront the possibility that the country which has established a heavy industry may still be markedly dependent on imports of raw materials and of equipment items. Contrary argument based on the proposition that agriculture is inferior to heavy industry because it lacks backward linkage would seem to miss the point that the process of producing an item of goods needs to have a beginning.

demand in a setting such as this where there is no shortage of paper money? Inequality in income distribution is part of the answer. But for the present, let us look at another aspect of the problem.

Involved are customary eating habits, institutional phenomena par excellence. Innumerable examples could probably be cited of new products which simply did not take with the consumers. There was a case, I believe, involving an individual in the state of São Paulo in Brazil, who showed some worthwhile initiative in raising chickens only to find that he could not develop market outlets. Does this mean that everybody in Brazil has as much meat (or even as much chicken) as he would like? Does it mean that this individual would have been better advised to promote a steel mill than a chicken coop?

It may merely mean that marketing channels need to be improved. Improved marketing channels are many things. For one thing, they involve the supermarket and its impressive displays of handsomely packaged food. The supermarket alone is probably capable of creating an eating-habit revolution in Latin America. And yet there may be something to the claim that the Latin American supermarket may quickly become as big a mess as the old public market. Certainly a supermarket may need to be policed and organized differently in Latin America than in the United States. But that is merely to emphasize the point that Latin America must create its own institutional forms. It may even be that the public market, somewhat reorganized, especially in terms of its procurement arrangements, would be substantially the same thing as the supermarket somewhat modified from the *norteamericano* model.

Policing a retail establishment involves a good deal more than the prevention of theft. It involves restraint on the fingering of merchandise, and it means the throwing away of goods of adultered quality by the store manager as a continuing process. People do not like to buy already fingered merchandise, although they may have a strong compulsion to finger the goods themselves. But better packaging, refrigeration, the control of fingering, and larger selling units should minimize the loss due to deterioration. The alleged preference of Latin American women for the individual attention of the small store will be found an easily surmountable institutional hurdle. They will love the greater choice and better assurance as to quality offered by the large, diversified store.

Working out the distribution problem will involve experimentation (1) with differing assortments of merchandise (2) in relation to various possible store sizes, and (3) with the location of the store in relation to the population and (4) the means of transport available to the buyers. The Latin American situation, where there are far fewer cars in relation to population and where, in the cities, the population is much more concentrated, would seem to create location problems substantially different from those in the United States. Perhaps the local Latin American supermarket should carry a wider range of items, involving much less choice in particular types of commodities, a regular dispersal of stores over the city, and much more drastic policing of the merchandise, including the effective barring of small children from the food display section of the store. Chains of stores of this type would seem to be necessary to make it possible to mobilize and coordinate more effective procurement methods. Whether the foregoing comments provide an effective formula, it is undoubtedly true that at present Latin American merchandising is fantastically inefficient and unsanitary.

There is a good deal to marketing beside the supermarket. There is the problem of food preservation, both in transit and in the store. Refrigeration, canning, bottling, and various forms of paper packaging offer possibilities for avoiding spoiling and for improving the odds against ptomaine and dysentery. They also offer the possibility for preserving food better so that a far larger proportion of the production will ultimately be consumed. And refrigeration equipment, canning, bottling (and bottle manufacturing), and the preparation of packaging offer possibilities as new industries which should have a high priority in economic development planning.

More effective transportation and marketing is an integral part of the sequence (farm production → transportation → processing → transportation → wholesaling → transportation → retailing).

That marketing practices and procedures need study and improvement was recognized in the 1960 program of the Mexican Partido de la Revolucion Institucional: "The distributive apparatus is severely overburdened and works in general on the margin of minimum norms of equity in the setting of prices, in giving honest weight and, above all, in the quality of the merchandise." [3]

There is probably not a great deal to be gained by trying to identify particular industries that might be developed in Latin America (except the proof that the author is a poor prophet). Many things would be

[3] *Trimestre Económico,* January, 1964, p. 148.

included in such a list that would turn out to be fiascos and many things omitted that would turn out to be bonanzas. The consumer goods industries are not going to develop in the framework of well-thought-out comprehensive long-run plans anyway. They are going to develop by trial and error. Of course, each new decision should be taken on the basis of the best knowledge available at the moment. But the success or failure of each new project is going to condition the appropriateness of later projects. It is not possible to plan very far ahead, and certainly not possible for one person to identify effectively the whole range of new products that might be developed. The main thing is that there be a lot of imaginative experimentation in this area. In spite of this, the author has probably not done his duty unless he makes some comments about possible new or expanded industries, at least in part to indicate something of what is involved in decision making in this area.[4]

Refrigeration in particular is an area that can stand development. One problem is at the level of an adequate supply of ice or of cooling for the small warehouse, store, or restaurant. There are currently available small machines for making ice that could deal with this problem. John Watt of the Mechanical Engineering Department of the University of Texas, for example, has perfected such a machine. Their manufacture in Latin America would represent a type of equipment manufacture that could well be developed.

Brazil and Ecuador might steal from the Dutch and Swiss the processing of cacao into high-grade chocolate and become a prestige source for chocolate products.

The boxing of bananas on the plantation improves the ultimate product and makes it likely that a larger proportion of the crop will be sold before it rots. Plantation boxing of bananas involved virtually none of the product in 1959. By 1961 it involved 20 percent of the production.

Outside of Argentina and Uruguay, meat and protein consumption in Latin America is low. A recent United Nations study indicates that vari-

[4] It would be useful to have a group, perhaps several hundred, industry studies which would identify the things that the promoter needs to look for in determining whether it would be a good idea to establish a particular industry at a given time and place. There was some discussion of the desirability of industry studies in Chapter Thirteen. It might be emphasized here that one of the main jobs of planning is to create the conditions that will make the industry studies as meaningful as possible. And one of the chief considerations is that price comparisons and cost comparisons be as meaningful as possible. One of the chief troubles with international trade restrictions as a device for encouraging development is the manner in which they make price and cost comparisons difficult.

ous countries in Latin America, for example Colombia, Venezuela, and Mexico, have substantial unutilized stock-farming potential; and slaughter, processing, and sanitary conditions down to the butcher shop are crying for improvement.[5] And in areas where stock farming already exists (even in Uruguay) meat yields are low. Major improvements in livestock production and yields are possible with some technical help and a modest amount of investment. Dairying also (and milk, cheese, and egg production) can contribute to improving the nutrition and health of Latin Americans. Colombia, Mexico, Guatemala, Venezuela, Peru, Bolivia, Chile, Argentina, Brazil (in reality, all of the Latin American countries) can and should make major advances in dairying with promptness. The Argentine situation is worth emphasizing. What with the fact that the demand for beef is probably price elastic and income elastic, Argentina could well reemphasize her beef production. The country seems to have made little effort to improve technology in the cattle industry for thirty years. Specifically, a thoroughgoing effort to eradicate the foot-and-mouth disease needs to be pressed.

It was reasonable several years ago for a United Nations mission in Bolivia to decide that Bolivia was suited for the development of a dairy cattle industry and that Switzerland, being also a high country, was a good source for the cattle. The idea went awry because of the resistance of the Bolivian Indian to making the appropriate institutional changes. (In fact, it is said that they slaughtered and ate much of the livestock.) This does not mean that the idea was poor nor does it even prove that a dairy industry based on Swiss breeds of cattle will not flourish in Bolivia in the years to come. But it does mean that some institutional attitudes need to be reconciled; and it may mean that the ideamen on the project did not stick around long enough to see the implementation through.

Additional flour mills seem to be needed in many of the Latin American countries.

Obviously, there are major possibilities for expansion through the whole range of consumer goods industries: cotton textiles, wool, hemp, ramie fiber, soap, pharmaceuticals, household appliances.

Albert Hirschman has been imaginative in finding a continuing role for handicraft industry. He conceives "that small and inexpensive addi-

---

[5] United Nations, *Livestock in Latin America. I. Colombia, Mexico, Uruguay, and Venezuela* (New York, 1962); *II. El Brasil* (México, 1963).

tions of capital equipment, made available at easy credit terms and combined with technical education and cooperative marketing," could enable the handicraft industries to play a larger role.[6] He might have added that Sears Roebuck would be glad to market a lot of such goods both in Latin America and in the United States.

A world-famous industry which can probably stand some expansion and some improved marketing methods exists in Ecuador. At Jipijapa and Monte Cristi, to the north of the Gulf of Guayaquil, the authentic Panama hats are made. Panama has had little to do with the industry except for marketing the hats to people in transit at the isthmus.

Argentina should be one of the prestige woolen-textile and clothing centers of the world, given the sheep industry of the country as a basis. In fact, under the influence of the British, the manufacture of woolens, using various British processes, developed decades ago to a respectable level of competence. But I believe the generalization is correct that the industry has stagnated of recent decades. Although much of the cloth is of respectable quality, the tailoring is on the whole poor, especially on ready-made, medium-priced suits as distinguished from the more expensive made-to-measure suits.

The palms of the tropics ought to serve as the basis for considerable expansion in manufacturing in the range of soaps, oils, waxes, resins, and phonograph records. Latin America should be able to develop a considerable export market for phonograph records in addition to the domestic market. And yet, possibly because the raw materials have been cheap to transport, many of these raw materials have been exported and the manufacture has occurred elsewhere.

One need only look around the typical Latin American city five minutes to appreciate that the drug and pharmaceutical business is thriving and guess that it has possibilities for thriving a good deal more in a region where most people cannot afford doctors and the pharmacists practice a little medicine on the side. Latin America is naturally endowed with pharmaceutical raw materials. The region was the original source of a long list of drugs from quinine, to cocaine, to curare. True, in many cases, the production center has moved from Latin America to other areas, but with some conscientious attention to quality in production

---

[6] Albert O. Hirschman, *The Strategy of Economic Development* (New Haven, Yale University Press, 1958), p. 130.

and to the developing of marketing channels, Latin America might become the prestige source of a considerable amount of the world's manufactured pharmaceuticals.

Building materials (brick, wood, cement, structural shapes) are enjoying a seller's market in Latin America and will continue to enjoy a seller's market for a long time to come. In the summer of 1964, there was a critical brick shortage in Peru (but the production facility President Belaúnde was talking about expanding was the steel mill at Chimbote). Teodoro Moscoso has mentioned that in Ecuador there is experimentation with the use of sugar-cane waste and banana stems for producing inexpensive wallboard. In the Dominican Republic, they are using pressed wood chips sprayed with cement. And it would be hard to find a Latin American country that could not to advantage do some experimenting with new building materials and expand the production of standard building materials. (There was some discussion of the building-material problem in connection with the discussion of housing in Chapter Seventeen.)

Apart from housing proper, furniture manufacturing offers possibilities for another use for wood, metal, and assorted synthetics. Furniture manufactured from tropical hardwoods should find a responsive market in the United States and western Europe. Demand is probably income elastic. But there are difficulties. The manufacturing (woodworking) stage needs to take place in larger, more mechanized, more efficient plants. But beyond this is the marketing problem. Organized, and financially powerful, marketing organizations need to be utilized. Outlets through retail chains in the United States and Europe that can place the goods before millions of people need to be assured. (In the current state of marketing procedures, it is little wonder that an imaginative small-scale manufacturer of mahogany furniture in Port-au-Prince or Belem may not be able to expand his operation.)

Glass manufacturing—both plate and blown glass—should be expanded very substantially in Latin America. For the most part, local sand can be used to produce glass for the local building trades or for bottles and glassware. The labor force has admirable potential for such work. Latin America ought to be able to develop a prestige glass industry that would enjoy substantial export popularity in the United States and western Europe as well as provide for local flat glass and bottle needs (notably beer bottles). The capital costs would be relatively small, and a high proportion of the raw material would be available locally.

Latin America exports many semiprocessed or semimanufactured products to other countries for further processing. A considerable amount of the additional processing might well occur in Latin America. The sugar centrals in Latin America turn the cane into raw sugar which is then, for the most part, shipped abroad to be refined. Much refining could well occur in Latin America. Part of the dissatisfaction in pre-Castro Cuba was due to circumstances such as these. The smelting of minerals is a major manufacturing industry in Mexico, Chile, and Peru. More refining and fabricating could well occur there as well. Failure to do this is one of the reasons for the poor image that American Smelting and Refining and the Anaconda Copper Company have in Latin America. Latin American countries are now making an effort to force the foreign oil companies to refine the oil in the local producing country rather than in such places as Aruba and Curaçao. Policy makers could well concentrate more on this sort of encouragement of domestic processing before export and less on import substitution.

There is no good reason why Latin America should not establish itself as the prestige source of some of the high-value-in-small-bulk items such as clocks, optical instruments, transistor radios, cameras, and what not. The Japanese have done it, starting from rather modest beginnings—and with little help from the already developed countries.

Steel

One of the reasons for the popularity of the steel industry with the development planner may be that it is easy to say "steel mill" and not so easy to advance a good suggestion in the area of consumer goods production. Coking coal and iron ore are the two crucial ingredients in the development of a steel industry. To point out that the whole of Latin America now produces less than 2 percent of the world's iron ore, less than 1 percent of the world's coal, 3.4 percent of the basic metals, and 1.6 percent of the metal products is merely to prove that heavy industry does not yet exist there. The future might change that.

In the state of Minas Gerais, Brazil has some of the largest iron ore reserves in the world. Venezuela has major deposits in the lower Orinoco

Valley; and Mexico, Chile, and Cuba have reserves of respectable size. In terms of iron ore reserves, there is the basis for the efficient existence of heavy industries of at least moderate size in several of the Latin American countries—Brazil and Venezuela and perhaps Chile and Mexico—but not in Argentina. The lack of coking coal is a major problem everywhere.[7]

The chief Brazilian steel mill is at Volta Redonda and is operated by the Companhia Siderúrgica Nacional, which is controlled by the Brazilian government. The mills use Rio Grande do Sul low-grade coal mixed with United States and English coking coal. In Mexico the government, through Nacional Financiera, has sponsored the establishment of a steel mill at Monclova by the Altos Hornos Company. A steel complex has been developed by the Venezuelan government (Siderúrgica del Orinoco) near the juncture of the Caroní and Orinoco rivers. Steel mills which may or may not be economical have been built by the Compañía de Acero del Pacífico at Huachipato in Chile; at Chimbote on the Santa River in Peru; at Paz del Río (Belencito) northeast of Bogotá in Colombia; and at San Nicolás on the Paraná River in Argentina.

Light Metals, Heavy Chemicals, and Atomic Power

The Latin American planner has not evidenced the mania to develop light metal and heavy chemical production that has characterized his attitude on the steel industry. And yet the various light metals and new alloys are surely among the promising developments of the future. A country, such as Brazil, with adequate water power and bauxite, can well emphasize aluminum production.

Latin America also has the raw material base for some important development in heavy chemicals. The oil industry of Venezuela offers possibilities for developing a petrochemical complex, the sulphur deposits of Mexico possibility for developing sulphuric acid.[8] Cuba, on the basis

---

[7] United Nations, *A Study of the Iron and Steel Industry in Latin America* (New York, 1954), compares production costs in various countries.

[8] For a general study of the problems and prospects of the chemical industry, see, United Nations, Economic Commission for Latin America, *La Industria Química en América Latina* (New York, 1963). The study indicates various branches of the chemical industry that might be established in Latin America and which would probably be internationally competitive (p. 108). However, the comparisons attempting to establish which industries should be established in which countries are distorted by the use of prevailing foreign exchange rates in

of sugar as a raw material, is endowed to develop the production of a variety of chemical products. The guano of Peru is probably not available in sufficient quantity to offer major possibilities for the long-run fertilizer business; but the nitrate of Chile and the petrochemicals of Venezuela would seem more than adequate.

The development of the chemical industry involves more than the usual amount of uncertainty; and planning for the development of the industry should involve even more than the usual leeway in keeping plans flexible.

Both light metals and heavy chemicals are examples of jumping-to-the-technological-frontier. And they involve an approach to development that various of the Latin American countries should consider further. The development of atomic power is another possible technological frontier-type industry that might be emphasized in Argentina.

Industrial Equipment

The steel industry needs to be close to coal or iron ore, preferably coal. But industrial equipment manufacturing firms can be located close to the demand with much less cost sacrifice because a high value added in the manufacturing process is involved. This should mean that a country like Argentina that is probably not well advised to promote a major steel industry may have justification for establishing a substantial industrial equipment industry. Farm machinery and Jeep-type cars and trucks would seem to be industries suited to Argentina. In fact, Henry Kaiser has participated in the establishment of a plant to manufacture Jeeps in Córdoba.[9]

What jumping-to-the-fronier means in terms of equipment is that the region should insist on new, technologically advanced, and efficient equipment. But this is not the same thing necessarily as labor-saving

making the international comparisons. This method has the effect of making Venezuela, which naturally has major advantages especially in petrochemicals, look like a high-cost country. The Venezuelan bolívar is overvalued on the foreign exchange market. This is another example of an artificial rigging of international economic relations which is working to the detriment of development.

[9] For discussion of the industrial equipment industry, see the series of which the following is one: United Nations, Economic Commission for Latin America, *La Fabricación de Maquinarios y Equipos Industriales en América Latina. III. Los Equipos Básicos en la Argentina* (New York, 1963).

equipment. It is probably not particularly desirable for various of the Latin American countries to emphasize highly automatic production processes. Although in general the Latin American development problem is somewhat different from that of south and east Asia, where the labor supply (highly unskilled) is running out of the continent's ears, the Latin American labor force is growing rapidly; and a specialization on relatively simple industrial equipment which will give more employment per unit of capital investment is most desirable.

On the whole, there is more and better technology involved in the equipment field than in the steel industry proper, the steel industry being (or having been until quite recently) a rather notorious technological laggard anyway. To the extent the Latin American countries feel a strong urge to develop heavy industry, they might do better in terms of accumulating technology and in terms of increasing welfare to concentrate on equipment. This would be especially true of Argentina and Mexico, both of which already have respectable equipment industries and could well emphasize expansion. Brazil and Venezuela could also well develop substantial equipment industries corollary with their steel industries—however, Venezuela can afford to do this only if she can assure herself of access to the Latin American Free Trade Association market. It behooves Venezuela to forget her misgivings about that organization and join. She very likely has more to gain by membership than any other Latin American country.

Consumer Durables

The sky is the limit on consumer durables. Like industrial equipment, they have the advantage of involving a high value added. Their production is bound to expand in Latin America and involve an ever-widening range of new items. But there is very little point in trying to guess what the chief new items will be five or ten years from now. The role of planning in the consumer durables area should be to keep track of what is going on elsewhere in Latin America so as to be able to warn producers against the development of the same product in too many places at once, and to keep track of what is going on outside the area so as to imitate with speed when that is appropriate. This is one way the complementarity concept might be implemented. And this procedure should be an important feature of a helpful hemisphere-wide planning, either under the wing of LAFTA or under the wing of the Alliance for Progress.

Conclusion

The economic development of Latin America is proceeding and already has a considerable degree of momentum. The time is past when planning might have shaped the development in its basic particulars. And the time probably never was when foreign investment could have made a significant contribution to the development. But the international movement of people and technical knowledge can yet play an important role in accelerating the process.

Governments can play and are playing a role in providing the infrastructure and social-overhead ingredients of the process. Light industry, directed primarily to providing consumer goods, deserves the highest priority in the industrial sector. In the field of industrial equipment emphasis should be on relatively inexpensive equipment which makes relatively large use of labor. In fact there are major possibilities in this specialization, especially since equipment provided from the United States is frequently unnecessarily complex.

PART FIVE

TRADE AND FINANCE

CHAPTER NINETEEN

INTERNATIONAL TRADE PATTERNS

General Trade Patterns

COMMODITY COMPOSITION. *Exports.* During the nineteenth century the exports of Latin America were chiefly the raw products of land and mine: sugar and rum, gold and silver, tobacco and coffee, wheat and meat. Occasionally a unique product enjoyed a spectacular, temporary boom. Guano enjoyed such a boom in Peru in the mid-nineteenth century, as did nitrate in Chile and rubber in Brazil at the turn of the century.

At the close of World War II there was a brief period when manufactured goods, such as textiles, increased respectably their share of Latin American exports. But the Latin American textile industry, based on obsolete equipment and strangling work rules, did not manage to maintain its position after the recuperation of the textile industries of the belligerent countries.

If industrialization bears fruit in Latin America, manufactured goods should come to represent a much larger proportion of total exports. But meanwhile raw commodities continue to dominate the scene: 91 percent of the total in 1962. Petroleum alone runs some 27 percent of the total and coffee 17 percent. During the last thirty years there has been a notable decline in the role of wheat and meat exports, a decline which is in some important degree a reflection of the stagnation of Argentina.

Imports. Through much of the nineteenth century, manufactured goods, such as textiles, represented a principal import of Latin America. But with the development of textile industries in Latin America in the late nineteenth century, the phenomenon that would now be called import substitution operated, and the relative share of textiles in the import picture declined.

In recent years imports have been a mixture of capital goods, industrial raw materials, luxury consumer goods, and consumption necessities. In 1962 machinery was 39 percent of the total; chemicals and other manufactures were 34 percent (making a total of 73 percent for manufactures); raw materials (including fuel) were 14 percent; food was 11 percent. However, 25 percent, or so, of the imports of manufactures were probably intermediate or semiprocessed goods. This would mean that slightly under half of Latin American imports were finished manufactured goods.

During the decade of the 1950s there was a substantial increase in the share of industrial raw materials and fuel in total imports. This may be an indication that in planning economic development too little attention has been given to basing new industries on locally available raw materials.

IMPORTANCE TO COUNTRY. *Trade/National Income Ratios.* For the Latin American countries as an average, exports run about 16 percent of national income. (By comparison, exports run about 4 percent for the United States.) International trade thus plays a far more important role for the typical Latin American country than it plays in the case of the United States. In general the trade dependence is higher for the smaller Latin American countries, running 20 or 30 percent in their cases. For the larger Latin American countries, such as Brazil, the figure is lower, 9 percent in 1960.

It should be emphasized that this dependence on trade is due to the fact that the countries are small; it is not primarily due to the fact that they are underdeveloped or poor. (One finds the same high-percentage dependence on trade in the case of developed small countries, such as Belgium, the Netherlands, and Denmark.)

However, this dependence on trade seems to be declining somewhat. Before the Great Depression exports ran on an average 25 to 30 percent of the national incomes.

Per Capita Trade. The situation looks somewhat different when it is put in terms of per capita trade. For example, the per capita exports (total exports divided by the population and stated in current dollars) were as follows:

	1928	1962
Latin America	$30	$ 43
United States	43	116
World	17	44

On a per capita basis Latin American exports are close to the world average. But they used to be far higher.

IMPORTANCE OF COUNTRIES. In 1962 Latin American exports ran $9.3 billion. And Venezuela provided almost exactly a fourth of the total. The leading exporters were:

	Millions of dollars
Venezuela	2,585
Brazil	1,214
Argentina	1,210
Mexico	929

The pattern was somewhat different on the import side. Total imports into the twenty republics in 1962 were about $8.8 billion.

	Millions of dollars
Brazil	1,475
Argentina	1,357
Mexico	1,143
Venezuela	1,096

The dominance of relatively small Venezuela on the export side is striking and is, of course, explained by petroleum. A major shift in importance during the last twenty years has involved an Argentine decline. Argentina accounted for 35 percent of the exports of Latin America in 1928, in 1962 for only 13 percent.

DIRECTION OF TRADE. Table 16 indicates the percentages of total Latin American exports going to various regions. The percentage of total Latin American imports coming from the various regions is only moderately dissimilar from the export pattern.

If the countries of the world are rather arbitrarily divided into developed and underdeveloped countries, the trade pattern becomes tripartite, involving (1) trade among the developed countries, (2) trade between

Table 16

PERCENTAGE SHARES OF LATIN AMERICAN EXPORTS

Percentages going to	1953	1962
United States	47.3	42.1
United Kingdom	7.9	7.9
European Economic Community countries	13.8	19.7
USSR and associated countries	0.5	7.2
Other Latin American countries	9.5	6.7

Source: Various United Nations publications.

developed and underdeveloped countries, and (3) trade among the underdeveloped countries.

Since World War II, trade among the developed countries has grown at a very rapid rate. The Latin American countries, and underdeveloped countries generally, tend to complain because the trade between the developed and underdeveloped countries has grown at a much slower rate—especially because their exports to the developed countries have grown slowly. But a rather significant relation that has been little mentioned is that trade among the underdeveloped has been the slowest grower of all.

In 1950, 28 percent of the exports of underdeveloped areas went to other underdeveloped countries. In 1960, 23 percent of their exports went to other underdeveloped countries.[1] A similar comparison is that, in 1953, 8 percent of world exports went from one nonindustrial country to another nonindustrial country. In 1962, the equivalent figure was 5.8 percent. It is substantially accurate to say that trade among the underdeveloped countries has stagnated.

LATIN AMERICAN SHARE OF WORLD TRADE. Table 17 indicates Latin American shares of world population, exports, and imports. Latin America has been and still is a relatively important trading region. Her share of the world's exports is roughly the same as her share of the world's population. But the share has fallen substantially from the peak of the 1940s and has reached a level perceptibly below that prevailing earlier. Such data provide a basis for the Latin American concern as to

[1] United Nations, *World Economic Survey, 1962*, I, 15; General Agreement on Tariffs and Trade, *International Trade, 1962*, p. 7.

Table 17

LATIN AMERICAN SHARES OF WORLD TOTALS

	Percentage share of world population	Percentage share of world exports	Percentage share of world imports
1913	4.5	8.0	6.4
1928	5.0	9.0	7.1
1938	5.4	7.8	5.9
1948	6.0	11.2	9.7
1962	6.8	6.6	5.9

Source: Data from miscellaneous United Nations publications, and also: Pan American Union, *The Foreign Trade of Latin America since 1913* (Washington, 1952); United States Tariff Commission, *The Foreign Trade of Latin America* (Washington, 1940). The data are distorted somewhat by the proliferation in the number of countries in recent years.

the ability of their exports to carry the chief burden of the financing of the imports needed to facilitate industrialization.

Imports indicate relatively the same pattern. However, they have held up rather better than exports. Foreign aid, or foreign investment, or changes in debt-service arrangements have permitted the relative maintenance of imports.

THE BALANCE OF TRADE. Latin America collectively, and most Latin American countries individually, has had an export balance of trade with marked consistency since the early nineteenth century. Remittance of debt service to foreign creditors financed this export balance between the two World Wars and before World War I. And it continues to be an important factor financing the export balance. During the 1920s, the existence of the export balance was rather unambiguously revealed by the commodity trade statistics. The manner in which the statistics have generally been presented has worked since World War II somewhat to obscure the existence of this export balance. Exports are generally quoted f.o.b. and imports c.i.f. Exports do not include ocean shipping costs; imports include such costs. The difference can be significant. The cost of ocean shipping is likely to run at least 10 percent of the value of the goods shipped. This difference alone would suggest that Latin America had an export balance of about $1 billion in 1962 instead of an import balance of $100 million, such as has been indicated by some of the presentations. However, even the data in terms of f.o.b. exports and c.i.f. imports, for the full period 1946 through 1962, give Latin America a cumulative merchandise export balance of $5.5 billion.

Certain questions still remain. For example, who paid the ocean freight? Consequently, one might say, the more meaningful balance is the goods and services balance, rather than the goods balance. But the use of the goods and services balance injects some new difficulties in terms of coverage. For example, there is the question as to whether debt service should be included or omitted.

Accumulated data for the period 1946 through 1961 indicates that for the whole period Latin America, on goods and services (debt service included) had an import balance of $9.8 billion (U.S.).[2] But if one omits the imputed imports which are the counterpart of the debt-service entries, the situation is changed drastically. For the same period the accumulated goods and services balance of Latin America (debt services excluded) involved an export balance of $6.1 billion.

A major share of the Latin American export balance is the Venezuelan export balance. Data presented earlier in this chapter indicate that in 1962 the Venezuelan export balance was almost $1.5 billion, a very considerable sum of money.

A slightly different approach to the statistical evidence that Latin America has an export balance is found in the relation, mentioned in Table 17, to the effect that in 1962 Latin America accounted for 6.6 percent of world exports and only 5.9 percent of world imports.

Latin America strives to have an export balance. It has one, but then tends to deny that it has one.

Trade with United States

LATIN AMERICAN ROLE IN UNITED STATES TRADE. Table 18 indicates the importance of the United States trade with Latin America. These figures run higher than do the similar figures indicating United States dependence on trade with Latin America, shown in Table 19. Trade with the United States plays a more significant role for Latin America than does trade with Latin America for the United States.

[2] The data are compiled from the International Monetary Fund, *Balance of Payments Yearbook(s)*. A slight error exists as a result of lack of coverage for Cuba for 1960 and 1961.

Table 18

	Percentage of Latin American exports going to U.S.	Percentage of Latin American imports coming from U.S.
1913	30.8	25.0
1928	31.5	36.7
1938	33.2	33.4
1948	37.2	57.7
1962	42.1	41.0

Source: George Wythe, *An Outline of Latin American Economic Development* (New York, Barnes and Noble, 1946), pp. 252–53; and various United Nations publications.

But there seems to be no clear-cut pattern in terms of whether the United States buys more from Latin America than it sells to the region, when the figures are put in terms of total money values. Generally in

Table 19

	Percentage of U.S. exports going to Latin America	Percentage of U.S. imports coming from Latin America
1913	14.4	26.0
1928	16.0	23.1
1938	16.1	23.1
1948	24.7	35.5
1962	15.3	20.7

Source: George Wythe, *An Outline of Latin American Economic Development* (New York, Barnes and Noble, 1946), pp. 252–53; and various United Nations publications.

the period before World War II United States imports from Latin America seem to have exceeded exports. In the period since World War II the pattern has been the reverse. But neither relation has been pronounced.

RECIPROCAL TRADE. It has sometimes been said that James G. Blaine, as Secretary of State of the United States, promoted the Pan-American movement because of a desire to increase exports to Latin America. Very probably this was an important factor. Certainly trade problems received much attention at the initial conference in 1889 and continued to receive major attention at succeeding conferences. At that first conference one of the committees reported its endorsement of the idea of working toward "unrestricted reciprocity" and a customs union.[3] What did such a pronouncement mean in terms of the actualities? Little. The United States was interested in fostering exports, not in increasing imports. Chile and Argentina, embittered by the spectacle of increased United States tariffs on hides and wool, dissented from the recommendation on the ground that the gestures toward freer trade made by the conference were not likely to be given effective meaning.

Since that first conference, the American countries at their periodic meetings have repeatedly paid lip service to free trade, freer trade, customs unions, and the like.

The Reciprocal Trade Agreements Act of 1934 (United States legislation) provided that the President, by agreement with foreign countries, could change the tariff rates charged by the United States on imports within a range of 50 percent. Agreements to reduce the tariff on a certain commodity were to be negotiated by the State Department with the principal supplier of the article. Thus, the agreement concerning the oil tariff rate was reached in the agreement with Venezuela, that concerning many kinds of woolen cloth in the agreement with England, and so on. The procedure was followed because the principal supplier was generally the one willing to reduce his own tariffs the most for the concession. Concessions so made were then generalized as stipulated in the most-favored-nation clause.

Since World War II much of the negotiation with the Latin American countries on the subject of tariff reduction has occurred in the setting of the multilateral General Agreement of Tariffs and Trade rather than in two-sided negotiations involving the United States and one foreign country at a time. Otherwise, however, the approach continued to involve much the same sort of reciprocity as had been practiced since 1934.

UNITED STATES RESTRICTIONS. The United States has no trade barriers against many Latin American products, such as Brazilian coffee. Similarly, before Castro, the United States gave a reduced tariff rate to sugar coming from Cuba. But the United States quota system on sugar probably kept a certain amount of Latin American sugar out of this country, and benefited domestic production from Colorado and Loui-

---

[3] *Minutes of the International American Conference* (Washington, 1890), p. 295.

siana accordingly. The United States maintains tariffs or the threat of tariffs on the various metallic minerals such as copper, lead, and zinc. A combination of tariff and quota arrangements applied to petroleum imports into the United States reduce the import of Venezuelan oil and help keep the world price of crude high (a high price which incidentally is much desired by the Venezuelans themselves). So the United States attitude toward imports from Latin America is somewhat ambivalent.

UNITED STATES TWO-PRICING, P. L. 480, ETC. United States businessmen worry about the competition of new production in Latin America. Latin American businessmen worry about the competition of United States exports.

The two-pricing of agricultural exports by the United States creates some of the problem. The United States exports many crops (for example, cotton and wheat) at prices lower than the domestic price in the United States. The difference is financed by a United States government subsidy to the exporters. Such arrangements create difficulties for Latin American cotton exporters such as Mexico, and wheat exporters such as Argentina.

This United States program of export subsidies represents in several respects a significant disservice to Latin America. United States agriculture has a major comparative cost advantage over Latin American agriculture to start with. In addition, prices are kept high artificially in the United States. This should make the United States an attractive market for Latin American agriculture except for the fact that the United States uses quotas, health quarantines, and so on, to keep out such Latin American products as are competitive with United States production. Then to cut itself in on the world market, in competition with such Latin American products as wheat and cotton, the United States pays substantial subsidies to the exporters of these items. Thus, the United States compounds its comparative cost advantage with artificial price rigging to the general detriment of Latin American agriculture and consumer goods production. The disservice the United States does to Latin America in this way may be substantial. And the policy places Latin American planners in a real quandary when they try to decide whether to commit substantial resources to agriculture and compete with a United States agriculture which is both low cost and subsidized. Some productive effort is probably being driven out of agriculture, which efficiency considerations might indicate ought to stay there, both in Latin America and in the world economy in general.

Even such well-intentioned gestures as the supplying of food to the world's poor under Public Law 480 and the Food for Peace program create problems. To what extent does a shipment of Food for Peace wheat to Pakistan cost Argentina wheat markets? How can one judge the good and the harm of such arrangements?

EFFECT OF LATIN AMERICAN GROWTH. Will United States industries suffer as a result of losing some of their foreign markets to the new industries of Latin America? Is it really to the disadvantage of an industrialized country to encourage the development of manufacturing in undeveloped regions?

At first glance, it might seem probable that new industrialization would be detrimental to established industries elsewhere. And the possibility certainly exists that a particular industry in the developed region will be injured by the competition of some new industry. United States exports of farm machinery to Latin America might be reduced by the development of farm machinery manufacturing in Latin America. On the other hand, they might not. For the moment, we will assume that such reduction may occur. What is the significance? If a new, more efficient industry is established and takes some of the market from the old, less efficient enterprise, this is a desirable result from the point of view of consumers in general.

May the adverse effect extend to industry as a whole in the developed country? The answer would seem likely to be in the negative. In the underdeveloped country, the new development will bring larger investment, larger payrolls, larger profits, and so on. It will bring an increase in purchasing power. This increase in purchasing power will tend to diffuse itself not only to other industries in the underdeveloped country but also to other countries. Developed countries need not fear that the industrialization of backward areas will mean loss of purchasing power there. With the development of manufacturing in western Europe and in the United States in the latter part of the nineteenth century, trade increased, both among the countries of western Europe and between them and the United States. England, which at that time was already industrialized, also found that instead of losing by these developments, she was experiencing an expansion of total trade. Thus, contrary to the impression that new industrialization will result in a decline of trade, the opposite is probably the result as a consequence of the diffusion of a greatly increased total purchasing power. There is considerable reason to believe that the development of industrialization in Latin America will in the end lead to a greater demand for the products of the United States. A particular industry in the United States may be injured; but industry in general in the United States will probably be benefited.

But this argument does not dispose of the question to the entire satisfaction of people who are fond of thinking in terms of power politics. They point out that, if industrialization goes far enough in the backward areas, the developed areas may find themselves eclipsed in terms of relative power. And so they may. But they would probably do better to defend their power position by fostering their own growth than by trying to retard the growth of their neighbors.

The industrialized countries will do well to participate intelligently in the industrialization of backward areas, at least in the promotion of industries that are economically sound. The total world production of goods and the total world purchasing power will be greater as a result.

Incidentally, part of the United States difficulty in marketing goods in Latin America may be that this country is trying to sell too fancy a product. In the appliance area Latin America, for the most part, has need of simpler products than those generally provided from the United States—and of more of them at lower prices.

Trade with the Soviet Bloc

Trade between the U.S.S.R. and the various Latin American countries has not been significant in amount in recent years. However, there have been specific brief periods when the trade of certain countries under bilateral agreement with the Soviet Union has represented a significant proportion of the national trade. This was the case for a time with Uruguay. And since 1958, of course, the trade of Cuba with the Soviet bloc has constituted a significant proportion of total Cuban trade. But Cuba is a rather special case.

Such trade as there has been with the Soviet Union has been conducted within the framework of bilateral agreements attempting to specify the quantities of various items of goods which would move back and forth. It seems that in general the implementation of these bilateral agreements has been sporadic and incomplete. In fact, trade under bilateral agreements seems to have been more of a feast and famine sort of trade than has been the case with trade with the United States and western Europe.

This is significant. The Latin American countries have, in recent years, reacted very violently against trade with the United States and western Europe precisely on the ground that the trade has been subject to violent ups and downs in value. It has been emphasized that these fluctuations have been a counterpart of the violence in price fluctuations. The Latin American countries have in consequence turned somewhat away from trade with the Western countries. Some of the sentiment for developing trade with the Eastern countries has been a result of the desire to establish more stable and reliable trading relations. It should be especially a cause for concern then, that the Eastern trade, instead of being more reliable and even in quantity, has fluctuated relatively more violently.

The United States has shown some tendency to try to coerce, or perhaps one should say induce, the Latin American countries into abstaining from trading with the Soviet Union. For psychological reasons United States initiative in this regard is rather more likely to push the Latin American countries into attempts to further such trade rather than to abstain. A better policy for the United States might well be to keep out of such negotiations. The Latin American countries will just have to find out some things the hard way. And if trade with the Soviet bloc turns out to be a fine thing rather than a fiasco, that might not be so bad either.

Policy making in the area of Cuban-Soviet trade took an odd turn during the spring and summer of 1963. Apparently the Cubans had expected the Soviet Union to underwrite the machinery, and so on, that would be necessary in pushing a major development of industrialization in Cuba. But Khrushchev seems to have given Castro to understand, during a visit by Castro to the Soviet Union in the spring of 1963, that the role of Cuba for the ascertainable future vis-à-vis the Soviet Union was to be that of raw commodity supplier. This apparently is what the principle of "international division of labor" within the Soviet bloc means to Cuba. Cuba seems to be back with its sugar monoculture and some of those who denounced Western capitalism for imposing that monoculture on Cuba must be wondering.

CHAPTER TWENTY

TRADE AND DEVELOPMENT

In this chapter we speculate with regard to possible causal relations between international trade and economic development.[1]

Role of Trade Restrictions

TARIFFS. *General.* The principal nineteenth-century trade restriction in Latin America (and elsewhere) was the tariff. The tariff, during that period, was an unsystematic revenue-raising device frequently intended to have also a protective effect.

Tariffs in Latin America have been assessed against both imports and exports, unlike the situation in the United States where they have been levied only against imports. However the tariff rates assessed against imports have generally been substantially higher than those assessed against exports. The over-all tariff structure favored exports relative to imports, just as it does most places. In Latin America, as a matter of practical politics, it was possible to have the export duties at all because the exports that were generally affected were owned by foreigners (Chilean nitrates and copper, Mexican minerals, and so on).

For the most part, Latin American tariffs have been specific rather than ad valorem. The tariff payment per unit of physical quantity (per pound or per cubic foot) was set at a fixed amount rather than being a percentage of the money value, the ad valorem case. Even tariffs that were ostensibly ad valorem were actually specific in the case of the so-called *aforo* system. In this system the aforo valuation was essentially

[1] Various works on Latin American international trade policy include: Rómulo A. Ferrero, *Comercio y Pagos Internacionales* (México, Centro de Estudios Monetarios Latinamericanos, 1963); Rafael Izquierdo, "Protectionism in Mexico," in Raymond Vernon, ed., *Public Policy and Private Enterprise in Mexico* (Cambridge, Harvard University Press, 1964); United Nations, *World Economic Survey, 1962. I. The Developing Countries in World Trade* (New York, 1963).

a traditional value rather than an estimate of current price, and consequently the real impact of the tariff was much the same as in the case of the specific tariff.

In some ways specific tariffs give more effective "protection" than do ad valorem tariffs. A foreign company trying to dump goods finds that the tariff per article is as high as it would be if the goods were valued at the going market price. But the situation is somewhat different in periods of rising prices. At such times specific duties become less and less effective as protection against imports; and such times have been common in Latin America.

As a result of the limited effectiveness of specific tariffs as protective devices the Latin American countries, beginning in the 1930s, made increasing use of ad valorem and of compound tariffs (that combine ad valorem and specific features). They also turned to other devices such as quotas, licenses, and exchange control. And they have increased the amount of executive discretion in changing rates.

In fact in Latin America the executive branch generally has the power to vary tariff rates as it chooses. This is, for example, the situation in Mexico. Its behavior is not so likely to be closely controlled by the law and the legislature as is the case in the United States.

Height of Tariff Walls. Just as had been the case with the United States, many of the Latin American countries began their independent existences reacting against mercantilism and under the influence of the free trade ideas of Adam Smith. Consequently, for many of the Latin American countries the initial tariffs of the 1820s were quite low, revenue tariffs. But also, just as was the case in the United States, within a decade or two the demands of particular business groups for protection and efforts by government officials to encourage industrialization (for example the efforts of Lucas Alamán in Mexico in the 1830s) led to the increase of various tariff rates. So, the rates came to reflect a mixture of uncoordinated protectionism and desire for revenue. And by the end of the nineteenth century this hodge-podge of protectionism and revenue-raising elements had resulted in some tariff walls which were extremely high. It was, for example, said of the Venezuelan tariff wall of the early part of the twentieth century that it was the highest in the world. At the present time, in Brazil, the rates are as high as 150 percent on many types of consumer goods.

The quantitative comparison of the height of one tariff wall with another is a tricky bit of statistical business. It is obviously not enough just to average all the rates. Some items are more important than others. But the selection of a reasonable method for weighting the relative importance of different items runs into almost intractable difficulties, chiefly because an effective tariff keeps out the goods against which it is applied and therefore makes that item look unimportant in the trade picture.

Consequently, an inspection of a tariff pattern by a knowledgeable observer may be as good a basis for saying a tariff wall is high or low as is a meticulous statistical study. On such subjective grounds, it is probably valid to say that by 1930 the Latin American tariff walls were generally extremely high. But there seems little to be gained by attempting any fine classification as to which one was a little higher than another, or as to whether the Latin American pattern was higher or lower than the United States pattern. The United States wall was also very high in 1930.

Tariffs as Revenue Raisers. In the typical Latin American country tariffs raise 30 or 40 percent of the national revenue. They used to provide 70 or 80 percent. In 1792 the United States government raised 94 percent of the federal revenue from customs duties. But with the passage of the years, and the changed economic structure of the United States, tariffs have come to provide less than 1 percent of such revenue.

OTHER TRADE CONTROLS (GIMMICKRY). Exchange control, multiple foreign exchange rates, quotas on imports and exports, embargoes and bilateral trade treaties have also been extensively and intensively used, considerably in Middle America, somewhat more in South America.

None of these tools accomplishes much that could not be done with tariffs, except that they have the additional "virtue" of adding complication; and complexity has the "virtue" of inhibiting trade.

Like most governments, Latin American governments seem to have a built-in faith that meddling with commercial policy can stimulate enterprise and influence industrialization.[2] Quite contrary to physical laws indicating that, as the effect of primary disturbances spreads in all directions the effect becomes weaker (as the square of the distance), the idea of commercial policy seems to be that if you penalize an import, a manufacturer (who has no connection with the import deal) will conjure up

---

[2] Rafael Izquierdo, "Protectionism in Mexico," in Raymond Vernon, ed., *Public Policy and Private Enterprise in Mexico*, pp. 243 *et seq.*

a gold mine. The infant industry argument for tariffs, and other commercial policy tools for encouraging industrialization, seem to be largely of this Rube Goldberg remote-control type.

Latin American international trade policy is replete with gimmicks. Import surcharges are used (or have been recently) by at least seven countries; advance deposits against imports, by at least seven; multiple exchange rate patterns, by six; quantitative restriction on imports, by eight; restrictions on capital transfers, by at least eight. (There is nothing definitive about these numbers.) The conclusion is that Latin American government planners are as busy as little beavers manipulating trade restrictions.

One should not deny the possibility that trade restriction might encourage domestic production sometime, somewhere. But for the advocates of restrictions to generalize this possibility into a proposition that extensive use of trade restrictions effectively encourages general development is probably a major disservice to the cause of development. The Economic Commission for Latin America in one aspect of its work has shaken loose from these trammels in advocating the Latin American Free Trade Association. But, in general, the faith in the usefulness of restrictions is still firmly held. And the smaller the country, the more intense the restriction phobia.

At a more mundane level, having little to do with the grand questions of economic development, miscellaneous trade controls have been used by the Latin American countries as devices for freezing foreigners out of trade. If that can be done, the substantial profits to be made from trading accrue to the local businessmen rather than to the foreigners. Considerable profits are to be made from trade especially if one can get an import quota which gives the importer a monopolistic position in the domestic market.

In the regulation of the trading process by means of quotas and licenses, the ingroup (politically speaking) and the old hands in the trade are likely to get preferences and priorities. But even in the situations where there is administrative impartiality, the allocation of quotas, which is generally done on the basis of some sort of formula giving quota shares on the basis of the share of the trade enjoyed in some earlier base year, ensures the perpetuation of the old trade shares. The Latin American merchant class is far from opposing the quota system in an effective way. They may complain about the red tape. But anyone already in the business must relish the system which ensures to him his historical market share and facilitates the obtaining of a sort of monopoly profit resulting from the fact that the existence of the quotas precludes much of the potential competition.

BILATERAL AGREEMENTS. Bilateral trade agreements, in which two countries try to plan the relation between the trade going one direction and the trade going the other direction, began to be used extensively, especially by South American countries, during the 1930s. Their use has decreased somewhat during the last five or ten years. But they are the chief method used in setting up trade arrangements with countries in the Soviet bloc and are occasionally used among the Latin American countries themselves or between a Latin American country and some other non-Soviet-bloc country.

INFANT-INDUSTRY ARGUMENT. At least since Alexander Hamilton, it has been argued that new industries in poor countries need to be protected from the competition of established industries in richer countries by infant industry tariffs.[3] The argument is obviously correct in posing the possibility that the old, established industries may (and frequently do) sabotage the new industries if they can get away with it. But that consideration leaves a good deal unsaid. Is the tariff the best means to provide the needed protection?

England and Spain both practiced protection up to the hilt between 1500 and 1800. In 1500 Spain was probably as advanced as England, in any important meaning of the expression advanced. By 1800 she was far behind in spite of her mercantilistic policies. The United States and the various Latin American countries began their independent existences (circa 1800) under the influence of the free trade views of Adam Smith. Early tariffs were nominal in both regions. Then from 1800 to 1930, tariffs (many based squarely on the infant-industry argument) proliferated in both the United States and Latin America. The United States

[3] It would take too much space here to deal with all of the arguments that have been advanced to justify the use of tariffs to help with economic development. For a discussion of, and I believe a refutation of, the arguments of Manoilesco, W. Arthur Lewis, and E. E. Hagen, which try to justify protection on the grounds that wage rates in manufacturing are too high relative to wage rates in agriculture, see the article by Hla Myint, "Infant Industry Arguments for Assistance to Industries in the Setting of Dynamic Trade Theory," in Roy Harrod and D. C. Hague, ed., *International Trade Theory in a Developing World* (New York, St Martin's Press, 1963), pp. 175-180.

grew apace and Latin America stagnated. One might suspect that there was some other explanation than the tariffs.

Since the early 1930s the United States has decreased its tariff protection very considerably. The various Latin American countries have continued to compound the use of tariffs. Whether the Latin American countries have closed the standard-of-living gap perceptibly on the United States since the 1930s would seem debatable.

Essentially the use of infant-industry tariffs to encourage development involves the use of a tool that requires considerable self-sacrifice. Countries which are already poor are asking their citizenry to take a standard-of-living beating in the form of less goods at higher prices during a transition period of indeterminate length. To make matters worse, the industries whose financial success is thus being aided are likely to practice the standard low-volume, high-unit-profit approach. As a consequence of this attitude the new company is likely to restrict production below plant capacity, charge prices as high as the tariff wall will permit, produce goods of a quality as poor as the tariff wall will permit, and grind monopoly-type profits out of the situation. The situation is even more incongruous when the protected firm is a joint venture with a foreign company (for example, the tire-manufacturing companies Goodrich-Euzkadi and Goodyear-Oxo in Mexico) and is nevertheless practicing the low-volume and high-unit-profit approach.

Use of infant industry tariffs tends to sacrifice a country's own consumers during the transition period. If there is any other way to protect the infant industry, there is a presumption that it would be preferable. And if there is a means that would constrain the protected infant to practice a high-volume, low-unit-profit approach, such means should surely be used.

Perhaps the production subsidy, financed by funds raised locally, offers possibilities. One thing that has never been in general short supply in the Latin American countries is the local currency. It is true that there are problems involved in terms of mobilizing local financial resources to pay a local production subsidy. But such measures are within the competence of the Latin American countries themselves, provided they are willing to tax the oligarchy (or, and this is probably less desirable, willing to create the necessary funds.)

In a setting where the production subsidy guaranteed the infant industry against bankruptcy, dumping by foreigners (instead of destroying the new industries) would merely represent a goods bonanza to the commodity-short country. One might guess that, under such circumstances, the dumping itself would be a short-lived phenomenon.

Very seldom in Latin American writing does one see the proposition stated that during the transition period it would be desirable to have more imports instead of less—if only the bankruptcy of the local companies could be avoided. One rare exception to this is a statement by Rómulo Betancourt of Venezuela in which he recommended increased meat imports during the period that the Venezuelan cattle industry was being built up.[4]

Jack Baranson, in describing the impact of such problems on Central America, has said that the Central American businessman has become so accustomed to protectionism and tax exemptions that it has become something of a disease with him.[5] The protection has not contributed to development, it has merely been a response to vested interest pressure—and been rationalized on the infant industry argument. He described the Central American businessman as being scared silly of new and "ruinous competition." And ruinous competition is any new plant either foreign-owned or domestically owned. Baranson concludes that it is about time the protectionist approach to the encouragement of industrialization was dropped in Central America.[6] And yet the countries are so small (even the region as a whole is so small) that it is hard to imagine that there is any satisfactory solution to the region's problems short of a larger customs union, one much larger than Central America itself.

Recently the Economic Commission for Latin America seems to have developed misgivings with regard to the use that Latin American countries have made of protection in their efforts to foster development. Some of those misgivings are reflected in the following statements:

> As is well known, the proliferation of industries of every kind in a closed market has deprived the Latin American countries of the advantages of specialization and economies of scale, and, owing to the protection afforded by excessive tariff duties and restrictions, a healthy form of

[4] Rómulo Betancourt, *Posición y Doctrina* (Caracas, Editorial Cordillera, 1959), p. 113.
[5] Jack Baranson, "Industrialización y Regionalismo en Centroamérica," in *Combate,* October, 1962, pp. 52–8.
[6] *Ibid.*

internal competition has failed to develop, to the detriment of efficient production.

．　．　．　．

The closed industrialization fostered by excessive protectionism, as well as the unduly high customs tariffs applied to some staple agricultural commodities, have created a cost structure which makes it extremely difficult for Latin America to export manufactured goods to the rest of the world.

．　．　．　．

In industry, too, the edge of the incentives to technical progress has been blunted by excessive protection and the positions of privilege it creates. Private enterprise needs constant applications of the spur of competition to keep it on the alert. And in Latin American industry as a whole, competition is seldom very keen. . . .

Protection carried to excess affords no encouragement to train efficient workers and make good use of their services. Production equipment is often misguidedly used, with the result that its performance is inferior to that registered even in countries with medium industrial yields, not to mention those where productivity is high.

．　．　．　．

In the shelter of high tariff barriers and other import restrictions or prohibitions, anti-competitive practices, if not virtually monopolistic combines, have become widespread. Well-equipped establishments operate alongside others whose costs are high, in a sort of tacit mutual benefit society, the latter safeguarding their marginal existence and the former reaping the big profits that accrue from the cost differential.[7]

On a slightly different level of generalization the proliferation of uncoordinated protective measures also creates problems. It may be a bit naïve for economists to study production and pricing by assuming competition and then analyzing how a system characterized by competition would work. But effective planning and decision making require that certain fairly reliable yardsticks be available to the planner. They have all too few as matters stand. Planning would be made easier if prices accurately reflected costs and were reasonably comparable as between companies and as between countries. Planning devices, such as tariffs, quotas, exchange control, and bilateral agreements which tend to isolate the prices and costs of one region from those of another have

[7] United Nations, *Towards a Dynamic Development Policy for Latin America* (New York, 1963), pp. 47, 71, 72.

as their chief effect, not the stimulation of development, but the obfuscation of the planner.

DISCRIMINATION TO INFLUENCE THE LOCATION OF PROCESSING. If, in spite of everything, Latin America is bound to use trade restrictions in an effort to encourage local industrialization, it might be better for the region to emphasize taxes on raw commodity exports in order to encourage domestic processing. For example Argentina has taxed linseed exports to encourage the domestic processing of linseed oil.[8] But relatively little along this line has actually been done by comparison with the fantastic amount of manipulation of import restrictions.

In the Trade Expansion Act of 1962, in a section ostensibly designed to benefit the tropical countries, the United States provided for the possibility of removing completely the trade barriers to various imports from those countries. But the coverage of the provision was limited to raw commodities and unprocessed goods. And this provision, which ostensibly was designed to favor the poor countries, turns out to be a device for keeping them active in raw commodity production and suppressing their manufactures.

Various of the European countries also have provisions designed to encourage raw commodity import and discourage processed goods import. For example, the European Economic Community, in its Common External Tariff, seems to be fabricating an instrument designed to discriminate against processed goods and semi-manufactures and in favor of the import of raw materials. The Common External Tariff on soluble, roasted, and decaffeinated coffee is in the 25 to 30 percent range, on coffee beans it is in the 16 to 21 percent range. It is 22 percent on cacao butter and 9 percent on cacao beans, and so on.[9]

Such discrimination inhibits Latin American industrialization and is a practice against which Latin American governments might legitimately protest vigorously at international conferences. Thus, one of the significant discriminations that the developed countries practice to the detriment of the underdeveloped countries is the rigging of a tariff pattern that places the highest duties against manufactured imports and the

---

[8] *Foreign Crops and Markets,* May 23, 1960.
[9] United Nations, *World Economic Survey, 1962. I. The Developing Countries in World Trade* (New York, 1963), p. 79.

lowest duties against raw material imports. And if the developed countries will not remove the discrimination, it could well be judicious for the underdeveloped countries to counteract such a tariff pattern by a pattern of export duties which is highest on raw commodity exports and nonexistent on manufactured goods exports.[10]

Export Promotion

Latin Americans are fond of arguing that their exports are fated to decline in value because they are chiefly raw materials. And historically, the relative importance of raw materials in the productive process is falling.

In trying to use import substitution policies involving the replacement of imports with domestically produced manufactured goods, they are likely to pay scant attention to the possibility of making the new manufacturing industry competitive in world markets. But if Latin American planners would pay a little more attention to quality and to the uniformity of standards and make their chief argument at international trade conferences one for equal access to world markets, they might surprise themselves in terms of how well they could do in stimulating exports. Latin American exports of handicraft articles have languished in some considerable degree, no doubt because they are not of consistent quality. The middlemen and consumers have not been able to count on what they were getting. As the Mexican Partido de la Revolución Institucional said in a recent program: "Our prospects for exporting finished and semi-finished products to more industrialized countries (such as the United States and Europe) will be progressively better, if we succeed in setting up genuinely efficient industries."[11]

Comparative Cost

GENERAL. The classical economic theory of Adam Smith and David Ricardo alleged that free trade combined with geographical specializa-

---

[10] However such procedure is likely to run into trouble as a result of the non-cooperation of one or two of the raw commodity-producing countries. (There is one in every crowd who will attempt to take advantage of the market possibilities resulting from the high export tariffs of the participating countries to push his own raw commodity exports.)

[11] *Trimestre Económico,* January, 1964, p. 149.

tion would permit production to occur where it could be carried on most efficiently. And consequently the supply of goods available would be larger. The Ricardian comparative cost refinement put this argument in terms of relative efficiency and contended that the world would be better off if each country specialized in the production of and exported the items in which it was relatively most efficient.[12] Ricardo argued that it would be to the country's advantage (and the world's) for it to specialize in the production of and export of the thing in which its comparative disadvantage was the least. This was obviously more productive than remaining idle would be.

Under the aegis of Raúl Prebisch and the Economic Commission for Latin America it has become stylish for Latin American economic circles to denounce the classical position on the advantages of free trade and particularly to excoriate the doctrine of comparative cost—as though those concepts had somehow done major wrong to Latin America. The argument seems to be that, as a consequence of the application of the doctrine of comparative cost by the developed countries to Latin America, the region was condemned to emphasis on raw commodity production, while Europe and the United States connived to emphasize manufacturing. And there is some natural law to the effect that the standard of living is higher in a manufacturing country than it is in a raw-commodity-producing country.

The standard of living would seem to be higher in the United States and in western Europe than in Latin America. What that proves is not unambiguous. The economies of western Europe and the United States have also been characterized by oligopoly and monopoly for the last hundred years or so. Perhaps the oligopolies, rather than the theory of comparative cost, should be blamed for the Latin American plight. And perhaps what has really done the damage in Latin America has been the failure to practice free trade and to apply the comparative cost principle.

In rationalizing the need for protection Latin American spokesmen are prone to speak of the cost disadvantage they are under in relation to the developed countries. For their part the developed countries are likely to complain of the cost advantage which cheap labor gives the poor countries.

---

[12] The possibility that a country could be high cost in all (or many) things was created by the assumption of the international immobility of certain of the factors of production and by the assumption of constant costs.

Prebisch and associates have been so busy denouncing the doctrine of comparative cost (on the ground that the Center has used the argument to exploit the Periphery for 150 years) that they have missed the chief message that the theory of comparative cost has to offer. That message has been that it is not absolute cost differences that determine whether something will be exported, but rather comparative cost differences. Classical international trade theory, as a corollary of the comparative cost proposition, argued that there is a basic necessity that a country's exports pay for its imports. And an absolute cost advantage is not necessary to permit a country's products to compete in world markets. The product merely need be one among those in which the country's production-cost disadvantage is relatively small.

AGRICULTURE. It seems to be that there is need of reinterpreting what comparative cost doctrine actually says about the orientation of specialization. Since Leontief's work on capital intensity in United States exports, it has been possible to argue that the United States comparative advantage in the international trade field is in agriculture rather, perhaps, than over the general field of manufacturing.[13] Leontief suggested that the relative importance of agricultural products in United States exports might indicate that the United Staes does not have a comparative advantage in capital-intensive products. What his argument may in fact mean is that United States agriculture is highly capital intensive.

Attitudes about the relation between agriculture and industry need to be rethought. In the United States we are prone to think of ourselves as the most industrialized country in the world. In the international trade field this presumably means that the United States has a comparative advantage over other countries in connection with manufactured goods, and we are at a comparative disadvantage in connection with production that does not require much capital equipment, that is to say, in raw commodity production and in agriculture. But increasingly there is evidence that this is not the case. Agriculture in the United States is in fact heavily mechanized, fertilized, sprayed (even oversprayed), and generally capital intensive. The mechanized agriculture of the United

---

[13] Wassily Leontief, "Domestic Production and Foreign Trade: The American Capital Position Re-examined," in *Proceedings of the American Philosophical Society,* 97 (September, 1953), 332–49.

States is an industrial sector in which the comparative advantage of the United States on the world scene is pronounced. This may be what Leontief really showed when he demonstrated the significant agricultural content of United States exports. Of course, it is a blow to some traditional ways of thinking to find out that the United States steel and petroleum industries are not, relatively speaking, the strongest of the country's industries. In fact, the much-maligned United States agricultural price support programs are the living evidence of the technical success of United States agriculture—unfortunate as those programs are in many respects.

This is one of the most important lessons that the Latin American countries can learn from looking at the United States. This is what they should see, rather than the steel industry of Pittsburgh. It is strange that the region that produced Rodó and the Idealist movement and has always enjoyed disparaging the production line in particular and modern industry in general should have become so enamoured of the steel industry.

In any case, the fantastic ability of the United States economy to turn out cheap agricultural products may indicate the desirability of a new assessment as to the areas where Latin American specialization is appropriate. It is almost certainly true that Latin America can develop meaningful comparative advantage at least in some significant areas of manufacturing. And Latin America had better plan development on the assumption that significant segments of Latin American manufacturing can be made (and had better be made) genuinely competitive on the international scene. The defeatist emphasis on manufacturing in a setting where it is assumed that Latin American manufacturing cannot compete effectively in world markets is not helping Latin American industrialization.

IMPORT SUBSTITUTION. The import-substitution mentality that has dominated Latin American thinking in recent years seems to conceive that any new production facility is good, almost regardless of cost, provided it turns out a product that can substitute for some imports. At times one gets the impression that the Latin American commitment to the principle of import substitution is so strong as to justify domestic production regardless of cost. And in giving the protection that is necessary for the high-cost industries, the Latin American governments will concede almost any tariff rate that the domestic manufacturer asks for.[14]

As justification for incurring an economic cost in protecting high-cost import substitutes, Latin American economists have argued that they cannot count on an increase in their own exports to provide the foreign exchange they need. They argue that this is the case because the terms of trade are running against them as a consequence of the low income elasticity of demand on the world markets for the typical Latin American exports. But even if true, the preceding argument is not a justification for high costs without limit in the import-substitute industries.[15]

It is difficult to test directly the effects of the import-substitution policies that have been used freely in Latin America in recent years. However, one bit of indirect evidence may be significant. The Statistical Office of the United Nations has compiled data comparing productivity changes.[16] Specifically what is compared is "average annual rates of change between specified years in output per engaged," i.e., per worker. The average annual rate of change in output per worker for the period 1938–53 in manufacturing was:

	Percent
Latin America	1.5
World	2.7
Northern North America	2.7

The figures were almost identically the same if the comparison was made for industry as a whole instead of just for manufacturing. The figures suggest that the import-substitution policies may be costing Latin America a good deal in terms of relative productivity. And this may be one reason the Latin American share of world trade is suffering.

One of the areas where tariffs based on the import-substitution argument are especially popular is luxury consumer goods. What policy could have more merit than one which avoids wasting precious foreign exchange on those lousy old luxury goods? But if the policy works, the

---

[14] Izquierdo, "Protectionism in Mexico," pp. 253, 256, 268.

[15] Harrod's example is: "But there is wastage if resources are directed away from an export commodity, their application to which would cause a 10 per cent deterioration in terms of trade in respect to that commodity, to an import-competing commodity requiring 20 per cent protection." Roy Harrod and D. C. Hague, eds., *International Trade Theory in a Developing World* (New York, St Martin's Press, 1963), p. 119.

[16] *Patterns of Industrial Growth, 1938–1958* (New York, 1960), p. 88.

industry that gets established as a result of the protection is the industry producing the questionable luxury consumer goods. And surely one thing the Latin American countries have little need for right now is a lot of high-cost industries producing luxury consumer goods. Patel and Sohmen have suggested that, in such cases, the appropriate tax policy is not an import tariff on luxury consumer goods but rather an across-the-board excise tax on luxury consumer goods which applies to all such goods regardless of where they are produced.[17]

Volume Per Se

The emphasis in Latin America on the export balance of trade and the restriction of imports has probably involved misplacing of emphasis. For one thing it is probable that an increase in the volume of trade, in and of itself, without especial regard for the balance of trade relation can make a significant contribution to development. What is involved is not just the usefulness of give and take in the trading process itself and the accompanying probability that the country will end up with more net real value of goods as a result. Perhaps more important is the stimulation in terms of improvement of production methods that will be a by-product of the increased exchange. Trade is an important channel for the transmittal of technical knowledge.

Discrimination and the Case against Reciprocity

Discrimination involves handling two people or countries differently; for example, applying different tariff rates or different quotas to their shipments. Such practice is likely to lead to international political bickering. This is not to say that virtue is necessarily connected with nondiscrimination and vice with discrimination. There are undoubtedly aspects of social behavior where discrimination is most appropriate. (If you do not care for a boor, you are entitled to shun his company.) Nevertheless there are important areas of social behavior where nondiscrimination is not only desirable but where society is obligated, in some important sense of the word, to impose nondiscrimination upon the would-be discriminator.

[17] I. G. Patel, "Trade and Payments Policy for a Developing Economy," in Roy Harrod and D. C. Hague, eds., *International Trade Theory in a Developing World*, pp. 319, 524.

Facets of international trade policy would seem to be examples of the latter necessity. Discrimination in trade policy against one foreign country and in favor of another is presumptively bad. This does not deny the possibility of the existence of special circumstances where discrimination would be appropriate. It means that the burden of proof is on the would-be discriminator.

Many cases of discrimination can be found. The United States used to discriminate in favor of imports from Cuba, perhaps because its conscience hurt as a result of the Platt Amendment and the way it handled Cuba after the Spanish-American War.

As a preliminary to the Geneva Conference on Trade and Development in 1964, the Economic Commission for Latin America formulated the proposition that it should be considered appropriate for the underdeveloped countries to place higher barriers against goods coming from the developed countries than the developed countries charged against goods going in the other direction. This conception, if put into practice by the trading nations, would be a significant change from the principle of reciprocity in tariff reductions which has been a cornerstone of the Reciprocal Trade Agreements program sponsored by the United States since 1934.

It may be that one of the reasons why the Geneva Conference on Trade and Development in 1964 had results that were rather unsatisfactory from the Latin American point of view was due to the nature of their argument against the principle of reciprocity. The Latin American delegations argued that the institutional arrangements in the international trading world are such that if they practice reciprocity in their relations with the developed countries they lose. They lose because, on the world scene, the income elasticity of demand for their chief exports, raw materials, is relatively inelastic over time.[18]

But apart from the question as to where Latin America's comparative advantage actually lies, it is a pretty tricky business to argue in favor of positive discrimination in one's own favor. This is what the Latin American countries were doing when they argued that they should be permitted to have relatively high tariffs. In view of the fact that all Latin America needed to do to net some major gains was to argue against positive dis-

---

[18] United Nations, *Towards a Dynamic* . . . , pp. 7, 73. This argument seems to assume a natural tendency for them to have their comparative advantage in the area of raw commodity production, a defeatist attitude which was discussed earlier in this chapter.

crimination against the region, without arguing for discrimination in favor of the region, it may have been a tactical mistake to make the key argument one against reciprocity.

Capacity to Import and the Usefulness of Imports

The economists of the Economic Commission for Latin America have risen above some of the misapprehensions connected with the export-balance-of-trade phobia and shown appreciation of the importance of volume per se in emphasizing the importance of increasing the capacity to import. The concept emphasizes that the usefulness of exports is in their ability to provide the financing for imports. The imports are the prime gain from the trading process. The commonly held belief that the loss of goods via exports is by some perversion of common sense a gain is, in this concept, discounted.

There is also another argument indicating the usefulness of imports that is worth mentioning. Because of this a point Hirschman has made in defense of imports becomes significant for Latin America.[19] He pointed out that the establishment of a new industry frequently waits until it has been proven that there is a significant market for the products of the industry. This would mean that the Latin American manufacturer would be more likely to start the production of something that has been imported in large quantities than to strike out on his own. The importation would be the proof he needed of the existence of a market. Consequently it is useful that the foreigner provide the service of developing the market. And the argument would mean that there is less likelihood that an industry will be established if there is a long-established tariff wall that has been doing the job of keeping goods out.

But these arguments indicating the usefulness of imports have not particularly influenced most of the Latin American governments, any more than they have influenced the average United States senator. And it can be alleged with reasonable accuracy that, by and large, Latin American governments are busy trying to restrict imports and to encourage exports by all sorts of artificial means without any especial concern for the ultimate effect of those measures on goods availability within their own countries and without real appreciation for the effect of those

[19] *Strategy of Economic Development* (New Haven, Yale University Press, 1958), pp. 120–25.

measures on development. There is in general almost blind acceptance of the attitude that keeping out imports is a good thing. And if a few tariffs help, more of them are bound to be better.[20]

Terms of Trade and the Gains from Productivity

It has been argued by the Economic Commission for Latin America in a document of considerable historical interest that the terms of trade have tended to run against the underdeveloped countries as a long-run trend.[21] A sophisticated statement of the relation runs to the effect that, during the nineteenth and early twentieth centuries, the increased output resulting from increased productivity was reflected, in the underdeveloped countries, in a fall in prices and was reflected in the more developed countries in a rise in wages and returns to the other factors of production. If correct, this argument meant that much of the gain from increased productivity in the poorer countries was transferred to the wealthier countries in the form of cheaper goods. But the gain from increased productivity was generally kept at home in the developed countries as export prices remained about the same and the purchasing power needed to buy the increased stocks of goods in the developed countries was chiefly in the hands of the local workers and businessmen. This tendency has allegedly been made worse by a tendency for the demand for raw materials to rise more slowly than the demand for manufactured goods.[22] These propositions have been much debated during the last ten years. And the arguments are worthy of respectful attention whether or not the currently available statistical data clearly support them.

In any event the terms of trade concept is probably largely irrelevant to the proposition that the country where a major increase in productivity occurs will be the chief beneficiary of that increase in productivity. And if Latin America desires really to obtain a substantial improvement in welfare, the region had better foster industries where considerable advantage is to be obtained from increased productivity. It is not enough for the increased productivity to occur in the developed centers and hope that it will trickle down to Latin America.

---

[20] Izquierdo, "Protectionism in Mexico," pp. 241-89.
[21] See the discussion in Chapter Six.
[22] United Nations, *Towards a Dynamic* . . . , pp. 7, 73.

CHAPTER TWENTY-ONE

COMMON MARKETS

At the time of the first Pan American Conference in 1889 there was talk of the formation of a customs union to include all of the Latin American countries and the United States. This was an abortive effort, however, as were several attempts to establish customs unions involving smaller groups of countries such as those in the region of the River Plate or in the Caribbean or Grancolombian areas.

Theory and Motivation

Latin America has been motivated to establish a common market or two by the apparent success of the European Economic Community and by the decline in the relative importance of the region's exports since World War II, if not since 1929.

THEORY. The customs-union theory that enjoys prestige is that developed by Jacob Viner in the early 1950s and subsequently elaborated by J. E. Meade.[1] Let me rather cavalierly allege that the theory which they elaborated in static, general equilibrium terms has very little to offer in indicating the implications of customs unions for Latin America.

A more significant argument may well be that the enlarged markets created by the existence of the customs union will increase national income; and the national income increase will result in an increase in international trade both among the member countries and between the customs union and the outside world. The chief circumstance that will

---

[1] Jacob Viner, *The Customs Union Issue* (New York, Carnegie Endowment for International Peace, 1950); J. E. Meade, *The Theory of Customs Unions* (Amsterdam, North Holland Publishing Co., 1955); Bela Balassa, *The Theory of Economic Integration* (Homewood, Ill., Irwin, 1961). The Balassa book is the best single source of information on customs-union theory.

lead to the income increase is the fact that the Latin American countries are now so desperately small. This point calls for further discussion.

TOO-SMALL COUNTRIES. Many products, to be efficiently produced, require plants capable of supplying many times the market of a whole Latin American country—especially when the country is Honduras, Paraguay, or Haiti. There is the example of the button factory in Nicaragua that could produce in three months as many buttons as Nicaragua could absorb in three years, and so on.[2]

There seems to be a tendency for the standard of living to be higher in large countries than in small countries. At least this is true as between countries similarly situated. (It is probably well to admit that the standard of living in Brazil is lower than that in New Zealand, even though Brazil is a larger country.) And as among the Latin American countries, at least in recent years, the bigger ones seem in general (and with exceptions) also to have the more rapid growth rates and the higher standards of living. Felipe Herrera, a Chilean who is head of the Inter-American Development Bank, remarked in December, 1962: "It is interesting to note that six countries—Brazil, Argentina, Mexico, Venezuela, Colombia and Chile, in the order of the size of their share—produce 87 percent of Latin America's gross domestic product and that the same six countries account for 76 percent of the population. The other fourteen countries, with 24 percent of the total population, contribute 13 percent of the product." [3]

Even the middle-sized Latin American country, such as Colombia or Peru, finds it difficult properly to time the progression in a particular industry from one plant to two, or from three to four. Most of the time there will be a significant amount too much or too little productive capacity. When countries as large as France and West Germany find it desirable to fuse into larger economic units, it suggests that even Mexico, Brazil, and Argentina may be a bit small for economic efficiency in the modern world.[4]

---

[2] New York *Times*, June 11, 1958, p. 49.
[3] Inter-American Development Bank, *News Release*, December 5, 1962(cc), p. 3.
[4] This argument indicates the difficulty with the suggestion of Aldo Ferrer that what Argentina needs is an economy integrated around a highly developed basic industry. Argentina is not big enough and does not have an adequate raw material base to support a major basic industry complex like the Ruhr. See Aldo Ferrer, *La Economía Argentina* (México-Buenos Aires, Fondo de Cultura Económica, 1963), esp. pp. 155 *et seq.*

The ramifications of the too-small-country difficulty extend beyond the problem of plant size. For an industrial concentration (a pole of development) to evolve, there needs to be a rather substantial reservoir of laborers trained in the various skills as machinists, mechanics, and so on. One industry or company can complement another in various ways. A highway will be more useful if it is serving several companies instead of only one. There is thus a considerable gain in efficiency from what might be termed the economies of agglomeration. The customs union may facilitate industrialization by facilitating the growth of industrial complexes in a setting where the growth of one firm may complement the growth of another.

Haiti, the Dominican Republic, Paraguay, and Honduras are certainly too small. They are too small to command respect in world society. They are too small to develop satisfactory, diversified production patterns. They are too small to provide (in a world of trade barriers) a profitable market for goods produced by plants of anything like optimum size in many lines of enterprise. In fact, the opinion may be hazarded that any country that has a serious monoculture and diversification problem is too small. It is too small for the good of its citizenry. However, it may be about the right size to provide a private domain to gratify the ego of some dictator or about the right size to be dominated by a foreign fruit company. The small country is generally at a great disadvantage merely because it is small. Some little countries had better do some fusing, even at the terrific cost of having one president where there were formerly two. To paraphrase Henry G. Aubrey: The world needs a few more declarations of interdependence and somewhat fewer declarations of independence.

Types of Common Markets

There are three chief possible types of common markets: (1) the customs union involving (a) the elimination of trade barriers among the members and (b) the establishment of a common pattern of trade barriers facing the rest of the world; (2) the free trade association, which also involves (a) the elimination of trade barriers among the members but, so far as the barriers facing the rest of the world are concerned, (b) retains the miscellaneous and different barriers of the various different member countries; and (3) the economic union, which would go beyond the customs union in establishing common fiscal, monetary, and perhaps other economic policies.

The European Economic Community is a customs union seriously considering economic union and even political union. The Latin American arrangement growing out of the Treaty of Montevideo of 1960 is a free trade association which has talked some about the possibilities of becoming a customs or an economic union—but which seems to view political union as anathema. The Central American arrangement is, more or less, a customs union with some intentions of integrating economic policy, and perhaps even of establishing political union.

LAFTA

The Latin American Free Trade Association was set up by a treaty signed at Montevideo in 1960. The members of the resulting organization (1964) are Chile, Argentina, Paraguay, Uruguay, Brazil, Peru, Ecuador, Colombia, and Mexico.[5]

The treaty provided for action with respect to the tariffs among the member countries in a pattern that would lower them 8 percent a year (as a minimum) for twelve years, thus accumulating to an ostensible reduction of at least 96 percent. This reduction formula has posed several problems. In the first place it does not provide assurance of eliminating the tariffs among the members by the end of the twelve-year-transition period. It would, on the contrary, seem to create the possibility of a residue of tariffs that might involve continued, irritating administrative protectionism.

The international discrimination which is a by-product of the establishment of customs unions has generally been granted to be acceptable (as not being in violation of most-favored-nation clauses in trade treaties) provided the members of the customs union unambiguously go all the way in establishing free trade among themselves. But it has generally been agreed that a pseudo-customs union, which only goes part way down this road, is to be condemned as a subterfuge for discrimination. And it becomes legitimate for other countries to adopt retaliatory

---

[5] Good general books on the subject are: Víctor Urquidi, *Free Trade and Economic Integration in Latin America: The Evolution of a Common Market Policy* (Berkeley, University of California Press, 1962); and Sidney S. Dell, *Problemas de un Mercado Común en América Latina* (México, Centro de Estudios Monetarios Latinoamericanos, 1959).

measures accordingly. The LAFTA countries may have a hornets' nest on their hands if they do not establish meaningful free trade among themselves by the end of the transition period.

The procedures for implementing the 8 percent a year reductions are fairly complicated.[6] And considerable maneuvering is involved each year as between each pair of countries in determining what commodities will be subject to negotiation during the current round. The commodities which it is agreed are subject to negotiation are then placed on the so-called national schedules.

But in addition to the national schedules there is a grouping of commodities called common schedules to which items are moved from the national schedules. Every three years 25 percent of the goods traded among the members is to be transferred to these common schedules. This is supposed to mean that the tariff reductions already negotiated in connection with those commodities are irreversible. A limitation on the efficacy of the procedure is that the proviso for the fourth three-year period covers, not the final 25 percent, but rather calls for coverage of "substantially all such trade." Only time can tell whether this provision will be a significant loophole in the tariff elimination process.

At the end of the first three-year period in 1964, the proviso for putting goods representing 25 percent of the intra-area trade on the common schedule might have been met by putting only two items on the schedule: wheat (representing 17.58 percent of the intra-area trade) and sawn lumber (representing 9.54 percent). But a disagreement as to the items to be included developed, which had not been resolved at the time of writing.

There is quite a range of escape, or partial escape, clauses spread through the treaty. One such clause is devoted to agriculture. Since trade in agricultural products has represented almost half of the intra-Latin American trade, the agricultural exceptions are not to be taken lightly. (However, the negotiators of the treaty anticipated a decline in the relative importance of agriculture, a development which might mitigate the importance of these clauses.) The agricultural exceptions involve some

---

[6] The formula actually runs: "Each Contracting Party shall annually grant to the other Contracting Parties reductions in duties and charges equivalent to not less than eight (8) per cent of the weighted average applicable to third countries, until they are eliminated in respect to substantially all of its imports from the Area. . . ." (Article 5). The Protocol to the treaty then elaborates at some length the procedures to be involved in the computation.

loosely worded paragraphs that are difficult to interpret. Perhaps agriculture in the end will be substantially excluded from the working of the treaty, perhaps not.

In addition there have been special lures to induce the poorer Latin American countries (Paraguay, Haiti, Ecuador, and Bolivia) to join LAFTA. The chief lure has been to recognize them as "relatively underdeveloped" countries, a recognition which would permit them to retain certain tariffs to protect local industry. Ecuador and Paraguay have been formally identified as being entitled to such preferential treatment. This being the procedure, one might almost wonder why they bother to join the customs union at all.

All of the Latin American countries are too small. But especially the poorer countries are too small. And if they join LAFTA and continue to use their tariffs to maintain their economic smallness, they are failing to take advantage of the characteristic of the common market (its economic size) that makes the whole operation worthwhile.

It is a kind of combination of the comic and the tragic to see the poorer Latin American countries using the same arguments against their richer neighbors that the richer Latin American countries have used against western Europe and the United States. They say: "The poor countries are no match for the rich countries in a free trade world, therefore we need protection."

The Economic Commission for Latin America has trouble defending its thesis that the Center exploits the Periphery without granting that there may be something to the thesis that the Latin American Center exploits the Latin American Periphery.

It was hoped that the provision for granting special status and the possibility of continuing protection to the poorer countries would encourage more of them to join. But many of the small countries seem to have rationalized not joining LAFTA on the grounds that the larger, more developed countries will get relatively most of the gain (perhaps due to conglomeration effects) and the little countries will lag relatively. This is probably a regrettable attitude. The small countries may lag if they join; they are certain to lag if they do not.

One may suspect that a more important reason for the abstinence of several of the smaller countries is the jealousy of the rulers. The presidents and *caudillos* (and their delegates to the United Nations and their diplomatic corps) of countries such as Haiti, Guatemala, and Honduras may quite correctly anticipate a loss of status relative to the larger countries if they participate in the free trade area. Also they may anticipate the possibility of some kind of political union following the economic union. Perish the thought that that should happen. They would really lose their perquisites then, and it would be a sad day for the New York City restaurant business, too.

With regard to the tariffs facing the rest of the world, the Treaty of Montevideo provided that each country would retain its own pre-LAFTA pattern of rates, which would be subject to modification in future negotiations with outside countries perhaps through the machinery of the General Agreement on Tariffs and Trade. It is this characteristic which makes the LAFTA a free trade association rather than a customs union. This characteristic may also necessitate a complicated administrative machinery to see to it that goods are not imported from outside LAFTA into the member country with the lowest tariff on the particular commodity in question and then transshipped to a member country with a higher tariff on that commodity. And of course even more subtle possibilities for evasion exist than crude transshipment.

The original planners of the LAFTA apparently hoped that the elimination of tariffs would be especially significant in connection with manufactured goods. They planned that a pattern of complementarity would be developed. One region would specialize in the development of one new manufactured item, another region in another. And production and productivity in the region as a whole would be greater as a result of the geographical specialization and free trade. But the original set of rules for tariff reductions did not provide for getting the tariff rates applicable to previously untraded goods automatically into the negotiating machinery. As the negotiating machinery stands they may never get in. In addition difficulties have developed in the negotiation of the complementarity patterns. (These difficulties were discussed in Chapter Thirteen, Planning, and Chapter Eighteen, Industrial Priorities.)

The Free Trade Association offers possibilities for making a major contribution to Latin American industrialization. The stimulating effect of the increased ability to trade can be immense. But the realization of the gain requires that trade not only be permitted to increase but that it does increase. And, for this to happen, improved land transportation facilities among the Latin American countries seem to be an essential corollary of the removal of trade barriers. Also important is the genuine freedom of movement of people about the area. As matters stand (despite the homogeneity of the people of Latin America) the region is plagued with restrictions and police-type harassment on the movement of people. Along the same line, the existence of twenty or more monetary systems, with their exchange controls, multiple exchange rates, and so on, represents a formidable barrier to trade even after the commercial barriers are removed.

Latin America has a lot to do before the area will realize from the LAFTA the pattern of gains that seems to be accruing to the continental European countries from the European Economic Community.

In fact there is considerable resistance to the effective implementation of the Treaty of Montevideo even in the countries such as Argentina, Chile, and Uruguay which were most active in promoting the treaty. As the Economic Commission for Latin America has commented:

> The problem of the Latin American Free-Trade Association is more difficult, for the very reason that the development of industrialization in watertight compartments has created vested interests and prejudices which oppose reciprocal trade without taking account of the serious effects of such an attitude on economic development.[7]

The Treaty of Montevideo is a masterpiece of ambiguity and complicated provisions. But if there is a real will in Latin America to implement a customs union the wording of the treaty will not prevent the development. However, if the forces that really do not want a genuine free trade area prove sufficiently strong (and not much strength may be necessary for this situation to result) the complexities and ambiguities of the treaty will make it easy to frustrate the substantial implementation of regional free trade. And the difficulty of too-many, too-small countries will remain to plague Latin America.

Procedurally whether a free trade area will actually have come to exist in twelve years as the result of the operation of the processes provided in the treaty is an open question, the answer to which depends much more upon the spirit in which the annual negotiations are conducted than it does on the literal wording of the treaty.

The trade statistics for some of the countries, Mexico for example, indicate that there has already been a substantial increase in the intra-

---

[7] United Nations, *Towards a Dynamic Development Policy for Latin America* (New York, 1963), p. 7.

area trade since the LAFTA was established. But it is much too early to read any very conclusive meaning into such statistics.

Central American Common Market

Eleven of the Latin American countries, including especially the smaller and less-developed countries and Cuba, are not as yet members of the Latin American Free Trade Association. Five of them (Guatemala, El Salvador, Honduras, Nicaragua, and Costa Rica) are, however, participating in a Central American customs union, which, on paper, seems to do much the same thing among them that the LAFTA tries to do for the region as a whole. The Central American arrangement, however, in one respect goes further than LAFTA and envisages a common external tariff. But all of the Central American countries together do not add up to a single decent-sized country. And those countries surely need to join a yet larger unit to obtain significant gains from economic integration.

Evaluation

A common market, including a small group of countries, may well be beneficial in a limited way. But there are dangerous possibilities if it engenders a bond of common interests that sets the group off antagonistically in relation to the world.

In view of the fact that the existence of customs unions may tend to stimulate interregional antagonisms, it might seem more desirable to encourage the effort to lower trade barriers across the board in the most-favored-nation type of procedure that the General Agreement on Tariffs and Trade follows. Nevertheless, a series of customs unions would probably be better than high tariff walls among all nations.

The freeing of trade any way it can be done has advantages. And LAFTA should permit lowering costs consequent on the enlargement of markets in a manner which will permit economies of large-scale production and conglomeration. The international price comparability that would become a possibility in a setting where trade barriers were largely eliminated should also make possible much more intelligent decision making than is now possible in a setting where intelligent comparisons of alternatives are made almost impossible by the price discrepancies occasioned by trade barriers.

Trade is itself an engine of growth. The exchange of goods and services is bound to have a dynamic and stimulating effect on the people that participate in the process. The use of trade barriers to encourage development is almost bound to have a by-product stultifying and enervating effect on the people who are isolated by the barriers. Latin America has had about all of that it should stand for.

It is likely that there cannot be any really effective implementation of the free trade association without some quite substantial abridgment of the sovereignty of various of the twenty or so Latin American countries. The European Economic Community, in spite of major language differences and centuries of bloody internecine wars, has found it possible to orient its goals toward an effective political unity to complement the economic unity.[8] The Latin Americans, in spite of much greater language similarity and the general absence of international wars in their historical backgrounds, have generally roundly denounced any implication that the free trade association might lead to closer political ties among the countries. This is odd.

[8] DeGaulle may make this argument inaccurate.

CHAPTER TWENTY-TWO

THE MONETARY STANDARD AND THE FOREIGN EXCHANGES

Bimetallism was the prevailing monetary system in Latin America (and the United States) until about 1900. Gold and silver coins—escudos of gold, *reales* of silver, pesos of gold and silver, duros and *ducados*—circulated, or were supposed to circulate, side by side. Generally either gold coins or silver coins circulated at one time but not both. Gresham's law operated. Whether it was gold or silver coins that circulated at a given time depended on which was currently overvalued at the mint relative to the market price. In accordance with the changing relative market values of gold and silver, the mint ratios between the two were changed by the Spaniards several times during the colonial period and ranged between 1:9.57 and 1:16.64, silver being the cheaper.

After independence was gained the new countries retained bimetallism as the prevailing monetary standard, for they were accustomed to it. But the standard was retained under difficulties. The gachupines, when they left the New World to return to Spain, took with them a substantial proportion of the metallic money, and for a time there was a shortage of currency in circulation. This led to experiments with paper (fiat) money issues. Mexico, for example, tried such an experiment shortly after gaining independence. The results were disastrous, the value of the paper money declined, and the issue eventually was repudiated. When paper money began to be generally used in the latter part of the nineteenth century, the commercial banks became the usual issuing agency, although some of the paper money was issued by the government.

About 1900 there was a shift by several of the Latin American countries from bimetallism to the gold standard. Argentina, for example, went on the gold standard in 1899. By the turn of the century, political leaders in several of the countries were conscious of the fact that Latin American traders and borrowers were at a disadvantage in the international money markets because their domestic monetary and financial structures were not based on the gold standard, which was the respectable monetary standard endorsed by the trading center, England. In most cases the standard adopted did not correspond exactly with the textbook norms describing the gold standard. Silver still played an important role. But, then, probably no country in the world ever had a gold standard which did correspond with those norms.

Generally speaking, the gold standard period in Latin America lasted from the turn of the century until just after the beginning of the Great Depression in 1929, although the period after World War I might more properly be identified with the gold exchange standard. The period of gold standard ascendancy was roughly the same in Latin America as in western Europe and the United States. But there were interludes, even during the 1900-29 period, when the standard was actually not in operation in many of the countries which avowedly had adopted it. Mexico, for example, had an assortment of fiat paper money issues during the period of revolutionary fighting from 1910 until 1920.

The gold exchange standards of the 1920s worked somewhat as follows: The currency of the country on the gold exchange standard, instead of being backed by gold (or fractional reserves of gold) alone, was backed by gold plus foreign exchange, and the country on this sort of a standard was obliged to redeem its paper money in gold or in a bill of exchange drawn on some gold standard country such as the United States or England. The scheme really needed the cooperation of the gold standard country, which had to give some assurance that payment in gold on such bills of exchange would not be stopped. The scheme was supposed to effect an economy in the use of gold, that is to say a given amount of gold was supposed to support paper money issues in both the gold standard and the gold exchange standard countries. But the system generally did not work that way. The gold standard country felt safer if it set aside the gold backing the gold exchange standard currency.

In December, 1929, following a period of substantial although not exhausting gold exports, Argentina suspended gold payments and went off the gold (exchange) standard. By 1932 all the Latin American countries were off the gold standard in fact, and most of their currencies had declined relative to the dollar or been subjected to exchange control. In 1933 the dollar itself went off the gold standard, although the United States government continued to buy and sell gold internationally in unlimited amounts at a new price—$35 an ounce, a change from $20.67 an ounce.

After abandoning the gold standard many of the Latin American governments set up stabilization funds to hold and manipulate the reserves of gold, foreign exchange, and the like, owned by the monetary authorities. The idea was that, if the local currency tended to decline on the foreign exchanges, quantities could be bought by the stabilization fund with their foreign exchange reserves and the price forced back to some approximation of the former level or vice versa.

The monetary ties of some of the Middle American countries, such as Panama and the Dominican Republic, with the United States have been very close. Federal Reserve notes and other United States currency have actually functioned as much of the circulating medium in the Dominican Republic until very recently. The price of several of the Central American currencies has been held in a stable relation to the dollar for many years.

At the time World War II began in 1939, the monetary situation in Latin America might be summarized as follows: Although the countries were off the gold standard, they continued to keep quantities of gold and foreign exchange as part of the legal reserve behind their currencies. The law was likely to specify that the central banks must have gold and foreign exchange reserves of, say, 25 percent behind its note issue. But individuals who possessed paper money could not obtain the gold or foreign exchange freely for it. Gold was used to settle international balances in some cases, but it was not freely available for this purpose. The international value of many Latin American currencies was maintained by the ability of the stabilization funds to buy and sell currencies at the desired rates. Inadequate foreign exchange reserves might result in devaluation or exchange control.

The Internal Standard

In general in the Latin American countries a paper money circulates that is not directly redeemable in anything else, at least so far as the domestic holder of the money is concerned. The monetary unit is the paper peso of the Bank of Mexico, the paper quetzal of the Central Bank of Guatemala, and so on. Typically, the governments, or the central banks, have rules establishing the reserve requirements backing these various paper money issues. It may be required that the bank of issue must have in reserve some stated percentage of the supply (currency plus demand deposits). The reserves are probably specified as gold or convertible foreign exchange (dollars on deposit in New York, or pounds on deposit in Britain). These typical Latin American arrangements are unlike the United States arrangement in that in Latin America the basic reserve is a minimum of gold plus foreign exchange reserves. In the United States it is a reserve in terms of gold, or gold certificates, only.

The holder of the paper money cannot generally convert his paper money into gold at his personal discretion. There is little or no free convertibility into gold. There is considerable freedom to convert into foreign exchange in the northern countries of Latin America, relatively less in the southern countries.

At any given time the gold plus foreign exchange reserve requirements control the ability of the central bank to manufacture paper money. But this is not to say that this is the basic, long-run, controlling force. In spite of loss of reserves it is possible for the legislature (or perhaps for the executive branch, by decree) to change the reserve requirement percentages. Or the monetary authorities may disregard the reserve requirements. By such devices the monetary supply can be expanded almost without limit.

Foreign Exchange Rates

IMF PARS. Most of the Latin American countries are now members of the International Monetary Fund, which began to operate in 1946. This means that the resources of the Fund are available, at the discretion of the Fund, to help the national stabilization funds maintain the international values of the different Latin American currencies. Those foreign exchange rates are ostensibly expressed as the par values of the national currencies and are stated in terms of gold and/or United States dollars. For example, the par value of the Mexican peso is now (1964) 12.5 to the dollar, or .0710937 grams of gold; the par value of the Venezuelan *bolívar* is 3.35 to the dollar, or .265275 grams of gold. Several countries, however, are at least temporarily without par values: Peru, Argentina, and Paraguay.

Under the treaty setting up the Fund, it is the legal obligation of the stabilization fund (or central bank) of the member country to keep the foreign exchange rate on the dollar within 1 percent of par. The Fund stands ready to consult with the local monetary authorities as to measures that may assist in this effort, and the Fund has substantial resources in various currencies that it may lend to the central bank which is running short of foreign currencies. For example, in February, 1964, the Fund placed $25 million (U.S.) at the disposal of the government of Chile. The Fund may place certain conditions on such assistance; for example, balanced budgets or control of expansion of the money supply. Similarly the stabilization funds of various other national governments may also provide aid to currencies in trouble. The United States Treasury has maintained varying amounts ($40 million or $50 million) at the disposal of the Bank of Mexico most of the time since 1938.

The Fund agreement provides for the possibility of changing exchange rates under certain conditions. A country may change the rate as much as 10 percent away from the initial par merely by reporting to the Fund its intent to do so while alleging it is afflicted with fundamental disequilibrium. For changes of more than 10 percent the approval of the Fund is required. And the free 10 percent can be used only once. A succession of 9 percent devaluations is not an alternative. It was the intent of the planners that changes in the exchange rates would be utilized only to correct a fundamental maladjustment of some sort, that such changes would not be frequently resorted to, and that the use of the power to change the exchange rate would cease to be a weapon in the hands of governments pursuing a nationalistic policy.

But the Fund does not have the power to control the creation of money and credit internally, and expansion in the money supply can affect the purchasing power of a currency so greatly that no given rate can be maintained without exchange control. The IMF will most certainly have failed in its purpose of freeing the exchange markets from the exchange controls which were so common during the 1930s if it is forced to allow rationing of currencies (exchange control) as a common phenomenon. And yet, because of this inability to control internal credit extension, there is question as to whether the present arrangements are inherently viable.

After Per Jacobsson became the managing director in 1956, the Fund began an effort to influence the credit policies of the member countries using as leverage the withholding of Fund credit. Jacobsson influenced several of the Latin American countries (Peru, Chile, Argentina, and others) to adopt stabilization policies, that is to say statements of intention to curtail the expansion of the internal money and credit supply and to balance their budgets. His effort to influence Kubitschek in Brazil, however, seems to have been notably unsuccessful.

In a more limited setting, the Central American countries are ostensibly in the process of establishing a monetary union and perhaps even a Central American peso. Much remains to be done in the working out of the details. However, a Central American Clearing House, established in 1961, is already in existence, with headquarters in Tegucigalpa. It clears the financing of much of the trade among the countries of the region.

EXCHANGE CONTROL. International shipments may be controlled indirectly by government regulations requiring that exporters turn their foreign currency earnings over to their central bank in exchange for local currency and also requiring that importers obtain the foreign currency to finance their imports from the monetary authorities.

Exchange control, used in this way, may be made a tool for regulating imports and exports. Argentina in particular and most of the South American countries in general have made use of such power to allocate exchange in order to restrict the importation of nonessential goods, or goods not particularly desirable in the opinion of the government. Countries which have made less intensive use of exchange control include those closer to the United States—Mexico, the Dominican Republic, Haiti, Guatemala, El Salvador, and Panama.

MULTIPLE RATES. By the end of the 1930s the situation in several countries, especially Argentina, Brazil, Chile, Colombia, and Uruguay, had grown complicated. Foreign exchange was being bought and sold by the monetary authorities at various rates in terms of the local currency, the rates depending on the degree of government approval of the transactions in question. In addition, there might be a free market which could be legally used for some purposes (or a black market which might be illegally used for many purposes). This situation has been simplified somewhat in recent years; but several countries, including Brazil, Venezuela, Colombia, Costa Rica, Ecuador, and Uruguay still, in 1964, had multiple rate structures. For example, in Venezuela the par value of the bolívar was 3.35 to the dollar, but there also existed a so-called official free market rate of 4.5 to the dollar which might be allowed in various cases.

CURRENCY DEVALUATION. For some reason the view is widely held that currency devaluation increases exports and that there is some inherent virtue in increasing exports. Perhaps an increase in exports will make domestic production more profitable and thus encourage domestic production. One might suspect any line of thought that seems to assume that a country makes itself better off by foisting more of its goods off on foreigners and rejecting imports. Nevertheless the idea that it is better to export more and import less seems deeply ingrained in the way of thinking of the Western countries in general as well as the Latin American countries in particular.

A case history of devaluation that has been repeated over and over again in Latin America runs somewhat as follows: The central bank increases the supply of money and credit. It may rationalize this action on the grounds that additional money is desirable to finance economic development. And also the increase in the money supply, it is thought, will operate somewhat like autonomous investment in the Keynesian-national-income-theory model. The marginal propensity to consume will determine the size of the multiplier. And national income will be increased by a corresponding multiple which will be three or four times the original increase in the money supply. Other factors influencing the central bank to increase the money supply may be that influential friends of the government want to borrow money, speculators need funds to finance inventory hoarding to permit them to make a killing by cornering the market in some necessity, and so on. The interaction of the various elements in this motivation may result in some increase in goods production; and such increase in goods production, if it occurs, will be a factor inhibiting inflation. But much of the monetary expansion will be purely inflationary in its effect. Prices then rise in the country in question relative to the rest of the world. This makes the Latin American country a relatively unattractive place in which to buy. Consequently imports rise relative to exports, and the foreign exchange reserves are decreased, if not exhausted. After this process has gone sufficiently far the central bank will no longer have foreign exchange reserves adequate to defend the foreign exchange rate which, by agreement with the International Monetary Fund, it is obligated to defend. Devaluation is the standard patent medicine for dealing with such a problem. And one devaluation may well lead to another as the fact of devaluation itself gestates lack of confidence in the devalued currency. Since World War II this process has been repeated in Latin America more times than one can readily count (for example in Mexico in 1948 and 1954).

A matter that is likely to be left out of account in discussing the effect of a currency devaluation is its role in influencing income distribution. The result of devaluation is likely to be a shift of income to the merchants in the export sector and, if they pass a little of the increase along to their workers, a shift of income to people in the export sector in general. Celso Furtado has pointed out this effect in connection with various Brazilian devaluations.[1] Money income is shifted to the export sector; and since real income in the country may well be decreased by the worsening terms of trade that are a rather likely counterpart of the devaluation, the shift in real income to those in the export sector is likely to be even more marked than the monetary shift. This is an especially serious result of devaluation because of the fact that the export sector is likely to be a relatively high-income sector anyway. A likely effect of devaluation is: "To him who hath shall be given."

Latin American governments have frequently, in connection with their devaluations, attempted to recapture some of this gain from the export sector by means of increased export taxes and such like devices. But it nevertheless seems clear that generally there has been a rather substantial income redistribution effect. And the export taxes have been used effectively only against foreign companies or against individuals out of political favor. The political ingroup has generally managed to capture a considerable income gain from devaluation. And many a Latin American minister of finance has probably made his private fortune by speculating against his own currency in the certain knowledge that his country was about to devalue.

There are alternatives (to a system which features sporadic or occa-

---

[1] Celso Furtado, *Formação Econômica do Brasil* (Rio de Janeiro, Editôra Fundo de Cultura, 1959), p. 188; Celso Furtado, *Desenvolvimento e Subdesenvolvimento* (Rio de Janeiro, Editôra Fundo de Cultura, 1961), p. 236.

sional devaluation) for dealing with problems such as those described. There is the fairly unlikely possibility that appreciation of the currency, rather than devaluation, might increase the value of exports relative to imports and thus improve the foreign exchange reserve situation. By and large, countries just assume that devaluation is the appropriate medicine, without considering the possibility that it may be exactly the wrong thing.

But, more important, thinking in terms of occasional devaluation or appreciation may involve working in the wrong frame of reference. If governments are going to insist on working themselves into difficulties tending to exhaust foreign exchange reserves, they might better use a system of freely fluctuating foreign exchange rates and thus avoid the periods of uncertainty, confusion, and profiteering that characterize the sporadic devaluations.

In addition, it should be mentioned that somewhat more judicious use of credit control powers might create situations where the original addition to the money supply would result in more expansion in production and less inflation. If expansion in the money supply is compensated for by additional goods production rather than by inflation, the pressure against the foreign exchange reserves may never develop.

CHAPTER TWENTY-THREE

BANKING

Banking practice might be cited as an example of an institutional barrier to development. It may not be too unfair to bankers to allege that they are influenced in their lending habits by customary preferences for one industry by comparison with another, by a more understanding attitude toward the problems of members of their own clubs, and lodges, and so on. They tend to be heavily influenced by whether the would-be borrower has borrowed before. Someone with no borrowing history and no record as a depositor (but with innate honesty and a good project) had better not go into a bank with any optimism that he will succeed in borrowing money. Such banker attitudes are an important influence on who gets credit and who does not, an influence apart from and additional to the purely rational pursuit of profit maximization.[1]

Foreign Banks

The first Banco do Brasil, which was established in 1807, might be considered the first real bank in Latin America, although there had been earlier institutions which performed certain banking functions. The Monte de Piedad, which was established in Mexico in 1775, for exam-

[1] Various general books on Latin American banking include: Bruno Brovedani, *Bases Analíticas de la Política Monetaria* (México, Centro de Estudios Monetarios Latinoamericanos, 1961); Benjamín Cornejo and others, *Sistemas Monetarios Latinoamericanos* (Córdoba, Argentina, Imprenta de la Universidad de Córdoba, 1943); Ernesto Lobato López, *El Crédito en México* (México, Fondo de Cultura Económica, 1945); O. Ernest Moore, *Evolución de las Instituciones Financieras en México* (México, Centro de Estudios Monetarios Latinoamericanos, 1963); David H. Shelton, "The Banking System: Money and the Goal of Growth," in Raymond Vernon, ed., *Public Policy and Private Enterprise in Mexico* (Cambridge, Harvard University Press, 1964); Frank Tamagna, *La Banca Central en América Latina* (México, Centro de Estudios Monetarios Latinoamericanos, 1963).

ple, made loans against the pledge of articles in pawn as security. But, by and large, banking did not become an important phenomenon until the influx of branches of foreign banks in the last half of the nineteenth century. This development was caused, in part, by the desire of foreign traders and investors to establish, in the "backward" countries, financial institutions of the sort with which they were familiar.

In the early years of banking, then, the principal banking institutions in many of the Latin American countries were foreign-owned. And foreign-owned banks are still active in Latin America: the Chase Manhattan Bank (New York), the First National City Bank (New York), and the First National Bank of Boston have been the principal United States banks with branches widely spread over Latin America. The principal British bank has been the Banco de Londres y América del Sud. But there are many more foreign banks with branches in Latin America: Italian, German, French, and Canadian banks.

Commercial Banks

The foreign banks were generally commercial banks. With this model before them, it was perhaps rather natural that, as the Latin Americans themselves came to establish banks, they would be of a similar type.

The commercial bank has been a fairly uniform species the world over. In Latin America it makes short-term commercial loans and receives deposits (both sight and time) just as in the United States. Especially in the early period, there was a tendency to make loans to favored individuals, rather than to individuals on the merit of the commercial transaction they had in mind. The loans were likely to be repeatedly renewed. If they were called, the borrower was likely to default, with the result that the portfolio of (apparently) short-term loans turned out to be not liquid at all. Such conditions forced the bankruptcy of the whole Mexican banking system between 1910 and 1915. The ostensible procedures have been improved in the last forty years, but some of those old characteristics keep cropping up.

Commercial banks at times and in different countries have had the power to issue their own bank notes, but in both the United States and in Latin America this power has generally been lost. Bank note issue is now, as a general rule, a monopoly of the central bank.

Several differences in commercial banking practices exist, as between the United States and Latin America. In the first place, checks play a much larger role in the making of financial settlements in the United States than is the case in Latin America, where paper money, coins, and even barter play a relatively more important role. In the second place, in Latin America there has not been a pronounced effort to confine the activities of commercial banks to short-term loans. In the United States it used to be considered almost immoral for commercial banks to go in for real estate or long-term financing, although attitudes have changed somewhat on this score. In Latin America there has been a tendency on the part of the government to encourage commercial banks actively to engage in long-term and other types of nonliquid investments.

BRANCH BANKING. In the United States, for a variety of reasons, there is little branch banking. The system in Latin America more closely resembles that of Europe in that branch banking is extensively used. For example the Banco do Brasil had some 500 branches in 1962.

INTEREST RATES. Ostensible interest rates in Latin America run substantially higher than is the case in the United States. High-grade commercial credit such as might run 5 or 6 percent in the United States is likely to run 8 to 12 percent, or even higher, in Latin America. This circumstance has been cited as a source of developmental difficulties; and probably it is, but not necessarily because it means that the real interest rate in Latin America is substantially higher than is the case in the United States. A 5 percent rate of inflation would approximately offset a 5 percent difference in nominal interest rates and reduce a 5 percent difference in nominal rates to no difference in terms of real rates.

There may be no difference in real interest rates operating as a barrier to development; but the confusion connected with the monetary inflation which eliminates the interest rate difference probably has itself been a significant hindrance to development.

Whether, after allowance is made for inflation, real interest rates in Latin America are effectively higher than in the United States would seem to remain an open question. The generally heard statement is that they are.[2] But this may be a case where the generally accepted interpretation is in error.

---

[2] The Banco Central de Venezuela recently endorsed this position in its *Informe Económico, 1962* (Caracas, 1963), p. 33.

Central Banks

ORGANIZATION AND CONTROL. Uruguay's central bank, which was set up in 1896, may be considered the first central bank in Latin America. The establishment of central banks became stylish in Latin America during the 1920s, when a Princeton economist, Edwin W. Kemmerer, went up and down the west coast of South America setting up such banks; and during the 1930s and 1940s most of the remaining countries established central banks. Brazil and Panama do not have central banks in the strict sense. But the Banco do Brasil performs some of the functions and also plays the role of Brazil's chief commercial bank.

Latin American central banks are either (1) owned entirely by the government, as are the Banco Central in Argentina, the Banque Nationale in Haiti, the Banco de la República in Uruguay and several others; or (2) owned jointly by the government, affiliated banks, and general public as is the case with the Banco de la República in Colombia, the Banco Central in Chile, and the Banco de México; or (3) owned jointly by the government and the general public as is the case with the Banco Central in Venezuela; or (4) owned jointly by the government and the affiliated banks as is (or was) the case with the Banco Nacional in Cuba; or (5) owned jointly by the affiliated banks and the general public as is the case with the Banco Central de Reserva in El Salvador and the Banco Central de Reserva in Peru.

Regardless of ownership, however, effective control of policy rests generally with the government. Central bank policy making is not substantially autonomous in the United States manner.

FUNCTIONS. *Private Banking.* Unlike the Federal Reserve banks in the United States, several Latin American central banks transact an extensive business with private customers. Some of the central banks, for example the Uruguayan, handle much of the commercial banking of the country through an extensive system of branch banks. Others, such as the Mexican and Argentine central banks, stay pretty much out of the commercial banking business. The trend seems to be toward withdrawal from commercial banking.

Note Issue and Central Bank Credit. Central banks are now generally given a monopoly of the note issue privilege (the right to issue legal tender money). They may also create "money" by opening accounts to the credit of other banks or the general public. Although in increasing disuse, in general the laws provide that the central banks must have in reserve behind their notes and credit: (1) certain minimum percentages of (a) gold (and silver) and (b) convertible foreign exchange. The required percentages are likely to be in the range between 25 percent and 50 percent. The Mexican and Argentine figures are 25 percent. The presence of foreign exchange reserves in the reserve requirement possibilities is to be contrasted with the United States law that allows only for gold certificates and not for foreign exchange. (2) The balance of the reserves is likely to be in (a) government bonds or (b) acceptable commercial paper. (3) The possibility also exists that there may be other criteria such as bank assets or bank capitalization involved in the reserve requirement. For example in Colombia, central bank credit is limited to 120 percent of the central banks' capital and reserves.

Credit Control. (1) *Qualitative and Quantitative Distinction.* Quantitative credit controls are primarily designed to influence the total amount of money and credit in the country, without being especially concerned as to the particular use of the credit. Qualitative credit control is more concerned with the use to which the credit is put than with the total amount of credit. There is in general in Latin America no shortage of money and credit in terms of the total quantity. The important problem is qualitative. Who gets the credit and for what purpose?

Latin American planners have expressed themselves many times as appreciating that qualitative credit control can play an extremely important role. But in general the implementation of this concept seems to occur at the wrong levels. The channeling of credit away from the private sector to the government, as the Bank of Mexico has tried to do, has been an example of qualitative credit control. But it has not been qualitative control at a level that distinguished among private projects on their merits. Following 1956 the Bank of Mexico shifted its policy and began a planned effort to pass off its holding of government debt onto the private banks. The success of this operation tended to reduce the power of the private commercial banks to lend to the private sector. And one can guess that, as the commercial banks limited credit to the private sector, it was not their associates in the oligarchy who chiefly felt the impact of the limitations, but rather the small independent borrower.

Qualitative credit control seems to be practiced in Latin America at the level of the individual borrower with a great amount of caprice. A qualitative distinction is made between one borrower and the next by loan officers, but it is likely to be on highly personal, if not on professionally dubious, grounds.

The level at which Latin American banks really need to practice qualitative credit control is somewhere between the macro level (involving choices as to whether or not more lending shall be made to the government or to the private section) and the level of the individual borrower. Also the distinction favoring lending to manufacturing by comparison with commerce is not at a low enough level to deal with many important problems. There need to be impartially enforced qualitative credit controls at the level of "type of project in a given community." Banks in Recife might discriminate in favor of sugar processing, banks in Bahia in favor of cacao processing, banks in Porto Alegre in favor of some branch of the textile industry. And all of this discrimination might well be in a setting where effort is made to develop standards that would permit discrimination in favor of the small, independent producer, the new producer, and the outsider (rather than the insider).

These problems are appreciated in thoughtful circles in Latin America, even though not much has been done as yet to come to grips with them. An example is the following quotation from a leading Mexican economics journal:

In its program of industrialization, the government of Mexico, in recognition of the needs of small business, established in 1953 the Fondo de Garantía y Fomento a la Industria Mediana y Pequeña; its operations, nevertheless, have developed on a scale much too reduced to assure an adequate flow of credit to this industrial group.[3]

In contrast to the difficulties experienced by small enterprise in financing its growth, it seems to be generally true that the large industrial groups, generally, have an adequate supply of credit available for financing such growth as they may want to engage in. This is true because the large industrial groups are generally integrated with banking groups. Particular banks may dominate particular industrial groups, or vice versa. Such connections are part of the reason the banks are close-

---

[3] *Comercio Exterior* (Banco Nacional de Comercio Exterior), February, 1964, p. 99. Along the same line the Partido de la Revolución Institucional stated in its program that "small and medium firms have the doors of credit closed to them." (*Trimestre Económico*, January, 1964, p. 161.)

fisted in dealing with credit-worthy outsiders, who might become competition for the bank's industrial associates.[4]

Another qualitative difficulty involves the standard commercial bank function, the financing of merchants in inventory holding. Inventories are excellent security for a loan. But sometimes it is rather difficult to distinguish between the holding of an inventory pending sale and the holding of an inventory in an effort to corner the market, run up the price, and make a killing. And it may happen that Latin American bankers occasionally collude a bit with the inventory speculators. At any rate, funds created by banks seem to find their way into market-cornering efforts rather frequently in Latin America. Such activities make a double contribution to Latin American inflation: the contribution of additional funds and the contribution of removing goods from the market.

(2) *Rediscounting*. A standard credit-control device, which has not been much used in Latin America, is the regulation of rediscounting. The central bank might influence the amount of borrowing the commercial banks did from the central bank by varying the so-called rediscount rate. However, Latin American commercial banks have not made borrowing from the central banks a common practice. And the central banks have only rarely changed the rediscount rates.

(3) *Commercial Bank Reserve Requirements*. Commercial banks are required by law to maintain reserves of various percentages behind their deposits, and generally to keep those reserves with the central bank. In Colombia, the commercial banks in 1964, for example, were required to keep reserves in the range between 19 percent and 12 percent behind "basic" deposits of various types, and 62.5 percent behind so-called marginal credit. These percentages may be changed by the Monetary Board.

Argentine Central Bank action in December, 1963, provides another example of the possibilities along this line. Argentina wanted to increase the amount of credit available to certain industrial activities. To effect this result, "the additional reserve requirements applied against increases in deposits" [5] were reduced from 12 percent to 6 percent for

---

[4] Frank Brandenburg, "A Contribution to the Theory of Entrepreneurship and Economic Development: The Case of Mexico," *Inter-American Economic Affairs*, 16 (Winter, 1962), 3–24.

[5] *International Financial News Survey* (International Monetary Fund), January 31, 1964, p. 32.

the greater Buenos Aires area and abolished for certain banks in the interior. It was specified that lending capacity made available by these changes in reserve requirements should be used for loans to the textile, clothing, and footwear industries and, in the case of the interior banks, also to industries processing agricultural and livestock products. "Eligibility for these loans will depend on a commitment by the firms concerned to raise production and to maintain stable prices. . . ."[6]

A variation of the reserve requirement regulations which permits reducing the percentages in cases where the commercial bank has invested in the manner recommended by the monetary authorities provides a means of injecting a qualitative element into the reserve requirement procedures. Mexico has done this sort of thing.

Fractional reserve requirements mean that the commercial banking system is in a position to increase its lending and credit creation by some multiple of its reserves. The exact figure depends upon the reserve requirement percentage.

In Latin America, as in the United States, credit control through control of the reserve requirements of commercial banks has proved more effective on paper than in practice. The trouble lies principally with the fact that control of the "percent of reserve" required does not give control of the figure against which the "percent of reserve" is computed. Thus government or central bank creation of new currency or government flotation of a new bond issue may broaden the base available for lending at the same time that effort is being made to reduce the amount of commercial bank lending by raising the reserve requirements.

(4) *Portfolio Ceilings.* This is a type of control which has become rather popular in Latin America but which has not been used much in the United States. It is common for Latin American banking legislation to provide for regulation of the percentage of the outstanding credit of the individual commercial bank that may be in some certain type of lending. For example the 1950 banking legislation of Honduras provided that the Central Bank could establish such portfolio ceilings applicable to commercial banks. Another example has been the Mexican regulation of September, 1959, raising the proportion of private bank lending that must go to industry and agriculture from 45 percent to 65 percent.

This is probably a very useful credit-control device with considerable

[6] *Ibid.*

unrealized potential. It could be used to force lending outside the inner circle of the oligarchy and to specific segments of industry and to particular geographical areas.

(5) *Government Sector* (a) *New Issues*. A central bank may lend to the government, perhaps against the security of government bonds. And the government bonds may then serve as part of the backing behind central bank credit. There is significant potential here for enlarging the supply of money and credit by enlarging the amount of government debt. As an example of the possible role of the government relation to the central bank, the Argentine developments of the 1962–63 period may be cited. The government of President José María Guido raised the "permissible level of Central Bank advances to the government from 15% to 30% of Treasury receipts during the preceding 12 months. The second reform authorized the Central Bank to hold government securities equivalent to 25% of total deposits in the nation's banks, compared to the 10% originally stipulated. . . ."[7] Such procedures are frequently the hard core of the explanation of inflation.

There is considerable variation from country to country in the matter of loans by the central bank to the government. Short-term loans made by the Banco do Brasil to the government have at times exceeded similar loans to commercial banks. This has also been the case in Bolivia, Paraguay, Ecuador, Mexico, and Peru. Some of the central banks have extensive holdings of government bonds (Argentina, Chile, Bolivia, and Mexico); others have little or none.

(b) *Open-market Operations*. Open-market operations are a credit-control device much emphasized in the United States. The central bank may buy or sell government bonds on the open market and thus influence the amount of money available to the public and to commercial banks. There is in Latin America, however, no ready market for government bonds, and therefore this credit-control device is little used. The development of a satisfactory market in which government bonds could be bought and sold and in which the central bank could engage in open-market operations might do much to improve the popular opinion of government bonds.

(6) *Commercial Bank Interest Rates*. The maximum or minimum interest rate may be set by law, or at the discretion of the central bank, or the relationship between the commercial bank rate and the rediscount

---

[7] *Hispanic American Report*, XVII (March, 1964), 73.

rate may be specified. Thus there is in Latin America a far more direct monetary-authority control of the commercial bank interest rate than is the case in the United States.

For example, in Brazil the maximum legal interest rate on commercial loans has been 12 percent. In Guatemala the maximum legal rate has been 6 percent. Countries which permit the monetary authorities to vary the rate within some established range have included: Brazil, Chile, Peru, Ecuador, Nicaragua, and Honduras. The situation in Mexico in 1962 was described as one where the Bank of Mexico did not "control" commercial bank interest rates but recommended that the interest rate on loans for production not exceed 12 percent.[8]

(7) *Advance Deposit on Imports.* It is likely to take from one month to six months (or longer) between the initial placing of an import order and the actual importation of the goods. If the importer is required to deposit the purchase price with the central bank at the time of the initial order (or at the time the central bank promises him the foreign exchange he needs), such procedure can reduce the money supply during the ensuing interval.

(8) *Installment Credit.* Installment credit is a device for promoting mass sales, especially of durable consumer goods. However, the extensive use of installment credit probably requires as a prior condition the existence of a quite large credit-worthy middle class. In the absence of an extensive standardized system of installment credit the regulation of installment credit can hardly function as a very important credit-control power. But as purchasing power grows in Latin America, and especially as the demand for consumer durables increases, the regulation of installment credit should become a control power of considerable potential.

Financial Intermediaries

Financial intermediaries other than commercial banks are of assorted varieties. They may specialize in long-term (*inmobiliario* and *hipotecario*), medium-term (*refaccionario* and *avío*), and short-term (*prendario* and *quirografario*) loans. Some are privately owned banks making loans against mortgages on property (the Chilean Caja de Crédito Hipotecario). Some are government-owned or sponsored: Nacional Finan-

[8] *Comercio Exterior,* October, 1962, p. 674.

ciera in Mexico and the Corporación de Fomento de la Producción in Chile. Some have specialized in agricultural credit (Banco Nacional de Crédito Ejidal in Mexico), others in mining credit (the Banco Minero in Bolivia), others in industrial credit (the Banco Industrial in Venezuela), and still others in consumer credit (the Monte de Piedad in Mexico).

Recent interest in institutions of this sort results from a desire to provide long-term credit on a more satisfactory basis to implement development.[9] And this is especially important because of the failure of capital markets for stocks and bonds to develop on a substantial scale in Latin America.

An example of such an institution is the Mexican Nacional Financiera, set up by the government in 1934. It supplements the funds for new industry made available through ordinary banking channels. It has helped finance several enterprises including Industria Eléctrica, manufacturing electrical equipment, and Altos Hornos, a steel mill at Monclova, Coahuila. Nacional Financiera may obtain funds from a wide variety of sources: (1) the government, (2) the Bank of Mexico, (3) the Export-Import Bank (United States), (4) the International Bank for Reconstruction and Development (international), (5) by floating security issues of its own on the market—or by guaranteeing the security issues of those establishments it wishes to encourage.[10]

Even though the financial intermediary cannot create "money" against fractional reserves, in an important sense it can create credit instruments: bonds, and so on. It can thus play a role in proliferating the quantity of credit instruments or monetary claims in the society and in influencing their composition and in identifying who gets credit. These activities can have significant effects on prices, production, and goods distribution.

Conclusion

Of course, money and credit do not automatically come into use because banks have the power to create them. Somebody needs to be willing and qualified to receive the credit. The trouble is not generally

---

[9] These institutions are also discussed in Chapters Thirteen and Fourteen.
[10] Calvin P. Blair, "Nacional Financiera: Entrepreneurship in a Mixed Economy," in Raymond Vernon, ed., *Public Policy and Private Enterprise in Mexico* (Cambridge, Harvard University Press, 1964).

with the inability of the banks to find willing recipients. The difficulty comes with the effort to find willing recipients who have projects that banks consider acceptable.

So far as the contraction of credit is concerned, it is possible for the central bank to enforce contraction, even though private holders of money do not want to be cooperative. Their loans can be called in or canceled at maturity, whether they like it or not. But such powers must be used with discretion. Banks do not keep friends by refusing to renew loans. And such credit contraction can play a major role in accentuating depression.

Credit, once extended, may be used constructively and be canceled out when it has served its purpose in such a manner that it has little or no inflationary impact. Such usefulness may be either in connection with commerce or with processing. On the other hand, the manner of use of a quantity of new credit may involve effects that are largely inflationary. This will probably be the case if the credit finances consumption or commodity speculation.

CHAPTER TWENTY-FOUR

PUBLIC FINANCE

In recent years an increasing amount of attention has been given to the relationship between fiscal policy and economic development.[1]

Tax-and-Spend Patterns

There has been much talk to the effect that the Latin American governments practice considerable intervention in the operation of their economies. The relative role of public finance in the economy would seem to be one test of the degree of intervention of the governments. But this test would not seem particularly to bear out the claim that the Latin American governments are interventionist. One study of these relations is given in Table 20. Note that the figures for the large Latin American countries, Mexico, Brazil, and Argentina run especially low.

Table 20

CENTRAL GOVERNMENT REVENUE AS A PERCENTAGE OF NATIONAL INCOME, 1959

Venezuela	27.1	Brazil	10.1
Chile	21.9	Haiti	9.9
Peru	19.3	Colombia	8.3
Guatemala	15.9	Mexico	8.1
Argentina	11.1		

Source: U Tun Wai, "Taxation Problems and Policies of Underdeveloped Countries," in *Staff Papers* (IMF), IX (November, 1962), 428–48.

[1] Works on Latin American public finance include: Walter F. McCaleb, *The Public Finances of Mexico* (New York, Harper, 1921); Daniel Martner, *Tratado de Hacienda Pública* (Santiago de Chile, Universidad de Chile, 1941); Pan American Union, *Ecuador: Hacienda Pública y Política Fiscal* (Washington, 1954); Carls S. Shoup and others, *Informe sobre el Sistema Fiscal de Venezuela* (Caracas, Ministerio de Hacienda, 1960); Henry C. Wallich, *Public Finance in a Developing Country: El Salvador* (Cambridge, Harvard University Press, 1951).

The equivalent median figure for a group of countries having relatively high income (averaging over $500 per capita per year) was 25 percent. The equivalent figure for the United States was about 17 percent. It would seem that government taxes as a percent of national income play a minor role in Latin America by comparison with wealthier countries. Percentages relating government expenditure to national income would not be far different from these tax-to-income ratios.

In view of the high degree of centralization of Latin American governments and the minor role of states and provinces, the inclusion of local government in the data would probably make the importance of Latin American governments in the economies appear to be even smaller.

Expenditures

The chief function performed by Latin American governments up to about 1930 was to protect the interests of the property owners and of the relatively small clique in power. The army has protected the vested interests of the hacendados against the Indians and has also protected its own vested interest (or rather the officer's interest) in salaries and power. It has been frequently pointed out, somewhat jokingly but more than half truthfully, that revolutions have come at times when the budget was so far unbalanced that there was real difficulty in paying officers' salaries.

Planned expenditures on the military as a percentage of central government expenditure in various 1962 or 1963 budgets are given in Table 21.

Table 21

	Percent
Argentina	15.8
Brazil	17.8
Mexico	10.8
Venezuela	10.8
United States	45.8

Source: *Statistical Abstract of Latin America 1963* (UCLA), p. 76.

It is easy to say that even these percentages are too high and that the Latin American countries should trust to the peace-keeping machinery of the OAS and the United Nations and cut their military expenditures effectively to zero. (And this is probably good advice.) But United States expenditures on the military run far higher than do those of the Latin American countries; and the United States is supporting the development of the Latin American military establishments with funds and equipment. The important result may not be so much ability to resist Communism as that the Latin American military establishments have become sufficiently overpowering so that virtually no effective coups can occur except on the initiative of the military. Thus, whether or not they provide any especial safeguard against Communism, the military in Latin America is in a position, in important degree, to dominate the political structures and the decision-making processes in Latin America.

In the past, large expenditures for justice and for internal affairs (police) have, along with expenditures on finance and the army, supported the group in power. Through most of the history of Latin America these items (the military, justice, police, and finance) have constituted not most, but well-nigh all, of the expenditures of the governments.

Within the last thirty or forty years the situation has changed somewhat. Beginning with the Revolution of 1910–20, Mexico began to incur expenditures to aid the landless and the lower classes generally. Expenditures, in that country, for land reform, education, and so on have increased tremendously in the period since 1910. Inspired partly by the Mexican example, and partly because world social pressure has made it the thing to do (also partly because foreigners have borne much of the immediate cost through severance taxes), many of the other countries have recently begun to make expenditures in fields designed to serve the general benefit: public works, agriculture, education, public health, infrastructure, and social overhead generally. This process is significant.

Revenue System

ECONOMIC CHARACTERISTICS. *Regressiveness*. A tax which takes from an individual a larger proportion of income the lower the income may be defined as regressive. It may be debated whether the Latin

American tax system is unambiguously regressive in terms of this definition. It has been estimated that the rich and poor paid taxes in the late 1950s in roughly the pattern shown in Table 22.

Table 22

THE PROGRESSIVENESS OF THE LATIN AMERICAN TAX SYSTEM IN THE LATE 1950s

Percentages of total population	Percentage of the income of the group paid out as tax
I. The poorest 50 percent	12.8
II. The next 45 percent	19.8
III. Bottom 3 percent of richest 5 percent	16.5
IV. The richest 2 percent	20.5

Source: United Nations, *El Desarrollo Económico de América Latina en la Postguerra* (New York, 1963), p. 74. *See also,* Josué Sáenz, "El Principio de Lucrecio," *Trimestre Ecónomico,* XXV (October, 1958), 621–37.

In terms of the relation between groups II and III the system would seem to be regressive by definition. Elsewhere the pattern is very slightly progressive. That a society in the 1960s should let its wealthiest citizens off with a tax averaging only 20.5 percent of income may seem like an anachronism, and it probably is. The similarly situated group in the United States probably pays 50 or 55 percent of income in taxes—not the 90 percent that one might believe from the nature of the lamenting on this score.

It is not difficult to recommend measures that could lessen the regressiveness of the tax system. One is a series of personal income tax laws that would be more progressive than those currently in effect and that would apply more effectively to property income. But progressive taxes are just the point where the local, entrenched, and vested interests balk. And to the extent that they control and influence government their balking is successful and economic development is delayed.

Even many sincere advocates of economic development in Latin America allege that the institutional resistance to progressive taxes is too powerful and that development, consequently, must be financed by circumlocution. Víctor Urquidi of Mexico is such a person. But maybe this is exactly the battle that had better be fought.

Marginal Propensity to Pay Taxes. This is jargon for the idea that in Latin America people who manage to obtain an increase in income are likely to be very successful in avoiding paying taxes on the increase. The apparent prevalence of this condition indicates the inadequacy of tax administration.

To the extent that this condition prevails, it means that an increase in income results in a fall in the ratio of taxes to national income. The whole process would seem to leave a larger percent of a larger income in the possession of people at the upper income levels. Because of the behavior tendencies of such people, relatively more money is saved, banked abroad, or spent on luxury housing. Also there is a tendency to shift expenditures from necessities to consumer durables. The government, already lacking tax revenues, suffers yet more; and the government tends to compensate with deficit financing and inflation.

INDIRECT TAXES. Through the years the various Latin American governments have raised most of their revenue by means of indirect taxes, the rich having been effective in resisting the implementation of property taxes or of income taxes.

It has been estimated that for Latin America as a whole in the late 1950s, indirect taxes accounted for 61.8 percent of total revenue (direct taxes for 31.6 percent and social security payments for 6.6 percent).[2] In the United States, for all levels of government, indirect taxes probably account for about 35 percent of revenue.

Tariffs. Historically the most important revenue raiser among the indirect taxes has been the tariff. Import duties alone, in many of the Latin American countries, have provided a third to a half of total government revenue during most of the period since independence was gained. Chile's export tax on nitrates supplied about half of the government's total revenue for a period of some fifty years before World War I. In recent years, the proportion of total revenue obtained from tariffs has declined considerably. The heyday of the tariff as a revenue raiser is past in Latin America, but it remains the poorer Latin American countries that make the greater use of tariffs, Argentina, Mexico, Chile, and Venezuela raising a much smaller percentage of their revenues by means of tariffs.[3]

---

[2] United Nations, *El Desarrollo* . . . , p. 74.
[3] U Tun Wai, "Taxation Problems and Policies of Underdeveloped Countries," *Staff Papers,* IX (November, 1962), 434.

Tariffs are excises, in the sense of being taxes on goods as they move through the channels of trade, and are probably generally regressive. And yet one should not deny the possibility that the tariff might be made progressive. High tariff rates on the import of luxury consumer goods may be a sort of second-best solution to the problem of injecting some progressiveness into the tax structure. However, as was argued in Chapter Twenty, it would probably be better if the indirect taxes on luxury consumer goods were general excises covering both imports and domestically produced goods, rather than imports alone.

Excises. A second group of indirect taxes includes the internal taxes on the manufacture, sale, distribution, or consumption of commodities: the so-called excise taxes.

Ordinary excises are fairly common in Latin America, being levied on such items as alcohol, cigarettes, tires, sugar, gasoline, matches, and coffee. The list varies considerably from country to country. These taxes now bring in more revenue than do the customs duties in the larger Latin American countries, such as Argentina, Brazil, and Mexico.

Several Latin American governments monopolize, either directly or by farming out, the sale of such commodities as tobacco, salt, alcohol, explosives, matches, and so on. To the extent that these monopolies bring in revenue they have about the same impact as excises.

It seems safe to generalize that the over-all burden of these excises is regressive. However, this does not preclude the possibility, as was mentioned above, that a carefully selected pattern of excises on luxuries could have a progressive impact.

Severance Taxes. Taxes on raw material production are of various kinds. The kings of Spain formerly collected a royal fifth (or tenth) of such production. At the present time in connection with taxes on mineral production there are various possibilities: (1) a charge may be made in connection with the acquiring of a concession, (2) annual taxes may be based on the geographical area being exploited, and (3) taxes may be paid on the value or volume of production. These latter are the severance taxes proper. In addition, there are taxes on the export of minerals (such as the Chilean tax on nitrate export); these are generally classified as an export tariff rather than as a severance tax.

The severance tax rates vary from country to country and from mineral to mineral. One of the most important is the 16⅔ percent applied to Venezuelan oil.

The countries that are major raw material producers (Chile, Venezuela, and Mexico) have obtained substantial revenue from this source.

In general, severance taxes would seem to be a second-best alternative. (That is to say, the taxing by an international agency of international corporations directly on their total operations, combined with a grant-in-aid system for distributing the proceeds back to the individual nations, would seem preferable.) But in the second-best world we know, there is a good deal to be said for severance taxes levied against physical quantities of production. They get at the profits of international corporations in a rather simple and straightforward manner. Tax administration difficulties are kept to a minimum. The problems of getting at the corporate books to determine over-all profitability and of determining the proportion of profit properly assignable to the particular country are finessed.

To the extent that the severance taxes are actually paid by foreigners living in wealthier countries, the tax serves a certain role in distributing the burden from the poor to the rich.

DIRECT TAXES. Direct taxes are taxes which the original taxpayer cannot transfer to someone else. They include the property tax, the income tax, and the inheritance tax. During the nineteenth century the Latin American governments obtained virtually no revenue from such taxes, although nominal property taxes were not uncommon. Only very recently have they begun to obtain significant revenue from these sources.

For the Latin American countries as a whole they average about 32 percent of total revenue. The low-income countries of Latin America get especially little of their government revenue from direct taxes, for example: Guatemala (9 percent), Haiti (8 percent), and Ecuador (17 percent).

Property Tax. In the period since independence, and because land has always been concentrated in the hands of a very few, the equitable enforcement of a general property tax would have made the whole tax structure much less regressive than it has been. But the propertied groups have been able to control the governments so that no effective general property tax has been enforced in most of the countries. Nominal property taxes exist in quite a few, however. The various Mexican states generally have had such taxes. But by and large, use of the property tax has been neglected in Latin America.

Increased use of the property tax in Latin America could have at least two major advantages. (1) It could make the tax system somewhat more progressive, and (2) the tax pattern could be set up in a manner to encourage more effective use of the land.

Income Taxes. All Latin American countries now have income taxes. (I believe this is correct.) Generally the larger countries, such as Mexico, Argentina, and Brazil, have had such taxes since before World War II; but some of the smaller countries have enacted the laws only within the past five or ten years.

Latin American income tax rates range far below those in the United States, where the highest surtax (on income over $200,000) is 70 percent under the 1964 law, and the basic rate is 14 percent. In Argentina the tax starts with a basic rate of 1.5 percent and proceeds up to a highest surtax of 45 percent. In Venezuela the highest surtax is 26 percent; in Mexico (on wages and salaries) it is 50 percent; in Panama it is 16 percent; and in Brazil it is 65 percent. In the 1964 Chilean law the highest surtax was set at 60 percent.

Unlike the situation in the United States, most Latin American income tax laws deal with personal income and corporate income in the same statute. This is not to say that the rates on the two are necessarily the same. The Latin American statutes generally classify income in several ways: by *cédulas,* or schedules. In the Mexican law the schedules are: (1) commercial income, (2) industrial income, (3) income from agriculture, (4) wages and salaries, (5) income from professional fees, (6) income from vested capital, (7) royalties, rentals, and concessions. Different rate structures are then applied to the different types of income. But on the whole the rate structure seems to be progressive in about the same mild way on personal and corporate income. The only one of the schedules with a rate structure higher than that on wages and salaries, where the highest rate is 50 percent, is the rate structure on royalties, where the highest rate is 55 percent. Generally there is some discrimination against income from wages and salaries and in favor of property income.

The fragmentation of the Latin American income taxes into schedules makes the real progressiveness of the rate structure much less than the ostensible progressiveness (just as is the case with the community-property provisions of the United States law).

The income tax is appropriate for Latin America. But there may be unfortunate implications as a result of the manner of implementation. For example, the income tax implemented in Guatemala, July 1, 1963, involved a provision for deduction from salary similar to that in effect in the United States. That was fine as far as it went; but the trouble was that that seemed to be about as far as it went. There was no effective machinery for assuring that the very wealthy paid the tax on income from sources other than wages and salaries. Thus there is the possibility that the new or augmented income taxes in Latin America may become merely an additional burden upon middle-income, employed people.

Foreign companies exporting raw materials from a Latin American country to themselves (or another subsidiary) have a temptation to underinvoice their exports. This procedure reduces the ostensible value of the exports and consequently cuts the government's tax receipts. The degree of seriousness of this problem is difficult to determine. The participants do not advertise their activities. But enough discussion of incidents does come to light to suggest that the procedure is fairly common. In 1959 the Venezuelan government investigated the Orinoco Mining Company (United States Steel) and Iron Mines Company (Bethlehem Steel) in connection with claims that the Venezuelan subsidiaries had been charging the parent companies prices less than prevailing market prices for iron ore, and that consequently the income taxes paid to Venezuela might have been artificially low.[4]

The Latin American wealthy have resisted the income tax by arguing that it would cut into their saving; in the best tradition of pre-Keynesian economic theory, they argued that the savings of the wealthy were needed to finance investment. However, the Keynesian theory has pretty much discredited this position by indicating that autonomous investment can occur in a manner which subsequently and automatically draws out an equivalent amount of saving.

A more important and relevant argument would probably be that effective demand will be increased by taking some of the tax burden off the sore backs of the poor. And the resulting increase in effective demand should encourage entrepreneurs and businessmen to expand their activities.

Because of the system of cédulas, the tax rates on income from capital and property are low. In Latin America, property income of one type or another runs 30 or 40 percent of total income. And the share of

[4] *Hispanic American Report*, September 1959, p. 388.

income going to wages and salaries is a relatively low 40 to 60 percent. And yet the share of income going to property owners (and investors) pays in general lower tax rates than does the income going to wages and salaries. An increase in the tax rates applicable to property incomes, which would only bring them about up to the level endured by wages and salaries, could make a significant contribution to government revenue.[5] A tax rate averaging about 30 percent (instead of 15 percent) on these incomes could well raise about $8 billion instead of $4 billion in revenue in Latin America.

Not only are the tax rates generally higher on income from wages and salaries, but also they are less subject to evasion—because of the techniques for withholding at the source. Generally speaking, income from wages and salaries gets a relatively raw deal in Latin America. Successful evasion and avoidance of taxes seems to be much more prevalent among those getting their income from property.

Along a slightly different line it might be mentioned that one of the things a too-small country really has trouble doing because of its smallness is implementing an income tax. The oligarchs, who both own and rule the country, much prefer that the mass of the population pay the taxes through the venerable excise and tariff channels.

50:50 (or 60:40). In the early 1940s Venezuela developed the idea of taxing the profits of the foreign oil companies at a 50 percent rate. The companies were permitted to deduct as a credit against the tax the amount of certain other taxes they had already paid, the most important of these being the 16⅔ percent tax on the gross oil production. Taxes of this sort have subsequently been used by the governments of most of the oil-producing countries of the world. And the rate pattern has been edged up in various countries. The Venezuelan figure, for example, has come to approximate a rate of 60 percent on the profits.

OTHER REVENUE. As is the case with countries generally, those in Latin America derive a small percentage of revenue from assorted licenses, fees, sales of public domain, rents, and from such assorted government properties as wharves, state-owned railroads, and land. The government of Peru over the years has even derived considerable revenue from the exploitation of guano deposits in the Chincha islands.

[5] Arnold Harberger has had some things to say on this count. *See* his, "Aspectos de una Reforma Tributaria en América Latina," in *Economía Latinoamericana.* I (November, 1963), 127–49.

Profits also have been made from government operation in the foreign exchange markets. Both Argentina and Brazil have profited this way. (They have also lost money in the foreign exchange markets.) During the Perón period Argentina also derived considerable revenue by paying Argentine farmers fixed prices for wheat and other products and then selling them at higher prices on the world markets.

Another source of revenue is the lottery. The policy of the Latin American governments with regard to gambling is rather different from that of the United States. In the United States gambling is handled largely by racketeers, who get the profits; and the gambling public is pretty much at their mercy. In the Latin American countries, where the governments usually operate the lottery, the profits go to the government, and the "sucker" comes nearer to having a chance than he does in the United States. The distribution of the gross receipts may be somewhat as follows: 70 percent as premiums, 10 percent to the vendors, 10 percent to cover administrative expense, and 10 percent to the national treasury—plus, perhaps, a tip to the vendor by a winner.

Also characteristic of the revenue systems is the extensive use of the stamp tax, in a manner that makes its economic impact quite similar to the impact of the sales tax.

STATE AND LOCAL TAXES. In general the Latin American countries are highly centralized and most governmental revenue is collected by the national government. Even in the cases of the countries with a federal system somewhat like that of the United States, a large share of total tax revenue is collected by the central government. Nevertheless the states or provinces do have tax systems.

Local governments have made limited use of the property tax, in Mexico for example.

The *alcabala* has historically been one of the more notorious of the state and local taxes. It is a tax on trade which has served as a major barrier to the shipment of goods from one region to another. Fifty or sixty years ago, major efforts were made to eliminate these taxes. However, vestiges of the alcabalas remain in many parts of the region.

By and large, the finances of state and municipal governments are dependent on the national governments. In Argentina, for example, the excise taxes are, in general, collected by the national government and some of the proceeds are turned back to the provinces in a form of grant-in-aid.

TAX ADMINISTRATION. Tax administration in Latin America is horrible. Raúl Prebisch has said on the subject: "There are cases where evasion runs 50 percent in connection with the income tax. This is not an isolated phenomenon. . . . It is necessary to reform the fiscal structure. . . ."[6] In Latin America the collection of taxes would seem generally to be poorly administered, costly, and graft-ridden.

The Government Debt

Everybody knows, or thinks he knows, that Latin American governments are in debt up to their ears. The fact that everybody is wrong may suggest that some questions need to be asked about Latin American fiscal policy in relation to the government debt.

On the whole Latin American governments may be said to be less in debt than is the United States government, if one compares debt to government revenue or to national income. For example, the federal debt in the United States is over 60 percent of national income, and it has been higher. By contrast, a rough computation that includes all of the large Latin American countries and most of the other countries indicates central government debt to average under 20 percent of national income. The Argentine figure is higher than the average, the Mexican is lower, and the Brazilian is about the average.

Debt-service expenditure as a percentage of total central government expenditure runs between 11 and 12 percent for the United States. For Argentina it is about 5 percent, for Brazil 1 percent, for Mexico 4 per cent.

The more backward of the Latin American countries are consistently the ones with the lowest per capita debt. It is enough to make one wonder if large debt may not have something to do with causing welfare improvement. But this would probably be a wrong identification of cause and effect.

The fact that the Latin American debts are relatively small on the

[6] *Combate,* January, 1961, p. 25; *see also, Boletín Quincenal* (Centro de Estudios Monetarios Latinoamericanos), April 10, 1964, p. 106.

basis of most of the comparisons that might be used to evaluate them does not mean that an increase in debt would automatically work miracles. The causal relation is probably the other way around. The low level of development combined with fiscal irresponsibility makes borrowing difficult. Nevertheless, these relations should indicate that increase in Latin American government debt is not, a priori, a bad thing, provided the money is used effectively.

Financing investment in capital equipment with budget deficits is more likely to be inflationary than financing by means of tax and spend would be. But if expansion in the productive capacity of the country increases more or less in step with the growing debt, there is no reason to be especially concerned about the debt. Given the resistance to the income tax on the part of the wealthy, some measure of debt financing of government investment is probably a virtual necessity if the government is to finance a meaningful amount of infrastructure.

However, there is another side to this argument. The wealthy and the ingroup prefer the easier route of debt (foreign or domestic), not only to avoid taxes, but also because of the intriguing possibilities that debt creation offers for the middlemen to siphon off something for themselves.

The government can pay for some capital creation by issuing some bonds and selling them at home or abroad on terms involving varying degrees of onerousness. With regard to this process, it may be said that, historically, the default record has been scandalous and domestic bond issues have generally been floated in manners that had an inflationary impact.

On the basis of such a background, it can only be said that, if used judiciously, the financing of government expenditures by debt creation is not necessarily the worst alternative.

Fiscal Policy as a Development Tool

TAX EXEMPTIONS. New industries are frequently excused from various taxes for a period of years. Also they may be excused from various import tariffs applicable to their raw materials or equipment.

A Mexican law of 1954, for example, classified some industries as either "new" or "necessary"; it then classified new industries as to whether they were basic, semibasic, or secondary; it classified necessary industries in the same way. The classification was then used for staggering the amount of tax exemption the industry would receive. Considerations influencing these decisions in the Mexican case have been, according to the Pan American Union's *A Statement of the Laws of Mexico in Matters Affecting Business:*

(a) quantity and quality of manual labor to be used; (b) degree of technical efficiency; (c) the extent of use of equipment and machinery; (d) volume of raw materials and finished or semifinished products of national origin which are to be utilized; (e) percentage of the domestic market to be supplied; (f) amount of the investment; (g) use for which the articles to be produced are intended; (h) the benefits greater than those legally required which are to be granted to employees; (i) importance of research laboratories that may be established.[7]

The exemptions will be canceled under the following circumstances:

(a) When the profits of an enterprise, excluding reinvested profits, are greater than the amount of its investment in fixed assets on the date on which production began;

(b) When an exempted enterprise shall not have begun its operations within a year from the time set in the resolution for operations to begin or within a year from any extension thereof;

(c) When an exempted business disappears;

(d) When grave social or economic damage is threatened;

(e) When the beneficiaries of the tax exemption commit serious infractions either of the law, the regulations or the resolution.[8]

Certainly standards need to be established identifying industries which are to be more or less discouraged (or encouraged). But the Mexican law seems to be more of a catch-all than a meaningful classification. Or, better put, it leaves the really meaningful decisions to administrative officials. And one may suspect that there may be a good deal more *personalismo* than impartial criterion at that level, although it would probably be a mistake to put rigid criteria into the law. But there does need to be a clear-cut set of administrative standards which are knowable to the general public and which are then implemented promptly and impartially by the responsible officials. It is the latter condition that is generally lacking in Latin America.

Mexico also gives special tax concessions on profits plowed back into the expansion of the enterprise. Is this really desirable? It may encourage

---

[7] Pan American Union, *A Statement of the Laws of Mexico in Matters Affecting Business* (3d ed., Washington, 1961), p. 99.

[8] *Ibid.,* pp. 99–100.

investment; but it also may encourage concentration. And the oligopolistic character of Mexican industry seems to be one of the barriers to development.

A recent (perhaps overdone) example of the use of tax incentives has been cited in *International Financial News Survey:*

> With the object of stimulating investment activity in the virtually unexplored, rich, and sparsely inhabited regions of Peru lying east of the Andes, the Government has decreed tax exemption for a period of ten years from all major taxes in an area almost half the size of the entire country. Exemptions are provided from import duties for items to be used exclusively within the zone, and from export duties, stamp taxes, business income taxes, personal and business surtaxes, banking taxes on interest and over-drafts, etc.[9]

The tax exemption tool is a tricky thing. It might be a healthier situation if tax burdens were uniform and without exception (at least in so far as possible). New businesses would have a better conception of their long-run responsibilities if they were paying taxes from the beginning in the pattern that they would have to carry permanently. And taxes in the formative years would probably be low anyway if profits were low. (If they were high, they ought to be taxed.)

Benjamin Franklin indicated long ago that the abatement of taxes is not as important as some taxpayers tend to think: "The taxes are, indeed, very heavy, and if those laid by government were the only ones we had to pay, we might easily discharge them; but we have many others, and much more grievous to some of us. We are taxed twice as much by our idleness, three times as much by our pride, and four times as much by our folly; and from these taxes the commissioners cannot ease or deliver us by allowing an abatement."

PRODUCTION SUBSIDY. The chief problems of a new company are how to obtain basic initial financing and how to compete pricewise with already established companies. Tax exemptions are not immediately geared to help with either of these problems. If one is going to fish in these waters at all, the production subsidy should be better bait than the tariff. (Any red-blooded promoter of sport stadiums knows this.) A simple model of the economic world might be constructed involving only

---

[9] February 7, 1964, p. 40. The International Monetary Fund publication cites the source of this information as being the *News Letter* of the Banco Continental of Lima. *See also,* New York *Times,* January 10, 1962, p. 71.

three stages: (1) production followed by (2) commerce, and concluded with (3) consumption. If the goal is to increase production, it is better to use a policy tool that impacts directly on production rather than using a tool that impacts on commerce and thus affects production only indirectly. The effects of action dissipate as one gets further away from the source. This would suggest that policy tools had better be applied pretty close to the thing they are supposed to affect. J. E. Meade has said: "There is always a presumption that the direct method will do less harm than an indirect method." [10] It is on this ground that the production subsidy is to be preferred to interference, such as the tariff or trade subsidy, at the commerce stage.

The production subsidy (if one has decided to show the new industry some favoritism) has some major advantages over other sorts of favoritism. It has the advantage that it can be financed with local monetary resources: taxes or credit. It has the advantage over the tariff that it encourages goods availability rather than goods scarcity during the transition period.

It probably is desirable to include in the law setting up the subsidy some automatic provision for its removal. It is difficult to get special privileges removed at a later date, if positive action is required to effect the removal. One thing institutions do with desperate energy is to protect their vested interests. But probably the production subsidy is no worse on this point than the tariff, and it may be a good deal better. It has been devilishly hard to get tariffs that were established on the basis of the infant-industry argument repealed after the infant has grown up.

Why do producers so much prefer the tariff to the production subsidy? Perhaps it has something to do with the free private enterprise mentality. The tariff-protected businessman can better gratify his ego with the thought that he is a self-reliant, independent, free, private enterpriser. But maybe this is yet another argument for the production subsidy.

Another point: If business is to be subsidized, let the subsidy be as a separate operation, handled by the government department dealing with economic development rather than by the finance or treasury department in connection with its tax work. A remark about the shoemaker sticking to his last might be appropriate.

---

[10] *Trade and Welfare* (London, Oxford University Press, 1955), p. 457.

CHAPTER TWENTY-FIVE

CYCLES, GROWTH, AND THE MONEY SUPPLY

National Income Theory

National income theory was formulated by Keynes to deal with business-cycle problems such as depression unemployment. Some of the problems connected with the effort to apply the theory to economic development were discussed in Part Four, especially in Chapter Fourteen, Capital Formation: Domestic.

A word about the possible role of national income theory, taken as business-cycle theory and applied to Latin America, may be appropriate at this stage. In terms of the Keynesian analysis, countries having a low national income and a high marginal propensity to consume (the Latin American case) should be able to achieve full employment with relatively little new investment. Because of this circumstance the Keynesian analysis may be of minor importance so far as the Latin American countries are concerned.

Actually the Latin American countries in the past have not had a serious employment problem in the sense which was bothering Keynes. For the most part everyone who wanted a job had one. But the pay has generally been wretchedly low. The hacendados, estancieros, and fazendeiros were willing to hire more and more labor at the pittance being paid. Or to put the matter another way, they did not discharge in hard times but rather kept all their workers, albeit on a reduced diet.

Under these conditions it can be seen why in the discussions of 1946–47 in the United Nations Economic and Social Council the representatives of the underdeveloped countries did not view full employment in their own countries as the major economic problem.[1] After they have raised their standards of living and acquired an unemployment problem, they will be glad to worry about it. Incidentally, that day may have virtually arrived in the overcrowded Latin American cities.

International Problems

BUSINESS-CYCLE PATTERNS. It is useless to argue that the business cycle is harder on underdeveloped countries than it is on developed countries, or vice versa.[2] There is too much difference in terms of the conditions that create hardship in the different types of countries. For the Latin American countries one of the pronounced unhappy results of the cycle is violence in the fluctuations in the prices of the major exports of the region. What does this mean in terms of hardship? Certainly it is hard on the exporters (one of the wealthier groups in the Latin American countries), and it is hard on the workers associated with the export industries. But such considerations do not establish a case for a particularly disastrous hardship for the economy as a whole. Subsistence agriculture, such as provides occupation for much of the population in many of the Latin American countries, passes virtually unscathed through the fluctuations of the international business cycle. Subsistence agriculture may be affected in a terrible way by drought and flood, but that is another story.

One should not be scornful of the adverse effects of price fluctuations on the export sectors of the Latin American economies. But one can be excused for believing that they are not of the earth-shaking importance that a Latin American finance minister, whose business background was the export sector, would have the world believe.

Violent price fluctuations affecting the export sector will occasion fluctuations in total export earnings. And, so far as appraising the effect on the domestic economy is concerned, it is probably true that the effect on total export earnings is more important than the effect on prices

---

[1] *Weekly Bulletin* (United Nations), March 18, 1947, p. 254.
[2] Some general books on international financial problems include: Virgil Salera, *Exchange Control and the Argentine Market* (New York, Columbia University Press, 1945); Henry C. Wallich, *Monetary Problems of an Export Economy: The Cuban Experience (1914–1947)* (Cambridge, Harvard University Press, 1950); John P. Young, *Central American Currency and Finance* (Princeton, Princeton University Press, 1925).

alone. One might expect that the violent price fluctuations would compound into effects on total export earnings that would mean greater fluctuations in such earnings for the Latin American countries than for the developed countries. However, there is some uncertainty as to whether this has been the case. Statistical findings of Joseph D. Coppock indicate that total export earnings fluctuate more violently for the developed countries than they do for the underdeveloped countries.[3]

With regard to the relative severity of depression impact on the United States and Latin America, Furtado has cited the following example in relation to Brazil: During the Great Depression, national income in Brazil fell by 25 to 30 percent. In the United States it fell by 50 percent.[4] From that point of view, the depression plight of the Latin American countries was, then, not demonstrably worse than that of the developed countries.

There is another aspect to the cycle situation that has been pointed out by Furtado.[5] It seems that in Brazil, during the 1930s, the disastrously low price of coffee was combined with a situation where the price of Brazilian imports remained relatively high. That is to say, the terms of trade ran very unfavorably against Brazil. But the effect of this compounded adversity was beneficial. Domestic manufacture was stimulated to expand production to substitute for the high-priced imports (and the lack of foreign exchange). And it seems that Brazilian industrialization obtained much of its early impulse during that period and as a result of that combination of circumstances.

The chief impact of international depression on the Latin American countries seems to have been violent price fluctuation in connection with the leading exports of the region. By contrast the manufacturing industries of the developed countries seem to have had the power to defend the price levels applicable to their products much more effectively. The prices of manufactured goods have held up rather well. What has suffered has been the volume of production and, even more important, the volume of employment. The serious impact of depression in an indus-

---

[3] Joseph D. Coppock, *International Economic Instability* (New York, McGraw-Hill, 1962), pp. 33, 37; see also, Benton F. Massell, "Export Concentration and Fluctuations in Export Earnings: A Cross-Section Analysis," in *American Economic Review*, LIV (March, 1964), 47–63.

[4] Celso Furtado, *Formação Econômica do Brasil* (Rio de Janeiro, Editôra Fundo de Cultura, 1959), p. 215.

[5] Celso Furtado, *A Economia Brasileira* (Rio de Janeiro, Editôra a Noite, 1954), pp. 83–187.

trialized country is on employment; in underdeveloped countries, on price.

RAW COMMODITY PRICING. The prices of raw commodities fluctuate more violently than do the prices of goods in general. This is an important symptom of the business-cycle-depression disease. And it is a symptom that in and of itself has unpleasant effects on many people. The suppression of the symptom would be worth a good deal, whether or not the suppression of the symptom "solved all problems." United Nations experts have pointed out:

> The decline in primary product prices in the recent recession, together with the continued inching up of industrial prices in 1957/58 represents a loss of more than $2,000 million in both the real income and the capacity to import of primary producing countries. . . . The loss is estimated in import capacity equivalent to about six years' lending to the underdeveloped countries by the International Bank for Reconstruction and Development at 1956/57 rates.[6]

In Chapter Six, in the discussion of raw commodity control schemes, a plan was suggested for protecting the producers from violent price fluctuations. But there are other levels of concern: (1) effects on other aspects of the economies of the raw-commodity-producing country, and (2) especially effects on the foreign exchange earnings of the nation.

But pending amelioration of price fluctuations it remains important to analyze some of their effects. Take Brazilian coffee as an example. During periods of high prices it seems that the gain is largely concentrated as high profits for the fazendeiros. In periods of low coffee prices the loss is largely socialized by means of currency devaluation.[7] Gain is thus privatized while loss is socialized. But the percentage fall in national welfare does not correspond with the percentage fall in the price of coffee because subsistence agriculture claims a large proportion of the population and because the by-product effects of coffee's hardship may work to the benefit of the industrialization of the economy. One might suspect from this combination of circumstances that in addition to arguing at international conferences for amelioration in the fluctuations in the export price of coffee, Brazil might well take additional measures to recapture from her own producers more of the bonanza

---

[6] *United Nations Review,* July, 1959, p. 7.
[7] Furtado, *A Economia Brasileira,* pp. 103–4.

profits of good times or else she might argue for a sort of international cooperation that would do more than just protect the fazendeiros in their profits.[8]

POLICY ON FOREIGN EXCHANGE RESERVES. The foreign exchange earnings of the Latin American countries do fluctuate violently over the cycle. Whether or not they fluctuate more than the earnings of the developed countries, they fluctuate markedly; and this fluctuation makes difficult the orderly planning of economic development.

About twenty-five years ago there began to be proposed arrangements for dealing with such foreign exchange problems. Robert Triffin made some proposals in this area before World War II. He suggested that there be some procedure for freezing the foreign exchange earnings of good times so that they would not become the basis for an expansion in credit at the time they were received. If they were used as the basis for an expansion in credit at the time they were received, they would almost certainly occasion a substantial increase in imports. And the purchasing power generated by the large exports of the prosperous period would later not be available for maintaining imports during the depression years.[9] So, according to this approach, the central bank should curtail credit expansion within the country during the prosperity phase of the business cycle if possible and expand credit during the depression phase. This is not the standard procedure of the international gold standard, which would have involved a credit expansion at the time reserves increased.

Another proposal involves the sale of government bonds to the public during the period of prosperity so as to sop up the excess purchasing power. This would permit the government to pay off the debt to banks incurred during depression.[10] But all kinds of problems arise

---

[8] Actually the Brazilian government does capture some of the profits of the low-cost Brazilian coffee industry by the use of discriminatory foreign exchange control measures.

[9] Robert Triffin, *Monetary and Banking Reform in Paraguay* (Washington, Board of Governors of the Federal Reserve System, 1946); Henry C. Wallich and Robert Triffin, *Monetary and Banking Legislation of the Dominican Republic, 1947* (New York, Federal Reserve Bank, 1953); Banco Central de la República Dominicana, *Legislación Monetaria y Bancaria de la República Dominicana* (Ciudad Trujillo, República Dominicana, 1948), p. 214.

[10] L. Kanesathasan, "Export Instability . . . ," *Staff Papers* (International Monetary Fund), VII (April, 1959), 46–74.

in connection with the willingness of the public or the exporters voluntarily to buy such bonds.

Another approach would be to tax the foreign exchange proceeds of good times so as to subsidize exports in bad times. This proposal also encounters institutional resistance in application. Is the export subsidy in bad times to go to the same individual who pays the tax in good times? Such a proposal would be difficult to implement. If it goes to other individuals, the original exporters will probably object.[11]

STABILIZATION OF FOREIGN EXCHANGE EARNINGS. Violent raw commodity price fluctuations (1) at one level pose a threat to the income of individual producers, (2) at another level a threat to the foreign exchange earnings of the nation. The problem in terms of the income of the individual producer has already been discussed.

And since there are other threats to a country's foreign exchange earnings than fluctuation in raw commodity prices, it is probably desirable to divorce the problem of fluctuation in foreign exchange earnings from the raw commodity pricing problem. It is not desirable that foreign exchange earnings fluctuate violently—whatever the cause and whichever the country involved.

The International Monetary Fund has taken a modest step in the interest of trying to stabilize export proceeds.[12] But this step does little more than give a tentative promise that under some highly circumscribed conditions a country suffering loss of foreign exchange earnings as a result of raw commodity price fluctuation may have a modest amount more access to the resources of the Fund.

It would seem desirable that there be some sort of generalized machinery for guaranteeing to every country that its foreign exchange earnings will not decline drastically and suddenly. Perhaps the guarantee could take the form of a Fund commitment to provide foreign exchange in an amount that would bring a country's earnings up at least to 95 percent of what it obtained the year before. Such a plan might require substantial modification of the functioning of the Fund; such modifications are due.

---

[11] C. G. F. Simkin, *Instability of a Dependent Economy* (New York, Oxford Press, 1951), p. 203.
[12] International Monetary Fund, *Compensatory Financing of Export Fluctuations* (Washington, 1963).

Inflation and Growth

STATISTICAL DATA. In Latin America there has been much speculation as to the relationship between the money supply, inflation, and growth.[13]

Table 23 provides information on the relation between growth rates

Table 23

RELATION BETWEEN INFLATION AND ECONOMIC GROWTH, 1945–1959

	Rate of growth of gross domestic product (average percent per year)	Average annual rise in cost of living (index units)
Venezuela	8.3	4
Mexico	5.9	16
Brazil	5.4	57
Cuba	3.5	2
Chile	3.1	340
Argentina	2.6	185
Haiti	1.8	negligible
Bolivia	1.1	1,257

Source: *Economic Bulletin for Latin America*, October, 1962, p. 234.

and inflation during the 1945–59 period. Some countries enjoying violent inflation seem to have stagnated (Argentina and Chile); one which enjoys the benefits of price stability continues to have a desperately low level of living (Haiti). Two large countries with impressive growth records (Brazil and Mexico) have experienced a significant but not runaway inflation. Venezuela has grown without inflation.

The significance of inflation for economic development has been debated much of late. In fact, a veritable tempest in a teapot called the monetarist-structuralist debate has emerged as a major battleground.

THE MONETARIST POSITION. The International Monetary Fund has been a leading exponent of the monetarist position. A leading Latin

---
[13] Frank W. Fetter, *Monetary Inflation in Chile* (Princeton, Princeton University Press, 1931); Edwin W. Kemmerer, *Inflation and Revolution: Mexico's Experience of 1912–1917* (Princeton, Princeton University Press, 1940).

American monetarist spokesman has been Roberto de Oliveira Campos. The leading exponent of the structuralist position has been the Economic Commission for Latin America.[14]

The monetarists object to inflation, believing that inflation is a controllable result of irresponsible monetary management and that the vigorous inflation that has gone on in several Latin American countries has contributed to their stagnation. They believe that substantial expansion of the money supply and unbalanced budgets are generally reprehensible practices.

The International Monetary Fund, since Per Jacobsson became managing director in 1956, has expressed especial alarm concerning inflation and its undesirable repercussions. And in the late 1950s the Fund became active in fostering stabilization programs in various Latin American countries as a condition for granting them financial assistance. Latin American countries that became involved in these (generally abortive) stabilization efforts included Peru, Bolivia, Chile, Argentina, Brazil, and (as late as February 1964) Colombia.

The Fund may have been, in several cases, overenthusiastic in imposing stabilization programs in a setting where the programs have had unfortunate implications in the domestic political setting. For example, during the Frondizi presidency in Argentina (about 1960 while Alvaro Alsogaray was in charge of the economic program of the government) charges were rampant that the economic program of the government was being run to the benefit of business and the disadvantage of the workers. There was some basis for these charges. The government was avowedly engaged in a program involving the turning over of certain government enterprises to private interests and was contracting with foreign oil companies to permit them to expand their operations, especially in Patagonia around Comodoro Rivadavia. In this setting, Alsogaray found it expedient frequently to suggest in his public addresses that the unpopular policies were imposed on Argentina by the International Monetary Fund. Thus, the Fund, which was probably only trying to make the Argentine government keep down the money supply and balance the budget, got the discredit for some policies with which it probably had nothing to do (or with which it should have had nothing

---

[14] Albert Hirschman, *Latin American Issues: Essays and Comments* (New York, Twentieth Century Fund, 1961), pp. 69–124, gives a good deal of attention to the debate between the structuralists and the monetarists.

to do). The Fund has enough trouble without carrying that additional cross—the responsibility for economic policies outside its proper financial sphere.

The Economic Commission for Latin America has commented about these activities:

> Anti-inflationary policy means a sacrifice by the lower strata of the population such as could only be tolerated from the psychological and political standpoints if an expansionist policy were simultaneously introduced to stimulate the use of the economy's idle capacity, with the ensuing rapid rise of income, and a policy of austerity in respect of the higher groups to reduce their consumption sharply and promote an increase in investment. . . . Thus monetary stabilization is not conceivable except in relation to a policy of economic development and social justice.[15]

The problem has been rendered difficult because the pattern of principles apparently fostered by the Fund as it has encouraged governments to adopt stabilization programs would seem to leave something to be desired. The Fund has endorsed the idea of keeping wages and salaries down (as well as money supply and prices) in the effort to obtain stability. The Fund could have avoided some of the psychological difficulty that it has gotten into if it had also vigorously advocated curbs on profits. But the Fund has said little or nothing about curbing profits along with wages and salaries. And it has seemed to the working men from Argentina to Mexico in recent years that, whatever else has been going on, profit taking has been flourishing.

THE STRUCTURALIST POSITION. Many monetarists would probably not subscribe to the preceding, oversimplified statement of their position. But the difficulty involved in summarizing the monetarist position is as nothing compared with the difficulty involved in summarizing the structuralist position. For one thing it is not clear (1) whether the structuralists wish to defend the proposition that inflation is positively a good thing for encouraging development, or (2) whether they merely wish to argue that inflation is an inevitable (perhaps, in and of itself, undesirable) result of circumstances. In either case they argue that inflation is a result of the working out of the structural relations among different sectors of the economy.

---

[15] United Nations, *Towards a Dynamic Development Policy for Latin America* (New York, 1963), pp. 51, 52; see also, "Colombia Unions Seek Ruling Role," New York *Times,* May 3, 1964, p. 27.

CYCLES, GROWTH, AND THE MONEY SUPPLY 381

A crude version of the Keynesian theory may be used to justify an expansion of the money supply in the name of economic development, it being alleged that in some sense an expansion in the money supply is analogous with new investment.

The more sophisticated structuralist argument of recent years may be stated, with some misgiving, in the following manner: Examples of structural difficulties involve continuing low productivity in agriculture at times when the population in the cities desperately needs more food, long-run worsening of the terms of trade, inequality in income distribution, and problems arising as such structural conditions try to mesh with other structural elements in the economy. In general, the interests and behavior of one sector of the economy are at odds with the interests and behavior of other groups. With regard to inflation, the structuralists would say that the expansion in the money supply, which may be the immediate cause of inflation, may be the result of these structural clashes and the pressures they put on the banks and monetary authorities. Or the structural clashes might result in inflation independently of an expansion in the money supply.

Some examples of structural-type difficulties have been identified by the Economic Commission for Latin America:

> The power of certain social groups to exercise an arbitrary influence over the distribution of income is what lies behind inflation in Latin America. . . .
> But when increases in wages, social security contributions and indirect taxes are not or cannot be absorbed by entrepreneurs' profits, as is generally the case, they force up costs and are transferred to prices, thus promoting credit expansion, and leading to new increases in wages, security benefits and taxes, in the all-too-familiar spiral. . . .
> This does not mean that some of the workers and employees do not generally succeed in recouping themselves for the effects of price increases, and even in more than offsetting them; but they do so only at the expense of other social groups. . . .
> The chief victims are the rural workers, who have no trade union power, generally receive little or nothing in the way of social security benefits, and do not enjoy the same State services as people in the towns.[16]

In general the new industries of Latin America (protected by their tariff walls) seem to be characterized by relatively high costs, and by prices that "did not fall much after the new industries had gained a foot-

---

[16] United Nations, *Towards a Dynamic* . . . , pp. 49–51.

hold." [17] And the program of the Mexican Partido de la Revolución Institucional has commented:

> It is the high price at which national industrial products are sold which contributes in a pronounced way to reduce the purchasing power of the Mexican and which, also, results in the idleness of a substantial part of national installed capacity.[18]

Latin America is frequently afflicted with unsalable surpluses of certain consumer goods and with monetary inflation at the same time. How can there be surpluses of, say, textiles in a land where people dreadfully need more clothing at a time when there is a redundancy of money? The structuralist's answer is that the wrong people have the money, the wrong types of goods are being produced, and so on.

But it still makes a good deal of difference in the nature of the structuralist argument whether the structuralist goes on to defend inflation as a useful shot-in-the-arm to development. Unless the structuralist is prepared to defend the shot-in-the-arm position, there may not be any important argument between the monetarists and the structuralists, provided the monetarist is willing to grant that there needs to be some explanation as to why the expansion in the money supply occurred in the first place. The bystander to the monetarist-structuralist debate might merely observe that it is desirable to take the factors identified by both groups into account. Irresponsible expansion of the money supply certainly has contributed to inflation in Latin America. Also the clashes between interest groups contribute to forcing an expansion in the money supply such as is inflationary. However, it should be pointed out that a clash between interest groups (which did not force an expansion in the money supply) could not have very much continuing inflationary impact by itself. Some structuralists have seemed to suggest that the structural clash alone, without the intermediation of expansion in the money supply, could lead to significant inflation. This is surely not the case.

The shot-in-the-arm argument runs to the effect that higher prices give the entrepreneurs higher money profit and the illusion that things are going well whether or not the higher money profit is canceled out by inflation. They respond by expanding plant and production with the result that there really are more goods in the society and higher standards

---

[17] Hirschman, *Latin American Issues* . . . , p. 90. The relevant comments are by David Felix.

[18] *Trimestre Económico*, January, 1964, p. 146.

of living. With regard to this argument, it may be said that, of course, a modest amount of inflation may play this role (or it may not, depending on the way businessmen react). But a major, continuing inflation will almost certainly have a disorganizing effect on an economy and be an inhibitor of growth. The chief by-product effect of runaway inflation will not be production expansion, but rather inventory hoarding and the running up of the price of land, if not riots.

Celso Furtado's explanation of Brazilian growth (mentioned earlier in this chapter) involves a structuralist-type argument that includes price changes as part of the sequence of events only incidentally. Much of the research of econometricians is structuralist in nature. Much of the analysis done with national income theory tools is structuralist. The institutional theory might be thought of as emphasizing structural relations. Structuralist-type relations are important for understanding economic processes in general, whether or not they justify inflation in particular.

THE INSTITUTIONALIST POSITION. The foregoing considerations failed to identify a general principle describing the relation between inflation and growth. On the one hand, there was the argument that rising prices and rising money profits are psychologically stimulating. On the other hand, there was the argument that rising prices are disturbing; they disturb normal financial operations, disorganize businessmen, and inhibit growth. Available statistical testing methods provide no clear basis for choosing between the arguments. The argument that a little inflation helps while a lot hurts is not much help, although it may well be true. But nobody in the argument has defended runaway inflation anyway.[19]

In this impasse the institutional theory may provide some helpful explanation. Reaction to inflation is in significant degree an institutional attitude, just as the opinion as to how high the profit rate needs to be to be attractive is very largely dependent on an institutional attitude. If it had been drummed into him when he was young that inflation was ominous, a businessman would react negatively to it. If the figures on money profits dominate the man's thinking, he will probably be encouraged by inflation. Too simple?

It seems that any simple generalization to the effect that inflation is

[19] United Nations, *Economic Development Planning and International Cooperation* (Santiago, Chile, 1961), p. 38.

either good or bad for development serves little purpose. A statistical approach which tries to relate the change in the quantity of money to the growth rate yields indeterminate results. What happens depends too much on who gets the money and what he does with it. This thought brings us back to qualitative credit control as one of the most important of the devices for influencing economic growth. It is not the quantity that matters, it is the quality.

The term qualitative credit control is used to mean the taking into account of the use to which the borrowed money is going to be put, in addition to the other circumstances connected with the loan. Not only must the borrower be worthy of credit in the sense of formal reliability, he must also be going to use the money for purposes that offer real possibilities for expanding production. (See Chapter Twenty-three, Money.)

The effect of increasing bank credit in a setting where only quantitative controls are used is to provide increased demand potential. But will producers respond with higher prices (so that inflation is the result), or by increasing production? This is a largely unanswered mystery. But we can be sure of one thing, that the answer comes largely out of institutional attitudes rather than out of the rationale of supply-and-demand theory.

It is easy to say that primary attention ought to be given to the quality of credit. And if underdeveloped countries would emphasize this consideration, they might be well able to finance their own growth. But it is sometimes said that credit-worthy borrowers with fine projects do not grow on trees. (This is a point much made by one group of economic development economists, which finds the lack of good projects, the so-called lack of absorptive capacity, to be a major barrier to development.) And a bank cannot lend to credit-worthy people with good projects unless such people come in the bank door; and not very many such people walk in the doors of Latin American banks. Of course, there is a sense in which this has been true. But such thinking, offered as an excuse for not making a major effort in the area of qualitative credit control, would seem to miss the point as to why responsible people with worthwhile projects have not darkened the doors of Latin American banks more frequently. It may be that such people know they will not be received considerately when they do.

Skepticism about the availability of numerous, worthwhile small projects has been an excuse for emphasis on the grandiose government-owned steel mill or the big dam. In fact, it might be much better if the economic planning agencies were to consider that their main task is to facilitate the creation of the small-scale, credit-worthy project—dreamed up by imaginative, competent people who do not have financial resources. There are many such people in Latin America, especially in the handicraft sector; and there would be many more if they were given half a chance and some more of the right kind of education. But the way things have been, such people have had no chance of carrying a project to realization. And the attitude of both the banks and of the economic development agencies toward emphasis on this sort of thing has hardly been a help. A certain amount of lip service, certainly, has been paid to the desirability of helping the small manufacturing plant. But this has more often meant little in concrete terms. The industrial and financial oligarchies are all too capable of diverting funds, ostensibly made available for small-scale enterprise, to the financing of small plants and small companies in which they themselves own most of the control.

CONCLUSION

This book is much more an expression of opinion than it is a rigorous report of research findings. The author is not nearly as sure of some of the conclusions as the dogmatic language may have suggested. As matters stand, one should be dogmatic about very little in connection with Latin America. But surely some things need to be said and discussed.

In Latin America there seems to be a potential to develop that is expressing itself in spite of very considerable obstacles. To a great extent, it is no doubt the dynamic power of technology (as distinct from capital) that is causal, and development is occurring in the countries where the institutional resistances are the weakest and the resources, human, raw, and mental, are the largest.

All in all, the destruction of the institutional barriers to change is pretty much up to the people of the region themselves. And good (or bad) as the judgment of norteamericanos may be with regard to what should be involved in the institutional revolution in the area, it is not the place of that sovereign nation the United States to play a leading role in imposing the content of the change. It is as important for Latin Americans to realize this as for North Americans.

The world now possesses the technical knowledge necessary to provide every man, woman, and child with enough food, clothing, and shelter so that all may live in decent comfort. But adequate food, clothing, and shelter are actually not available to all. This is because the knowledge of production techniques is not fully utilized, and the distribution problem has not been solved. This is as true for Latin America as it is for the rest of the world. A few points of special relevance for that region may be reiterated.

Production needs to be integrated with international trade in some kind of a pattern that reasonably contributes to the increase of welfare. The use of import substitution as a primary criterion for identifying whether a particular new industry should be established is to invite emphasis on hopelessly high-cost production and would seem to occasion too much diversification in very small countries.

A far better criterion for identifying new industries would be: Is it possible for our country to become relatively efficient and reasonably low cost in the production of the goods in question? Emphasis on effective production and pride in workmanship is not going to hurt the Latin American development effort in the long run. On the contrary such emphasis is necessary to keep the new industries from being hothouse phenomena that will tend to wither on the vine—as some of them have perhaps been doing since 1955.

Whether or not the region now has the sort of business and governmental organization best calculated to supervise the process of increasing productivity is a question. Just as is the case in the United States, Latin America needs somehow to keep its corporations from overemphasizing production restriction and high prices in an effort to raise profits. So far as the governments are concerned, some major improvements in public administration need to occur.

The income tax suggests itself as part of the solution to the income distribution and government revenue problems. But the privileged people need to accept that and other institutional changes with a good grace and go about their work. The tendency of the privileged and their cohorts to resist fanatically any minor abatement of their privileges is a heavy hand stifling the progress of Latin America.

Whatever institutional order emerges from these times of trial in the Western Hemisphere will need to be primarily the work of the people concerned. This must be true if the resulting system is to have a chance of working.

SELECTED BIBLIOGRAPHY

GENERAL BOOKS ON LATIN AMERICAN ECONOMIC PROBLEMS

Brief bibliographies of specialized books on specific topics are included as footnotes in the text when that has seemed appropriate.

Adams, Mildred, ed. Latin America: Evolution or Explosion? New York, Dodd, Mead, 1963.

Benham, Frederic C. The Economy of Latin America. London, Oxford University Press, 1960.

Checchi, Vincent. Honduras: A Problem in Economic Development. New York, Twentieth Century Fund, 1959.

Combined Mexican Working Party. Economic Development of Mexico. Baltimore, Johns Hopkins Press (for the International Bank for Reconstruction and Development), 1953.

Cooke, Morris L. Brazil on the March. New York, McGraw-Hill, 1944.

Ellis, Howard S. and Henry C. Wallich, eds. Economic Development for Latin America. New York, St Martin's Press, 1961.

Ellsworth, P. T. Chile, An Economy in Transition. New York, Macmillan, 1945.

Foreign Policy Association. Commission on Cuban Affairs. Problems of the New Cuba. New York, 1935.

Furtado, Celso. The Economic Growth of Brazil. Berkeley, University of California Press, 1963.

Glade, William P., Jr., and Charles W. Anderson. The Political Economy of Mexico. Madison, University of Wisconsin Press, 1963.

Gruening, Ernest. Mexico and Its Heritage. New York, Century, 1928.
Hanson, Simon G. Economic Development in Latin America. Washington, Inter-American Affairs Press, 1951.
Harris, Seymour E., ed. Economic Problems of Latin America. New York, McGraw-Hill, 1944.
Herring, Hubert C. Good Neighbors. New Haven, Yale University Press, 1944.
Hirschman, Albert O. Journeys toward Progress. New York, Twentieth Century Fund, 1963.
Hirschman, Albert O. Latin American Issues: Essays and Comments. New York, Twentieth Century Fund, 1961.
Humboldt, Alexander von. Ensayo Político sobre el Reino de la Nueva España. México, Robredo, 1941. Originally published about 1818.
Hunter, John M. Emerging Colombia. Washington, Public Affairs Press, 1962.
International Bank for Reconstruction and Development. Basis for a Development Program for Colombia. Washington, 1950.
International Bank for Reconstruction and Development. Economic Development of Guatemala. Washington, 1951.
International Bank for Reconstruction and Development. Economic Development of Nicaragua. Baltimore, Johns Hopkins Press, 1952.
International Bank for Reconstruction and Development. Economic Development of Venezuela, Baltimore, Johns Hopkins Press, 1961.
International Bank for Reconstruction and Development. Report on Cuba. Washington, 1951.
May, Stacy. Costa Rica: A Study in Economic Development. New York, Twentieth Century Fund, 1952.
México: Cincuenta Años de Revolución, Vol. I: La Economía. México, Fondo de Cultura Económica, 1960.
Mosk, Sanford. Industrial Revolution in Mexico. Berkeley, University of California Press, 1950.
Pike, Fredrick B., ed. Freedom and Reform in Latin America. Notre Dame, University of Notre Dame Press, 1959.
Portnoy, Leopoldo. La Realidad Argentina en el Siglo XX, II, Análisis Crítico de la Economía. México, Fondo de Cultura Económica, 1961.
Powelson, John P. Latin America: Today's Economic and Social Revolution. New York, McGraw-Hill, 1964.
Robock, Stefan H. Brazil's Developing Northeast. Washington, Brookings, 1963.
Seers, Dudley. Cuba. Chapel Hill, University of North Carolina Press, 1964.
Stark, Harry. Social and Economic Frontiers in Latin America. Dubuque, Iowa, Wm. C. Brown, 1961.
Teichert, Pedro C. M. Economic Policy Revolution and Industrialization in Latin America. University, Miss., Bureau of Business Research, University of Mississippi, 1959.

United Nations, Economic Commission for Latin America. Analyses and Projections of Economic Development. II. Economic Development of Brazil. New York, 1956. There are similar books in either Spanish or English on El Salvador, Panama, Bolivia, Argentina, Peru, Honduras, and Colombia.

United Nations, Economic Commission for Latin America. El Desarrollo Económico de América Latina en la Postguerra. New York, 1963.

United Nations, Economic Commission for Latin America. Economic Development Planning and International Co-operation. Santiago de Chile, 1961.

United Nations, Economic Commission for Latin America. Economic Survey of Latin America. New York. This was an annual publication from the late 1940s through 1958.

United Nations. Towards a Dynamic Development Policy for Latin America. New York, 1963.

United States, Congress, Joint Economic Committee. Economic Policies and Programs in Middle America. Washington, Government Printing Office, 1963.

United States, Congress, Joint Economic Committee. Economic Policies and Programs in South America. Washington, Government Printing Office, 1962.

Urquidi, Víctor L. Viabilidad Económica de América Latina. México, Fondo de Cultura Económica, 1962.

Vernon, Raymond. The Dilemma of Mexico's Development. Cambridge, Harvard University Press, 1963.

Vernon, Raymond, ed. Public Policy and Private Enterprise in Mexico. Cambridge, Harvard University Press, 1964. The four essays are by Miguel S. Wionczek, David H. Shelton, Calvin P. Blair, and Rafael Izquierdo.

Wythe, George. Industry in Latin America. New York, Columbia University Press, 1945.

INDEX

Agency for International Development, 178, 206
Agriculture, 139, 143, 151, 186, 278 f., 318, 366
Alamán, Lucas, 189, 308
Alba, Victor, 33
Alberdi, J. B., 17, 18, 189
Alemán, Miguel, 65
Alexander, Robert, 109n., 114, 149, 173, 182
Alianza de Obreros y Campesinos de México, 112
Alliance for Progress, 26, 35, 132, 178, 206 f., 247, 261
Alsogaray, A., 192, 379
Amado, Jorge, 167
American Federation of Labor, 111
Antitrust legislation, 66 f.
AOCM, 112
Arango y Parreño, F., 16
Argentina, cattle industry, 75.; colonial trade, 11, 15; credit control, 350 f.; economic development, 258, 285 f.; exchange control, 366; foreign investment, 246 f.; growth rate, 225 f., 246 f.; medicare, 128; monopoly, 69; price floors, 73; railroads, 101
Army, 162, 358
Asamblea general de accionistas, 42
Asimow, Morris, 180
Asociación de Banqueros, 63
Asociación de Fabricantes de Drogas, 59n.
Asociación de Industriales de Latinoamérica, 63
Aubrey, Henry G., 327
AVIANCA, 120
Ayres, Clarence, 6, 159
Azpiazú, J., 22

Balassa, Bela, 325n.
Ballesteros Porta, Juan, 26n.
Banchero Rossi, Luis, 64
Banco Comercial Mexicano, 61n.
Banco de Comercio, 61n.
Banco de la Nación Argentina, 220
Banco do Brasil, 344, 346, 347
Banco Industrial de la República Argentina, 220
Banco Nacional de Desenvolvimento Econômico, 220
Banco Nacional de México, 61n., 215, 217
Bancroft, Hubert H., 14n.
Banking, 344 f.; branch, 346; credit, 353; credit control, 348; Garza Sada group and, 61; installment credit, 353; loans, 353; note issue, 347; portfolio ceiling, 351; rediscounting, 350; reserve requirements, 348, 350
Bank of Mexico, 339, 348
Bank of the Northeast (Brazil), 165
Baranson, Jack, 313
Baranyai, L., 84n.
Batlle y Ordóñez, 100
Beckerman, W., 158n.
Behrman, Jack N., 175
Belaúnde Terry, F., 209, 287
Belgrano, Manuel, 14, 15
Bermúdez, Antonio J., 53n.
Betancourt, Rómulo, 313
Blaine, James G., 301
Blair, C. P., 61n., 98n., 218n., 354n.
Bogotá, Act of, 206
Bolívar, 14
Bolivia, 54, 247, 285
Bonifacio, José, 15
Brandenburg, Frank, 60, 61n., 183, 184n., 350n.

Brazil, antitrust, 68; capital formation, 225; coffee, 84 f., 374, 375; economic development, 374; foreign investment, 176, 236, 246; independence, 15; industrial priorities, 181–2, 258; iron ore, 288; minimum wage, 123; railroads, 267; the Estado Novo, 30, 73; transportation, 270
Bresser Pereira, L., 161n.
Brizola, Leonel, 105
Brovedani, Bruno, 344
Brown, Lester R., 279n.
Buffer stock, 88, 91
Building materials, 287
Bulnes, F., 17
Bureaucracy, 164
Burnett, Ben G., 109n.
Business cycles, 79 f., 372 f., 373 f.
Business organization, 39 f.
Butler, William F., 272

Calvo clause, see Mexico
Câmara, Cardinal, 150
Cámara Nacional de la Industria de Transformación (CNIT), 63, 64
Cámaras de comercio, 62
Cámaras de industriales, 63
Campos, Roberto de Oliveira, 72n., 379
CAP, 97
Capital coefficients, 226
Capital formation, domestic resources, 213 f.; foreign resources, 231 f.
Capital goods, 251 f.
Capital investment, 222 f., 228 f.
Capitalism, 22
Capital/output ratios, 225 f.
Cárdenas, Lázaro, 110
Cardoso, Alfonso, 64
Castro, Fidel, 28, 90, 306
Catholic Church, 10n., 14, 21 f., 63, 110, 214; falange movement and, 23
Catholicism, 163
Cattle industry, see Meat
Cavers, David F., 104
Cayrú, Visconde de, 15
Ceiling prices, 71
Central America, 313
Central American Bank for Economic Integration, 193
Central American Clearing House, 340
Central American Common Market, 333
Central American Free Trade Association, 193, 328

Central banks, 347 f.; open-market operation and, 352
Cerro de Pasco, 54, 57
Chan Kom, 213
Chile, 51, 57n., 128, 157, 209, 247, 248
Chincha islands, 365
CINVA-Ram, 274
Cisneros, Viceroy, 15
Clark, Marjorie, 109
CLASC, 111
Colombia, 59n., 98, 247, 350
COMIBOL, 120
Comisión Nacional de Abastecimiento, 74
Comissão Federal de Abastecimento e Preços, 71
Commercial agriculture, 278 f.
Commercial banks, 220, 221
Common markets, 325 f.
Communism, 22, 34 f.
Comodoro Rivadavia, 379
Companhia Siderúrgica Nacional, 289
Comparative cost, theory of, 316 f.
CONASUPO, 71, 74
Confederación de Cámaras Industriales (CONCAMIN), 63
Confederación de Cámaras Nacionales de Comercio (CONCANACO), 63
Confederación de Trabajadores de América Latina, 111
Confederación General del Trabajo, 112
Confederación Latinoamericana de Sindicalistas Cristianos, 111
Confederación Obrera Panamericana, 111
Confederación Patronal de la República Mexicana, 63
Confédération Internationale des Syndicats Chrétiens, 111, 113
Consejo de administración, 42
Conselho Nacional do Petróleo, 73
Consorcio Pesquero del Perú, 64
Consumer durables, 291
Consumer goods, 251 f.
Contract law, 117
COPA, 111
Coppock, Joseph D., 79n., 374
Cornehls, James V., 25n.
Cornejo, B., 344
Corporación Argentina de Productores de Carnes (CAP), 76 f., 97
Corporación de Fomento de la Producción (Chile) 98, 192, 220, 354

INDEX

Corporación de los Valles del Magdalena y del Sinú, 191
Corporate state, 29 f., 113
Crawford, W. Rex, 17n.
Credit control, *see* Banking
CROM, 110
CTAL, 111
CTM, 110, 112
Cuba, 16n., 28 f., 34 f., 64, 82, 114, 123, 258, 305 f., 322
Currie, Leonard, 273
Customs union, 327
Cutler, F., 245n.

Dávila, Carlos, 131
Davis, Tom E., 157
Debt peonage, 20, 123
Deductive method, 10n.
DeGaulle, Charles, 334.
Dell, Sidney S., 328n.
Departamento Nacional do Café, 86
Devaluation of currency, 341
Dewey, John, 24
Díaz, Porfirio, 17 f., 109, 115, 246
DNOCS, 165
Droguerías Aliadas, 59n.
Drugs, *see* Pharmaceuticals

Economic Commission for Latin America, 5, 58, 82 f., 137, 164, 169, 194, 196, 216, 261, 310, 317, 322, 324, 330, 380, 381
Economic development, 153 f., 189 f., 368 f., 372 f., 377 f.; balanced growth of, 257; cartorial state and, 32; complementarity and, 250 f., 261 f.; conglomeration and, 256; dams and, 271; dictatorship and, 162; diversification and, 256; external economies in, 159; flour mills and, 285; in Ceará, 180; in colonial period, 9 f.; 257; level of living versus power in, 252; manpower and, 259; planning and, 189 f., 209, 261; priorities and, 250 f., 265 f., 277 f.; productivity and, 147, 324; resources for, 187 f.; skipping versus repetition, 258; Spanish language and, 169 f.; the Científicos (Mexico) and, 17; unbalanced growth of, 257; unprogrammed planning and, 202 f.
Ecuadorian Fruit Import Corp., 71n.
Education, 275; literacy and, 136; progressive, 24
Ejido Bank (Torreón), 26

Employment, structure of, 142 f.; sectar shares, 143
Entrepreneurship, 165
Ericcson, L. M., 105n.
Escarpenter, Claudio, 102n., 270n.
European Economic Community, 328, 332
Exchange control, 340
Export-Import Bank, 233, 237
Export promotion, 316
Exports, 295; angostura bitters, 279; bananas, 284; beef, 75, 284 f.; carnauba wax, 56, 279; coffee, 84 f.; quinine, 279; monoculture and, 81 f.; quebracho, 279

Federación Sindical de Trabajadores Mineros de Bolivia, 119
Federal Maritime Commission, 103
Felix, David, 62n., 161, 382n.
Ferrer, Aldo, 253n., 280n., 326n.
Ferrero, Rómulo A., 307
Fetter, Frank W., 216, 378n.
Feuerlein, Willy, 231n.
Fillol, Tomás R., 69n.
Financial intermediaries, 218, 353
Fish Meal Exporters Organization, 64
Flores, Edmundo, 25n.
Flores Magón, 109
Flota Mercante Grancolombiana, 102
Food and Agriculture Organization, 134
Food consumption, 134
Food for Peace, 304
Foreign aid, 247
Foreign companies, 59; American Smelting and Refining, 57; Anaconda Copper, 54, 57; Canadian Light, 99; Creole Petroleum Co., 53; Gath & Chávez, 60; Harrod's, 60; International Telephone and Telegraph, 99, 105n; McKesson and Robbines, 59n.; Royal Dutch Shell, 53; Sears Roebuck, 60, 167
Foreign exchanges, 338; earnings of, 377; multiple rates and, 340; rates, IMF pars, 338
Foreign investment, 174 f., 222, 231 f., 237; accretion of, 242; Baring crisis and, 247; direct, 242; immature/mature borrower/lender, 238
Foreign investors, 43 f.; branch plants, 44 f.; Westinghouse, 176
Franklin, B., 370
Free trade, 15

Free trade association, 327
Friedmann, Wolfgang, 46
FSTMB, 119
Fund for Special Operations, 194
Furtado, Celso, 119, 149, 158, 181–82, 246, 342, 374, 375n., 383

General Agreement on Tariffs and Trade, 331, 333
Geneva Conference on Trade and Development, 322
Germán Parra, Manuel, 258
Gold standard, 336
Gompers, Samuel, 111
Goodrich, Carter, 247
Goodrich-Euzkadi, 312
Goodyear-Oxo, 312
Gordon, Lincoln, 176, 177n.
Goulart, João, 237
Government: bonds, 352; business, 94 f.; debt, 367; expenditures, 357; fiscal policy, 368; lottery, 366; revenue, 358; saving, fiat money, 221; subsidy, 242, 370
Great Britain, 239
Gresham's law, 335
Growth, *see* Economic development
Growth rates, employment and product, 146, 226
Guatemala, 34, 35, 70

Hacienda store, *see Tienda de raya*
Hagen, E., 165, 166, 311n.
Haiti, 43, 136, 234
Hannan, Elizabeth, 231n.
Hansen, Alvin, 159
Hanson, Simon G., 100n.
Harberger, Arnold, 365n.
Harrod, Roy, 225, 227 f., 240n., 320n.
Health, 133
Herrera, Felipe, 194, 326
Hidalgo, Father, 14
Hirschman, Albert O., 62n., 156, 159, 161n., 165, 216, 248, 254, 264, 285, 323, 379n.
Hospitalization, 128
Hostos y Bonilla, E., 17
Housing, 135, 272; density of habitation in relation to, 135

ICFTU, 111, 113
Idealism, 18 f.
Imperialism, 234 f.
Import, capacity to, 323

Imports, 295; advance deposit on, 353
Import substitution, 319 f.
Income distribution, factor shares, 148; inequality, 148; sector shares, 146 f.
Indian empires, pre-Spanish: Aymará, 8; Aztec, 7 f.; Chibcha, 7 f.; Inca, 7 f., 213; Jivaro, 8; Maya, 7 f.
Indigenous question, 6, 23
Inductive method, 10n., 18
Industria Eléctrica de México, 176
Industrial equipment, 290
Industrialization policy, 11, 12; *see also* Economic development
Industrial priorities, 277 f.
Industrial production, 138; bauxite in, 289; of chemicals, 289;
Industrial Revolution, 10
Industry: airline, 270; handicraft, 285; heavy, 255; infant-industry argument, 311 f.; light, 279; linkages, 263 f.; service, 144
Infant-industry argument, 311 f.
Inflation, 378 f.
Infrastructure, 101 f., 251 f., 265 f.
Ingenieros, José, 17
Input-output matrix, 199
Institutional theory, 5 f., 159, 383
Institutions, 6, 7, 10, 14, 155 f., 159
Instituto Brasileiro do Café, 73
Instituto de Fomento Industrial (Colombia), 98
Instituto do Açúcar e do Alcool, 73
Instituto do Cacau de Baia, 73
Instituto Nacional de Reforma Agraria (INRA, Cuba), 29
Instituto Nacional do Mate, 73
Instituto Nacional do Sal, 73
Instituto Rio Grandense do Arroz, 73
Insurance, 218
Inter-American Coffee Agreement, 87
Inter-American Council of Commerce and Production, 63
Inter-American Development Bank, 135, 194, 206
Inter-American Economic and Social Council, 194
Inter-American Housing and Planning Center, 274
Inter-American Institute of Agricultural Sciences, 186
Interest rates, 346, 352
International Bank for Reconstruction and Development, 106
International Basic Economy Corp., 273

INDEX

International Chamber of Commerce, 63
International Coffee Agreement, 87
International Confederation of Free Trade Unions, 111
International incorporation, 52
International investment, *see* Foreign Investment
International Monetary Fund, 174, 240, 338 f., 342, 377, 379
International Railways of Central America, 70
International Raw Commodity Control Schemes, 78 f.
International Sugar Agreement, 90
International Tin Committee, 88
International trade, 295 f., 307
International Trade Organization, 87, 91 f.
Izquierdo, Rafael, 254n., 307n., 309n., 320n., 324n.

Jacobsson, Per, 340, 379
Jáuregui Hurtado, Arturo, 111
Jenks, Leland, 231n.
Job, right to a, 118; hiring for a, 177; discharge from a, 118
Juárez, Benito, 15
Julião, Francisco, 119
Junta Nacional de Granos, 73
Junta Nacional de Carnes, 73, 76
Junta Reguladora de la Producción Agrícola, 73
Just price, 22

Kafka, Alexandre, 167, 216
Kaiser, Henry, 290
Kanesathasan, L., 376n.
Kemmerer, Edwin W., 347, 378n.
Kennedy, John F., 34, 206
Kepner, Charles D., 231n.
Keynes, J. M., 163, 215, 222, 224 f., 229 f., 341, 364, 372, 381
Khrushchev, N., 28, 306
Kidd, Charles V., 183
Knight, M. M., 231n.
Kubitschek, 206, 340

Labor: arbitration, 115 f.; *bracero,* 51, 124; child labor, 126; conciliation, 115; female labor, 126; forced labor, 13; mediation, 116 f.
Labor movement, 109 f.; collective bargaining and, 115; collective contracts and, 117

Labor unions, 109 f.; organization of, 113
LAFTA, *see* Latin American Free Trade Association
Land grants, 242
Landholding: *altepetlalli,* 8, 23; *ayllu,* 8; *calpulli,* 8, 23; *chacras,* 21; *colonos,* 28; *estancia,* 13, 20; *fazenda,* 13, 20; *hacienda,* 13, 20
Landowners, 161
Land reform, 24; *baldíos,* 21; *caballerías* and *peonías,* 21; dotation, 24; *ejido,* 23 f., 278; *fraccionamiento,* 24; *latifundio,* 20
Land tenure, 13, 14, 20; Creoles and, 14; *encomienda,* 13
Lastarria, José, 17
Latin American Free Trade Association, 193, 256, 261, 268, 291, 310, 328 f.
Latin American Institute for Economic and Social Planning, 194
Lechín, Juan, 119
Lenin, V. I., 28
Leontief, Wassily, 318
Letelier, Valentín, 17
Levine, Flavian, 209
Lewis, Oscar, 144
Lewis, W. Arthur, 257n., 311n.
Liebhafsky, H. H., 200n.
Life expectancy, 133
Light metals, 289
Limantour, José, 17, 189
Lipsey, Robert E., 79n.
Lloyd Brasileiro, 102, 103
Lobato López, Ernesto, 344n.
Lombardo Toledano, V., 111, 113
López Camara, F., 242n.
López Michelson, Adolfo, 58
Low-volume—high-unit-profit, 58 f., 61, 62

McBride, George M., 131
McCaleb, Walter F., 356
Macrovariable model, 196
Manufacturing, 137, 145, 266, 277; furniture, 287; glass, 262, 287; of Jeeps, 290
Marginal propensity: to consume, 224; to pay taxes, 359 f.
Marketing, 57; middlemen and, 57
Market organization, 37 f.
Márquez, Javier, 174
Marshall, Alfred, 159
Marshall, Chief Justice, 52n.

INDEX

Martner, Daniel, 356
Marxian Socialism, 24
Massell, Benton F., 374
Matarazzo, F., 60, 217
Mattei, Enrico, 96
Mauá, Visconde de, 17, 189
Maximum prices, 71
Mayobre, José A., 194
Meade, J. E., 252, 325, 371
Meat, 75 f., 134, 284 f., 313; beef, 75, 284 f.; foreign packers and, 75
Medicare, 128
Mercantilism, 10
Mexican Revolution, 23 f.; monument to, 232
Mexico, Calvo clause, 235; credit control, 351; Constitution of 1917, 23, 24, 67, 115, 130, 325; devaluation, 342; foreign investment, 43, 231, 246; housing, 135; Labor Code of 1931, 117; labor movement, 109, 116; land redistribution, 24; land tenure, 8, 23 f., 358; Mexican Revolution, 23 f.; oligopoly, 60 f.; Petróleos Mexicanos, 53; planning, 192, 198; prices, 71; profit sharing, 130; program of Mexicanization, 46; propensity to consume, 224 f.; restraint of trade, 67, 68; *sinarquismo* movement, 23; social security, 127; sulphur deposits, 289; tax exemptions, 368 f.; the Reform, 15, 24; wages, 123
Mikesell, R. F., 231n.
Mill, John Stuart, 180
Mills, J. C., 84n.
Minerals, ownership of, 52; *cateo* concession and, 53; *de beneficio* concession and, 53; exploitation concession and, 53
Minimum Price Law, 76
Minimum wage laws, 122 f.
Miranda, F., 14
Mixed companies, *see Sociedad mixta*
Monetarists, 378 f.
Monetary standard, 335 f.
Money supply, 372
Monte de Piedad, 344, 354
Montevideo, Treaty of, 193, 261, 328, 332
Moore, O. Ernest, 344n.
Mora, J., 16
Moreno, Mariano, 14, 15
Moscoso, Teodoro, 287
Mosk, Sanford, 63

Mújica, Emilio, 148
Mutual unions, 22, 109
Myint, Hla, 216n., 255, 311n.
Myrdal, G., 159

Nacional Financiera, 192, 220, 289, 354
National income theory, *see* Keynes
Nationalization, 119
National Railways of Mexico, 101
Navarrete, Ifigenia M. de., 149
Nazas river, 26, 272
Nehemkis, Peter, 150
Nelson, James R., 104n.
Nolen, Herman C., 59n.
Northeast (Brazil), 119, 165, 173, 191, 271
NRA, 30
Nurkse, R., 159, 174, 257n.

Ocean shipping, 102 f., 270
Oil, *see* Petroleum
Old-age pensions, 127
Oligopoly, 60 f.
Operation Pan America, 206
Ordem e Progresso, 17
Organización Regional Interamericana de Trabajo, 111
Organization of American States, 35 f., 193
Organization of Central American States, 193
Organization of Petroleum Exporting Countries, 89
ORIT, 111
Ortiz Mena, Antonio, 60, 272

Pachuca, 97
Packaging, 282
Packers Control Act, 76
Panama, 43
Pan American Federation of Labor, 111
Pan American Highway, 256, 269
Pan American Union, 193
Pan American World Airways, 120
Partido de la Revolución Institucional, 31, 62n., 205, 283, 316, 349n., 382
Patel, I. G., 321n.
Pazos, Felipe, 209
Peace Corps, 178, 275
Peasant Leagues, 119
Per capita income, 139 f.
Per capita trade, 296
Pérez Jiménez, 236, 243

Perón, Juan, 23, 31, 77, 101, 112, 164, 366
Perroux, François, 159
Peru, 8, 9, 64, 67, 131, 204; guano industry in, 95
Petroleum, 89 f., 99, 243 f., 361; petrochemicals and, 289
Pharmaceuticals, 59, 234n., 286
Phonograph records, 286
Pius XI, 22
Pizer, Samuel, 245
P.L., 480, 303
Platt Amendment, 322
Poblete Troncoso, M., 109n.
Political democracy, 14
Ponte, Conde da, 15
Population growth rate, 136 f.
Portnoy, Leopoldo, 62
Positivism, 17 f.
Powelson, John P., 193n.
Prado, Manuel, 131
Prebisch, Raúl, 5, 149, 194, 196, 253, 264, 317, 367
Preconquest South America, 7 f.
Price floors, 73
Price fluctuations, 79n.
Primum mobile, 156, 158
Production, 137
Production subsidy, 370
Profit motive, 156
Profit sharing, 130
Programming, linear, 200
Propensity to import, *see* Trade/national income ratio
Public utilities, 101 f.

Railroad Commission (Texas), 89
Railroads, 96, 97, 101 f., 120, 267 f.
Ramírez, Raúl, 274
Raw commodity control schemes, 78 f.; base-year quotas and, 87, 90
Raw commodity pricing, 375
Ray, Philip, 248
Reciprocal trade, 301, 321 f.; agreements, 302
Redfield, Robert, 56, 213
Revenue (government), 358
Ricardo, David, 316
Rio Grande do Sul, 105
Río Negro, 191
Rippy, J. Fred, 231n.
Rivera, José E., 56
Roads, 268
Robinson, Joan, 160, 223

Roca-Runciman, 77
Rockefeller, Rodman, quoted, 273
Rodó, José E., 19
Rojas Pinilla, 236
Roosevelt, F. D., 233
Rosenstein-Rodan, P. N., 140n., 142, 159, 257n.
Rostow, W. W., 156, 159, 258
Rubber, 56, 173, 279
Ruiz Galindo, A., 65

Sáenz, Josué, 359
Salera, Virgil, 373
San Martín, J., 14
San Nicolás, 43, 97, 289
Sanz de Santamaría, C., 211
São Francisco Valley Commission, 165
São Paulo, 85
Sarmiento, Domingo, 17
Saving, corporate, 217; government, 221; individual, 215
Scholasticism, 10, 10n.
Schumpeter, Joseph, 156, 158
Scientific method, 10n., 18
Scitovsky, Tibor, 257
Securities, 219; the *financiera* and, 219 f.
Sewerage, 135
Shelton, David H., 344
Shipping lines serving Latin America, 102, 103
Shoup, Carl, 356n.
SIAM di Tella, 60
Siderúrgica del Orinoco, 120, 289
Silva Herzog, J., 17n.
Simkin, C. G. F., 377n.
Simonsen, Mario H., 62, 150
Simpson, Eyler, 25n.
Singer, Hans W., 159, 216n.
Single proprietorship, 40
Smith, Adam, 14, 15, 61, 308, 316
Socialism, 28
Socialization, 99
Social overhead, 251 f., 265 f.
Social Progress Trust Fund, 194, 207, 276
Social security, 127 f.
Sociedad anónima, 42
Sociedad de responsabilidad limitada, 41
Sociedad en comandita simple, 41
Sociedad en nombre colectivo, 41
Sociedad Mexicana de Crédito Industrial, 61n.
Sociedad mixta, 42, 97

Solís M., Leopoldo, 11n.
SOMISA, 97
Soothill, Jay H., 231n.
Soviet Union, 90, 305
Spanish law, 12, 23
Spanish Succession, War of the, 11
Specialization, 256
Special-purpose banks, 220
Stabilization, 377
Staley, Eugene, 52n.
Standard Fruit and Steamship Co., 71n.
Standard Oil Co. of N. J., 53, 102, 243
Stark, Harry, 140n.
Steel industry, 9, 12, 43, 99, 253 f., 263, 288 f.; Acero del Pacífico, 289; Altos Hornos, 97, 289, 354; at Chimbote, 289; at Huachipato, 289; at Paz del Río, 98, 254, 255, 289
Strikes, 115 f.; at Cananea mines, 109
Stroetzel, Donald S., 274n.
Structuralists, 381
Sturzo, Luigi, 22
Subsidy, 242, 370
Subsistence agriculture, 278; coca leaf and, 278; pulque and, 278; yucca and, 278
SUDENE, 165, 191
Sugar, 82, 90 f., 123, 173, 288, 302
Superintendencia de Abastecimientos y Precios, 71
Syllogistic logic, 10n., 163

Tamagna, Frank, 344n.
Tannenbaum, Frank, 18n.
Tariffs, 307 f., 360 f.; *aforo* system, 307
Tawney, R. H., 163
Tax administration, 367
Taxes, 46 f., 368 f.; *alcabala,* 366; Bethlehem Steel and, 364; direct, 362; discriminatory, 51; excise, 361; exemptions, 242, 368 f.; income, 363 f.; indirect, 360; Iron Mines Co. and, 364; local, 366; Orinoco Mining Co. and, 364; progressiveness of, 359; property, 362; regressiveness of, 358; severance, 361; state, 366
Tax exemptions, 242, 368 f.
Technology, 6, 8, 9, 159 f., 172 f.
Teléfonos de México, 105n.
Terms of trade, 79 f., 324
Textile industry, 286
Tienda de raya, 20, 123
Tin, 87 f.

Tin-mining companies: Aramayo, 54, 87; Hochschild, 54, 87; Patiño, 54, 87
Trade, balance of, 238, 299
Trade associations, 62
Trade controls, bilateral agreements, 311
Trade Expansion Act of 1962, 315
Trade/national income ratios, 296
Trade regulation, 11; *Asiento* agreement and, 11
Trade restrictions, 307 f.
Transportation, 267 f.; urban, 103
Triffin, Robert, 376
Trotsky, Leon, 28
Trouyet, Carlos, 61n., 105n.
Tupac Amaru revolt, 13
Turlington, Edgar, 231n.
Two-pricing, 303

Unemployment, 129
United Fruit Co., 49, 70, 71n., 102
United Nations, 35 f.
United States, debtor status, 239; international investment position, 237, 241; trade with Latin America, 300
Upton, T. Graydon, 273
Urquidi, Víctor, 328n., 359
Uruguay, 49, 127, 128, 347
Utilities, p. 103 f., 271
USSR, *see* Soviet Union

Valorization of coffee, 86
Vargas, Getulio, 23, 30, 73, 113
Veblen, Thorstein, 6, 159, 255
Velázquez, Fidel, 112
Venezuela, 14, 53, 89, 141 f., 243, 300, 308, 341, 361
Venezuelan Petroleum Corp., 89
Vernon, Raymond, 31, 63n., 65, 100n., 158n.
Viner, Jacob, 325
Volume per se, 321
Vorágine, La, 56

Wages, 122 f., *aguinaldo,* 130; Christmas bonus, 130; hours worked, 122; security and, 122 f.
Wai, U Tun, 356
Wallace, Henry, 281
Wallich, Henry C., 356, 373n., 376n.
Watt, John, 284
Welfare, 107 f.

Western Hemisphere Trade Corporation, 45, 48
WFTU, 111
Wickham, H. A., 173
Williams, Walter, 166
Winkler, Max, 231n.
Wionszek, Miguel S., 104n.
Workmen's Compensation, 126 f.
World Federation of Trade Unions, 111, 113

Wythe, George, 301

Yanaconazgo, 123
Yerba mate, 56, 73, 279
Young, John P., 373

Zamora, Fernando, 57
Zarka, Claude, 138
Zea, Leopoldo, 17n.
Zimmermann, Erich, 160, 174, 187, 190

4820-00-026